· English Medieval Romance

# Longman Literature in English Series

**General Editors: David Carroll and Michael Wheeler
University of Lancaster**

For a complete list of titles see pages x and xi

# English Medieval Romance

W. R. J. Barron

**Longman**

London and New York

LONGMAN GROUP UK LIMITED,
Longman House, Burnt Mill, Harlow,
Essex CM20 2JE, England
Associated Companies throughout the world.

Published in the United States of America
by Longman Inc., New York

First published 1987

BRITISH LIBRARY CATALOGUING IN PUBLICATION DATA
Barron, W. R. J.
    English medieval romance.—
    (Longman literature in English series)
    1. Romances, English—History and
    criticism    2. English poetry—Middle
    English, 1100–1500—History and
    criticism
    I. Title
    821′.1′09        PR321
    ISBN 0-582-49221-1    CSD
    ISBN 0-582-49220-3    PPR

LIBRARY OF CONGRESS CATALOGING IN PUBLICATION DATA
Barron, W. R. J. (William Raymond Johnston)
    English Medieval romance.

    (Longman literature in English series)
    Bibliography: p.
    Includes index.
    1. Romances, English—History and criticism.
    2. English literature— Middle English, 1100–1500—
    History and criticism. I. Title. II. Series.
    PR321.B37    1987        820′.9′001        86–15388
    ISBN 0–582–49221–1
    ISBN 0–582–49220–3 (pbk.)

Set in 9½/11pt Bembo (Linotron 202)
Produced by Longman Singapore Publishers (Pte) Ltd.
Printed in Singapore.

# Contents

# Editors' Preface

The multi-volume Longman Literature in English Series provides students of literature with a critical introduction to the major genres in their historical and cultural context. Each volume gives a coherent account of a clearly defined area, and the series, when complete, will offer a practical and comprehensive guide to literature written in English from Anglo-Saxon times to the present. The aim of the series as a whole is to show that the most valuable and stimulating approach to literature is that based upon an awareness of the relations between literary forms and their historical context. Thus the areas covered by most of the separate volumes are defined by period and genre. Each volume offers new informed ways of reading literary works, and provides guidance to further reading in an extensive reference section.

As well as studies on all periods of English and American literature, the series includes books on criticism and literary theory, and on the intellectual and cultural context. A comprehensive series of this kind must of course include other literature written in English, and therefore a group of volumes deals with Irish and Scottish literature, and the literatures of India, Africa, the Caribbean, Australia, and Canada. The forty-six volumes of the series cover the following areas: pre-Renaissance English Literature, English Poetry, English Drama, English Fiction, English Prose, Criticism and Literary Theory, Intellectual and Cultural Context, American Literature, Other Literatures in English.

David Carroll
Michael Wheeler

# Longman Literature in English Series

**General Editors: David Carroll and Michael Wheeler
University of Lancaster**

### Pre-Renaissance English Literature

* English Literature before Chaucer *Michael Swanton*
  English Literature in the Age of Chaucer
* English Medieval Romance *W. R. J. Barron*

### English Poetry

* English Poetry of the Sixteenth Century *Gary Waller*
* English Poetry of the Seventeenth Century *George Parfitt*
  English Poetry of the Eighteenth Century, 1700–1789
* English Poetry of the Romantic Period, 1789–1830 *J. R. Watson*
  English Poetry of the Victorian Period, 1830–1890
  English Poetry of the Early Modern Period, 1890–1940
  English Poetry since 1940

### English Drama

English Drama before Shakespeare
English Drama: Shakespeare to the Restoration, 1590–1660
English Drama: Restoration and the Eighteenth Century, 1660–1789
English Drama: Romantic and Victorian, 1789–1890
English Drama of the Early Modern Period, 1890–1940
English Drama since 1940

### English Fiction

English Fiction of the Eighteenth Century, 1700–1789
English Fiction of the Romantic Period, 1789–1830
* English Fiction of the Victorian Period, 1830–1890 *Michael Wheeler*
English Fiction of the Early Modern Period, 1890–1940

### English Prose

English Prose of the Renaissance, 1550–1700
English Prose of the Eighteenth Century
English Prose of the Nineteenth Century

## Criticism and Literary Theory

Criticism and Literary Theory from Sidney to Johnson
Criticism and Literary Theory from Wordsworth to Arnold
Criticism and Literary Theory from 1890 to the Present

## The Intellectual and Cultural Context

The Sixteenth Century
The Seventeenth Century
★ The Eighteenth Century, 1700–1789 *James Sambrook*
The Romantic Period, 1789–1830
The Victorian Period, 1830–1890
The Twentieth Century: 1890 to the Present

## American Literature

American Literature before 1880
American Poetry of the Twentieth Century
American Drama of the Twentieth Century
American Fiction, 1865–1940
American Fiction since 1940
Twentieth-century America

## Other Literatures

Irish Literature since 1800
Scottish Literature since 1700

Australian Literature
Indian Literature in English
African Literature in English
Caribbean Literature in English
★ Canadian Literature in English *W. J. Keith*

★ *Already published*

# Author's Preface

Of the three volumes in this series given to pre-Renaissance literature, two deal with a wide variety of forms and types over lengthy periods; this volume, the third, surveys a group of texts from the same periods on the assumption that they constitute a distinctive genre, Medieval Romance. Yet at first glance their variety seems to defy classification: written in prose and in verse of many kinds, ranging in date over more than three centuries, in length from a few dozen to many thousands of lines, in subject-matter from the legendary conquests of classical heroes or kings of old to the Robin-Hood adventures of simple yeomen, in form from ballad to chronicle, in social setting from oriental court to cottar's hearth, in literary achievement from stumbling naïvety to subtle sophistication. But many generations of readers and critics have felt that they have something in common, some core of meaning which sets them apart from other forms of medieval literature.

In search of that core of meaning students of romance have commonly looked for guidance to the dominant cultural influence of contemporary France, from whose literature both the term and the form emerged. Knowledge of that tradition, until recently rather general and impression-istic than precise, suggested basic characteristics – aristocratic milieu, preoccupation with love, supernatural plot-machinery, an atmosphere of fantasy – which the English examples only sporadically and imperfectly display. They are no more faithful to the formal criteria associated with the French tradition: extended episodic structure, verse medium almost wholly restricted to octosyllabic couplets, rhetorical elaboration as part of a con-sciously literary approach to an educated audience. Growing dissatisfaction with both sets of criteria as constituting a conception of the romance genre which has served to diminish and undervalue most English texts has suggested that they ought rather to be judged by their own evident aims and formal characteristics.

The approach adopted here gives primary importance to certain fundamentals – the basic attitude to human experience as part fantasy, part reality, the superior powers credited to the protagonists, the balance of idealism and realism in the values celebrated – which constitute the perennial romance mode. The historical importance of the French tradition in re-embodying that mode is acknowledged in a limited survey of the creation of the medieval genre sufficient, it is hoped, to show the variety of forms it assumed and, by the standards of the age, the rapidity of its evolution. The varying and disparate relationship of English romance to the French tradition, the random selection of texts preserved by chance, their general anonymity and uncertainty of date, prevent the continued tracing of any evolutionary process. Since the substitution of any structure of examination based upon a modern conception of the nature of the texts would risk the imposition of irrelevant values or misleading perspectives, that used here, based on the origins of the story-matter, reflects a contemporary view of the material and, in outline, the early evolution of medieval romance. It is hoped that a structure largely independent of the concept of genre will allow appreciation of the extent to which the English romances adhere to the established tradition without prejudging their originality as necessarily a deviation from its norms.

In any assessment of tradition and originality in the English romance the romances of Chaucer pose particular problems. Some, such as his 'Knight's Tale' and *Troilus and Criseyde* treat traditional matter in a manner which seems to expose the limitations of the mode as a means of presenting human experience. Others, such as the Wife of Bath's and Franklin's tales, suggest gentle amusement at the ease with which its inherent idealism can become a means of self-deception. Elsewhere Chaucer mocks the conventions of the genre as meaningless without the informing spirit of the mode, gently out of context in the Miller's fabliau and the Nun's Priest's beast fable, uproariously in his own parody *Sir Thopas*. Yet all, not least the parody, show an intimate appreciation of the nature of romance and the distinctive characteristics of the English examples. Full appreciation of Chaucer's romances requires not only the kind of reassessment of the English corpus aimed at here but also the wider context of his other works in which established genres are similarly transformed by his genius. Considerations of space apart, its treatment seems more appropriate to another volume in this series dealing with Chaucer's poetry as a whole.

I owe a debt of gratitude to the friends and colleagues who advised me on such matters of scope and structure, especially those who read parts of the book in draft form: Marian Glasscoe, Tony Hunt, Elspeth Kennedy, Roy Owen, Sue Powell, Jane Taylor, and Michael Wheeler. The patience and good guidance of the General Editors have saved me from many errors. I must take responsibility for those which no doubt remain.

WRJB
October 1985

# List of Abbreviations

In addition to the standard abbreviations used as titles of periodicals:

AUMLA:      *Journal of Australasian Universities Modern Language and Literature Association*
ELH:        *Journal of English Literary History*
PMLA:       *Publications of the Modern Language Association of America*

the following abbreviations are employed throughout the Notes and Bibliography:

EETS:       Early English Text Society
EETS, ES:   Early English Text Society, Extra Series
STS:        Scottish Text Society

# Chapter 1

# Introduction: the Nature of Romance

Romance, though we scarcely recognize it, is so much with us, penetrating so many aspects of our lives, that the objective attention needed to define it confuses and embarrasses us. Living in the shadow of Armageddon, we pride ourselves on our realistic cynicism; yet the publications of Mills and Boon sell better year by year and long-running fantasies – *Dallas, Dynasty, Falcon Crest* – flicker across our television screens, most of them products of that society which most loudly boasts its pragmatic mastery of the real world. In the age of quick divorce, we assure ourselves that romance is dead; yet the popular press continues to chronicle the mating of the much-married in the confidence that all the world loves a lover still. Guided by consumer-protection societies, we shop for the best buy, technical survey in hand; while the advertisers, appealing as ever to hearts rather than heads, promise us romance in everything from a perfume to a package holiday. Masters of science, manipulators of birth and makers of mass death, we dream of flight from a polluted earth to clean new worlds beyond the stars, calling it romance and rivalling each other to make it reality. Confused by the complexity of its forms – ideal or entity, escapist fantasy or a facet of reality, reasonable aspiration or a delusory aspect of human temperament? – and bemused by our own ambivalence towards it, we equate romance with fiction, fiction with falsehood, and flick through *True Romances* on the bookstall without noticing the contradiction in terms.

The roots of this semantic confusion lie in the history of the word, which originally designated that form of vulgar Latin adopted as their vernacular by western regions of the Roman Empire. *Romanz* first distinguished the vernacular from the classical language, then the secular texts written in it from learned writings in Latin, then particular types of literature favoured by the lay aristocracy who were the patrons of the age. But even in France, where it was first applied to the emergent romance genre, the term long continued to be widely and loosely used. And as the genre evolved and ramified through the centuries it charged romance with multiple meanings and emotional associations which underlie our ambivalent response to it today.[1]

The gradual restriction of *romanz* from linguistic medium to literary form suggests the futility of searching for the origins of the genre or defining it on the basis of the texts to which the term was initially applied. Many characteristic features of romance had already appeared in the literature of ancient Greece in a variety of evolving and interrelated forms; the story-matter presented there was to contribute much to the later development of European romance, the forms themselves very little. In the course of that development, the terms 'romance', 'romantic' were associated with such numerous and varied types of literature and acquired so many extra-literary overtones that, if we think of them as literary terms at all today, it is merely in a secondary sense referring to a minor, and critically suspect, category of the novel. Though the medieval romance was one of many roots of the modern novel, any attempt to define it by its affiliation with that remote and highly ramified genre would be to classify the acorn in terms of the oak. What the romantic novel shares with other examples of the form, as its medieval counterpart with other texts in *romanz*, are superficial accidents of structure and medium; what distinguishes romantic fiction across the ages is the characteristic mode in which it presents human experience. Critics increasingly prefer to define the medieval romance in terms of mode rather than genre.[2]

The critical basis for such a definition is supplied by Aristotle. In the *Poetics* he proposes to classify the fictions through which men attempt to express their relationship to the universe according to the hero's power of action, which may be greater than ours, less, or roughly the same. Of the categories established by Aristotle, three are relevant here:

1. That in which the hero is superior in *kind* to other men and their environment, since he is a divine being, the subject of a *myth*.
2. That in which the hero is superior to other men in *degree* (not necessarily, though frequently, in rank, but rather in personal qualities) and to his environment by virtue of his superlative, even supernatural, abilities which make him the characteristic protagonist of *romantic* fiction.
3. That in which the hero is superior neither to other men nor to the environment in that, however admirable or abject his personal qualities, he is subject to the criticism of others and to the order of nature in his actions, which are related in various types of *mimetic* or realistic fiction.

In classical and European literature these three fictional modes – mythic, romantic, mimetic – though associated with various genres, are not exclusively confined to any particular form. In application to periods and types of literature, the terms indicate the predominance of certain elements rather than the presence of a fixed canon of characteristics identified with a specific genre.[3]

The fluid relationship between the various modes is illustrated by the way in which the borderline between the mythic and the romantic is blurred as ageing myths lose their original religious significance, providing story-tellers with a mass of narrative incident freed from the restrictions of realism by its original mystic function and the charismatic powers of the hero. With the coming of Christianity to Western Europe, bringing a new body of oriental myth, the mythology of preceding cultures, Roman, Celtic, and Teutonic, was freed from its sacred associations to provide fit subjects for romance. And in turn the saints and martyrs of the Church were celebrated in romanticized legends scarcely distinguishable from the contemporary romances of chivalry. Both betray their mythic inheritance by the frequency with which their plots are resolved by violation of the laws of nature and the charismatic ease with which their heroes dominate their environment and lesser men.[4]

In the long centuries of general illiteracy such demythicized material was less likely to become literature than part of the vast amorphous category of folk-tale, a subdivision of the romantic mode whose characteristic concerns are personal, psychological, and social rather than formally religious or ethical. Their universal and perennial relevance is reflected in the ease with which folk-tales survive from age to age and pass from one culture to another largely unaltered. Rationally judged, they are full of inconsistencies and improbabilities, but their patterns of repetition, their pictorial images, magical transformations, and disguised or changing identities have a logic of their own akin to that of dreams in which the unconscious seeks through a language of images both to express and disguise the contents of the mind; to disguise because, like traditional tales, dreams are frequently concerned with disturbing subject-matter – hate, incest, parricide – which the conscious mind does not care to realize. Such tales derive their lasting appeal from the universal nature of the emotions which the listener is invited to share by identifying with the hero (or, quite commonly, heroine) in the exploration of experience through feeling rather than conscious thought: maturation through struggle, independence from parental influence, self-realization, the establishment of wider personal relationships, and integration with society. Such basic human aspirations often underlie the more consciously formulated social ideals which are the concern of the literary romance, which, none the less, may draw its plot from folk-tale and its appeal from the underlying dream of wish-fulfilment.[5]

Folk-tales and fairy-stories seem entirely alien to the mimetic mode which measures the hero and his environment against the reader's experience of men and society. But many of their inconsistencies and absurdities lie only at the literal level where they make no pretence of offering an overall, consistent, and plausible imitation or 'mimesis' of normal life. They disregard mimetic truth in favour of a deeper meaning which underlies the surface events; their logic lies not in the improbable adventures which befall the hero but the resultant testing of his powers, not in the magic machinery which manipulates the plots but the variety of experience provided for him, not in the fantastic objects of his quest but in the achievements which such trophies symbolize. Details and incidents which seem implausible when they are read as accounts of material cause and effect appear perfectly plausible when seen as part of a self-consistent pattern expressing the inner stresses, desires, and aspirations to which the mind, conscious or unconscious, is subject. Such stories, though symbolic rather than mimetic in their methods of expression, are realistic in that they are concerned with fundamental and universal realities. 'Though they are not at all, in one sense, "like life", they have given many generations of hearers and readers . . . a deep conviction that they tell us in some way "what life is like".'[6]

To the fundamental human concerns of the folk-tale, the romance proper adds a social ideal based not upon life as it is known through the senses but as the imagination, inspired by a vision of what might be rather than by objective fact, dreams of it. Though its idealism can express itself at many social levels, romance is inherently aspiring, often aristocratic; yet in values as in setting it aims not at pure escapism or fantasy but at the conviction of reality. It is not satisfied with the trappings of realism but strives for the conviction that the world it projects has existed in some past golden age, or will be in some millennium to come, or might be if men were more faithful to their ideals than experience suggests them capable of being. The romance mode, indeed, cannot ignore reality since its idealism is constantly challenged in readers' minds by their knowledge of the imperfect world in which they live. From age to age, in order to meet that challenge, it repeatedly changes the nature and form of the perfection which it seeks to express: selfless chivalry inspired by love in the courtly romance of the Middle Ages, nobility in the service of the well-governed state in the allegorical and pastoral romances of the age of Elizabeth, escape from the aridity of reason to imagination, sensation and the dark underside of consciousness in the Gothic romance of the late eighteenth and early nineteenth centuries, the vision of a man-made brave new world in the scientific romances of the early twentieth and, in modern space fiction, flight from the failure of that dream to some perfect planet where man has truly mastered the universe.[7]

At the heart of the romance mode in all its manifestations certain values remain constant. From ancient Greece to our own age, the search for the ideal has been constantly concerned with the same essential experiences: love, honour, valour, fear, self-knowledge. Whatever genre the romance mode may adopt, they find expression through the same conventional motifs: the mysterious challenge or summons to a mission; the lonely journey through hostile territory; the first sight of the beloved; the single combat against overwhelming odds or a monstrous opponent. The conventions may be variously disguised, particularly in an age when the mimetic mode is dominant, but the power of their conventional nature can be felt through the trappings of realism. They may be marshalled in an infinite variety of ways, but the essential formal medium is always adventure. However the incidents are related, as independent episodes in the hero's career or in mounting sequence to a climactic adventure, the underlying structure is always a quest. And the quest, whether it is pursued on horseback through the trackless forests of the Middle Ages or by spaceship beyond the outer galaxies, is always to some extent symbolic.[8]

The need to express fundamental human concerns in the heightened terms of idealism leads the authors of romance to exploit a technique of superlatives: extraordinary, even supernatural, incidents, exotic settings, fabulous trappings, and properties which function as images as much as objects. 'And as they move from the realms of common experience the romance writers, of necessity, move into the realms of analogy; those realms in which, as in the realms of religious experience, actuality can be described only by metaphor. We are therefore, as it were, balanced between a realm of experience, the sensible, and a realm which has to be interpreted by means of the sensible.'[9] In the medieval romance, these expressive conventions, like those of narrative form and structure, though often deep-rooted in folk-tale and myth, draw much of their evocative power from their continuous corporate use. Their dual nature, mimetic and symbolic, puzzling to modern readers, presented fewer problems to an age accustomed to see all physical, mental, and spiritual phenomena as interrelated expressions of the divine will and to read all narratives at more than one level of meaning. Their recognition of symbolic overtones in ordinary objects and situations was not necessarily more conscious, more of a distraction from the pleasures of the narrative, than our appreciation of the lost slippers, magic lamps, exchanged rings, and awakening kisses of fairy-tale.[10]

The same duality marks the treatment of characters, presented in black and white terms according as they oppose or forward the ideal to which the quest is dedicated. Their roles are representational rather than individual, and in so far as they are subject to social criticism – a mimetic element invading romance – it is their conduct in relation to the ideal which is under scrutiny rather than their personal, psychological motivation. Whatever traits of personality or contemporaneity they may show, the figures of romance are essentially stereotypes in the service of its didactic purpose.[11]

The expressive conventions of the literary form reflect in their antithetical nature – adventure and instruction, fantasy and idealism, symbolism and realism – the mixed nature of the romantic mode, poised between the mythic and the mimetic. The tension between the various expressive means reflects the paradox within the mixed mode, which in turn reflects the dual nature of man as sensualist and idealist, escapist and moralist. From age to age, the shifting balance between the two sides of the human temperament finds different social expression and romance flourishes or dwindles.[12] Throughout the Middle Ages it was all-pervasive, showing itself not only in almost every literary genre, including the professedly mimetic categories of chronicle, history, and biography, but in the other arts and even the forms and ceremonies of courtly life.[13] In so far as the medieval romances can be recognized as a group, it is by the particular aspects of the age and its aspirations which they seek to express rather than by any distinctive characteristics of form or literary means. The external characteristics which associate them as a genre are less significant than the fundamental attribute they share with the romances of other ages: that they represent life as it is *and* as it might be, as imperfect reality *and* imagined ideal in one.

The scanty records of civilization suggest that Man has told himself stories from the beginning of time, partly for the simple pleasure of it, partly in order to understand himself and the world about him. But just as scientific explanation of the universe was still beyond him and record-keeping too rudimentary to let him see his past in historical perspective, so a wholly objective view of the human condition was neither possible nor appealing to him. A particular truth about the fate of Smith or Jones would have seemed too limited, a factual description of the world about him too narrow to be worth repetition through the ages. Instead, he produced in myth imaginatively convincing accounts of the origin of the universe and his relationship to the gods who shaped his destiny; and in legend versions of his past which, however slight their conformity with history, satisfied his need for racial significance through association with giant figures of the past, real or imaginary. He credited their pro-tagonists, gods, demi-gods, and heroes, with supernatural powers which overrode all the limitations of his own humanity, providing imaginative fulfilment protected from reality by religious belief and respect for ancestral tradition.

But this mythic mode of viewing the universe could not satisfy Man's need to see himself in relation to it, since daily experience demonstrated the limitations of his own powers. The most he could do was to credit his representatives in the folk-tales he invented and repeated down the ages with powers which mimicked those of the heroes of myth and legend, but exceptional in degree rather than supernatural in kind, human qualities of body and mind beyond the limitations of common men. Upon them he could project his dreams of what might be achieved in the difficult world of his daily experience by wit and muscle, beauty and charm beyond those of which he knew himself possessed. At one level of his mind he acknowledged the real nature of the world around him and his own human limitations; at another his imagination defied reality and dreamed of what might be possible given courage, daring, luck, and the occasional supernatural intervention in which science had not yet undermined his belief. Hovering between a too acute awareness of reality, which produced depression and cynicism, and an over-ready indulgence in dreaming, which induced fantasy and escapism, he evolved stories in the romance mode which could inspire hope and raise aspiration, moderated but undaunted by the likelihood of failure.

The stories of *Jack the Giant-killer* and *Cinderella*, of *Tom Thumb* and *The Sleeping Beauty* and their variant versions in many cultures, told and retold down the ages, embody universal ideals of exceptional personal qualities tested in strange adventures which prove the power of wit, strength, and goodness to triumph over evil, allowing their possessors to attain maturity, win a marriage partner, and live happily ever after. Their expressive means like many of their motifs, the cruel stepmothers, rival siblings, cloaks of invisibility, flying carpets, helpful talking animals, may change from age to age, from one culture to another, but the central values remain constant; they acknowledge the real world and men's dreams of surmounting or circumventing its difficulties. Such basic embodiments of the romance mode never lose their validity, are independent of the literary fashions of any particular age or society, and endlessly adapt themselves to new expressive means as they arise.

But the romance mode may also embody the specific idealism of a particular society or class and express itself in distinctive literary forms peculiar to the culture of an age. With the passage of time, as the pattern for the good life which such literature proposes is in part achieved in part outmoded by changing social circumstances, the revolutionary instinct underlying the romance mode, always eager for new worlds to conquer, offers an alternative model based on other ideals. The old idealism as it fades into the mists of time is seen in false perspective as part of a golden age whose dreams had become reality, distanced, exotic, romantic, inspiring the new age in its attempt to define its own ideals.

The reincorporation of the romance mode which took place in Europe in the Middle Ages seems in the apparent suddenness of its emergence a new creation. But the poets of northern France who gave it fresh expression in the twelfth century had partial models in their ancestors' *chanson de geste* which expressed martial codes still valid in their own age, in contemporary adaptations of classical stories where women were associated with male idealism as inspirers or rewards of valour in arms, and in newly circulating Celtic legends whose dominant, passionate heroines inspired the concept of valour in the service of love. What was new was the frankness and fascination with which the *romanz* narratives expressed the interests of the age, above all the concept of a love demanding absolute, mutual commitment devoid of the social restrictions and self-interest of feudal match-making, inspiring and controlling for socially valid purposes the chivalric energies which were a threat to good order in a violent age.

The skill with which the French poets devised expressive means for the reincorporated mode, partly invented, partly adapted from the classical texts which had been their rhetorical models in the schoolroom, strengthen the impression of a newly created genre. The motifs which they found most useful for their purpose – the court gathered round an archetypal feudal monarch in embodiment of chivalric values, the challenge to those values which its reputation provoked, the solitary quest of its representative along forest pathways to answer that challenge, the temptations which beset him in welcoming wayside castles, the lovely woman wooed and won among a maze of adventures, the eventual victory in combat against the challenger and triumphant return to court – were to be used and reused until they came to seem synonymous with *romanz*. But like the literary technique which made the new genre so seductive – the fluid octosyllabic couplet equally effective in narrative and dialogue, the monologue of reflection and self-examination expressive of feeling, the supernatural interventions, unquestioned and unexplained, conveniently supplying the plot-machinery, the discreet narrator directing reactions by comment and irony – the characteristic motifs were the accidents of medieval romance subject to time and changing fashion. The historical survey of the evolution of the genre in Chapter 2 shows how rapidly they were modified, extended, and replaced as new subject-matter was drawn into the courtly literature of France, from native history and legend, from classical literature, from the oral tales of Celtic Britain, from European and oriental folklore. As the new matter was used to express new aspects of courtly idealism, religious as well as secular, as the rising bourgeoisie were drawn to romance by its adventures rather than its ideals, the genre changed in motifs, expressive means, and in the balance of fantasy and reality. What remained constant was the core of the mode, the characteristic tension between the real and the ideal which French *roman courtois* shared with the romances produced by other ages and cultures.

In the aftermath of the Norman Conquest England inherited the French tradition, but inherited it piecemeal without discriminating between the various subject-matters, between early versions and late, between aristocratic idealism and popular adventure stories. Nor was the English tradition merely derivative; its makers showed their independence in selection of source material, in the radical nature of their redactions, and the freedom with which they intermixed them with native folklore. The random selection and chance survival of English versions, their uncertain dating and unknown authorship, the undefined nature of their audience make the establishment of any evolutionary tradition impossible in the present state of our knowledge. Even the grouping of texts for study and comparison risks the imposition of modern perceptions of structural or thematic similarity. The arrangement adopted here, related to the story-matters successively incorporated into French *romanz*, allows appreciation of the loose relationship of the English versions to that tradition and of their own distinctive identity. The variety of forms in which they intermingle convention and originality, imitate and invent motifs, will demonstrate the futility of judging them by the superficial characteristics of the genre. It is by the fundamentals of the mode, by their success in incorporating the perennial tension between ideal and reality peculiar to romance that they are entitled to be judged.

## Notes

1. The term was, for example, applied to the pseudo-chronicle of the *Roman de Brut*, the psychological allegory of the *Roman de la Rose*, the *Roman de Renart* beast fable, and even to a Life of Christ. On the range of reference in English see Dieter Mehl, *The Middle English Romances of the Thirteenth and Fourteenth Centuries* (London, 1968), pp. 13–22.

2. 'It is doubtful whether the romance can be indeed regarded as a genre at all. . . . The romance is in origin merely a narrative in the vernacular and the texts that we call romances merely a somewhat arbitrary selection from medieval narrative. . . . It seems preferable to speak of a romance mode' (Pamela Gradon, *Form and Style in Early English Fiction* (London, 1974), pp. 269–70).

3. 'The words "romantic" and "realistic", for instance, as ordinarily used, are relative or comparative terms: they illustrate tendencies in fiction, and cannot be used as simply descriptive adjectives with any sort of exactness' (Northrop Frye, *Anatomy of Criticism* (Princeton, New Jersey, 1957), p. 49). Frye helpfully restates and extrapolates Aristotle's theory (see pp. 33–52) and develops his own conception of romance in *The Secular Scripture: A Study of the Structure of Romance* (London, 1976).

4. See W. P. Ker, *Epic and Romance*, reprint (London, 1908), pp. 40–41.

5. 'The romance is nearest of all literary forms to the wish-fulfilment dream. . . . In every age the ruling social or intellectual class tends to project its ideals in some form of romance, where the virtuous heroes and beautiful heroines represent the ideals and the villains the threats to their ascendancy' (Frye, *Anatomy*, p. 186). See also Anne Wilson, *Traditional Romance and Tale: How Stories Mean* (Ipswich,

1976), pp. ix–x, and Derek Brewer, *Symbolic Stories: Traditional Narratives of the Family Drama in English Literature* (Cambridge, 1980), p. 10.

6. Brewer, p. 1.

7. '. . . there is a genuinely "proletarian" element in romance too which is never satisfied with its various incarnations, and in fact the incarnations themselves indicate that no matter how great a change may take place in society, romance will turn up again, as hungry as ever, looking for new hopes and desires to feed on. The perennially child-like quality of romance is marked by its extraordinarily persistent nostalgia, its search for some kind of imaginative golden age in time or space' (Frye, *Anatomy*, p. 186). The varieties of English romance are briefly outlined in Gillian Beer, *The Romance* (London, 1970).

8. See John Stevens, *Medieval Romance: Themes and Approaches* (London, 1973), p. 16 and Frye, *Anatomy*, pp. 186–87.

9. Gradon, p. 226.

10. '. . . in order to grasp the essence of a medieval work, we must extend our feeling for the symbolic nature of the world to every object and every action. . . . There will be moments during a story when we can give ourselves up entirely to the charm of the narration. But suddenly there may come a passage in which things appear in an unexpected light and there is a sense of mystery; the medieval reader, accustomed to look for the reality behind the veil, would pause, baffled but thoughtful, and gradually let himself be permeated by the deeper meaning of what he was reading, hearing or seeing' (Stevens, p. 153).

11. 'The romancer does not attempt to create "real people" so much as stylized figures which expand into psychological archetypes. . . . That is why the romance so often radiates a glow of subjective intensity that the novel lacks, and why a suggestion of allegory is constantly creeping in around its fringes' (Frye, *Anatomy*, p. 304).

12. The psychological factors which account for the enduring appeal of the romance mode are examined by Kathryn Hume, 'Romance: A Perdurable Pattern', *College English*, 36 (1974), 129–46.

13. See Stevens, pp. 227–37 and Gradon, pp. 269–72.

# Chapter 2
# The Evolution of European Romance

Medieval romance evolved in twelfth-century France, at that time the dominant culture of Western Europe. The nation state as we know it today did not then exist. Among other heirs to the shattered empire of Charlemagne, the King of France ruled in his own right only the north and east of the country, surrounded by territories held by his kinsmen or by the Angevin kings of England either directly or under his nominal suzerainty and bounded to the east by Burgundy, still part of the Holy Roman Empire. But the legal and literary heritage of Rome and the mutually intelligible dialects of Vulgar Latin (*romanz*) in use there gave these territories a cultural unity which was to become largely a political reality by the early years of the following century.[1]

The cellular state of France was characteristic of medieval Europe, divided into a patchwork of feudal fiefdoms held by great noblemen from a royal or imperial overlord in return for their allegiance and services, divided by them in turn among a host of minor vassals on similar terms. Duchies and counties might pass from the suzerainty of one monarch to that of another by conquest or matrimony, non-heritable lordships be taken from one vassal and bestowed on another, but the network of feudal allegiances endured unbroken. At its intersecting nodes lay the palaces of great kings in the capitals of emerging nation states or the regional centres of their seasonal visitation where they dispensed justice and consumed their revenues in kind; the fortified cities of their princely cousins, petty kings in all but their allegiance to a greater; the fortress towns of local magnates; the isolated castles of country lords whose landless younger sons served any master who would arm and mount them. All formed part, at very different levels, of the same political, military and social systems and acknowledged with varying degrees of sincerity the same religious, corporate, and personal values. Their courts were each, in proportion to the cultivation and capacities of its members, centres of social sophistication, art, and literature.[2]

The dominant literary tradition of the era was Latin, inherited by the

Church from the Christianized late Roman Empire and made the basis of its educational work throughout the Middle Ages. In France that work was first centred in the monasteries, stimulated in the eleventh century by monastic reform and revival, then shared by episcopal schools in the growing centres of population and trade. Their primary aim was spiritual and theological enlightment, and their classical inheritance of history, grammar, and logic was as much valued to that end as the biblical commentaries of the Church Fathers. The key to both was the Latin language, close analytical study of which encouraged stylistic awareness and appreciation of the expressive resources of the vernaculars descended from it. With the Latin medium, medieval schoolmen inherited not only the Vulgate Bible but also a large part of the secular literature of imperial Rome and, through the translations and summaries of Boethius (c. 480–524), some of the fruits of Greek systematic observation and analysis in the works of Plato and Aristotle. Ecclesiastical libraries included poetry as well as theology, pagan as well as Christian authors. Even those whose professional interest in the pagan poets was limited to matters of style and technique could not resist the poetic power of Virgil, Statius, Ovid, Terence, Juvenal, Horace, and Lucan, read aloud during monastic meals or privately in hours of recreation, or the temptation to imitate them in their own writings. They may have been consciously valued as models of rhetoric, the art of presenting old truths persuasively, but their very success in that art made their contents insidiously attractive. The Latin literature of the schoolmen – panegyrics of royal defenders of the faith, lives of militant martyr saints, versified summaries of moral doctrine – is full of classical reminiscences. Such material, basically functional and didactic, was to endure throughout the Middle Ages and to evolve genres later exploited by secular poets writing in the vernacular.[3]

Meanwhile the clerics themselves, literate in Latin and native speakers of *romanz*, were potential producers of vernacular literature. Even in their professional capacity they served both Church and State, the greatest acting as royal administrative officers, others as teachers, doctors, jurists, the humblest as chaplains and stewards in the households of petty vassals. Those too ill-educated or lacking in patronage to find any employment, ecclesiastical or secular, wandered the Continent as perpetual students, drifting from school to school, or as 'pilgrims' haunting the shrines where alms or occasional offices might be acquired. These *clerici vagantes* were natural recruits to the ranks of the *trouvères*, finders or makers of secular literature, and willing co-operators with the *jongleurs* who sang or chanted it in market-place or castle hall. Much of their material existed only in oral form but its influence was widespread, travelling easily with its makers and performers across the internal boundaries of Christendom.[4]

## Vernacular literature and its audience

The literature of the masses, the tales told by the fireside and the songs sung in the inns from time immemorial, made its own immortality by its perennial appeal to popular taste. It was unlikely to achieve written form unless, by chance, it caught the attention of the clerics who controlled the expensive apparatus of literacy and who were liable to rework it in 'art' versions of their own. The earliest vernacular texts which they have left us, anonymous didactic works, sermons, and saints' lives, translated or adapted from Latin originals, show the clergy, long accustomed to preach in the vernacular, using the same medium to influence the literate classes. Their success led to the rapid development of other Latin genres for the entertainment of laymen, but French literature was still little more than an echo of the literature of the Church when, at the end of the eleventh century, both epic and lyric appeared, apparently simultaneously. The survival of texts from these centuries is so much a matter of chance that appearances may be deceptive. That no songs were heard in castle halls before the appearance of the courtly lyric is inherently improbable. As for the epic, there are allusions in Latin manuscripts to the reciting of poems on the heroic deeds of noblemen; many clerics were active participants in contemporary warfare, so martial values were not alien to them; the existence of Latin epic poems on the siege of Paris by the Normans (885) and on Germanic legends of the struggle against Attila shows their willingness to preserve material of military interest; many of the saints' lives they wrote in both Latin and *romanz* breathe the same martial spirit. The appearance of the *Chanson de Roland* (*c.* 1100), an epic fully formed and complexly structured, represents the maturing rather than the first flowering of a tradition of secular narrative in the vernacular.[5]

The audience for such literature did not exclude ecclesiastics, nor were the laymen for whom it was primarily intended entirely devoid of learning. Many princes of the Church were members of noble families, and younger sons, educated for ecclesiastical office, were sometimes required by family circumstances to return to secular life. Some of their brothers shared their knowledge of Latin and the classical authors to whom it gave access. But many of their country cousins were as ill-educated as the minor clergy and, more often than not, illiterate even in the vernacular. In an age when the supply of reading matter was limited by the high cost of producing individual copies on expensive parchment, illiteracy was a merely technical problem to be solved by employing the professionally literate. It carried little stigma for laymen who were judged by their social rather than their intellectual gifts nor, in an age of oral culture, did it necessarily mean that they were ill-informed or unenlightened. The nobleman to whom all books were closed might be no less socially perceptive, no less able to judge how his tastes and interests were expressed by the *jongleurs* who performed before him, or to appreciate the technical virtuosity of their performance.[6]

To please him they had to cater to his interest in the values, corporate and personal, uniting him to others in the network of feudal alliances which constituted the social structure of the age. Both codes had been moulded by historical forces and coloured by the complex cultural influences to which France was heir. In the chaos following the break-up of Charlemagne's attempted revival of the Roman Empire, men had fallen back on older bonds which promised security in an age of violence. Among the Germanic peoples to which their Frankish ancestors belonged, the mutual dependence of the kinship group, extending to remote degrees of cousinship, provided a degree of protection in peace and war. In war the chiefs surrounded themselves with a bodyguard of close dependants bound to them by the generosity with which they provided weapons, lands, and livelihood, owing them loyalty to the death in return. The peacetime value of family solidarity was recognized in the emerging corpus of law under which kinsmen were guarantors of oaths, avengers of murder, champions in trial by combat. Imperial Rome had had its counterpart in the system of patronage by which lesser men attached themselves as clients to those powerful enough to support them in civil and legal disputes, and elements of Roman law now served to regularize and codify the feudal system. Gradually the personal service of vassal to overlord in war and peace was formalized into lifelong fealty in return for the granting of a fief which the holder would strive to turn into a hereditary property. Late in the process, the Church added a gloss of sanctity to the dubbing ceremony by which young warriors were admitted to the service of an older, and the oath of fealty by which vassals swore loyalty to an overlord. Its approval served to strengthen the element of idealism in what was essentially a system of mutual self-interest: to die for one's lord, it declared, was akin to martyrdom, to kill him was unpardonable treason; he and his followers were in duty bound to protect the weak, right wrongs, and defend Holy Church.[7]

French history after the collapse of Charlemagne's empire is a record of the breach of those ideals in internecine war between Christian rulers, the abuse of seigneurial power, the rebellion of vassal against overlord, brutal disregard for the defenceless peasantry taxed and trampled upon by both, cynical neglect of feudal code and Christian morality. But even when such attention as men could spare from the struggle to retain and extend their own domains was given to resisting the central authority of the King, the old imperial dream still fascinated them. That, they could convince themselves, had been a golden age when Christian Europe had been united under a political and military genius to drive back the forces of paganism: Norsemen perpetually raiding down the western seaboard, Saxons threatening from the North, Slavs and Avars from the East, and in the South the incursions of Muslim Spain which in 732 had reached as far as Poitiers. By the eleventh century the tide had long turned: the Norsemen were settled in Normandy, the Muslims, riven by faction, were in retreat before the Christian reconquest of Spain, and in 1095 the Pope, invoking Charlemagne's example, launched the First Crusade for the recovery of the Holy Land. About that time was made the oldest surviving example of French epic, the *Chanson de Roland*.

## The Matter of France: *La Chanson de Roland*

Its central event is recorded in the royal annals under the year 778 when, as Charlemagne was returning from an abortive mission to take possession of Saragossa, promised him for military aid to one Muslim faction fighting another, his rearguard was attacked by Basques in the Pyrenean pass of Roncevaux where many nobles, including Roland, Count of the Breton Marches, were killed. The incident, a significant defeat for Charlemagne, was important enough to figure in the official history of his reign, but the poetic version is so distorted as to suggest that its sources were legend rather than history. In the 300 years between event and poem we have glimpses of the material in evolution, but the process of transmission remains obscure. Scholarship once favoured the idea of short songs made close to the events they celebrated, then woven together into full-scale epics; later the manifest clerical influence was attributed to co-operation between monks and *jongleurs* along the pilgrimage routes to Spain on which key events of the poem are located; recent opinion suggests the influence of Latin epics, Carolingian histories and lives of heroic saints at the culmination of a long, slow process of oral transmission and corporate elaboration over the centuries. Songs on epic subjects were circulating in the vernacular by the middle of the eleventh century; what resemblance they bore to the oldest text of the *Roland*, copied a century later, we cannot tell. But all opinions agree that that version bears the unified and integrated stamp of a poet of genius.[8]

The narrative can be seen as falling into four parts. *The betrayal*: having, after seven years in Spain, subdued all resistance except that of Marsile, King of Saragossa, Charlemagne receives a deputation from him promising submission. His nephew Roland, suspecting treachery, urges continuation of the war and is opposed by his own stepfather, Ganelon. Roland then volunteers for the dangerous mission to Saragossa to arrange the surrender, and when Charles refuses to risk losing him or any of his twelve peers, nominates Ganelon instead. Ganelon plots with Marsile to attack the French rearguard which will be commanded by Roland. *The battle*: as the French forces prepare to cross the Pyrenees, Ganelon nominates Roland to command the rearguard. In the pass of Roncevaux, Oliver sees the whole Saracen force emerging from ambush and urges Roland to blow his horn and call back the main French army. Roland refuses until the rearguard has been reduced to sixty men, then dies in the effort of sounding it with superhuman power. *The revenge*: hearing the horn signal, Charlemagne returns with ten divisions, encounters the Emir Baligant newly arrived from Babylon with thirty, defeats him utterly and captures Saragossa, before bearing the bodies of Roland and the other peers back to France for burial. *The punishment of Ganelon*: when he is accused of treason, Ganelon's guilt is proven in trial by combat and he is torn apart by wild horses.

To the age for which it was written this was a *chanson de geste*, a song of deeds and those deeds predominantly military. But though the action is so largely concerned with battle and the fundamental theme is an affirmation of feudal loyalty as the basis of salvation for Christian France, there is more to the poem than epic celebration of past triumphs. The historical perspective, partly distorting, partly interpretative, by which the political concerns and social values of *c*. 1100 are projected upon the reign of Charlemagne, gives his fictitious triumph inspirational significance for the age of the crusades. But there are ironic contrasts between present reality and epic past which can scarcely have escaped the poet's contemporaries: the power of Charlemagne, focus of patriotic sentiment and personal attachment, contrasted with the feebleness of the French monarchy, constantly undermined by its natural allies and dependants determined to escape from their feudal allegiances; the solidarity of Christendom contrasted with the perpetual feuding of Christian princes which made popes preach crusades as a desperate remedy for internecine strife. And there are ironies within the poetic myth itself: Charles the Great, symbol of Roman achievement and French aspiration, is now over two hundred years of age and his flowing white beard bespeaks a wisdom belied by the blind confidence with which he conducts military campaigns and his erratic control of councils of state; despite his victory at Roncevaux, the campaign which opened with virtual triumph in Spain closes with his weary expectation of future struggles to come. Without the Baligant episode, which some critics believe to be a late insertion, his victory would be less sweeping and the action as a whole more obviously centred upon Roland. Its inclusion increases the scale of the challenge to Christendom, but though the might and the military code of the Saracens is respected, their paganism irrevocably weakens their moral standing – 'paien unt tort et chrestiens unt dreit' (pagans are wrong and Christians in the right) the poet asserts. They serve as a focus for emergent French nationalism, but the real moral challenge to that society comes from within.

Parallel to the theme of national resistance to external challenge runs another of conflict within the network of feudal relationships: of Roland and Ganelon as kinsmen and rivals for repute and honour; of Roland and Oliver as brothers in arms radically different in temperament; of Charles overdependent upon his vassals, by turns indulgent and inflexible in his control of them. His instability, which allows the enmity of individuals to threaten the safety of the State, may reflect feudal prejudice against monarchical authority; the emotional roots of that enmity, reminiscent of folklore, universalize the personal conflict beyond its feudal context. It is tempting to see Ganelon as the wicked stepfather, motivated by pure malice to destroy Roland, ignoring the feudal law that any attack upon a vassal was an attack upon his overlord, so that his private enmity was treason to Charles. But the poet is determinedly fair-minded in showing him alienated by Roland's nomination of him to the perilous mission to Saragossa, courageous in fulfilling it, open in his defiance of his stepson before the whole court. The final verdict against him seems to turn on the fact that he had allowed natural resentment so to cloud his judgement that his private revenge imperilled the nation.

Yet the national disaster, whose inevitability is felt from the beginning of the poem, also depends upon similar defects in Roland. Ganelon plays upon his pride and impetuosity to ensure the tit-for-tat revenge which, like a well-set trap, leads to an Aristotelian tragedy rooted in the defects of a heroic personality. The definition of those defects is conditioned on the one hand by the comparison between Ganelon, blinded by self-interest, and Roland who seems to equate his personal reputation with the national interest, and on the other by the contrast with the equally courageous but more prudent Oliver constantly underscored by the poet: 'Rollant est proz e Oliver est sage' (Roland is valiant, Oliver is wise). Some critics have seen the contrast between them as a personification of a familiar rhetorical opposition, *fortitudo* versus *sapientia*, as idealism opposed to realism. But if Oliver's rational and moderate behaviour typifies the quality of *mesure*, much praised in the age, it is the very extravagance of Roland's *demesure*, his intemperance in courting national disaster for the sake of personal honour, the irrationality of his refusal to summon help against overwhelming odds which most excites the poet's enthusiasm. Yet he does not blink at the disastrous results or spare his hero the criticism of his closest companions.

Attempts by modern critics to determine the poet's ultimate

assessment of his hero by striking a balance of praise and blame are
frustrated by the element of ambivalence in the behaviour he describes
and his withholding of any direct comment on it. He seems rather to be
exploring the paradox of heroism; by placing Roland in the archetypal
epic situation – the last resistance of a man driven into a corner – not
through the malice of enemies alone but by his own excess of heroic
temper, he implies that the ultimate test of the heroic nature is internal
and self-determined by its own code. So Roland, having first tried to
shatter his sword, the emblem of his identity as a warrior, dies as it were
by his own hand in rectifying the error into which his pride had drawn
him. And his self-sacrifice seems approved: angels bear his soul towards
heaven, the Saracens he has engaged are exposed to the French
counter-attack, and God causes the sun to stand still while Charlemagne
takes revenge on them. Through the magnificent folly of Roland,
martyr and victor, the nature of heroism has been explored, not with the
intention of demonstrating a thesis but of exciting wonder at and
celebrating the mystery it represents.[9]

This central concern, to which everything contributes, provides an
underlying coherence in a narrative whose elements rarely form a logical
sequence in time or in terms of cause and effect. A train of events, a
scene, a speech may be abruptly interrupted without reason only to be
resumed later without any rational link or transition. The attention is
totally preoccupied by each while it lasts and they follow one another
like a series of vivid tableaux, individual moments of great dramatic
intensity, rather than a unified drama. Yet there is an underlying unity
created by the balancing of episodes similar in nature contrasting in
significance (Marsile's council with his servile, flattering vassals
followed by Charlemagne's with his independent, quarrelsome peers),
and the continual restatement of themes in similar terms. Most characteristic is the technique of repetition with variation by which successive
verse paragraphs (*laisses*) repeatedly present the same episode, gradually
revealing more of the action or different aspects of an emotion, each
repetition giving a separate impression of the same event.

The effect is to reinforce the emotive significance of events which
constitutes the unity underlying the fragmented narrative. In the
original oral performance of the *jongleur*, the events of a traditional story
already known to the listeners were not of primary importance, so the
narrative is swift and taut, unhindered by analysis of motive, and the
characters are developed through their actions and their reactions to
others' deeds. Description is limited, vivid, and formulaic, presenting
statuesque attitudes and symbolic gestures, endowing repeated
evocations of the Pyrenees with an ominous atmosphere appropriate to
the events located there. Variety is achieved by changes of pace and
tone, lyrical passages alternating with fully orchestrated crescendos in

battle scenes and passionate tirades – direct speech occupies close to half
the poem's 4000 verses. The ten-syllable lines are grouped in *laisses* of
varying length by sharing a common assonance of the final stressed
vowel, less demanding than full rhyme for the *jongleur* filling out a
familiar narrative by improvisation. Linked only by this minimal effect,
each line is an independent unit juxtaposed with others, often
contradictory, often associated in patterns of repetition and variation.
Each makes its individual impact upon the sensibility, and the effective
as well as the syntactical relationship between them is often left for the
listener to determine.[10]

The confidence with which this oblique rhetorical method is handled in
*Roland* suggests a long-established tradition. Elements of it were to
reappear in other poems dealing with Charlemagne and his immediate
predecessors and successors, with the rebellions of noble vassals against
their unjust or inept rule, and with the crusades organized by the Church to
provide a focus for national loyalty and united effort in defence of the faith.
This Matter of France (see below, pp.89–108) continued to be a topic of
courtly literature into the fourteenth century, its distinctive themes and
methods of presentation gradually contaminated by those of other types of
narrative in *romanz*. But is the *Roland* itself romance? Its relationship to the
romance mode is most apparent in its transformation of history in the spirit
of myth and in the interplay of antithetical elements which results: its
projection of the ideal of Christian solidarity expressed in the crusades
upon the golden age of Charlemagne evokes awareness of the continuing
struggle against Muslim power uniting past and present, while its attempt
to define an ideal of individual behaviour within the network of feudal
relations, associated with wider issues of human relationship by its folk-tale
patterns of friendship and enmity, invites the judgement of readers who
shared the values evoked. Neither its distinctive verse medium nor many
of its expressive conventions were to figure in recognized examples of the
romance genre. But identification of the characteristics of the genre is a
matter of hindsight; the poets of the *chansons* may, like their romantic
successors, have valued the symbolic power of their narrative conventions
no less than their suitability for the oral recitation which gave their poems
that distinctive title.

It is hindsight too which debars works like *Roland* from association
with the romance genre because they ignore a particular element, that
idealized love between the sexes which later ages were to identify as the
essence of romantic literature. The rare women in the early *chansons* are
shadowy background figures: noble mothers, chaste wives, or patiently
waiting betrothed like Oliver's sister Aude whose twenty-five-line role
is confined to dying at the news of her fiancé Roland's death. Saracen
maidens who press their attentions on some heroes are welcomed as

companions in adventure or prizes of war rather than inspirers of passionate devotion. But poets trained in the schools to admire their classical predecessors as models of style could scarcely fail to be attracted by their subject-matter, in which relations between men and women were often very differently presented. The Roman poems and Latin versions of Greek works offered them many of the satisfactions of the *Roland*: the valour and prowess of supreme heroes in the context of conflict on which the fate of nations hung, epic grandeur of theme and vastness of scale, even a sense of historical involvement through their belief in France's imperial heritage and the supposed Trojan ancestry of the Franks. But these chronicles of the deeds of men, so similar to their own *chansons de geste*, also celebrated noble women; sometimes as passive participants in a male world, unwitting causes or prizes of war, sometimes as active protagonists, inspirers or furtherers of heroic enterprises, passionately involved with the men who often wrong but cannot ignore them.[11]

## The Matter of Rome: *Le Roman d'Eneas*

The anonymous poet who, about 1160, adapted Virgil's *Aeneid* dutifully reproduces the adventures of the Trojan Prince in flight from his ruined city on a god-destined mission to refound it at Rome. But he seems less inspired by the endless wars which that involves than by the episodes concerning two unfortunate women afflicted by love of the hero: Dido, Queen of Carthage, who, despite her devotion to the memory of her dead husband, gives him her heart only to die by her own hand when his mission calls him away; and Lavinia, engaged to his chief opponent but tormented by an irresistible passion for Aeneas. The situations derive from Virgil, but their handling in the *Roman d'Eneas* is quite distinctive, greatly elaborated and focused on the feelings of the women, afflicted with love as by an incurable malady. In both episodes it is they who take the initiative. Aeneas's response to Dido is made more ambiguous by the French poet's need to play down the power of pagan gods in directing his mission, his inevitable desertion casting doubt on the sincerity of his protestations of love. But Virgil's sympathy for the deserted Queen is modified to implied condemnation by the adapter, not because her love was extra-marital but because it was unequal in view of Aeneas's great destiny, excessive in relation to his feeling for her, and unnatural because initially inspired by Venus, an insidious *fole amor* leading to moral atrophy and sexual licence. Lavinia's experience of love, freely developed by the medieval poet from Virgil's brief account, is hardly less painful. At first overwhelmed by an emotion she scarcely recognizes, she slowly grows in understanding, reasoning out her response to a love both desired and feared, suffering because she does not know whether her feelings are reciprocated, risking a breach of convention by declaring them to Aeneas. Aeneas too has to progress beyond the self-interest of his relationship with Dido to a fuller understanding of the nature of love as mutual, trusting, a *leal amor* demanding conscious, personal commitment to a relationship eventually sealed by marriage.[12]

These episodes in which love replaces war as the focus of interest are limited, but they include situations and forms of expression quite foreign to the epic spirit of Virgil's poem. There is the unheroic spectacle of the middle-aged widower Aeneas tossing in sleeplessness, weeping and begging the god of love to let him off lightly. There is Lavinia who has just declared that she has no use for love, struck by Cupid's dart as she stands in a window watching the Trojans pass, exploring her feelings through sleepless nights in long monologues of interior self-examination before confiding in her mother and stammering out the name of Aeneas syllable by syllable. Both matter and manner have one predominant source in the works of Ovid: the whole psychology and physiology of love elaborated, with ironic intent, in his *Ars amatoria* (*Art of Love*) and *Remedia amoris* (*Remedies for Love*), love as sickness, love as combat, are presented here in deadly seriousness; his *Metamorphoses* repeatedly show women taking the initiative in confessing their love, confiding in nurse or companion, expressing their conflicting emotions in self-questioning conducted on rhetorical principles. The greatly increased descriptive element – detailed pictures of palaces, temples, tombs, of the wonders of the ancient world, natural and supernatural, of personal beauty, male as well as female – suggests a series of classroom exercises from the contemporary schools of rhetoric for whom Ovid was a favourite model.[13]

The schoolmen, probably clerks in minor orders, who produced the *Roman d'Eneas* and similar medieval adaptations of the Matter of Rome (see below, pp. 109–131) in the decades after 1150 created a new type of courtly narrative by their fusion of epic action and Ovidian sentiment. The former allowed them to project the predominantly male and military values of their own society into a golden age of the past in a double perspective; romantic in its larger than life heroes serving an absolute ideal, realistic in its recognition of the human passions, vices, natural disasters to which they are prey. The latter provided means for the expression of one of those passions: an overpowering love, often tragic in its conflict with other, social claims on its victims, yet idealized as *leal amor* which, restrained by *mesure*, can develop through mutual trust and enhanced self-awareness, inspiring socially useful conduct. It is seen in clear, if somewhat negative form, in two adaptations from Ovid's *Metamorphoses*, *Narcisus* and *Piramus et Tisbé*, stories of young love frustrated by its own *demesure*, being excessive, immature, misdirected, and in defiance of parental authority. In both it is the women who take the initiative, who display most sensuality, who show themselves most conscious of the problems of love, of heart and head, instinct and social convention in conflict. Through them the spirit of Greek romance spoke to an age initially attracted to the classical inheritance by its epic interest.[14]

## The *lais* of Marie de France

The common medium of these romanticized epics is a fluid octosyllabic couplet which allowed their authors to write at enormous length (30,000 lines in one case), while the adapters of Ovid limited themselves to a mere 1000 lines. The same metre, the same restricted format and Ovidian fascination with the psychology of love, recur in a dozen short poems composed, most probably in the decade before 1170, by that medieval rarity, a poetess. The gentlewoman, Marie de France, calls her works *lais* and for most of them claims a Breton source, supposedly sung to the harp by Celtic minstrels wandering from court to court. The precise connection between song and poem has not been established, but Marie's *lais*, though they pretend to authenticity, suggest oral rather than written sources and folklore rather than learned origins. They are all concerned with adventure, a fated intervention in human life promising happiness not always actually attained, but are otherwise very various in length (from 118 to 1184 lines) and subject-matter: a lover who must win his bride by carrying her to the top of a mountain scorns the drug which would give him strength and dies with her in the attempt (*Les Deus Amanz*); a lady plots her husband's murder in order to marry her lover, but dies with him in the scalding bath intended for the victim (*Equitan*); a young wife shut up by her elderly husband is visited by a fairy lover transformed into a falcon which the husband kills, but not before she has conceived a child who later avenges his father's murder (*Yonec*); a knight of Arthur's court, to save himself from false accusations by Guinevere whose advances he had rebuffed, declares that he is loved by a far more beautiful woman and, despite the fact that he has broken an undertaking to keep their love secret, his fairy-mistress appears, forgives him, and vindicates him by her beauty (*Lanval*). Quite unembarrassed by the magical elements, Marie presents every episode with the same spare concreteness, as if drawn from contemporary life.[15]

Despite their variety of incident, each of Marie's *lais* is unified around a single idea which always relates to love as a fatal power controlled with difficulty. It is a mutual passion requiring equal idealism, equal sacrifices from man and woman. But most often Marie's sympathies are clearly with the women whom she allows to take the initiative, to display their erotic interest and act pragmatically in matters of the heart. Her own attitude is amoral: religious issues are ignored, adultery is countenanced, but legal marriage is always the ultimate goal; the power of the institutions and prohibitions of her own society are acknowledged in the tragic outcome of some tales; but blame rests with the cruel fathers and jealous husbands rather than the lovers whose destiny justifies many devious shifts. Their overriding obligation is to remain loyal to the mutual vows voluntarily undertaken, even if their union can only be attained through death – their own or that of anyone who stands in their way. Despite the individuality with which she has applied her concept of love to a variety of inherited narratives, her Prologue to the *lais* shows Marie conscious of working in an established tradition: the *leal amor* of the *Roman d'Eneas* is at the root of her conception and the Ovidian language of emotional analysis is used by some of her lovers in their initial, dubious exploration of the new emotion.[16]

## Versions of the legend of Tristan and Iseult

Hereafter the *lai* was to develop in parallel with the *roman* in much the same relationship as the modern short story and novel. One of Marie's *lais*, *Chevrefoil*, deals with an episode in the archetypal story of romantic love which was to inspire full-blown romances in almost every European language. In so far as its evolution can be traced, the legend of Tristan and Iseult exemplifies the complexity of folklore tradition in an age of oral transmission and of literary development when creation was conceived of as the rehandling of the common stock of stories, motifs, expressive conventions made potent in meaning by their accumulated associations. The hero's name is that of an eighth-century Pictish prince; the core of the plot came from Ireland, where Grainne, betrothed to the elderly Finn, put magic on his nephew Diarmaid to make him elope with her; it passed to Wales, where the legendary King Mark of Cornwall took Finn's place in the triangle, and then apparently to Brittany where elements of Graeco-Latin and oriental mythology were added.

As early as 1130, *lais* dealing with elements of the plot were circulating on the Continent; if it achieved unified treatment at this early stage, that version is lost though large parts of it may be represented in the poems of Thomas and Béroul, both themselves fragmentary. A fated, tragic love is at the heart of all the versions: Tristan, bringing home his uncle's bride, the Irish Princess Iseult, unwittingly drinks with her the love-potion which her mother had prepared to ensure lifelong happiness with the elderly Mark. Thereafter it is death for the two young people to be apart for more than a few days and they are driven to ever more devious shifts to conceal their relationship from Mark, to convince him of its innocence, enjoying only a fugitive happiness until they are joined in death under the intertwined trees which spring from their graves. It is not religious morality which torments them but the knowledge that the clever devices by which they deceive the jealous courtiers who would slander them to the King are dishonourable, their deception of Mark treasonable in wife and kinsman bound to him by feudal obligations.[17]

The existing versions cannot be directly compared since their surviving sections cover different parts of the story, but the two poets clearly differ in their interpretation of it. Béroul's poem, though later (c. 1190) than Thomas's (1155–70), is in the spirit of the *chansons de geste*, swift-moving, presenting the characters through their words and actions, with the minimum of introspection and authorial comment. The poet's sympathies are with the young lovers and he implies, admittedly ambivalently, that providence too favours them: when Mark discovers their hideout in the wildwood, he finds them sleeping with a drawn sword between them, a fortuitous if misleading symbol of chastity. But Béroul is also conscious of the conflict of love and feudal duty: Mark spares the sleeping lovers but leaves his sword, ring, and glove as a sign to them that he has not surrendered his rights as overlord, husband, and king. To resolve the conflict, Béroul allows the power of the potion to diminish after a time, they become conscious of the harshness of their life as outlaws, Iseult returns to her husband and Tristan goes into exile. But their love survives as human passion drawing them back to each other again.

Thomas accepts the lasting power of the potion, celebrating love as destiny, overriding social duty, incompatible with marriage, driving its victims to masochistic extremes of self-abnegation: Tristan, to share the agony of Iseult torn between lover and mate, marries a Breton princess who has his beloved's name, but cannot bring himself to consummate the marriage. For this poet love is a mystery to be reasoned out in the long interior monologues of the *Roman d'Eneas*, a mystic communion in which the laments of the parted lovers echo each other, sealed by the ceremonial of their death in love; the wounded Tristan, deceived into thinking that Iseult denies him her healing powers, dies invoking her name and she yields up her life on his lifeless body. The question of their spiritual salvation, like the issues of adultery, feudal duty, and personal conscience, is ignored in this idealization of romantic love.[18]

## Social ideal and social reality in the age of the romance

We have come a long way in the first seventy years of the twelfth century; from *Roland* to the *Tristan* of Thomas, secular narrative in *romanz* has radically changed in matter and manner. As the romance mode reincorporated itself in medieval terms, the idealism at its core gradually expanded and ramified, the balance between ideal and reality changing from decade to decade, text to text. Whether or not one regards the *chanson de geste*, or at least the earlier examples, as a distinctive genre, the *Roland* already presents the world in dual perspective, projecting upon the age of Charlemagne a complex ideal of personal and social conduct whose appeal for contemporary audiences lay in its relevance to circumstances of their own age which demonstrated the need for such qualities. At many levels from personal prowess, the loyalty of comrades in arms, mutual trust in the bonds of kinship, reciprocal fidelity within the feudal system, to national solidarity in defence of faith and sovereign, it depicts the values by which life might be lived. And at the same time it illustrates the individual urge for pre-eminence, the misunderstandings between comrades, the mistrust between those who are kinsmen only by law not blood which can endanger the common cause, the vulnerability of the feudal bond to the intemperance of autocratic rulers, and the treason of resentful underlings all too familiar to a France threatened from without by the power of Islam and torn within by the private wars of feudal barons and the resistance of over-mighty subjects to the authority of the monarch. The ideals are confidently asserted, to the point of paradox in the case of the hero's personal code; but the tacit acknowledgement of human failings – over-confidence, ambition, jealousy, self-interest – produces the characteristic ambivalence of the romance mode, of life viewed both as it is and as it might be.

The re-establishment of the perennial mode in medieval terms becomes more apparent as it begins to incorporate ideals which the age had not previously thought it possible to entertain, a feminine counterpart to the personal prowess and comradeship of military heroes. The stories of the ancient world inherited as the Matter of Rome included, among the deeds of supreme warriors in the service of an imperial ideal in which the twelfth century recognized the values of its feudal aristocracy, episodes in which women devoted to such heroes abandon the passivity of the heroines of the early *chansons* to express their feelings with a frankness hitherto unknown in *romanz* literature. The eagerness with which French poets elaborated the sufferings of Dido, the dawning passion of Lavinia acknowledges the appeal of a novel idea: that relations between men and women might be governed, not by the dynastic, territorial, financial factors on which the marriages of the feudal aristocracy were based, but by an irresistible passion mutually experienced and confessed. Yet the suffering involved and, in Dido's case, the unhappy outcome of a love presented as excessive and potentially destructive acknowledges the gap between ideal and contemporary reality. The mutual commitment of Aeneas and Lavinia to a relationship ending in marriage is more acceptable as an adjunct to rather than a distraction from his imperial destiny. Both affairs are episodic, isolated from the epic context, as if the romance mode had not yet acquired the confidence to challenge reality at the emotional level as openly as at the level of military codes and feudal relationships.

The fortuitous combination of folk-tales largely unmarked by the values of any particular society and a poetess adept at making them vehicles for the social concerns of her own age produced in the *lais* of Marie de France expressions of emotional relations largely divorced from other considerations. In them love is a fatal power experienced equally by men and women, demanding equal sacrifices from both; they openly acknowledge the emotional needs and sexual appetites of women but celebrate an ideal of mutual commitment ending in marriage. Nothing, even adultery or death, is allowed to inhibit the emotional fulfilment of the lovers. Yet the barriers to their happiness – cruel fathers, jealous husbands, feudal custom, religious prohibition – reflect the reality of the age and its institutions, too powerful to be overcome even by love without the aid of supernatural agencies. In *romanz* versions of the Tristan legend such an agent, the love-potion, makes possible the romantic ideal of an overpowering love which surmounts and sweeps away all barriers – social, legal, and spiritual. But it does so at the cost of every other value of twelfth-century life: kinship, feudal duty, marital fidelity, personal honour. The lovers, driven from one desperate shift to another to be together, are tormented, exiled, ultimately separated by a passion which, since it is chemically induced, does not ultimately satisfy the need of the age to believe in love as an overwhelming emotional force naturally and instinctively conceived. The love-potion allows ideal to defy reality, but the characteristic ambivalence of the romance mode is uneasily underlined by the unnatural means and the destructive consequences.

The appearance of evolutionary development in which a feminine idealism of the emotions is superimposed upon and partly displaces a male idealism of action may be deceptive; the dating of texts is too uncertain to establish a progressive process and, as we shall see, there were other trends favouring harmonization of the seemingly conflicting values of love and war. Whatever the detailed timing of what was no doubt a complex process, the contrast between the *Roland* and the various *Tristan* texts implies a period of radical social change reflected in the rapid modification of the romance mode. It was accompanied by changes in the expressive means employed by poets so sweeping as to suggest the emergence of a new genre. The underlying evolution from a form of poetry essentially oral and dramatic to one inviting the reflection to which private reading is conducive, from one which celebrates established ideals to one which propounds and explores novel concepts in conflict with received opinion brought changes in the way experience was put before the audience. And, at the same time, the succession of story-matters drawn into *romanz* literature brought new types of supernatural agent for the ready manipulation of the action.

The oral technique underlying even the late literary texts of the *Roland* presents at every level from the single line to the isolated tableau moments of high drama, vivid but static, in which the heroic theme is exemplified in stark outline, only to be reiterated in the following line or scene. Like the flickering frames and sparsely captioned sequences of some silent film, the method relies upon the audience's familiarity with formulaic conventions, situations, and values to extrapolate meaning and theme from the discrete components. The self-consciously literary technique of the *Roman d'Eneas*, with its monologues of self-examination as aids to psychological understanding of motivation and its interest in feeling rather than action, seems almost at the opposite extreme of authorial intrusion. Marie, with her thematic concentration and dramatic concreteness, leaving striking incidents to carry their own significance with minimal commentary, makes adventure the characteristic stuff of romance, exposing her characters' values in their reactions to the unexpected and adventitious. The contrast between the *Tristan* of Béroul, with its dramatic narration concentrating on speech and action and a minimum of introspection in the manner of the *chanson de geste*, and the version of Thomas in which the interior monologues and laments of the lovers, in the manner of *Eneas*, express the mystery of love in emotional terms, demonstrates the coexistence of various expressive means. Despite the almost universal adoption of the octosyllabic couplet, the genre is no more uniform in literary method than in its reincarnation of the romance mode of literary perspective.

The medieval concept of romance is now clearly exemplified: myths whose original meaning has been forgotten serve to display the powers of heroes without wholly protecting them from the challenge of reality, the criticism of contemporary values. But now they are matched with heroines no less charismatic, and the ideals they serve have changed dramatically. The military values of a society organized for war are still at the heart of their code, but their chivalry is no longer confined to the physical and moral virtues of the heavy cavalry which once defined it. What was once a profession in the service of a social system has become, with the inheritance from father to son of duties, rights, feudal holdings, an aristocracy of birth anxious to define the nobility which sets it apart from lesser men. Muscular ability and skill in arms are still taken for granted, loyalty to overlord, defence of Christendom, protection of the weak still familiar shibboleths. But the qualities now stressed are personal: nobility of nature, generosity, contempt for fatigue, pain, death, concern for reputation and the praise of one's peers; their attainment may benefit society but their primary effect is to exalt the knight above lesser men, *chevalerie* above *vilanie*, the qualities of a *villein*, a rustic boor. At the same time, the Church has taken advantage of its increasing involvement in chivalric ceremony to inject a moral element, binding the knight by oath to religious observances, to moderation in battle (sparing a defeated adversary), to justice in his seigneurial role (shunning treason to superiors, coercion of inferiors). The Church in return has given its blessing to the social supremacy of what is now effectively a ruling class.[19]

The seat of its power, administrative centre, place of justice, focus of social converse and ceremony, is the court, great or small depending on the seigneur's place in the feudal hierarchy. And out of the court comes a new chivalric quality, *courtoisie*: good breeding, social and moral refinement, personal elegance, politeness, skill in the social arts of music, dance, chess, and conversation – everything which makes life at court civilized and rewarding. With the growing consolidation of vast estates in the hands of mighty princes heading a hierarchy of nobility, their courts have become magnets drawing lesser men to share in the power and prestige concentrated there; places where magnificence of display is a political instrument and courtly manners a means to preferment. Consolidation and increased security have brought greater prosperity, trade with the East new luxuries – silks, spices, perfumes, precious stones – and contact with Islam in trade and war something of its own chivalry and the social values which it had absorbed from ancient Greece, modern Byzantium, Persia, and India – among them some indefinable elements of the oriental attitude to women, cloistered, unapproachable and revered. In Western courts where the sons of his vassals are fostered by their overlord and bred up as landless knights in his service, they come under the refining influence of the chatelaine and girls of good family in her care. As that influence grows in the growing intervals between one war and the next, respect for and devotion to women becomes an essential component of *courtoisie*.[20]

*Courtoisie* was both a social and a literary manifestation, the product of social circumstances, duly reflected in courtly literature which in turn set a model for refined conduct. In expressing that aspect of the courtly code which concerns the adoration of women, the *trouvère* poets of northern France lagged behind the troubadours of the South. The first known troubadour, William IX, Duke of Aquitaine (1071–1127), was a libertine, repeatedly excommunicated, master of a harem stocked with Saracen girls, whose poetry can celebrate the qualities of women in terms of mares to be mounted. But mingled with the coarsest barrack-room ballads there are songs idealizing women, passive and rather remote, as objects of a humble service demanding from the lover the highest courtly qualities: *valor* (moral worth) and the renown (*pretz*) which it brings; *jovens* (youthful generosity, material and moral); *joie* (the quest for happiness in life); and *mesure* (self-discipline and moderation of desire). The relationship assumed social benefit as well as self-interest, modelled itself upon feudal service (the lady being addressed as *mi dons* – my lord), and saw the wife of the seigneur as the worthiest object of love because the most exalted. If consummated it was likely to be adulterous, and so secrecy and discretion were absolutely binding upon the lover.

For William and the host of poets, noble and humble, who followed him, this *fine amor* (commonly called courtly love by scholars) was an idealization of relationships between the sexes, amoral and detached from Christian values as a subject for lyric verse of enormous technical complexity. In so far as their art related to life, it was by inversion of social reality: aristocratic marriage, particularly in the South, defied the Church's teaching; men chose wives for their estates and sought pleasure and love outside marriage; brutality and neglect on their part were common and divorce frequent. The northern *trouvères*, though uneasy about the implications of adultery, welcomed an idealization of love which postulated a greater refinement of human relationships than their own *leal amor*. They and their successors struggled to define infinite shades of *fole amor* (carnal love), conjugal love, and *fine amor*, which resembles married love except that it is between single persons who love, without self-interest, for the good qualities they see in their partners and only secondarily for sexual pleasure. Ultimately, in striving to exalt human passion, they might identify the lady who was its object with Holy Church or the Virgin Mary, just as they related all forms of love to that sacred love (*caritas*) which mutually binds the Creator and his creation.[21]

## The evolution of the Matter of Britain

Courtly love could find full expression in narrative literature only in texts less committed to epic interests than the *Eneas*, less restricted in scope than Marie's *lais*, such as the malleable compound of *Tristan* – though only the version of Thomas reflects the concept clearly. Tristan, once an independent Celtic hero, has already become associated with King Arthur who was to be the dominant figure in this Matter of Britain (see below, pp. 132–76). Arthur, originally a war-leader in legends of uncertain historical validity concerning British resistance to the invading Anglo-Saxons in the late fifth century, became the hero of an embryonic epic of great psychological significance for the defeated Celts. His personality drew to itself others of similar stature, heroes of forgotten epics and gods of dead religions, and with them a mass of myth and legend from all the Celtic nations confounded by a complex process of oral transmission from one to another and confused in meaning by the passage of time. He and his companions with their often supernatural powers appear sporadically as assistants in some impossible task facing a folklore hero, or as rumbustious pagans defying the spiritual power of some Welsh saint, fortuitous survivals of a mass of unrecorded folk-tales. The Norman rulers of Britain after the Conquest encouraged the literary celebration of the epic Arthur, using his patriotic reputation to rally Celts on both sides of the Channel against their defeated Anglo-Saxon subjects and legends of his Continental conquests as propaganda for their own imperial ambitions there.

Their purpose was effectively served by the *Historia Regum Britanniae* (1136) of Geoffrey of Monmouth, a Welsh cleric teaching in Oxford, who blended quasi-historical fact gathered from the British chronicles with a mass of convincingly contrived fiction in a prose epic which gave Arthur the legendary stature of Aeneas or Charlemagne. Its immense popularity – 180 manuscripts still survive – owed something to the fact that it lent historical respectability to other Arthurian material already widespread in Europe: improbable adventures made possible by fairy magic, exotic names from no known geography or culture, allusions to strange customs, fantastic symbols, and images which appealed to the dawning romantic taste for the picturesque. Of the various adaptations into the vernacular, the *Roman de Brut* (1155) by Wace, coloured by the poet's talent for description of fashionable manners and décor, began the process of turning Arthur and his companions of the Round Table into a mirror for the courts of Western Europe.[22]

Wace dedicated his book to Eleanor of Aquitaine, granddaughter of the troubadour William IX, who married successively Louis VII of France and Henry II of England, and through her dominant personality and numerous progeny influenced literary tastes in half the French-speaking courts of Europe. Between 1170 and 1174, while she held court at Poitiers, ruling the duchy in the name of her young son Richard Cœur de Lion, she tried to reproduce there the luxurious life she had seen at Byzantium in the course of a pilgrimage and perhaps something of the social values of neighbouring Saracenic courts. Hundreds of young knights flocked to the tournaments regularly held in her domains, and her immediate circle contained many noble women as sophisticated as herself. We do not know the extent of their formal education, but they were literate in French if not in Latin, patrons of music and poetry, intellectually aspiring and socially refined.

For one of them, her daughter Marie, Countess of Champagne, the cleric Andreas Capellanus wrote a Latin treatise *De Amore* (*c.* 1184–86), modelled on Ovid's *Ars amatoria* but inverting his cynical description of the arts by which men seduce women to show woman as dominant, man as a vassal in her service. Though it acknowledges the concept of *fine amor*, it is less interested in the sufferings of troubadours than in the social effects of passion, debating whether a lover who had broken his vow of secrecy to defend his mistress from calumny could be forgiven, whether love was possible between different classes, whether true love could exist within marriage. Even behind the mask of an academic exercise in dialectic, tinged with conscious irony, there are signs of the chaplain's embarrassment at his defiance, no doubt at the Countess's dictation, of social reality and church precept. There *was* a court, he insisted, where such values were an integral part of the practice of chivalry, that of King Arthur. Even in his Arthurian epic, Geoffrey of Monmouth had asserted that love was an ennobling and refining force, inspiring knights to win it by their valour and ladies to deserve it by their chastity. Such a concept could appeal to both sexes; what was needed now were examples of its operation, free and unrestrained in an ideal society. The raw material had long been available in the tales of wandering Celtic story-tellers, such as that Welsh or Breton *jongleur* Breri who was at Poitiers *c.* 1135, tales in which the interests of women – fairy-mistresses putting magic on men or testing the fitness of heroes for their love – were dominant. All that such matter needed to appeal to Eleanor or Marie was the gloss of courtliness.[23]

## The romances of Chrétien de Troyes

That transformation came in the work of Chrétien de Troyes who, between 1170 and 1190 produced five poems which came to represent the classic type of the *roman courtois*. His name associates him with Champagne and at least once he wrote directly for the Countess Marie, mistress (during the minority of her sons) of a court served by many poets. The extent of Chrétien's learning suggests that he was a cleric, most probably in minor orders to judge from his thorough familiarity with courtly life and values. Among his other works were love-songs, versions of Ovid, and a lost poem *Del roi Marc et d'Iseut la Blonde* concerned, perhaps, with their marriage rather than her adulterous liaison with Tristan. These compositions, and the manifest influence in all his work of the Matter of Rome romances and Geoffrey of Monmouth, show him involved in the main literary currents of his day. The five Arthurian romances, despite their use of names, themes, and motifs of manifest Celtic origin, are highly original creations. The basic plots of three of them resemble tales in Welsh which, however, reached written form at a late and uncertain date bearing signs of French influence and can offer no more than evidence of a common source with Chrétien's versions. On that evidence his poems are radical reworkings, mingling material from other sources, with much invention of detail and reinterpretation of theme in courtly terms.[24]

The variety and complexity of Chrétien's work can only be inadequately exemplified by two related yet contrasting examples. *Erec et Enide (c.* 1170) falls into three clearly marked sections. *The hunt for the white stag*: while Arthur's court is engaged in the ancient custom of hunting the white stag, Erec, accompanying the Queen unarmed, is insulted by a stranger knight whom he follows to a town where next day there is to be a tournament for the prize of a sparrow-hawk. Erec borrows arms from a poor gentleman who offers him hospitality, falls in love with his beautiful daughter Enide in her ragged gown, and asks for her hand in marriage; next day he defeats the insulting knight Yder and presents the hawk to Enide. Returning to court, they find that Arthur, having killed the white stag, must kiss the most beautiful woman there; he chooses Enide, whose pre-eminence everyone recognizes, and so avoids any disharmony. This might well be a *lai* of Marie de France: an idyllic love between two young people, equals in beauty and breeding, defying worldly considerations of wealth and rank; a Cinderella heroine, her true worth perceived through her rags, carried off to court as the prize of her prince's valour; through his prowess and her beauty, joy and harmony are restored to that court, threatened with disorder by a mysterious custom, imperative yet self- imposed. But under the fairy-tale surface there are social issues closer to the reality of contemporary life: Erec, inactive in the hunt, is unprepared for Yder's assault on the integrity of Arthur's realm, but quick to vindicate his own honour in a chivalric contest for the prize of a sparrow- hawk; he claims Enide's hand from her father, urging his wealth and royal blood – as in the *chansons de geste*, the girl's feelings are not considered. Marriage, the ideal conclusion of the *lais*, leaves these issues unresolved.

*The quest*: after a magnificent court wedding, the young couple honeymoon in Erec's own land where they are so absorbed in each other that he is criticized for his neglect of arms and·chivalry. Overhearing Enide reproaching herself for distracting him from duty, Erec orders her to accompany him in a quest for adventure; each time danger threatens, she breaks his command of silence to warn him, and he triumphs against ever-increasing odds until they are reconciled in mutual trust and love. The issues left unresolved by their fairy-tale marriage surface again as soon as their relationship is exposed to stress: Erec, though love has brought him awareness of another existence than his own, throws himself into marriage with the same absolute absorption as into his self-centred chivalry, until shocked into renewed action by concern for his reputation; Enide, passive and inexperienced, cannot prevent herself feeling some concern over the public criticism of Erec nor hide her doubts from him. The test to which he then submits her in a quest for adventures proves a double one, furnishing repeated demonstrations of his prowess for her reassurance and of her fidelity to him as, time after time, she breaks silence to warn him of danger until he realizes that her earlier words too were motivated by love. Together they progress through expiations of their initial faults to maturation and greater understanding of themselves and the codes they serve: self-serving chivalry and self-absorbed uxoriousness are not the only alternatives, love and adventure are not mutually exclusive; married love can inspire chivalric prowess in the service of society not merely self, as the concluding episode demonstrates.

*The 'Joy of the Court'*: bent on renewed proof of the prowess inspired by his confidence in Enide's love, Erec penetrates into a garden surrounded by a wall of air, encounters the giant knight Mabonagrain whose love-service to his *amie* requires him to behead all comers, defeats him and frees him from bondage to the lady and the whole region from the dread of an evil custom. This episode structually balances the opening encounter with Yder while thematically inverting its values. In each, chivalry serves to vindicate a woman's reputation: but where in the first instance Erec was motivated by vainglory, he now fights in the interests of social order threatened by mindless self-interest which uses a good knight enslaved by passion as the instrument of its malign purpose. The tyranny of *fine amor* through which his *amie* misuses Mabonagrain's prowess is contrasted with the healthy marital relationship of Erec and Enide who, now self-controlled and confident in her husband's valour, instructs the lady in true love as a willing partnership of equal rights and services. The equilibrium of love and social duty, self-knowledge and self-control, which they have finally achieved becomes of service to the wider community as, on the death of Erec's father, they are jointly crowned in his realm.[25]

If, in *Erec and Enide, fine amor* is unfavourably contrasted with marital love, in *Lancelot* or *The Knight of the Cart* (1177–81) it becomes the predominant social value, the touchstone by which all relationships are to be judged. According to Chrétien both the subject-matter and the theme were dictated to him by the Countess Marie. The shadowy outline of the story is detectable in the Celtic myth of a woman carried off by a mysterious stranger and rescued from his other-world realm by her husband, and on the evidence of a bas-relief on Modena Cathedral (dated about 1120–30) the central role was early assigned to Guinevere. At the beginning of the poem, through Arthur's rashness and ill-judgement, the Queen is carried off by Meleagant into the land of Gorre where many of her fellow-countrymen are held prisoner; by the end all have been released through the valour of the hero.

*The quest*: Gawain, on his way to rescue the Queen, meets another knight on the same mission whose horse has been killed in combat; offered a lift in the kind of cart in which criminals are carried to execution, the latter hesitates for two paces, then mounts and is carried on his way through public mockery. Faced with two perilous entrances to the land of Gorre, Gawain chooses the easier underwater bridge while the Knight of the Cart lacerates himself on the terrible sword-bridge. Later, as he fights her abductor Meleagant, he manœuvres so as to keep his eyes on the Queen watching from a tower and she recognizes him as Lancelot del Lac. The rescuer is not her husband but her lover, the intensity of whose passion has been repeatedly demonstrated: by the trance which almost causes him to fall from a window as he watches her led past in captivity; by the fervour with which he adores the golden hairs caught in a comb of hers left lying by a spring; by his self-control when one of his wayside hostesses insists on sleeping with him; above all by his voluntary humiliation in the cart. Such lack of moderation contrasts with the *mesure* he shows in chivalry, sparing a knight he has defeated and yielding to the request of a damsel to kill him for an offence to her only when he renews his attack. Yet it is love which inspires his prowess, sustains him at the sword-bridge, and allows him to rescue the Queen while his foil, Gawain, more concerned for his own honour, will fail.

*Rejection and reward*: when Lancelot is brought into Guinevere's presence, she turns coldly from him; but she relents after a false report of his death, while he, hearing a similar rumour of her, attempts suicide. She ultimately explains that his fault had been the momentary hesitation before mounting the cart, forgives him and invites him to a rendezvous that night; tearing the bars from her window, he kneels as if to a saint and they are united in love-making. When Meleagant accuses the Queen of adultery with another knight, Lancelot fights him in defence of her honour and spares him for the second time on her intercession. The lovers exemplify *fine amor* in its most absolute form: Lancelot, his will destroyed by love, has learnt complete submission to the woman he idolizes as a goddess, to accept shame for her sake, recognizing that his hesitation at the cart, unusual in one who unthinkingly accepts every challenge in pursuit of renown, sprang from putting his self-regard before her interests; Guinevere, under the imperious mask of the troubadour *belle dame sans merci* which she wears as an inspirer of selfless chivalric service, is bitterly conscious that she has wronged her lover by her inflexibility, and rewards him with a passion which equals his own. The extreme form taken by their adulterous relationship and the exaggeration of convention bordering on parody, in which it expresses itself, may seem to the modern mind to exclude sincere feeling; but the Middle Ages associated high emotion with formalized expression which intensified and dignified it beyond everyday experience.

*Imprisonment and identity*: in search of the laggard Gawain, Lancelot is ambushed and imprisoned by Meleagant but released, by the help of his gaoler's wife, to attend a tournament where Guinevere, seeing through his incognito, first orders him to fight badly and then to do his best. Reimprisoned, he is freed by Meleagant's sister whom he had served by beheading the offensive knight, and arrives at Arthur's court just in time to defend the Queen against the accusations of Meleagant whom he finally defeats and kills. In the renewed quest which is to bring full self-awareness and integration of his chivalric personality, Lancelot expiates his fault in a way which mirrors its nature and form, exposing himself to public humiliation at Guinevere's command and without a second thought – love has triumphed over self-regard. His progress is marked by a series of incidents in which he promises his affection to other women – the wayside hostess, his gaoler's wife, Meleagant's sister – who forward his mission; paradoxically, to win Guinevere, he must be willing to serve others. Like Erec, Lancelot in his new identity embodies the balanced interrelation of love and prowess, but here there is one issue unresolved: can *fine amor*, outside marriage, sustain selfless service to a society whose overlord, Arthur, does not yet know that his chief lieutenant is committing sexual treason with his wife? Some critics, detecting signs of irony in the near blasphemy of Lancelot's religion of love and, noting that Chrétien left a fellow-poet to finish the work, suggest that he was ill at ease with the theme dictated by the Countess Marie; others believe that, within marriage or not, courtly love being devoid of self-love was, for him, an adjunct of Christian *caritas* in the struggle of good against evil.[26]

There is latitude for such variant interpretations in Chrétien's compositional method, explained by him in his prologues to *Erec* (ll. 9–22) and *Lancelot* (ll. 24–29) as that of drawing from the tale of adventure which supplied his *matière* a *mout bele conjointure* (a very fine arrangement, composition) to bring out its *sens*, the meaning he found inherent in it. Working with inherited folk-tales whose mythic significance had long been forgotten and transformed, he apparently saw no need to harmonize every element of the original matter with his *conjointure* of courtly meaning, and narrative inconsistencies, loose ends of plot, and magical objects and supernatural occurrences remain to puzzle the reader who loses track of Chrétien's *sens*. Though his *sens* is always concerned with the ideals of the feudal aristocracy, it is not openly stated as propaganda but suggested with an ambivalence which leaves it to the individual reader to interpret in the light of his own moral perception. The conventional values of the age may be attributed to Arthur's court, but Chrétien's heroes ride out from it and, through adventure, discover themselves more fully and realize their own hierarchy of values.

By juxtaposing the normal worldly values of his age with an aspiring idealism which rose far above them, Chrétien created a tension between actuality and aspiration, reason and feeling, stimulating to the imagination. At the same time he maintained an ethical neutrality which allowed him to present situations and project values which some of his readers might disapprove. The ideal interrelationship of love and prowess achieved in *Erec* is not possible in *Lancelot* where the supremacy of *fine amor* raises an ambivalence within the chivalric ideal and reveals the hero as both sublime and ridiculous; but Chrétien's personal judgement of both is obscured by irony, parody, and the presentation of events through the eyes of characters who often misinterpret what they see.[27]

In the absence of an authorial point of view, the reader's own response is conditioned by, among other means, the role of the narrator. Despite his evident concern to present his story as vividly as possible in conformity with contemporary reality, Chrétien constantly breaks the illusion by drawing attention to his conduct of the narrative, by warnings of future developments which create anticipation, by revelations not shared by the characters which create irony; the reader is made complicit with him in the narration and accepts its fictional nature. The omniscient narrator may, on occasion, withhold information. He does not explain Erec's harsh treatment of Enide on their quest; instead he changes the point of view to present most of the narrative through Erec's consciousness in the sparrow-hawk episode, through Enide's on the quest so that her reaction to his treatment rather than the reason for it becomes the focus of interest. We are made privy to her thoughts and reflections while the narrative continues to be predominantly concerned with Erec's actions. Chrétien is more concerned with psychological interest than with narrative incident.

That interest is not, as in the modern novel, centred in the characters as individuals but as representational figures, types of the good knight or the imperious lady, whose behaviour exemplifies the courtly code. Only the hero and, to a lesser degree, the heroine achieve any psychological development; minor characters present only such attributes as are essential to their function in relation to them: dwarfs are invariably malicious, stranger knights belligerent, wayside hostesses seductive or helpful as their role in the quest requires. Even the principal persons, though they display a range of emotions, do so as and when theme and narrative situation require, not as expressions of personality. Broadly speaking, they are presented in dual form as what they are and what they aspire to be; psychological development is represented by their gradual change from the one to the other, sometimes symbolized by a change of name, as the Knight of the Cart becomes Lancelot. At the crisis, the hero's personal reactions often appear to have been suspended by his obsession with his quest and he acts like an automaton without will except to pursue the search. But these critical periods of blind action are interspersed with static moments when, in long, introspective monologues which demonstrate Chrétien's mastery of the rhetorical tradition inherited from the Matter of Rome romances, the hero and heroine dissect their feelings and display their capacity for self-doubt and self-deception. Such analyses are not merely displays of Chrétien's virtuosity but a vital element in his *conjointure*; alternating with passages in which the reader is denied access to a character's psychology, they focus attention on those traits which are important to the poet's *sens*.

At the heart of the *conjointure* which reveals that *sens* is Chrétien's art of story-telling, seemingly artless, events presenting themselves to the reader much as they do to the protagonists but with an underlying architecture, of which he may remain unconscious, to guide his perception. Its inherent ambivalences, arising from the fact that the obvious narrative structure, frequently tripartite, does not coincide with the thematic structure, commonly bipartite, challenge the reader's understanding. The narrative divisions of *Erec et Enide* with their pattern of happiness gained, lost, and regained, do not coincide with the thematic structure of error and expiation whose crisis comes with startling suddenness in the midst of happiness. Up to that point, the romance might well be read as a celebration of conventional courtly values; the abrupt realization of the hero's flaw at the moment of crisis casts a critical light on his earlier behaviour. This retrospective realization of the nature of his failing is extended throughout the regenerative quest by the way in which its seemingly unstructured stream of adventures is patterned to relate the expiation to the original offence. So Enide by repeatedly breaking silence during the quest redeems her original fault in voicing her doubts. Similarly, Lancelot's tragic delay in mounting the cart is illuminated by his unhesitating choice of the sword-bridge as the shorter, if more dangerous, route to the rescue of Guinevere. This system of analogical relationships is often strengthened by the structural parallelism which places them in similar positions within related divisions of the poem.[28]

## The social relevance of *roman courtois*

Chrétien narrates with such economy in the flexible octosyllabic couplet he inherited as the medium of romance that he packs a mass of incident into the seven thousand or so lines which are his norm. Until quite recently modern critics saw little more in his works than narrative incident for its own sake. Increasingly, however, as they have learnt to understand his creative methods, they have become aware of thematic complexities unsuspected before and begun to read other twelfth-century romances more closely in the light of Chrétien's art. Many of their perceptions remain controversial, but they indicate some of the trends in current understanding of the romance.

In Chrétien's work the archetypal mingling of the mythic and the mimetic is apparent in the hero's passing from Arthur's court, to which the trappings and conventional values of contemporary society are attributed, into another world where agents and adventures, often mysterious and unexplained, test his charismatic powers and his understanding of those values to the uttermost. But opinions differ on the balance of ideal and reality and on the social relevance of Chrétien's work as perceived by the original audience. Very shortly others were to use the same social milieu, the same themes, the same narrative conventions in *romans d'aventure* where classical wonders and Celtic enchantments serve merely to free the heroes from the restraints which reality might place upon their adventures. Chrétien might, at first sight, seem to be exploiting the same freedom to present a heightened version of reality very flattering to contemporary values. In an age when the growing unity of France had led to increased tension between the central monarchy and the great vassals forced to recognize its authority, the voluntary adherence of so many outstanding knights to the Round Table, symbol of egalitarian unity round a king who is merely first among equals, might imply a model feudal relationship. But there are elements of ambivalence in Chrétien's presentation of the Arthurian world which suggest a critique of contemporary values. The essential bond in that ideal society is mutual loyalty, represented by faithful service on the part of the knights and gratitude on Arthur's part expressed through largesse, reflecting the reality of an economy increasingly based on money rather than land. Growing co-operation between the monarchy and the emergent bourgeoisie, controllers of the monetary economy, threatened the interests of the feudal nobility; the romance writers championed them by ignoring the rising middle classes as incapable of chivalry and making Arthur the exemplar of the chivalric qualities he shared with his knights. Yet Arthur is generally inactive in the exploits, often precipitated by some impulsive or ill-judged decision of his, in which they display their chivalry, so that his reputation suffers by the contrast. His ambivalent status is symptomatic of the conflict between ideal and reality unresolved in his fictional court in which the competing interests of the various feudal orders are supposedly reconciled.[29]

The *roman courtois* can be interpreted as forwarding the interests of the monarchy. The political power of the nobility rested upon the right to have recourse to arms; to limit the threat which they represented to the stability of the state in the relatively war-free period of the later twelfth century, the French monarchy strove to bring them within the rule of law, substituting the judicial inquest for the arbitrament of arms and trial by combat for mass engagements. The romance acknowledges this, not only by the frequency with which legal forms and issues figure in it but by the way its narrative, where knights errant frequently recapitulate before the court violent deeds done elsewhere, resembles the deposition of the judicial inquest. It also acknowledges contemporary reality by showing the law of force, and the injustice and disorder in which it results, operating in the world beyond the court. The knights who go out to encounter its challenge may commit acts which, if performed within the court, would bring them into danger of the law, but they do so inspired by ideals of gentleness, courtesy, and *mesure*, the principle of individual self-regulation, associated with Camelot as the model of the modern State. In expressing an ideal which would replace the personal ties of a feudalism in decline with self-restraint and the rule of law under a benign and generous monarchy the *roman courtois* was prophetic, projecting the struggle of a society in transition towards a new definition of itself.[30]

The solitary adventurers who are the focus of its action have been seen as representatives of the lowest of feudal orders, the landless knights, growing in numbers with the consolidation of fiefs in fewer hands, forced by the suppression of domestic conflict to seek their fortunes as knights errant in foreign wars. By projecting the idea of valour inspired not by gain but by an emotional experience, a selfless love, an individual voluntarily submitting himself to a test from which he gained in moral stature and others from his chivalric service, Chrétien and his contemporaries provided both a model and supportive propaganda for a class whose unemployed energies and unrestrained self-interest were a constant threat to good order. It was in the interests of the great nobles, patrons of literature, who needed the political support of lesser knights yet suffered from the ill repute they brought on the whole feudal order, to propagate a chivalric model both exemplary and exclusive to that hierarchy.[31]

It may be, however, that twelfth-century romance was less concerned to express the individual's relation to society than to himself, particularly through the experience of love which affords him a purely personal vision of happiness and fulfilment. In his quest for self-fulfilment the hero may be brought to realize that he has been distracted from true happiness by false or conventional values which exalt personal prowess above public duty or destructively oppose love and chivalry. The problematic interrelationship of these two aspects of the courtly code can best be solved, the poets imply, by the hero realizing in action the true self of whom he has become inwardly aware. The inner adventure may be as perilous as the outer: the gap between imagined self-fulfilment and actual frustration due to error or misjudgement may lead to self-loathing, madness, attempted suicide (as in Lancelot's case); or undue contradiction between personal desire and social situation may make individuality a disruptive force or one which seeks fulfilment through deceit and illusion. The poets' concern with individuality is displayed in various ways: by showing the hero's use of wit and ingenuity to solve problems that do not yield to the basic chivalric virtues of strong arm and faithful heart; by realistic portrayal of the society in which he moves and vivid evocation of his sensory perception and intellectual apprehension of it; by emphasizing his inner life – emotions, will, motivation – showing how his personal and subjective responses differentiate him from others. The effect upon the reader is a heightened awareness arising from the dual perspective given by involvement in a vividly realized world and simultaneous consciousness of it as a fiction controlled by the poets' art, of problems and ironies implicit in a situation when fragmented, self-interested viewpoints replace objective moral criteria as the basis of human action.[32]

## Literary means in the *roman courtois*

These concepts of the social and personal focus of the *roman courtois* need not be mutually contradictory; both levels of meaning may be present in the same text, the hero's struggles with obstacles that impede his quest serving as a metaphoric version of his inner struggle to control impulses which would lead him away from self-fulfilment. Opinions differ on the extent to which deliberate symbolism is involved. In an age of symbols it would have been natural for schoolmen skilled in the art of reading at more than the literal level, of seeking the grain of truth among the chaff of narrative incident, to apply their exegetical techniques in the *conjointure* by which they made meaningful many elements in their Celtic story-matter whose original meaning was lost to them. Their audience, accustomed to accept the coexistence of literal and symbolic significance in the same object or action, would be alert to other possibilities in the hunting of the white stag in *Erec* than an Arthurian custom; but the variety of meanings which tradition provided was so wide that definition must depend upon the relationship to other symbols in the wider context. If to them the garden of the 'Joy of the Court' episode suggested Eden, would they consequently have seen Erec and Enide as Adam and Eve and then associate Erec with Christ as God made man redeeming the sin of excessive carnal desire committed there? It seems more probable that symbols served a diffused and sporadic purpose in adding wider moral and spiritual implications to the social themes of romance, contributing to the *conjointure* on a harmonic rather than a structural basis.[33]

The coexistence of various levels of meaning suggests the possibility of irony arising from different perceptions of their interrelations. In a genre concerned with ideals which much in contemporary life contradicted, treated by poets inhabiting a courtly milieu but professionally debarred from participating in its pursuits, irony seems inherently likely. Medieval rhetoric with its roots in the classical tradition recognized *ironia*, specifically the expression of something by its contrary, as one of a group of figures which convey meaning through indirection. In Chrétien it is evident, at the verbal level, when one of their wayside hosts attempts to win Enide over to his plot to murder Erec, an act of disloyalty, by swearing on the loyalty inseparable from his rank as a count. The same effect is apparent in larger structures, one episode taking on an ironic meaning in relation to another with which it is associated in the narrative pattern, or in the eyes of the reader aware of facts of which the characters are ignorant, or retrospectively when information withheld from him is later revealed. Such ironies may reflect upon the values presented: the trial by combat in which Lancelot defends the Queen against Meleagant's charge of adultery loses its judicial character in the eyes of the audience conscious that, though wrongly framed because it named the wrong culprit, the general charge was true, casting a dubious light on contemporary judicial procedure. Similarly, when Chrétien stresses that after their marriage Erec and Enide are both lovers *and* man and wife, yet follows the declaration that whoever serves such an *amie* is made more worthy by the privilege with his account of Erec's unworthy neglect of chivalry, he seems to be ironically undermining the literary fiction of *fine amor* as an absolute value by querying its operation in relation to other social obligations.[34]

Many of these ironic effects depend upon a particular relationship between author and audience by which he shares with them narrative facts, insights into situations and judgements on values to which the characters are not privy, encouraging them to maintain a certain detachment, ironic, amused, and alert to weigh and judge. Chrétien compounds the effect by periodically abandoning his detached role as narrator, buttonholing the reader to comment on his sources, the mechanics of narration, or an impossible obstacle to the action which proves easily overcome. By intruding on the fiction he reminds the reader of reality and his own freedom to view the story objectively, observing the illusion in which the characters flounder from an aesthetic distance which allows moral judgement without destroying sympathy, consciousness of his participation in the creative process adding to his pleasure. Such intellectual involvement may seem foreign to our modern concept of romance which perhaps overvalues the escapist element, but the *roman courtois* exploited its freedom from the restraints of reality in search of truth. The classic instrument for that purpose in the Middle Ages was the logical analysis of texts from Scripture downwards. The second half of the twelfth century was the age of dialectic when the habit of mind acquired by schoolmen in grammatical analysis to define meaning, in juxtaposing contradictory authorities in order to reconcile them, inspired a questioning attitude towards established ideas and values which influenced both the form and content of courtly literature. It dictated not only the questioning mode of Andreas's *De Amore* but Chrétien's *conjointure* with its ordering of oppositions, complementary and contradictory, in a web of contrasts and correspondences. By presenting love and chivalry as opposed and associated ideals, making conflicting yet complementary demands upon the characters, involving constant tensions between extravagant commitment and *mesure*, action and inaction, the dialectic method of composition stimulated imaginative grasp of the *sens* through the resolution of often paradoxical oppositions. The outcome is not so much a thesis proven – Chrétien shifts his ideological ground from one romance to another – as an issue explored, a code critically examined. The process is open-ended and it is for the individual reader to determine by his appetite and capacity how far it should go. It requires time for reflection, reading and rereading socially or privately, intellectual detachment rather than the emotional involvement which the oral performance of epic, dramatic in nature and celebratory in function, must have called for.[35]

# Later developments

Chrétien's works have come to represent the classic form of the *roman courtois*, partly because his genius has excited exceptional efforts to understand them and because the complexity of their literary method provides a measure of the subtlety with which others have exploited its resources. It was to undergo manifold developments, formal and thematic, over the next three centuries, the most significant of which were rooted in Chrétien's own work. His last romance, *Perceval*, left incomplete at 9000 lines, seems designed on a larger scale than usual. The adventures of the hero, a boy of noble stock brought up in ignorance of arms and *courtoisie*, in search of his chivalric identity are intertwined with those of Gawain, whose model chivalry acts as a foil to his inexperience. But Perceval has a mystic experience which raises him above Gawain's worldly achievement: in a wayside castle he witnesses a mysterious procession in which are carried a lance dripping blood and a grail, a vessel brimming with light; in obedience to his newly learnt *courtoisie* he asks no questions, only to learn later that to have done so would have healed his host, the maimed Fisher King, and restored well-being to his stricken kingdom. The source of the Grail procession, most probably Celtic, and the meaning Chrétien intended it to have remain uncertain. But its fascination for his contemporaries produced six additions to his *Conte du Graal* by various hands, amounting to between sixty thousand and seventy thousand lines. Through a maze of adventures runs the quest for the Grail, now given a specifically Christian meaning as the vessel in which Joseph of Arimathea collected Christ's blood at the Crucifixion, and the central motif of Arthurian romance thereafter.

In the last years of the twelfth century, Robert de Boron carried on the development in his *Joseph d'Arimathie*, telling how the Emperor Vespasian, on conquering Jerusalem, released Joseph from the dungeon in which he had survived for many years nourished only by the Grail; how he, instructed by the Holy Ghost, made a table resembling that of the Last Supper on which to place the cup; and how his followers eventually carried it to 'the vales of Avalon' (Glastonbury). The mixture of sacred history and Arthurian legend was potent, producing in the first third of the next century an enormous prose compilation (some three thousand quarto pages in print) in five branches: the *Estoire del Saint Graal*, an expanded version of Robert's *Joseph*; the *Estoire de Merlin* elaborated from another poem of his bridging the gap from the first to the fifth century with the story of how the devils, furious at Christ's rescue of the righteous Jews from hell, plot to mislead mankind through a prophet, half human half devil, that Merlin who later aided Uther

Pendragon in founding the Round Table, modelled on the table of the Grail and, as in Geoffrey's *Historia*, in siring Arthur on another man's wife while magically disguised as her husband; the *Lancelot* in which Chrétien's romance is set in a mass of adventures from the hero's earlier career; the *Queste del Saint Graal* in which the Christian chivalry of Arthur's principal knights proves unequal to the experience of the Grail upon which only the virgin knight Galahad, Lancelot's son by the daughter of the Fisher King, can look openly; and finally *La Mort le Roi Artu* in which Lancelot, despite the humiliation which his love for Guinevere earned him in the Grail quest, renews his adultery, leading ultimately to a breach with Arthur, civil war, and the downfall of the Round Table.[36]

This Vulgate Cycle, which later authors who mined and quarried it for plots and motifs regarded as the standard text of Arthurian romance, shows the passion for completeness and order which characterized the thirteenth century, the age of the encyclopaedic summaries of universal knowledge. By providing the endless adventures of *roman courtois* with a 'historical' setting ultimately derived from Geoffrey's account of the Trojan ancestry of the British and the legendary empire of Arthur, it sought to give their idealism of personal achievement wider significance by associating it with the rise and fall of a society. To that metaphor of the ultimate human reality it added the Grail quest as a mission of mystic self-fulfilment and spiritual service for a messianic hero in the course of which the inadequacy of worldly chivalry is repeatedly demonstrated. The massive narrative scale and complex thematic integration required new artistic methods: long-running narrative threads are interwoven with each other, knights errant abandoning one quest to take up another, earlier or later adventures being recalled or announced in a way which allows a number of separate themes to be pursued simultaneously; numerous cross-references, made possible by the fact that the earlier branches were later additions, keep plots and themes constantly in the reader's mind; an explicit symbolism, an underlying allegorical framework, and a didactic commentary – notably in the *Queste* where Cistercian influence is evident – drive home the moral *sens*. Yet the ultimate effect of this coherence of matter is a deliberate ambiguity of meaning in the unresolved conflict of divine and earthly chivalry: only Galahad is capable of the supreme spiritual experience, the failure of others makes their quest for self-fulfilment seem delusive and transitory, and the conflicting demands of personal honour and social duty tear the Round Table apart.

Such complexity of narrative and theme was scarcely to be equalled in the centuries that lay ahead, but the diversification which the Vulgate represents in comparison with the work of Chrétien was to carry the romance in a dozen different directions before it lost itself in a variety of story forms in verse and prose – allegory, pastoral, romantic epic, picaresque tale – during the Renaissance. While Arthurian matter was made the vehicle for mysticism requiring more and more explicit commentary, other subjects were treated with increasing realism in contemporary settings and with topical allusions. As the rising middle class began to exert its patronage and claim a share in the literature of its betters, the values and techniques of *roman courtois* were often distorted, structure degenerating into the mere multiplication of episodes and chivalric *sens* being undermined by irony and parody. France lost her primacy in courtly literature, but already in Chrétien's lifetime the stories of Tristan, Erec, and Perceval had passed from *romanz* into other European literatures, beginning the long journey which was to carry them round the world.

# Notes

1. For a convenient summary of the process of political unification see C. W. Previté-Orton, *The Shorter Cambridge Medieval History*, 2 vols (Cambridge, 1975), II, 703–11.

2. See Pierre Le Gentil, *La Littérature française du moyen âge*, third edition (Paris, 1969), pp. 25–28, and J. C. Payen, *Littérature française: le moyen âge, I: des origines à 1300* (Paris, 1970), pp. 28–29.

3. See R. R. Bezzola, *Les Origines et la formation de la littérature courtoise en occident, 500–1200*, 5 vols (Paris, 1944–63), II, 19–45, and R. W. Southern, *The Making of the Middle Ages*, reprint (London, 1959), pp. 163–208.

4. See Gustave Cohen, *La Vie littéraire en France au moyen âge* (Paris, 1949), pp. 31–32, 46–47, and John Fox, *Literary History of France*, I, Part 1: *The Middle Ages* (London, 1974), pp. 15–17; Payen, *Littérature française*, pp. 31–32, 46–47.

5. See Le Gentil, *Littérature française*, pp. 16–21 and Payen, *Littérature française*, pp. 33–34.

6. See Bezzola, *Origines*, II, 129–39 and Marc Bloch, *Feudal Society*, translated by L. A. Manyon (London, 1962), pp. 79–81.

7. See Bezzola, *Origines*, II, 236–43; Bloch, *Feudal Society*, pp. 123–75; Payen, *Littérature française*, pp. 25–31.

8. See Bloch, *Feudal Society*, pp. 92–102; Fox, pp. 75–78; Pierre le Gentil, *La Chanson de Roland* (Paris, 1955), pp. 15–21.

9. Among the mass of publications on the *Roland*, our understanding of which is a continuing process, the following offer guidance on general issues of interpretation: Fox, pp. 60–70; Le Gentil, *Roland*, pp. 92–122; D. D. R. Owen, *The Legend of Roland* (London, 1973), pp. 59–142; V. R. Rossman, *Perspectives of Irony in Medieval French Literature* (The Hague, 1975), pp. 78–85; Eugène Vinaver,

*The Rise of Romance* (Oxford, 1971), pp. 11–14. Quotations are from the edition by Frederick Whitehead, Oxford, 1942 and the translation by D. D. R. Owen, London, 1972.

10. See P. Y. Badel, *Introduction à la vie littéraire du moyen âge* (Paris, 1969), pp. 137–42; Fox, pp. 70–74; Le Gentil, *Roland*, pp. 123–80; W. W. Ryding, *Structure in Medieval Narrative* (Paris, 1971), pp. 96–99, 117–18.

11. See Jessie Crosland, *Medieval French Literature* (Oxford, 1956), pp. 67–72; Fox, pp. 134–39; Jean Frappier in *Le Roman jusqu'à la fin du XIII^c siècle*, edited by Jean Frappier and R. R. Grimm, Grundriss der romanishchen Literaturen des Mittelalters iv (Heidelberg, 1978), i, 145–48; J. C. Payen, *Les Origines de la courtoisie dans la littérature française medievale: ii Le Roman* (Paris, 1967), pp. 5–14; Maurice Wilmotte, *Origines du roman en France* (Paris, 1941), pp. 172–77.

12. See R. M. Jones, *The Theme of Love in the Romans d'Antiquite* (London, 1972), pp. 30–42, and G. Raynaud de Lage in *Le Roman jusqu'à la fin du XIII^c siècle*, i, 174–78.

13. See Crosland, pp. 72–74, and Edmond Faral, *Recherches sur les sources latines des contes et des romans courtois* (Paris, 1913), pp. 73–157, 410–15.

14. See Badel, pp. 43–45, and Jones, pp. 3–18, 66–70.

15. See Crosland, pp. 93–102; M. J. Donovan, *The Breton Lay: A Guide to Varieties* (Notre Dame, Indiana, 1969), pp. 1–64; Fox, pp. 167–71; Ernest Hoepffner in *Arthurian Literature in the Middle Ages*, edited by R. S. Loomis (Oxford, 1959), pp. 112–21; Payen, *Littérature française*, pp. 152–55.

16. See Jones, pp. 71–76; Moshé Lazar, *Amour courtois et fin 'amors dans la littérature du XII^c siècle* (Paris, 1964), pp. 174–98; Payen, *Origines de la courtoisie*, pp. 15–18.

17. See Fox, pp. 139–45; Helaine Newstead in *Arthurian Literature in the Middle Ages*, pp. 122–33; D. D. R. Owen, *Noble Lovers* (London, 1975), pp. 76–100; Raynaud de Lage in *Le Roman jusqu'à la fin du XIII^c siècle*, i, 212–19; Frederick Whitehead in *Arthurian Literature in the Middle Ages*, pp. 134–44.

18. See Lazar, pp. 149–73; Payen, *Origines de la courtoisie*, pp. 19–25; Raynaud de Lage in *Le Roman jusqu'à la fin du XIII^c siècle*, pp. 220–30; Vinaver, pp. 44–52.

19. See Bloch, *Feudal Society*, pp. 316–19, and Georges Duby, *The Chivalrous Society*, translated by C. Postan (London, 1977), pp. 94–111.

20. See Bloch, *Feudal Society*, pp. 305–07; Jean Frappier, *Amour courtois et table ronde* (Geneva, 1973), pp. 1–5; Lazar, pp. 9–10.

21. See Bezzola, *Origines*, ii, 243–65; Fox, pp. 105–21; Frappier, *Amour courtois*, pp. 6–31; Douglas Kelly, *Medieval Imagination: Rhetoric and the Poetry of Courtly Love* (Madison, Wisconsin, 1978), pp. 13–21; Lazar, pp. 9–64; Payen, *Littérature française*, pp. 136–46. Like many other elements in this chapter, courtly love is the subject of continuing controversy, particularly with regard to its nature and ultimate origin; the various theories are surveyed by Roger Boase (*The Origin and Meaning of Courtly Love* (Manchester, 1977)) who defines it as 'a comprehensive cultural phenomenon: a literary movement, an ideology, an ethical system, a style of life, and an expression of the play element in culture, which arose in an aristocratic Christian environment exposed to Hispano-Arabic influences' (pp. 129–30).

22. See Fox, pp. 146–49; Frappier in *Le Roman jusqu'à la fin du XIII^c siècle*, i, 183–211; R. S. Loomis, *The Development of Arthurian Romance* (London, 1963), pp. 13–40.

23. J. F. Benton, 'The Court of Champagne as a Literary Center', *Speculum*, 36

(1961), 551–91; Lazar, pp. 268–78; J. H. M. McCash, 'Marie de Champagne and Eleanor of Aquitaine: A Relationship Reexamined', *Speculum*, 54 (1979), 698–711.

24. See Fox, pp. 145–49; Jean Frappier, *Chrétien de Troyes* (Paris, 1957), pp. 8–22; Jean Frappier in *Arthurian Literature in the Middle Ages*, pp. 157–64; Loomis, pp. 44–66. A recent investigation (C. A. Luttrell, *The Creation of the First Arthurian Romance* (London, 1974) ) suggests a briefer period, 1184–90, for the composition of Chrétien's romances.

25. On thematic aspects of *Erec et Enide* see John Bednar, *La Spiritualité et le symbolisme dans les œuvres de Chrétien de Troyes* (Paris, 1974), pp. 51–67; R. G. Cook, 'The Structure of Romance in Chrétien's *Erec* and *Yvain*', *Modern Philology*, 71 (1973–74), 128–43; Frappier, *Chrétien de Troyes*, pp. 85–105; Douglas Kelly, 'La Forme et le sens de la quête dans l'*Erec et Enide* de Chrétien de Troyes', *Romania*, 92 (1971), 326–58; N. J. Lacy, *The Craft of Chrétien de Troyes* (Leiden, 1980), pp. 72–80; Alexandre Micha in *Le Roman jusqu'à la fin du XIII^c siècle*, I, 232–39; L. T. Topsfield, *Chrétien de Troyes: A Study of the Arthurian Romances* (Cambridge, 1981), pp. 23–63.

26. On thematic aspects of *Lancelot* see Bednar, pp. 87–105; Frappier, *Chrétien de Troyes*, pp. 124–46; Douglas Kelly, *Sens and Conjointure in the 'Chevalier de la Charrette'* (The Hague, 1966), pp. 31–165; Lacy, pp. 88–92; Micha in *Le Roman jusqu'à la fin due XIII^c siècle*, pp. 247–55; Topsfield, pp. 105–74.

27. On *matière, sens*, and *conjointure* in Chrétien's works see Kelly, *Sens and Conjointure*, pp. 33–97 and Vinaver, pp. 15–23, 33–44. On the relationship of ideal and social reality see Erich Auerbach, *Mimesis: The Representation of Reality in Western Literature*, translated by W. Trask (New York, 1957), pp. 107–24.

28. On Chrétien's creative methods see Frappier, *Chrétien de Troyes*, pp. 210–39; Kelly, *Sens and Conjointure*, pp. 166–237; Lacy, *passim*; Ryding, pp. 48–49, 89–91, 126–30.

29. See Anthime Fourrier, *Le Courant réaliste dans le roman courtois en France au moyen âge* (Paris, 1960), I, 111–78 and Erich Köhler, *L'Aventure chevaleresque: Idéal et réalité dans le roman courtois*, translated by E. Kaufholz (Paris, 1974), pp. 7–76.

30. See R. H. Bloch, *Medieval French Literature and Law* (Berkeley, California, 1977), pp. 249–58.

31. See Köhler, pp. 77–102.

32. See R. W. Hanning, *The Individual in Twelfth-Century Romance* (New Haven, Connecticut, 1977), pp. 1–15.

33. See Bednar, *passim*, and R. R. Bezzola, *Le Sens de l'aventure et de l'amour* (Paris, 1947).

34. See D. H. Green, *Irony in the Medieval Romance* (Cambridge, 1979), and V. R. Rossman, *Perspectives of Irony in Medieval French Literature* (The Hague, 1975).

35. See Peter Haidu, *Aesthetic Distance in Chrétien de Troyes* (Geneva, 1968), and Tony Hunt, 'Aristotle, Dialectic, and Courtly Literature', *Viator*, 10 (1979), 95–129.

36. See Fox, pp. 163–67, 197–206; Frappier, Micha, & A. W. Thompson in *Arthurian Literature in the Middle Ages*, pp. 295–318, 319–24, 206–17; Frappier and Payen in *Le Roman jusqu'à la fin du XIII^c siècle*, I, 332–61, 536–89.

# Chapter 3
# English Romance: the Corpus and its Context

The history of the English romance does not begin until the thirteenth century, yet England shared in the development of the genre from its emergence. Tradition has it that the *Chanson de Roland* was sung on the battlefield at Hastings – though it can hardly have been the literary version preserved to us – and the oldest surviving text of that version was made in England. The outcome of the Battle of Hastings (1066) brought to the throne of England, William, Duke of Normandy, whose descendants were to rule half of western France, including those northern provinces from which came the earliest literature in *romanz*.

For a century thereafter, until the Norman dialect of the invaders took on a distinctive insular form, no clear division can be made between literature produced in northern France and in England; the same patrons employed writers on both sides of the Channel and many new developments in a revolutionary age originated on the English side. There, as on the Continent, the natural patrons were monastic orders and feudal courts; the monks, domestic chaplains, and lay clerks who served them wrote both in Latin and French, making no absolute distinction between learned and popular tastes. Surprisingly often, both patrons and poets were women.

The Conqueror's youngest son, Henry I (1100–35), strengthened his English roots by marrying a princess of the old Anglo-Saxon royal line, Matilda, for whom the monk Benedict translated from Latin the *Voyage of St Brendan*, a lively mixture of saint's life, adventure story, and spiritual vision charged with Celtic mystery. For his second queen, Adelaide of Louvain, were written a *Bestiary* and a verse history of her husband's reign. Even during the anarchy under Stephen (1135–54), the intervals of peace produced Geoffrey of Monmouth's *Historia Regum Britanniae*, the earliest of several verse translations of it – Gaimar's version, now lost – and the translator's sequel, the *Estorie des Engleis*, largely based on the *Anglo-Saxon Chronicle*. But the glory of the Norman dynasty came with the accession of Henry II (1154–89), extending the sphere of Anglo-Norman culture by the vast territories of his wife, Eleanor of Aquitaine. To her was dedicated a rival translation of the *Historia* by the Jerseyman Wace who abandoned his *Geste des Normans* in pique when her husband gave the same subject to Benoit de Sainte-Maure whose *Roman de Troie*, a romanticized epic like the *Eneas*, was also dedicated to the Queen. Henry II was most probably the King to whom Marie de France dedicated her *lais*, some, if not all, written in England, where too the *Tristan* of Thomas was certainly, that of Béroul very possibly, composed. And in his reign the nuns of Barking Abbey produced Lives of Edward the Confessor and St Catherine, both perhaps by the same hand. Of all the genres of *romanz* only the full-blown *roman courtois* is missing, though it seems unlikely that it would have been less welcome in Eleanor's English court than at Poitiers. The texts preserved to us are no doubt only a handful of those that once existed.[1]

But, though limited, they do not suggest the decline of a culture isolated from its native roots; there is innovation in the skill with which the *Voyage of St Brendan* fuses saint's life and romantic adventure and in the development of chronicle as secular entertainment, of which Gaimar provides the earliest example in French. Those which dealt with recent history no doubt gave the new rulers the feeling that they now had roots in the country they had conquered. But Geoffrey's *Historia* and its various vernacular derivatives glossed over their displacement of Anglo-Saxon rulers by associating them with earlier Celtic dynasties and their legendary Trojan ancestry through Aeneas's great-grandson Brutus, the supposed founder of Britain. The various *romans de Brut*, by presenting Arthur as an active imperial figure, rather than the passive presiding arbiter of romance, gave the British a patriotic figurehead to rival Charlemagne in the competition with his descendants, the French monarchs who were their nominal overlords, which was to continue in peace and war for the rest of the Middle Ages.[2]

## Social and linguistic consequences of the Norman Conquest

Continental rivalry was to be a more significant factor in social relations within Britain than any bitterness caused by the conquest of the island. The Conqueror had had some claim to the throne, success in war was regarded as God's judgement in his favour and he exacted the formality of election by the Witan. Much of the Anglo-Saxon nobility died at Hastings, most of the remainder in ruthless campaigns of

suppression over the next four years. Thereafter, William was pragmatic, efficient in his exploitation rather than deliberately brutal. He dis-
tributed the lands and titles of the English thanes to his followers and,
though he maintained the laws of England, ruled as absolute monarch
with the support of a court of his chief barons and royal officers. Each of
them maintained a similar court on his estates, attended by his own
tenants who were his followers in war. Soon the land was filled with
castles, each a centre of Norman influence. Effectively the feudal system
was established in England and many yeomen farmers, deprived of their
land, sank into serfdom. But feudalism largely completed and formalized changes which had been going on within the English social
system for over a century and its values were not entirely alien to the
small number of English nobles who managed to hold on to their
estates. Henry I, by his own example, encouraged intermarriage between the races and by the end of the twelfth century, we are told, it was
impossible to tell who was Norman and who English. But wealth, rank,
and office must long have distinguished them; for the great mass of the
English, landbound and illiterate, life went on untouched by the social
changes above them. The newcomers, though numerous, powerful, and
widely disseminated were never more than a minority. In the long run
that was to prove the decisive factor for language and literature.[3]

Anglo-Saxon was unique among the vernaculars of eleventh-century
Europe in having developed a literary prose so standardized in form that
it could be used as a medium of national administration. It continued to
be used for that purpose for some time after the Conquest and was
eventually replaced with Latin for functional rather than political
reasons. The new rulers of Church and State had no nationalistic bias
against English, but they felt no need to master the language of a
defeated people. With the displacement of the English ruling class, the
spoken language was largely confined to a land-bound peasantry whose
dialects grew more diversified in isolation, making them increasingly
unfit for any national function. Any administrative or educational purpose for which Latin was inappropriate – pleading in the law courts,
domestic documents, the education of nuns – was served by the
language of the new rulers which was also the language of polite society
and, naturally, of the literature addressed to it. As the language of power
and prestige, it was in the interests of every Englishman who wished to
rise in the world – from a surviving thane anxious for assimiliation with
his peers to the native steward of a baronial estate – to learn Anglo-
Norman as quickly and perfectly as possible. No statistical estimate of
linguistic distribution can safely be made; the variations between class
and class, town and country are too wide, the biographical details of
individuals perhaps too unrepresentative for generalization. For some

two hundred years after the Conquest, the ruling classes of whatever racial origin spoke Anglo-Norman with an increasing, if casual, knowledge of English; the great mass of the people spoke only English, and an ever-increasing body of men were, to a greater or lesser degree, bilingual, while some clerics were trilingual.

Early in the thirteenth century the linguistic balance began to shift. When, in 1204, King John lost Normandy in a dispute with his over-lord, Philip of France, each required his feudal dependants to pay allegiance only to him, abandoning their estates in the other's kingdom to younger brothers. The English crown retained its vast territories in the south of France from which many soldiers and clerics flocked to the court of Henry III, rousing anti-foreign feeling even among his subjects of Norman stock who began to feel that to be truly English they must speak English. At the same time, the cultural dominance of France, increasingly expressed through the emergent standard language, Francien, made them conscious that Anglo-Norman in its isolation had become a provincial dialect liable to excite ridicule in the courts of France. By the end of the century the children of the nobility were being taught French in the schoolroom and, as far as possible, in the Continental form. Slowly Anglo-Norman retreated and was replaced by English in schools, administration, documents, wills, parliamentary records, as the Hundred Years War (1337–1453) fanned English nationalism. Shortage of labour following the Black Death gave greater freedom and economic power to the peasants, the growth of towns to the rising middle class of merchants and craftsmen, increasing the status of English as their natural language. Its use by court poets in the age of Chaucer confirmed its return to universal employment and the estab-lishment of Caxton's printing press in London gave the dialect of the national melting-pot general currency as a standard written form. In speech and writing English was a national language again.[4]

## Literature in English: the two traditions

In the post-Conquest centuries, three literary traditions coexisted in Britain: Latin, French, and English, the last of which seemed to con-temporaries the least important and the most undeveloped. But the future was on its side and in the meantime it was nourished by both the others. Latin, as the vernacular of the learned, supplied not only pious source-matter for homilies, verse-sermons, debate poems, but, through such products of their leisure hours as Geoffrey's *Historia*, academic support for the interests and ideals of laymen – often, as in that instance, through the intermediary of Anglo-Norman versions. The social dominance of Anglo-Norman as the language of the aristocracy excluded English from court literature until the fourteenth century. But didactic and homiletic works in English, often closely paralleling their French counterparts, found an audience throughout the twelfth century. They may have been produced by the smaller monastic houses less subject to Norman infiltration but, like their counterparts in the thirteenth century, they show independence and confidence in blending and redeploying materials and techniques from the common literary stock of the period. Too much has been lost to establish the coherent development of a literary tradition in the various dialects of emergent Middle English, but the quality of individual works denies passive dependence on French or Latin models. From the beginning of the fourteenth, translations and adaptations of French in all genres abound and by the end of the century, when literature in English dominates the court of Richard II (1377–99), Chaucer, Gower, and Lydgate are fully masters of everything which scholastic training, Latin classics, and Continental literatures have to offer them.[5]

The half-hidden sources of this resurgence may be suggested by the survival of a native medium. In addition to its old-established tradition of vernacular prose, Anglo-Saxon England had a distinctive verse form in which half-lines of two stresses in a variable number of syllables are linked across a medial caesura by alliteration borne by two or more of the stressed syllables – e.g. wéox under wólcnum, wéorðmýndum þáh. The poetry, in which a variety of two-stress patterns were combined in a highly formalized way, expressed the ideals of a military aristocracy and, with the disappearance of the Anglo-Saxon nobility after 1066, apparently ceased to be composed. But the medium survived to reappear in a wide variety of forms – blank verse, unrhymed *laisses*, and closely rhymed stanzas – sparsely up to *c.* 1350, thereafter in texts of every type including romance. It flourished first in the south-west Midlands, then the north-west Midlands, then the North and the Scottish borders. The appearance of a sudden revival in the fourteenth century is perhaps deceptive, resulting from the loss of alliterative texts in earlier ages when writing in English had little prestige or durability. The variety of verse forms with which alliteration is associated and their remoteness from the rigidly structured Anglo-Saxon line suggest other sources for its survival. The prose of the *Anglo-Saxon Chronicle* often combines rhythmic patterning with alliteration and occasional rhyme and, at moments of high emotion, passes into alliterative verse more loosely structured than the classic form. Such verse continued to be written after the Conquest, just as late Old English sermons and homilies in a rhythmic prose whose phrases often fall into two-stress patterns linked by alliteration went on being copied into the twelfth century and apparently influenced a group of west Midland homilies and saints' lives in which alliterative patterns in the prose become so rhythmical at moments of heightened emotion as to be indistinguishable from verse. The survival of alliterative patterns in this prose context may have given English poets freedom to borrow and experiment with a native medium just at the moment when the decline of Anglo-Norman allowed them to inherit all its verse forms, previously associated with polite literature. The associations of the alliterative tradition were provincial but some of the works it produced, as experimental as the new medium, were among the most sophisticated of the age.[6]

## The corpus of English medieval romance

There are romances in both the traditions, in verse and in prose, in a few hundred lines and in many thousand, from every area of the country and from every period after the first quarter of the thirteenth century. The problem of imposing any sort of meaningful categorization on this diversity is compounded, as we shall see later, by the lack of any agreed definition of the genre. The generally recognized corpus is the result of scholarly consensus, but not all items included command equal support so that even the overall total remains uncertain. The principal bibliographical publication in the field gives the following analysis by date: 1225–1300: 8 texts, 1300–50: 19; 1350–1400: 36 (excluding the work of Chaucer and Gower); 1400–1500: 42; after 1500: 11. The total of 116 takes no account of variant versions of some romances so distinctive as to be considered separate works; there is no way of telling what proportion it represents of the original corpus, nor how representative the surviving examples may be. Such a breakdown by date is liable to constant alteration as advancing knowledge allows greater discrimination between manuscript date and date of composition; analysis by area of origin is equally liable to change with our increasing ability to identify the dialect of the original after copying and, perhaps, recopying in other areas.[7]

Only the most general distinctions can be made from age to age, largely on the basis of medium. The earliest English romances are clearly not experiments in a new form but versions of Anglo-Norman originals predominantly in a four-stress couplet derived from their octosyllabic form. In the fourteenth century a broad division can be made between romances in the four-stress couplet and those in a variety of tail–rhyme stanzas (based on the repetition of a rhyme, commonly in a shorter line, after the interval of at least two rhyming lines – e.g. $aa^4b^3cc^4b^3dd^4b^3ee^4b^3$). The fifteenth century is characterized by lengthy prose romances on the one hand and degenerate versions of earlier examples in abbreviated ballad form on the other. But this ignores the alliterative texts which span the whole period. It is doubtful if, on its own, such a formal categorization can tell us very much.[8]

## Readers and listeners, minstrels and poets

In the absence of direct information on who constituted the audience of the English romances, the forms in which they are preserved offer suggestive rather than conclusive evidence. The general contrast between the modest manuscript compilations in which most English romances are preserved and the richly illuminated, large-format French texts from contemporary libraries reflects the relative status of the two languages throughout much of the period. The relative numbers preserved tell the same story: the aristocratic prestige of French romance better justified the expense of laboriously multiplying copies on costly sheepskin to be willed as family heirlooms. English texts, of less material value, were less likely to survive in private hands; many were no doubt lost at the Dissolution of the Monasteries (1536–40), since a surprising amount of secular literature seems to have been tolerated there. So an occasional romance is found in a compilation which otherwise reflects clerical interests.

The British Library MS Harley 2253 (1330–40), possibly the work of a cleric in the household of the Bishop of Hereford, contains, in addition to some ecclesiastical matter in Latin, equal bodies of French prose and verse and English poems, religious and secular, complaints and satires on contemporary events, courtly love-lyrics, and the romance of *King Horn*. More characteristic is the contemporary Auchinleck MS (National Library of Scotland, 19.2.1), apparently the product of a London bookshop engaged in the copying of material likely to appeal to the newly literate bourgeoisie, anxious for edification but also for the type of entertainment favoured by their social superiors. It contains a mixture of didactic and devotional poems, satirical pieces, and fifteen romances, some of which have been adapted to this improving context, the endless adventures of *Guy of Warwick* having tagged on to them a treatise of religious instruction which capitalizes upon the hero's pious, if late, reputation as pilgrim and hermit.[9]

The survival of so many Middle English romances in such compilations indicates that those which could be seen as edifying and morally instructive had most chance of being preserved, but does not necessarily typify the tastes of the audience for which each was originally written nor characterize the whole corpus, so much of which has evidently been lost. The context should not condition critical judgement of the romances themselves; two of the most sophisticated English examples, most clearly conscious of the Continental tradition, are found in just such moral and didactic compilations: the alliterative *Morte Arthure* in the Thornton MS (Lincoln Cathedral Library A.5.2.) and *Sir Gawain and the Green Knight* in the British Library MS Cotton Nero A.x. The latter poses the problem most sharply: the manuscript is modest, the texts unique, the three religious poems as subtle and widely rooted in tradition as the romance. What audience can there have been for these and other alliterative poems of the north-west Midlands in the second half of the fourteenth century? Did it include the country gentry who were benefactors of local monastic houses and profited from their considerable libraries; great nobles who maintained households on and periodically visited their local estates; men of the region who sought advancement in the court of Richard II and found there others to whom the provincial alliterative medium was an acceptable vehicle for sophisticated moral and social ideas? The issue is unresolved, and as we shall see, other romances outside the bourgeois compendia pose the same problem in less clearly defined social contexts.[10]

Many, for example, even among the late and highly literary texts, make use of formulae associated with oral recitation; direct address to the audience, appeals for silence and attention, calls for refreshment and remuneration, initial blessing and concluding benediction. But this need not, as once supposed, imply that they were written by *jongleurs* for recitation before an audience of illiterates. Rather they reflect the cultural time-lag by which communal living and social preference maintained the habit of reading aloud almost into modern times, leading poets similarly conditioned to address ears rather than eyes long after growing literacy had made private reading possible for many in all but the lowest classes. It affected the way in which the most conscientious structured their narratives in linear sequence for easy absorption, patterning events by parallelism and contrast underscored by verbal echoes, and the way in which the less artistic used familiar phrases of everyday speech, gradually conventionalized, to fill out a line or supply a rhyme. Diction alone will not define the audience of a particular romance any more absolutely than manuscript format. Only late in the period, with the products of Caxton's press, does format imply the intended readership. With his shrewd commercial sense developed as representative of the English traders at Bruges and knowledge of the most refined literary tastes of the age acquired through contact with the Burgundian court there, Caxton designed his comparatively expensive productions, including many romances, for the Westminster court and the wealthy merchants who served it. It was left to his foreman and successor, Wynkyn de Worde, to move the press from Westminster to Fleet Street and print the cheap copies of verse romances whose success with ordinary readers kept some of them in print up to the nineteenth century.[11]

The lengthy prose romances published by Caxton were mostly his own translations from French originals, representing the late medieval take-over by laymen – the civil servant Chaucer, the knight Malory, Henry Lovelich the London skinner – of what had long been regarded as a clerical function. The secular subject-matter and, in many cases, the colloquial style and formulaic diction of the earliest verse romances once caused them to be considered minstrel compositions. The English *jongleurs*, like their French counterparts, ranged in status from royal servants to roving vagabonds, but there is little evidence to suggest that, even at the highest level, the varied entertainment, chiefly musical, which they provided included the recital, still less the composition, of extensive narrative poems. Variations in multiple texts of the same romance, not only narrative but verbal changes from line to line, have been seen as the results of oral transmission and some of the more modest manuscript compendia as representing the repertoires of individual minstrels. Length alone would rule out the memorizing of many Middle English romances; some of the shorter ones may have been improvised from memory with much use of those rhetorical clichés and verbal tags with which the less scrupulous scribes pieced out their copies. But for the most part they are literary productions, individually composed.[12]

With rare exceptions, they are anonymous and though the extent of their knowledge, often considerable, and the quality of their literacy suggest that most of the authors had some clerical education, their professions can only be guessed at: minor clerics, domestic chaplains, professional scribes with literary ambitions? As such they are likely to have written romance as a spare-time occupation, at the bidding of a patron, translating or adapting an existing work not from any absolute lack of originality but because the climate of an age of uncertainties favoured the preservation of existing knowledge; what had been popular in French was likely to please aspiring English readers and the imitation of established modes and patterns promised success. Many romances bear marks of originality and individual imagination, but they do so within a framework established by tradition and convention.[13]

## Definition and classification

The late emergence of the English romance occurred at a period when its French counterpart, model and frequent source had so diversified as to bear only a general resemblance to the classic form of Chrétien de Troyes. In the interim the diffusion of the romance mode had invaded literature in many genres: chronicle, in which chivalric idealism could be projected upon the martial deeds of ancestors, endowing them with contemporary values just as the manuscript illuminators pictured them in medieval chain mail; saints' lives, whose heroes displayed their spiritual charisma in adventures often indistinguishable from those of popular romance; dream-vision, such as the *Roman de la Rose*, in which the psychological workings of love are demonstrated in allegorical action; lyric verse, where the language, imagery, and relationships of *fine amor* are applied to the celebration of both sacred and divine love. As chivalry and courtly love became thoroughly established concepts reflecting dominant concerns of the age, the life of the aristocracy expressed itself through them in a multitude of forms: the chivalric orders founded in imitation of Arthur's Round Table; the tournaments in which contestants assumed the names and bore the arms of heroes of romance; the mock battles in which besieged ladies pelted their knightly assailants with flowers; the Courts of Love in which delicate issues of relations between the sexes were debated. As life imitated literature, the fantasies given concrete form in masques and interludes, in tapestries and paintings brought the atmosphere of romance into aristocratic society, blurring the distinction between ideal and reality, in turn inspiring other idealized expressions of contemporary concerns in literature and art.

In England the process was complicated, so far as the development of the genre was concerned, by the apparent ease of communication between literary and sub-literary forms, folk-tale nourishing formal romance in ways which are not always open to scholarly inspection. The result is an even greater variety of form and content than in the French tradition, defying definition of the genre except in terms so general as to have little practical value.[14] Critics are increasingly abandoning the concept of a romance genre as unhelpful, recognizing that it comprises as many types and sub-types as the modern novel. Attempts to distinguish sub-varieties have been inhibited by lack of agreement on the basic characteristics of the genre, by modern prejudices against the coexistence of entertainment and didacticism and by preconceptions, formed by the romanticism of later ages, as to the essential nature of the original. It is doubtful if contemporary readers – or, at least, the less sophisticated – would have made any absolute distinction between the oblique social and moral commentary of the romances and the overt didacticism of the highly entertaining, action-packed saints' lives. And although, from the seventeenth century onwards, it was the exotic settings of romance adventure, distanced by time and social change, the supernatural interventions in human affairs, and the treatment of passionate emotions which seemed characteristically romantic, the magic machinery is casually presented as a narrative convenience, the social effects of passion receive as much attention as the personal, and the morals, manners, and settings, however heightened, reflect contemporary reality.[15]

Such retrospective judgements, confounding the values expressed in the romances and the experiences and conventions in which they are characteristically embodied, have compounded the problem of definition. No absolute distinction between epic and romance on grounds of form and theme has proved possible; judgements which contrast the thematic seriousness, solidity and realism of epic with the implied triviality and unreality of romance reflect modern prejudices or relate to the social conditions which produced them rather than to their distinctive literary characteristics.[16] Instead, they are increasingly recognized as different varieties of the enduring mode of romance, 'for both spring from permanent impulses of human nature, the impulse to realize and the impulse to idealize.'[17] Definition of a romance genre was achieved by concentrating upon the characteristic incidents and conventions through which the mode expressed itself in a particular formative period, that of the *roman courtois*, but it has proved limiting and distortive, concentrating attention upon the expressive accidentals rather than the essential nature of romance. The conventions could be mechanically manipulated by hack poets without regard for the experiences and values which they were developed to convey, just as, in modern literature, the novel of ideas and the pulp novel of incident make use of similar types of episode, setting, and narrative procedures. The presence or absence of romance conventions in a particular Middle English work tells us comparatively little of the author's appreciation of the mode, still less of his literary ability.[18]

The corpus of English medieval romance, the largely random product of chance survival, presents problems of classification and evaluation. The variety of type and achievement represented has caused some critics to abandon classification, judging individual examples by the qualities to be found in good narrative art of any age, with the consequent risk of undervaluing the distinctive characteristics of medieval romance.[19] Others have attempted classification on the basis of metre and area of composition, of length, and of the relative predominance of hero and background, of individual achievement or the history of a society.[20] Though outline surveys based on such external criteria succeed in imposing some order on the mass of English romance, they do not resolve all the disparities which appear as soon as texts are subjected to detailed literary analysis.[21] Those confined to particular groups, selected on the basis of theme or subject-matter, reveal greater homogeneity at the risk of reflecting a modern rather than a medieval conception of the nature of romance.[22] No approach has so far commanded general acceptance.

That adopted here is rooted in the belief that mode offers a better guide to the essential nature of romance than does genre, especially in the case of the highly heterogeneous English corpus. Though the earliest examples offer some evidence of a distinctive native tradition and of evolution along individual lines, the effect is soon obscured by the overwhelming influence of French romance. Thereafter, neither date nor area of composition – even when they can be determined with some certainty – nor the nature of the source, nor the metrical forms adopted can provide an adequate basis for the grouping and analytical comparison of the English texts. Each criterion is relevant in some degree to most texts and each provides a fruitful basis for the study of limited groups whose redactive treatment of French sources or employment of the alliterative medium give them significant characteristics in common, even though other features may connect them meaningfully with different groups.

Since our critical understanding of romance, both as mode and genre, is still advancing, more helpful critical bases may in time emerge. In the meantime, any comprehensive survey should allow the reader freedom to form his own impression of the range and variety of English romance without imposing on the corpus preconceptions of how mode ought ideally to be embodied or what constitute the essential characteristics of the genre. The long-term perspective over the history of world literature suggests that each age, each culture has its own idealism seeking expression, its own conception of the balance to be maintained between ideal and reality, of the means of expression best suited to that end. Many of the genre characteristics – the quest for adventure, the sense of values under test, representative rather than individual characters, a plot-machinery, magical or scientific, which makes all things possible – endure from age to age because their function in expressing the mode remains valid. But they are secondary to the primary need of the mode to find literary expression.

In the following survey the arrangement adopted is based on the medieval classification of story-matters which both reflects contemporary interest in cultures to whose values the age felt itself heir and also retraces in outline the evolution of the European tradition of romance. The central chapters deal with the classic matters on which that tradition was based: the Matter of France, stories of Charlemagne and his vassals united against the power of Islam or opposed in a conflict of autocracy and independence; the Matter of Rome, stories of the ancient world whose heroic values have been partially recast in romantic terms; and the Matter of Britain whose Celtic folk-tales have been made the vehicle of the social ideals of twelfth- and thirteenth-century France. Shortly after the point, early in the thirteenth century, at which the outline of French *romanz* in Chapter 2 broke off, the evolutionary process was blurred by the drawing-in of story-matter from diverse sources which encouraged divergent expression of the romance mode and widened the expressive means of the genre at the expense of some loss of clarity in the conception represented by the classic *roman courtois*. In English the impression of ramification and intermingling of types of romance is compounded by the nature of the corpus, late in date, random in selection, and piecemeal in composition. A representative selection of the wide range of story-matter subjected to the process of romanticization is included in the final chapter of the survey. It opens, however, with examples of romances based upon native story-matter, demonstrating that, though England may have been subject to foreign influence in its development of the genre, the spirit of the mode was not alien to it. Throughout, though limitations of space have prevented detailed analysis of more than a selection of texts, an attempt has been to ensure that these are as representative as possible and to indicate the character and variety of the English corpus in terms of both genre and mode.

## Notes

1. See M. D. Legge, *Anglo-Norman in the Cloisters* (Edinburgh, 1950), pp. 110–36 and *Anglo-Norman Literature and its Background* (Oxford, 1963), pp. 1–107.

2. See Anthime Fourrier, *Le Courant réaliste dans le roman courtois en France au moyen âge* (Paris, 1960), I, 19–22, and Erich Köhler, *L'Aventure chevaleresque: Idéal et réalité dans le roman courtois*, translated by E. Kaufholz (Paris, 1974), pp. 64–71.

3. See A. L. Poole, *From Domesday Book to Magna Carta* (Oxford, 1951), pp. 2–35, and Margaret Schlauch, *English Medieval Literature and its Social Foundations* (Warsaw, 1956), pp. 99–113.

4. See A. C. Baugh, *A History of the English Language*, third edition (London, 1978), pp. 107–57; H. J. Chaytor, *From Script to Print* (London, 1966), pp. 30–36; Derek Pearsall, *Old English and Middle English Poetry* (London, 1977), pp. 85–89.

5. See Legge, *Anglo-Norman Literature*, pp. 369–73; Pearsall, *O. E. and M. E. Poetry*, pp. 89–118; R. M. Wilson, *Early Middle English Literature*, second edition (London, 1951), pp. 288–98.

6. See N. F. Blake, 'Rhythmical Alliteration', *Modern Philology*, 67 (1970), 118–24; Derek Pearsall, 'The Alliterative Revival: Origins and Social Backgrounds', in *Middle English Alliterative Poetry and its Literary Background*, edited by D. Lawton (Cambridge, 1982), pp. 34–53, 132–36; Thorlac Turville-Petre, *The Alliterative Revival* (Cambridge, 1977), pp. 6–36.

7. For the analysis by date see *A Manual of the Writings in Middle English 1050–1500: I Romances*, edited by J. B. Severs (New Haven, Connecticut, 1967), pp. 13–16. Except where otherwise indicated, the authority of the *Manual* has been accepted on matters of dating and provenance throughout.

8. For an outline survey see Derek Pearsall, 'The Development of Middle English Romance', *Medieval Studies*, 27 (1965), 91–116, and 'The English Romance in the Fifteenth Century', *Essays and Studies*, n.s. 29 (1976), 56–83.

9. For an outline analysis of romance manuscripts see Dieter Mehl, *The Middle English Romances of the Thirteenth and Fourteenth Centuries* (London, 1968), pp. 257–62; see also Pearsall, *O. E. and M. E. Poetry*, pp. 120–32, 143–49, and L. H. Loomis, 'The Auchinleck MS and a Possible London Bookshop of 1330–1340', *PMLA*, 57 (1942), 595–627. On the implications for the social status of the intended readership see Karl Brunner, 'Middle English Metrical Romances and their Audience', in *Studies in Medieval Literature in Honour of Professor A. C. Baugh*, edited by MacEdward Leach (Philadelphia, Pennsylvania, 1961), pp. 219–27.

10. On MS Cotton Nero A.x see Pearsall, *O.E. and M.E. Poetry*, pp. 169–73; on the possible audience see Elizabeth Salter, 'The Alliterative Revival', *Modern Philology*, 64 (1967), 146–50, 233–37, M. J. Bennett, '*Sir Gawain and the Green Knight* and the Literary Achievement of the North-west Midlands: the Historical Background', *Journal of Medieval History*, 5 (1979), 63–88, 'Courtly Literature and Northwest England in the Later Middle Ages', in *Court and Poet*, edited by G. S. Burgess (Liverpool, 1981), pp. 69–78, and Jutta Wurster, 'The Audience', in *The Alliterative 'Morte Arthure': A Reassessment of the Poem*, edited by K. H. Göller (Cambridge, 1981), pp. 44–56.

11. On oral formulae in the romances see Ruth Crosby, 'Oral Delivery in the Middle Ages', *Speculum*, 11 (1936), 88–110. On early printed versions see H. S. Bennett, *English Books and Readers: 1475 to 1557* (Cambridge, 1952), pp. 1–18, and N. F. Blake, *Caxton and His World* (London, 1969), pp. 46–100.

12. See Mehl, pp. 7–13, A. C. Baugh, 'The Middle English Romance: Some Questions of Creation, Presentation, and Preservation', *Speculum*, 42 (1967), 1–31, and R. F. Green, *Poets and Prince-pleasers: Literature and the English Court in the Late Middle Ages* (London, 1980), pp. 101–34.

13. The general conditions of medieval authorship and patronage are helpfully outlined in W. F. Bolton, *The Middle Ages*, Sphere History of Literature in the English Language, I, edited by W. F. Bolton (London, 1970), pp. ix–xxxvii; see also J. A. Burrow, *Medieval Writers and their Work: Middle English Literature and its Background, 1100–1500* (Oxford, 1982), pp. 1–55.

14. Where definitions once had a certain ring of confidence – 'a romance is a story of adventure generally involving a considerable amount of armed combat; love may or may not be an ingredient; when it is, it is often the occasion or the excuse for knightly prowess' (Baugh, 'The Middle English Romance', pp. 1–2) – increasing awareness of exceptions has reduced them to such generalizations as 'narrative designed for entertainment' (Pearsall, *O.E. and M.E. Poetry*, p. 145) or 'a good story' (Mehl, p. 17) until recent writers have been driven to the conclusion: 'The term "romance" itself has no clear generic meaning in Middle English' (Burrow,

*Medieval Writers*, p. 71). The variety of terms originally applied to narratives in the romance mode is described by Paul Strohm, '*Storie, Spelle, Geste, Romaunce, Tragedie*: Generic Distinctions in the Middle English Troy Narrative', *Speculum*, 46 (1971), 348–59.

15. See Dorothy Everett, 'A Characterisation of the English Medieval Romances', in *Essays on Middle English*, edited by P. Kean (Oxford, 1955), pp. 1–22.

16. On attempts to distinguish epic and romance see N. E. Griffin, 'The Definition of Romance', *PMLA*, 38 (1923), 50–70, and D. M. Hill, 'Romance as Epic', *English Studies*, 44 (1963), 95–107. Both seek distinctions in the social conditions reflected in the two genres, a matter of continuity and marginal contrast which I have elsewhere formulated as: 'Epic is the treatment in literary form, and therefore in heightened terms, of the ideals of a military society, through the medium of history and pseudo-history, usually that of the society itself; Romance is the treatment in literary form, and therefore in heightened terms, of the ideals of a chivalric society, through the medium of pseudo-history, myth and legend, including those of other societies and other ages' (W. R. J. Barron, 'Alliterative Romance and the French Tradition', in *Middle English Alliterative Poetry*, pp. 70–87, 140–2 (p. 71). Modern judgements on such social factors, particularly on the degree of heightening involved in their presentation, may not provide a reliable critical basis – witness the extent to which the escapist associations of romance in the modern mind have obscured the strong element of realism in many examples.

17. C. S. Baldwin, *Three Medieval Centuries of Literature in England: 1100–1400*, reprint (New York, 1968), p. 58.

18. The present position in regard to the whole problem of definition is effectively summarized by John Finlayson, 'Definitions of Middle English Romance', *Chaucer Review*, 15 (1980), 44–62, 168–81; previous attempts at classification are summarized in W. R. J. Barron, 'Arthurian Romance: Traces of an English Tradition', *English Studies*, 61(1980), 2–23 (pp. 2–6).

19. This is the approach taken by George Kane, *Middle English Literature* (London, 1951), pp. 1–103.

20. The bases are, respectively, those of A. M. Trounce, 'The English Tail-Rhyme Romances', *Medium Aevum*, 1 (1932), 87–108, 168–82; 2 (1933), 34–57, 189–98; 3 (1934), 30–50, and Pearsall, 'The Development of Middle English Romance'; of Mehl, *The Middle English Romances*; and of Kathryn Hume, 'The Formal Nature of Middle English Romance', *Philological Quarterly*, 53 (1974), 158–80.

21. Mehl's classification by length, though the basis of a detailed study, does not resolve the issue whether differences of scale are matters of kind or merely of structure and economy; he himself does not seem to find it wholly adequate, interpolating a chapter on 'Homiletic Romances' and finding no place for one of the most idiosyncratic and challenging texts, the alliterative *Morte Arthure*.

22. Such selective treatments tend to base their conception of romance on the twelfth-century *roman courtois* and to assess English examples on their conformity to it – Everett's 'romances of chivalry' ('A Characterisation') and the few English texts included in S. F. Barrow, *The Medieval Society Romances* (New York, 1924) – or as traditional tales or local legends of 'Trial and Faith' or 'Love and Adventure' transformed into romance guise by imitation of the conventions of the courtly romance (L. A. Hibbard, *Medieval Romance in England* (New York, 1924) ).

# Chapter 4
# The Matter of England

When, late in the twelfth century, a French poet summarized the topics of romance:

> N'en sont que trois materes a nul home entendant;
> De France et de Bretaigne et de Romme la grant . . .[1]
> (*There are only three subjects for anyone of understanding; France, Britain and great Rome* . . .)

he ignored a body of national legend which, had he known of it, he would probably have thought unworthy to rank with the others. Yet the Anglo-Saxon civilization which was overwhelmed by the Norman Conquest had had a national literature long before French achieved independent status as a language or became a literary medium. It included, on the evidence of a single surviving epic (*Beowulf*) and a number of fragments, narrative poetry celebrating the ideals of a military aristocracy in the legends of exemplary heroes set in the context of Germanic history. Inevitably it disappeared with the disappearance of its audience at the Conquest; but the oral literature of the folk-culture was probably no more affected by the change of ruler than the mass of the English people whose interests and values were shaped by their inheritance from the past.

## The Germanic legacy

Their common heritage, rooted initially in their pagan faith and the military code of a society constantly at war, was reinforced after 800 by the coming of the Vikings representing a more primitive Scandinavian variant of their culture, by whose barbarism and paganism the Christianized Anglo-Saxons were horrified. Their long struggle under Alfred and his successors to contain the invaders within their area of settlement (the 'Danelaw') created there an area of linguistic and cultural fusion extended to the nation as a whole when a fresh wave of invasions brought the Dane Canute to the throne of England in 1016. Though the Anglo-Saxon line regained the crown in the next generation, the Scandinavian threat continued to the very eve of the Battle of Hastings, to which the English army marched immediately after decisively defeating a Norse force to be equally decisively defeated by the Normans – themselves, ironically, Norsemen settled in France 150 years before.

This prolonged period of conflict and cohabitation, armed truce and breach of faith between peoples whose social concepts had many common elements – personal stoicism, unquestioning loyalty to the leader in war, mutual interdependence of the kinship group, growing belief in the value of law – produced a number of exemplary figures whose fulfilment of their codes could be idealized in folklore or recorded with cool realism in the sagas. But if sagas were written in pre-Conquest England they have not been preserved and though the fame of many Germanic heroes – Hunlaf, Attila, Hengist and Horsa – long survived the Conquest, the mass of legends in which they were once celebrated, largely in oral form, is represented only by chance literary references. As late as 1200 a monk of St Albans gave an account in Latin of the legend of Offa, fourth-century King of the Angles, incorporating memories of the much later Offa of Mercia; a thirteenth-century Latin sermon quotes a single stanza from a Middle English tale of Wade, perhaps originally a sea-giant, later famed in German literature as the type of the faithful retainer; Geoffrey of Monmouth and others remembered Wade's son Weland the Smith, legendary weapon-maker of Germanic mythology. In the years following the Conquest, stories of men who had resisted the invasion of their homeland had obvious appeal, and the guerrilla activities of Hereward the Wake in the Isle of Ely and the thane Eadric in the forests of the west Midlands were romanticized in the songs and stories of country folk; but we should probably never have heard of either if their improbable adventures had not caught the attention of the clerical chroniclers who recorded them. If the latter is that Eadric Wilde about whom, in the late twelfth century, Walter Map told an incredible tale of his winning of a fairy bride, his popular reputation had clearly made him a folklore hero. The chroniclers claimed to know ballads of Hereward and the *Gesta Herewardi* based its account on an English text as well as the reminiscences of his guerrilla comrades. But, in general, those heroes who passed from history to folklore entered English literature only through the intermediary of French romance.[2]

## King Horn and Havelok the Dane

In the earliest of the English romances, *King Horn* (*c.* 1225), history is so thoroughly absorbed into folklore that, though the period of the Viking raids provides the violent social context of the action, specific historical events and characters cannot be identified. The Anglo-Norman version, which predates it by half a century, seems independently derived from a common original, perhaps a folk-tale told by people of Norwegian descent in the west of England.[3] As a boy, Horn is set adrift with his companions by Saracen pirates (late substitutes for Viking originals?) who have killed his father, the King of Sudene; he lands in Westernesse where Rymenild, the King's daughter, falls in love with him. When his false companion Fikenild betrays them to King Aylmer, Horn is banished, sails to Ireland, and serves King Thurston, killing the Saracen giant who had killed his own father but refusing the King's daughter in marriage. Hearing that Rymenild is being forced into marriage with King Mody, he returns in disguise to Westernesse, kills the bridegroom, denounces Fikenild's treachery, and sets out with his faithful companion Athulf to regain his father's kingdom. Meanwhile Fikenild tries to force Rymenild into marrying him, but Horn again returns in disguise, kills him, rewards the faithful with kingdoms and brides, and reigns in his own land with Rymenild.

*Horn* is immediately recognizable as a folk-tale of the exile-and-return type involving the familiar motifs of revenge, recovery of the patrimony, and the winning of a bride. Its form is that of the multi-move story which several times repeats the same basic pattern of incidents: the victim hero suffers a misfortune or experiences a lack of something essential to him, leaves home, is tested by adventures involving a villain, emerges victorious to return home in disguise and be recognized by some token or test, only to recommence the pattern of events as the result of some new misfortune, villany, or continuing lack. The repeated pattern stands out clearly in *Horn*, though it involves the usual improbabilities and irrationalities of folk-tale. Horn conceals his royal birth in both the courts he visits for no apparent reason; by pretending to be a thrall he makes himself an unsuitable suitor for Rymenild, yet her father seems to feel his kingdom threatened by this humble stranger; the readiness with which the King lets Fikenild cow him into giving Rymenild to him is equally unexplained. The logic of folk-tale, however, is not that of reason but of feeling; it is a fantasy on which the rational mind has imposed sufficient order to allow the working out of the conflict between the hero's wishes and inhibitions.

Like someone engaged in a ritual, Horn goes through six moves, crossing water between each of them and in each enacting variations on the same theme. In Sudene he is a prince deprived of the protection and freed from the restraint of a father by circumstances for which he has no responsibility. In Westernesse he is a thrall whose love for Rymenild would threaten the kingdom; when she dreams that a fish has broken her net, Horn predicts that an ill-wisher will destroy their happiness, as if willing his own banishment. In Ireland, under the name Godmod (Goodmind), he avenges his father by killing the Saracen giant who slew him and, though he refuses the Princess offered him, serves her father for seven years. Back in Westernesse, he throws off his beggar's disguise to declare his true identity, joking with Rymenild about a net which has been set for seven years, shows no awe of her father the King, and kills the rival suitor, King Mody. Crossing to Sudene with his true friend Athulf, he claims his own throne. Returning to Westernesse, Horn overthrows Fikenild, his rival for Rymenild who once suggested that his love for her threatened her father's kingdom, and finally overcomes, now that he is king in his own right, his persistent feeling that to marry a princess and become a king is a disloyal act against a reigning monarch. The underlying theme is clearly that of the maturation of an individual: the various kings are representatives of the father-figure from whose control he struggles to free himself; the good and bad companions are aspects of his personality which further or inhibit his half-realized desire to rival his father and grow to full adult power and independence.[4]

It is impossible to tell how far the original audience, with its greater familiarity with folk-tale, would be consciously aware of this level of meaning where the modern reader sees only the shadowy outline of a male-Cinderella story. But just as today a fairy-tale can be the medium of pantomime or of political allegory, so in *Horn* a familiar folk-tale pattern contributes its underlying meaning to an exemplary poem on the making of a good king. The plethora of kings in the poem are not just the gilt gingerbread figures of fairy-tale; they exemplify, positively or negatively, the condition to which Horn was born and for which circumstances require him to demonstrate his fitness, reflecting, perhaps, the original shaping of the folk-tale in the Viking age when royal birth could not secure the succession without outstanding personal qualities. From the beginning, Horn's beauty (a useful adjunct to royal charisma) is stressed; he has courtly talents of manner, speech, skill in harping which earn him golden opinions at Aylmer's court; these qualities win him the love of a princess, which discretion and loyalty to her father as his overlord will not allow him to accept until he has achieved knighthood and proved his valour in battle; though it was Rymenild who made all the advances, he limits his claim on her fidelity to seven years, remains faithful to her through seven years of exile, but still refuses to demand her in marriage until he has regained his patrimony and can claim her as an equal.

The folk-tale pattern of repetition with variation serves this theme also. Of the three fights against pagans in which Horn proves his fitness for his father's role of defender of faith and nation, details of the first echo the King's last battle when Fortune overwhelms him with unfair odds only to favour his son when he is similarly overmatched; the second, a David and Goliath encounter in which he kills the giant who slew his father, shows him as the champion of a Christian society whose own leaders have failed to stem the pagan influx; the third, when he reconquers his own kingdom, demonstrates the fruits of valour in the rescue of his mother, the founding of churches, and revitalization of a Christian society. His valour is rooted in faith but also in love: the ring which Rymenild gave him serves as a talisman strengthening him in battle. His initial seduction by her makes him seem a puppet without will, but the inversion of that incident when he refuses a princess freely offered by her father shows him making a free choice in deference to prior obligations of duty to his deserted people and fidelity to Rymenild. Horn's changing status in the love relationship is indicated by the symbolism of Rymenild's dream, when he still fails to ask for her hand after being knighted, that a fish has escaped her net; when he returns in disguise to rescue her from King Mody, he identifies himself as a fisher come to fish! Horn in turn dreams of the drowning Rymenild thrust under by Fikenild and returns again to kill the false friend whose earlier treachery had found him still naïve and vulnerable. The fatherless castaway, with the aid of Fortune and his own physical and spiritual powers, has assumed the authority of a Christian king, scourge of pagans and protector of other kingdoms.[5]

The English version of *Horn* in some 1550 three-stress couplets, about a quarter of the French counterpart, has the spare and sinewy directness of saga. An omniscient narrator outlines action, introduces actors, switches locations but, apart from the occasional ominous phrase warning of dangers ahead, gives no insights into character or motivation. The terse couplets carry the action forward with the absolute minimum of detail needed to establish situation and imply motive:

> A morewe tho the day gan springe,    *when*
> The King him rod an huntinge.
> At hom lefte Fikenhild,
> That was the wurste moder child.
> Horn ferde into bure    *went*
> To sen aventure.    (ll. 649–54)[6]

The individual scenes, each a moment of intense dramatic action, follow one another without explicit connection, their frequently ironic relationship being implicit in the pattern of repetition and inversion. Each is self-contained, carrying forward Horn's feud against the Saracens and his winning of Rymenild alternately but largely independently, the episodes achieving their internal climax and resolution without affecting each other except at the causal level, separate phases in the development of the public and the private man. The public sphere provides the greatest variety of adventure and the long time-span which tests the constancy of the lovers, but their relationship remains the central focus kept continually in mind by Horn's desire to make himself worthy of Rymenild, by her ring which inspires his valour, by the dreams which betray their concern for each other even when apart, and by Horn's various disguises which stress the continuing threat to their union. The narrative procedure is formulaic, moving from episode to episode in a dozen words, scarcely varied, which sketch the repeated sea voyages:

> The whyght him gan stonde          *breeze, arose*
> And drof till Irelonde.
> To lond he him sette                     *disembarked*
> And fot on stirop sette.   (ll. 761–64)

They function like blackouts between the scenes of some experimental drama whose coherence depends upon the emotional interplay between episodes and the ability of the audience to interpret the conventions of parallelism and contrast in situations, themes, and characters.[7]

It is a production without décor; the schematic procedure has no place for description and even the repeated references to the hero's good looks have narrative function, moving his Saracen captors to spare the boy's life and causing Rymenild to distinguish him from his companions. Only Horn has any degree of individuality; the other characters are the formulaic stereotypes of folk-tale – father, faithful and unfaithful friend, foreign king, his marriageable daughter – and even Rymenild is presented only in terms of her passionate love for Horn and the passionate anger she turns on those who come between them. He responds with an undemonstrative fidelity, acting to remove the barriers between them with a simple, manly directness so devoid of courtly address that one might think him motivated more by need to avenge his father and advance his own career than deserve her love. When he expresses emotion, throwing off one of his many disguises, it is with the same directness with which he acts:

> He wiped that blake of his swere          *dirt, neck*
> And sede, 'Quen so swete and dere,
> Ich am Horn thin owe.                              *own*
> Ne canstu me noght knowe?
> Ich am Horn of Westernesse.
> In armes thu me kusse!'   (ll. 1213–18)

The highly dramatized action constantly breaks into speech, statements rather than dialogue, in which the characters declare their feelings and intentions where their French counterparts explain theirs. With characteristic economy, they convey the import of past action or prepare for events to come, the unemotional content made vivid by the sparse context, like speeches in a ballad.[8]

Failure to appreciate how the structural pattern of folk-tale serves the epic theme of a good king's survival as champion of Christian values in the face of paganism without and treachery within has, until recently, caused *Horn* to be undervalued in relation to *Havelok* where the popular appeal of a folk hero dominates the social theme.[9] His tale of exile and return, vaguely coloured by memories of the union of England and Denmark under Canute, was given undeserved authenticity by inclusion in Gairmar's *Estoire des Engleis* from which, about 1200, it was adapted as a brief Anglo-Norman poem in imitation of Marie's *lais*. Towards the end of the century, an English poet working, most probably, in Lincolnshire, made a much fuller adaptation from a related Anglo-Norman source.[10] It tells how, on the deaths of their parents, Goldborough, heiress to the throne of England, is entrusted as ward to Earl Godrich and Havelok, Prince of Denmark, to Earl Godard who usurps his throne and hands him over to the fisherman Grim to be killed. Recognizing his royal birth by a miraculous light shining from Havelok's mouth, Grim flees with him to England and founds Grimsby; the boy becomes a scullion in Godrich's castle at Lincoln, attracts attention by his great strength, and is married to Goldborough whom the Earl had promised her father to give to the strongest man in the kingdom. Havelok dreams that he will become a great king, returns to Denmark where his king-light wins him knighthood, defeats Godard, returns to England, defeats Godrich, and, after doing exemplary justice on the two traitors, rules in both kingdoms.

The similarity of the basic folk-tale pattern of the deprived boy winning back his heritage to that in *Horn* is evident. But this male Cinderella accepts the ashes as his element: growing up in Grim's cottage, his hearty appetite makes him ashamed to eat without working and he sells fish for him until, in a time of famine, he costs more to feed than he can earn, when his foster-father sends him to seek his fortune in Lincoln, barefoot and dressed in an old sail. He wins his first job carrying supplies for the Earl's cook by shoving the other porters into the mud and he labours in the castle kitchen, breaking firewood and carrying water like a beast of burden but 'Als he was strong, so was he softe' (l. 991):

> It ne was non so litel knave,                    *child*
> For to leiken ne forto plawe,                     *sport*
> That he ne wolde with him pleye;

> The children that yeden in the weye                    *ran*
> Of him, he deden all here wille,
> And with him leikeden here fille.
> Him loveden alle, still and bolde,                    *shy*
> Knightes, children, yunge and olde.    (ll. 949–56)[11]

In the new clothes with which the cook provides him, he is the hand-somest man in England, a novice yet champion stone-putter – but only because he is too 'sore adrad' to disobey the cook's order to compete. When, still a virgin, he is forced to marry Goldborough, to prevent her being shamed at court he takes her away to Grimsby where Grim's children, whose father is now dead, serve them as lord and lady. Only when his wife, alerted by the king-light which an angel explains to her in a dream, interprets his own prophetic dream of possessing Denmark and England does Havelok remember his childhood and pray for divine aid against Godard. On landing in Denmark with Grim's three sons to reconquer his heritage, his ignorance of arms is demonstrated by an incident in which he does great slaughter among the thieves who attack his lodging by flailing them with the bar of the door, impressing Earl Ubbe so that, recognizing him as Denmark's heir, he knights him and has him crowned king. Thereafter the blood royal begins to show as Havelok knights Grim's sons, captures and condemns Godard, invades England, defeats Godrich in single combat, makes the English do fealty to their true queen, and rewards all the friends of his youth, giving noble husbands to Grim's daughters and Godrich's earldom to his former cook, while his own union with Goldborough provides rulers for many kingdoms:

> He geten children hem bitwene                    *begot*
> Sones and doughtres right fivetene,
> Wharof the sones were kinges alle,
> So wolde God it sholde bifalle,
> And the doughtres alle quenes:
> Him stondes well that good child strenes.    (ll. 2978–83)    *begets*

The fairy-tale ending and the proverbial truism represent the dominant tone of *Havelok* with its naïve hero become a leader of men by force of circumstances, motivated by good sense rather than any awareness of natural superiority, its acknowledgement of harsh necessity in the fam-ine which causes Grim to send his foster-son away to the city, and practical piety in Havelok's foundation of a priory in Grim's memory. But instead of the generalized never-never-land of fairy-tale it is set in a polity which mirrors contemporary concepts of good and bad gov-ernment. The England of King Athelwold in which it begins is an idealized medieval state in which equity and good order are maintained by a stern but just monarch who enforces his laws with impartial rigour, earning the respect and love of all classes. England under the usurper Godrich and Denmark under Godard suffer all the ill effects of tyrannical rule: both demand oaths of loyalty from all subjects but allow them no part in the government; Godrich creates an oppressive bureaucracy to enforce his personal will and coerces his barons to support him in fighting Havelok by threatening to reduce them to thralls, a flagrant violation of law; the inherent weakness of Godard's tyranny is demonstrated by the attack on Havelok's lodging and the rapidity with which his barons desert the Earl to join their rightful prince. The view of kingship which emerges reflects contemporary English theory: the absolute power of a king ruling by divine right needs to be modified by the willing consent of the governed if it is not to degenerate into tyranny.

Against the record of contemporary failure in practice, Havelok's career reads like the idealized biography of an Athelwold: pious, selfless, just and generous. It is not the king-mark but his personal characteristics of courage, loyalty, strength, good sense, and amiability which distinguish him as he rises from the lowest social class to be doubly conqueror and king. In each he displays the virtues appropriate to his social position: slaving uncomplainingly as a porter, and as king rewarding loyal adherents however humble and punishing his opponents, after due legal process, with drastic penalties – Godard is flayed alive and Godrich burnt – which satisfy both the rigorous justice of folk-tale and contemporary precedent.[12] His development from the gentle giant who goes in fear of his master the cook to an imperious monarch may not be psychologically convincing, but it expresses the ideal of the virtues of the good king as rooted in the best qualities of the ordinary man which is at the heart of the poem. The English poet has fused the individual and social roles of his hero much more successfully than the author of the Anglo-Norman *lai* who, in putting a courtly gloss on the folk-tale, sets it in the age of Arthur, makes Grim a baron unaccountably given to fishing, and Havelok a rather passive figure carried along by events rather than one who, initially ignorant of his royal birth, earns the right to rule by his own efforts.[13]

The English redactor has not only taken much greater space, some three thousand four-stress lines, than either French version, but has structured the narrative to underline his dual theme of personal and regal virtues. Though Goldborough is inevitably passive, her role as victim parallels that of Havelok, allowing reduplication of the situation in which a land initially well ruled falls into the power of a man who breaks his feudal troth, usurps the right of the legitimate heir, and rules with the viciousness to be expected from one who lacks divine ordination. Their forced union, intended by Godrich as a degradation of the

Princess, has the opposite effect, uniting her with 'the best man' physically and morally and preparing the eventual triumph of right over wrong. Havelok's actions when he comes to power parallel those of Athelwold in a way which promises that under him England will be as well ruled as in the past. There, as in Denmark, the people admit their fault in submitting to usurpers, acknowledging that they have a part to play in government, just as the fidelity of Grim and his sons is contrasted with the treachery of their betters. The two countries, repeatedly evoked as 'al Denemark' and 'al Engelond', are made active participants, most vividly in the prophetic dream which the English redactor transferred from Goldborough to Havelok who sees himself embracing his future kingdoms in his arms.[14]

The emotional as well as the thematic significance of the action is heightened by the recapitulation of key episodes: repeated recollection of the scene in which Havelok saw his sisters killed on Godard's orders keeps the usurper's crimes in mind until retribution overtakes him; periodic appearances of his king-mark declare the hero's royal birth throughout his humble youth; frequent comparison of the two usurpers with Judas and the devil and references to the oaths of loyalty they have broken maintain animosity against them during their long absences from the action. Frequent interventions by the narrator, displaying his personal bias, direct the audience's reactions: he repeatedly curses the two traitors, calls down maledictions upon them or prays for a blessing or divine aid for hero and heroine; he draws attention to changes of scene and the progress of the action, allowing the minstrel who assumed his voice in performance to make direct contact with the listeners. The minstrel would also have been able to make effective use of the many passages of direct speech, not only dramatic dialogue but the monologues of Godard and Godrich meditating the fate of their wards, the dying speeches of their royal fathers, the speech of Ubbe exhorting the Danes to rally to their true prince, recapitulating his wrongs just when they are about to be revenged. The patterned structure and pointed narration achieve a clarity of outline which allows the poet to indulge in incidental detail, developing the minor characters, in particular Grim, beyond the folk-tale stereotypes on which they are based.[15] His delight in description gives the often brief scenes, particularly those of humble life, a vividness which has, perhaps, unduly influenced opinions on the popular character of the poem. But whoever designed the dual theme subtly interrelated, the clear-cut narrative, the economic style in which the swift-running couplets carry a mass of detail without falling back on line-filling formulae, rising to rhetorical tirades or crystallizing into popular proverbs which underscore meaning, he was more probably a trained cleric than a wayside entertainer.[16]

Both *Horn* and *Havelok* are manifestly in the romance mode, fantasies of wish-fulfilment which express a dual idealism of personal maturation and social stability while acknowledging the realities of life for a fatherless boy and the limitations of good government in a troubled age. Both show the structural pattern of repetition and variation familiar from the *Chanson de Roland* and the works of Chrétien, perhaps a legacy of their common folklore inheritance, but none the less with full appreciation of the value of such narrative procedures for thematic emphasis. In other respects their relationship to the romance genre is more various: *Horn*, with its stress on personal qualities of leadership employed in defence of faith and fatherland, inspired by a love which is served rather than indulged and whose goal is marriage for dynastic ends, shares the social values of the epic, the limited scale of the *lai* and the dramatic narrative elisions of the ballad; *Havelok* fills out a similar structure with a wealth of naturalistic detail and vividness of narration reminiscent of the popular tale rather than the distanced, atmospheric romance. Modern critics, attracted by *Havelok*'s realism, assume that their preference reflects that of a popular English audience to whom the style and conventions of *roman courtois* would have been alien but whose pious and sentimental tastes approved the moral rectitude of the hard-working hero, a model apprentice-boy, and the idealized picture of monarchic rule. But Havelok is essentially a Perceval-figure whose inherent qualities display themselves in a disparate context; the contrast between royal birth and humble circumstances can be appreciated from above as well as below and *Havelok* may not so much reflect what the lower classes thought of their rulers as what the ruling classes liked to think humbler people thought of them.[17] The effect of the human detail, the touches of comedy, the vivid style is to modify the dangers of piety, bathos, and exaggeration arising from the attempt to span social and moral spheres so widely separated. The same dangers exist in *Horn* but are avoided there by a strictly schematic presentation of all spheres, both humble and regal, in terms of familiar plot situations, a self-consistent version of reality which does not challenge comparison with the real world.[18]

However attractive to us, contemporary audiences do not seem to have found the realism of *Havelok* a more satisfactory solution. Though his association with Grimsby kept the hero's reputation alive in folk tradition and won him mention in later chronicles, the Anglo-Norman *lai* fathered no Continental adaptations and the English version did not live on in the chapbooks. The Anglo-Norman Horn story, on the other hand, was transformed into a pedagogic French prose romance which, though it smothered the primitive power of the original in using it to exemplify proper gentlemanly behaviour, found its way into English, German, Dutch, and Icelandic versions by the end of the sixteenth century. The English story reappears in *Horn Child* (*c.* 1320) stylistically

distorted by a particularly inept tail-rhyme stanza, while its true nature
was recognized by the ballad-makers of whose work nine examples
stretching back to the fourteenth century remained current until the
nineteenth. The fact that none of the surviving versions seems to derive
directly from another, and that the three texts of *King Horn* vary so
much in verbal detail that scarcely a line is exactly the same in all three
implies a lively, widely dispersed tradition acceptable at many social
levels.[19] The occurrence of *Horn* and *Havelok* in the Bodleian MS Laud
Misc. 108 in association with one of many texts of the *South English
Legendary*, a vastly popular compilation of saints' lives, folklore, natural
science, and recent history, has suggested that they too would appeal to
an audience of limited sophistication anxious for instruction and moral
edification. Such a context may indicate one aspect of their appeal, but
all that can be certainly known of the audiences for which they were
*originally* written is that they were not French-speaking; the quality of
the Anglo-Norman versions does not suggest that the interests, tastes,
and literary discrimination of those for whom the English texts were
composed were in any way inferior.

## Ancestral romances: *Guy of Warwick*

The shadowy history of England against which *Horn* and *Havelok*
are set was, to judge from their Anglo-Norman cognates, as interesting
to the new rulers as to the native population. But even those who had
committed their future to the conquered land did not feel entirely at
home there; some who had founded religious houses in England none
the less retired in old age to French monasteries. Others sought psychological roots in romances celebrating the past glories of their adopted
country to which an inventive poet could connect them through the
famous deeds of some supposed ancestor. Towards the end of the
twelfth century, the Anglo-Norman *Waldef* recounted the struggle of an
English king to regain his throne and the avenging of his death by his
sons; the poet claims an English source, in all probability a saga of tenth-
or eleventh-century East Anglia. The romance of *Fergus*, remotely based
on the adventures of a Viking to whom David I gave lands, was written
by someone who had first-hand knowledge of its Scottish setting,
perhaps to commemorate the marriage of Alan of Galloway, an English
magnate, to the niece of William the Lion in 1209. The career of Fulk
Fitzwarin gave rise to a romance – perhaps by a monk of New Abbey,
Allerbury, one of his family's foundations – tracing its fortunes since the

Conquest, Fulk's rebellion against King John, exile in France, improbable adventures in distant lands, and eventual burial at New Abbey. The original verse text of *c.* 1256–64 survives only in an early fourteenth-century prose redaction and the English text in alliterative verse which once existed has been lost, like the Middle English version of *Waldef* from which a monk of Thetford made a fifteenth-century Latin prose translation.

But English versions of two of these ancestral romances survived to become perhaps the most successful of all examples of the genre. The Anglo-Norman *Boeve de Haumtone* (*c.* 1154–76), perhaps intended as a compliment to William de Albini, Earl of Sussex, who had been granted the honour of Arundel, elaborates a historical fantasy of a pre-Conquest ruler of Southampton. Bevis, heir to the earldom of Southampton, is carried off by pirates and given to the Saracen King of Armenia whose daughter Josian promises to become Christian for love of him and presents him with the war-horse Arundel. When Bevis is imprisoned on a false charge of seducing her and she is forcibly married, Josian preserves her virginity by a charm until, after seven years, he escapes and rescues her. After numerous repetitions of a pattern of adventures in which Bevis, supported by the faithful steward who protected him in childhood, alternately returns home to fight for his heritage and dashes back to Europe to rescue Josian from various abductors, one of their twin sons becomes King of Armenia and the other heir to the throne of England by marrying King Edgar's daughter. Like *Horn*, similarly patterned, the poem has many features of the *chansons* derived from an earlier version whose core was, perhaps, a lost saga. Early in the thirteenth century a Continental French version bloated its spare, swift narrative with a mass of *roman courtois* incident whose appeal was nevertheless sufficiently popular to produce versions in many languages up to the nineteeth century, while the Anglo-Norman text inspired adaptations in Welsh, Norse, and Middle English which kept Bevis a hero of children's literature until living memory.

In many respects his career is matched by that of Guy of Warwick whose name may derive from that of Wigod of Wallingford, a famous cupbearer of Edward the Confessor, one of whose daughters married Robert d'Oilli, a member of the family to which the Earl of Warwick's mother belonged; another daughter married Brian Fitzcount, some of whose exploits may have contributed to what is otherwise a tissue of romance commonplaces. The compiler of the Anglo-Norman text (*c.* 1232–42), perhaps a canon of Osney Abbey, may have intended it as a compliment to the Earl of Warwick whose family were patrons of the house, but its popular appeal was enormous; through an English version of *c.* 1300 and a French prose adaptation it reached almost every country in Europe; in England it furnished matter for a separate romance *Guy and Colbrand*, episodes in respectable chronicles, sixteenth-century ballads, a seventeenth-century play, numerous chapbooks and children's stories, while relics of the legendary Guy are still displayed at Warwick Castle.[20]

Though the various surviving manuscripts and early prints of *Guy of Warwick* preserve the substance of the Anglo-Norman original, they differ in completeness, in wording and in verse form to an extent which suggests the complex textual history of a perennial best-seller. Most characteristic is the form it assumes in the Auchinleck MS (*c.* 1330), probably the product of a commercial scriptorium, whose compiler has divided it into three sections: Guy's career before marriage (ll. 1–6898 – octosyllabic couplets); after marriage (ll. 6899–10479); and the career of his son Reinbrun (ll. 10480–12000 – twelve-line stanzas with a complicated rhyme-scheme, like the second section). In part one, Guy falls in love with Felice, daughter of the Earl of Warwick, but she scorns him as the son of her father's steward; so he journeys overseas to win fame in tournaments, achieves such success that he is offered the hands of princesses of France and Constantinople, but can never forget his true-love; returning after seven years, he kills a dragon in Northumberland and marries Felice. The second part brings an abrupt change of heart: after only fifty days of marriage, Guy leaves his wife pregnant and sets out on a pilgrimage to atone for his earlier life of fighting; returning, disguised as a palmer, after many deeds of courage and self-sacrifice, he saves King Athelstan from the invading Danes under King Anlaf by killing their champion, the African giant Colbrond, and, on his deathbed, reveals his identity to Felice. Reinbrun's career in the third part follows a pattern reminiscent of *Horn* and *Havelok*: stolen by pirates at the age of seven, he is brought up by the daughter of King Argus of Africa, rescued by his father's faithful steward, and, returning to England, frees Amis, a knight imprisoned for aiding Guy.

To some critics this combination of sensationalism and piety characterizes the naïve tastes of the audience for such English romances, exemplified by the mixed contents of the Auchinleck MS whose text of *Guy* has tagged on to it the *Speculum Guy de Warewyke*, a treatise of basic religious instruction.[21] But the English romance was not originally written for that context, its Anglo-Norman counterpart is not notably more sophisticated, judged by the criteria of *roman courtois*, and both went through many transformations in response to the varied tastes of audiences who found something to admire in them over the centuries. Readers of the original are most likely to have been reminded of the various divisions of some cycle of the *chansons de geste* in which the son's adventures echo those of his father whose own career may end in withdrawal from worldly adventure to direct service as pilgrim or hermit of the God he has championed in the field – like William of

Orange in the *Moniage Guillaume* emerging from retirement in a hermitage to help King Louis break the Siege of Paris by the Saracens.[22] In terms of the romance mode there is no absolute distinction to be made between Guy's earlier and later life: in both he serves an idealism of chivalric service to love, to the defenceless and distressed and to God in a way which acknowledges the self-serving, socially disruptive and unchristian reality of much contemporary chivalry. The second part, like many literary saints' lives, makes use of all the expressive means of the romance genre – endless adventures in high society at home and exotic lands abroad, civilized tournaments with fellow-knights, battles to the death with giants and paynims, ambushes and betrayals – exploited in the first. The connecting thread which makes one continuum of them both is the personal development of the hero from a self-absorbed worldling to a mature, self-aware individual, to the borders of sainthood.

Guy's secular career follows a familiar romance pattern in which a hero of comparatively humble birth is scorned by the lady he loves until he has proved himself worthy of knighthood in a series of tournaments against ever-increasing odds. Even then Felice is slow to yield, fearing that assurance of her love may make him inactive and so damage his reputation; her fears echo those of Chrétien's Enide, his devotion to her is that of the courtly lover whose self-will is subdued by obedience to a higher power, and the knight-errantry to which she inspires him is socially valid. Again and again, as he is about to return and claim her, the call of someone in distress sends him off on a new series of adventures which involve him in a maze of incident and swiftly moving action. But narrative interest is not allowed to distract attention from his dawning self-awareness. When Duke Segyn seeks to be reconciled to the Emperor of Germany after accidently killing his nephew in a tournament, Guy acts as mediator, urging Christian mercy for a penitent rather than the family vengeance which Germanic usage requires; the Emperor is moved to forgiveness, but when one of his kinsmen objects to such leniency, calling Guy a traitor, the hero leaps on him in fury like a wild boar, unable as yet to match Christian precept to personal practice when his own reputation is questioned. In another incident, preoccupation with his knightly dignity causes him to strike dead a young man who demands his horse as a fine for trespassing in a private hunting-park; later, while he is being courteously entertained in the castle of Earl Florentin, his host's son is brought home dead and Guy, accused of his murder, has to defend himself with arms while pleading the claims of hospitality; his arguments secure his escape, but his taunts to the elderly Earl for his feeble efforts to revenge his son and the slaughter he wreaks upon his retainers show him still unable to subdue personal pride and violent impulse to the code he serves. When, returning home, he volunteers to kill the Irish dragon which is ravaging Northumberland, he refuses Athelstan's offer of 100 knights, dismisses the companions who follow him, and puts himself entirely in God's hands:

> 'God,' he seyde, 'fader almi3t,
> Þat made þe day and ni3t also,
> And for ous sinful þoldest wo,                    *endured suffering*
> And heldest Daniel fram þe lyoun,                       *preserved*
> Saue me fram þis foule dragoun.'   (p. 378, ll. 7222–26)[23]

Unlike some of his earlier victories, the fight is long and bitter and the dragon breaks three of Guy's ribs; but it brings him Felice as his bride at last.

Even before their wedding the Auchinleck version makes the switch from couplets to rhymed stanzas which marks a fundamental shift in emphasis. The Anglo-Norman compiler who, up to this point, has ransacked the storehouse of romance convention for prophetic dreams in which savage animals attacking the hero warn of danger, grateful beasts such as the lion Guy saved from a dragon which follows him like a faithful dog, historic weapons which have descended from Alexander, Hector, and Hercules, now turns to a different model, the legend of St Alexis who, on his wedding night, abandons his wife, sails to the East and lives in such holy poverty that, when he returns to beg for the rest of his life under the stairway of his father's house, not even his nearest and dearest recognize him. Even with this widely known legend to provide the didactic structure of his romance, the poet redoubles his efforts to make the moral explicit through the dramatic flow of the narrative. Guy's sudden change of heart, so much more improbable than that of the pious Alexis, is prepared in an episode which owes nothing to the saint's life. Returning from hunting shortly after the wedding, Guy goes up into a turret and is moved by the maze of stars in the summer sky to think of Christ:

> 'Allas,' he seyd, 'þat y was born:
> Bodi and soule icham forlorn.                          *damned*
>     Of blis icham al bare.
> For neuer in al mi liif biforn
> For him þat bar þe croun of þorn
>     Gode dede dede y nare;
> Bot wer and wo ichaue wrou3t,                     *wrong, harm*
> And mani a man to grounde ybrou3t:
>     Þat rewes me ful sare.                               *grieves*
> To bote min sinnes ichil wende                        *remedy*
> Barfot to mi liues ende,
>     To bid mi mete wiþ care.' (p. 398, st. 22, ll. 1–12)      *beg*

In the long scene with Felice which follows, the French *roman* concentrates upon the malign effects of Guy's love for her: his own
frustration and the deaths of those he has killed to prove himself worthy
of her. The extended English version dwells on that higher form of love
and service to God which he has neglected in pursuit of worldly honour.
Felice cannot see the two forms of love as mutually exclusive, nor the
need for a penance commensurate with the sin itself which Guy
reiterates: "'Þat iche haue wiþ mi bodi wrouȝt/Wiþ mi bodi it schal be
bouȝt'" (p. 404, st. 29, ll. 10–11). The departure of St Alexis is un-
opposed, his search for humility a natural extension of his blameless
existence; Guy's painful breach with Felice, the living symbol of the
worldly values on which he is turning his back at the moment of his
triumph, his struggle to make her realize that his sin demands an active
penance rather than the alms-giving she recommends dramatize the
conflict of values vital to contemporary readers. The process is continued in the adventures of Guy's subsequent career, contrasting in
motivation rather than nature with those of his earlier life which, indeed, they often parallel. When he now goes to the aid of those in
distress, his identity concealed by his pilgrim dress, he is treated with
contempt – often, ironically, by those who speak with awe of the
famous Guy – until success in combat heightened by his new self-
knowledge and selfless motivation declares his true nature. The reluctance of friends and opponents to recognize his new identity provides
occasion for direct didactic statement of the values Guy now represents.
The effect, dramatic and didactic, culminates in his last combat in
defence of England against the African giant Colbrond, champion of the
invading Danes, which parallels the climax of his secular career in
freeing the country from the Irish dragon – and may have raised patriotic echoes of the historical Athelstan's defeat of Anlaf at the Battle of
Brunanburh (937). He finds the court at Westminster fasting that God
may send them a champion; Athelstan, on angelic instructions, appeals
to the poor palmer 'for charyte' and Guy, magnificently armed, disposes
of Colbrond with the aid of God. Still unrecognized, he mingles with
the beggars at the gates of Warwick Castle, receives Felice's charity,
and, confident that now she fully shares his values, dies in her arms.[24]
The independent existence later assumed by the Colbrond episode
indicates the appeal of military action and patriotic sentiment for contemporary audiences. But if those were their only interests, redactors
might have mined *Gui de Warewic* freely for such incidents without
regard to their contribution to any overall theme. The various
adventures follow each other in apparently casual sequence, each easily
separable from the whole, the characters and situations so conventional
as to need little introductory explanation. The fact that the various
English redactors respected the integrity of the Anglo-Norman text

suggests that they appreciated the structural parallelism by which Guy's later adventures duplicate his earlier career in a different moral sphere. Throughout the story-telling is highly competent, swift-moving, packed with incident, unencumbered with explicit comment. The effect seems artless yet the impression left on the mind is strong, the connection between episodes logical, the minimal characterization of persons who reappear after long absence in conformity with that originally established.

Apart from the poet's opening comment that men should learn from past adventures, there is little open didacticism; the ordered sequence of Guy's dual career is left to make its own point as a record of growing self-awareness in which the reader is involved through empathy with the hero's human qualities, his lapses into anger, his gradual realization of the extent to which conventional chivalric behaviour falls short of the essential Christian values. Any impression that only the former is fit subject for romance and the latter a pietistic intrusion is a modern misconception; medieval readers, accepting them as parts of the same essential unity, needed no elaborate commentary to appreciate their interrelationship. The poet guides them by the occasional explicit comment on motivation, by the growing frequency of Guy's prayers and reiterated use of the language of penance, charity, and forgiveness. But for the most part the adventures are left to speak for themselves, the dramatic effect created by rapid action, incisive dialogue, and challenging interplay of personalities exemplifying the conflict of values more effectively than moral explication could have done. Both the verse media serve the narrative well, though the complex stanza is not without some of the minstrel mannerisms which Chaucer was to mock in his parody romance *Sir Thopas* – a tribute to Guy's widespread popularity.

## Romances of the greenwood: *The Tale of Gamelyn*

Among the heroes of English legend in the post-Conquest period there is a notable number of outsiders or rebels against the established order of society: Hereward, Eadric, Fulk Fitzwarin, Horn and Havelok in youth, Bevis during much of his career, Guy until he has earned the love of Felice. Quite apart from the obvious popularity of their stories with the Anglo-Norman ruling class, it would be a mistake to see them as cult-figures of a defeated people embittered by foreign rule; the *chansons* which dealt with barons in revolt against the Emperor and the reflections in the *romans* of tensions within the feudal hierarchy show that the Matter of England was not unique in expressing the resistance of individuals to oppressive authority in an age of absolutism inadequately restrained by the rule of law. Nor do they necessarily embody only the frustrations of the common people; from Robin Hood to Billy the Kid and Ned Kelly, men who resist and outwit established authority have fascinated those who lack the courage to rebel against the forces which repress them, but in the Middle Ages it was often men of rank and power, from Thomas Becket to Henry of Lancaster, who found themselves at odds with those above them. For them there might be no alternative between martyrdom and open rebellion; for lesser men there was always the greenwood where, outside the law, with prices on their heads like wolves, they could band together to prey on the ill-policed society around them. Their stories, transmuted by folk-memory, became the archetypal matter of romance: endless adventures in which, by their own inherent qualities of mind and muscle, they righted wrongs, took from the rich to give to the poor, and avenged themselves on their oppressors in a world which closely resembled contemporary reality, withdrawing when pressed into an idealized greenwood where English law and the English climate could be equally ignored.

Robin Hood, the prototype hero of the greenwood, unidentified among a host of historical outlaws and perhaps a conflation of two such legendary figures, features only in ballads implying a popular audience. But ballads were characteristically the work of professional minstrels who drew on many sources, including metrical romances, and compounded texts into miniature epics. Their initial audience may have been the yeoman class to which Robin himself belongs, a rising class after the Black Death; but their appeal is classless and they mirror the exploits of noble outlaws as readily as they glamorize the social standing of humbler ones. Two English romances of the fourteenth century suggest how the adventures of Robin Hood may have been treated if they ever attained that form. In *Athelston* (*c.* 1355–80) the shadow of English history hovers behind a plot, for which there is no known source, compounded of familiar folklore motifs. Athelston, having risen to the throne from humble origins, appoints three men with whom he has sworn brotherhood to high office, but when one of the three later accuses another of treason, the King reacts tyrannically until the third, appointed Archbishop of Canterbury, defies him and, by administering the ordeal by fire, proves that the real traitor was the false accuser. The King's name may be another echo of the hero of Brunanburh, and the rebellious Archbishop may reflect Becket's resistance to the absolutism of Henry II, but the theme of defiance of tyranny in the name of brotherhood and the rule of law is perennial. It finds another expression in *Gamelyn* (*c.* 1350–70), a compilation of stock wildwood themes made in the north-east Midlands, apparently without any French source. It is preserved in twenty-five manuscripts, more than any other English romance, always in association with *The Canterbury Tales*, suggesting that Chaucer may have intended to rework it for his Cook or Yeoman to tell.[25]

On the death of their father, a modest knight of the shire, his eldest son Johan appropriates the inheritance of the youngest, Gamelyn until, grown into a champion wrestler, he is strong enough to demand restitution, to beat up a party of clerics feasting at his brother's expense, and break Johan's back. He then flees into the greenwood with his father's faithful steward Adam, while Johan as sheriff declares him an outlaw and bribes the jurors to condemn to death their brother Ote who has gone bail for Gamelyn; he, however, arrives with his band of outlaws, seizes the court, and sentences Johan and the jurors to be hanged, takes possession of his inheritance, is made Chief Justice of the Forest by the King, marries, and lives happily ever after. The underlying pattern of folklore motifs stands out with copybook clarity: the benevolent father who provides equally for all three sons; the youngest left prey, as a child, to the malignity of the eldest, finding resource in his growing physical strength and the human qualities which draw men to him, supported by good brother and faithful servant, recognized as a natural leader by other outsiders, eventually winning his way to full adult status, social recognition, and sexual maturity. It is a timeless pattern, independent of specific social circumstances, as effective in a host of 'western' films as in *As You Like It, David Copperfield*, or Stevenson's *Kidnapped*.

The social circumstances to which it is fitted here are not primarily those of the greenwood which, like the West in much modern cinema, provides an escape from the more intractable facts of life into a simpler world where physical might can determine right and wrong and the inherent ability of an unsophisticated hero win rapid recognition. It is a world of young men, ready hospitality, easy manners, ironic acceptance of common misfortune – '"He moste needes walke in woode    þat may not walke in towne"' (l. 672)[26] – and democratic justice directed only against the unjust, such as the clerical landowners who are Robin Hood's frequent victims. Challenged on arrival in the forest, Gamelyn offers to take on a dozen at once and is immediately accepted at face value – 'Tho þey herde by his word    þat might was in his arm,/Ther was non of hem alle    þat wolde do him harm' (ll. 653–54) – and then equally effortlessly elected 'king' of the outlaws. Though he does little there, it is from the greenwood that Gamelyn draws his reputation and the power to coerce the outside world which is less ready to recognize it.[27]

As with other exile and return stories, it is the world to which the hero returns that is the real scene of his struggles and triumphs. Here it bears a resemblance to the world of contemporary English yeomen almost uncomfortably close for the romance mode. In it the traditional enmity of elder towards younger brothers and the abuse of the defenceless by an unjust society express themselves through the machinery of fourteenth-century law, precisely noted by the poet and no doubt appreciated by the audience. Their father having ignored the rule of primogeniture in providing for all his sons, an exception recognized in contemporary practice, Johan takes revenge by neglecting the lands and wasting the revenues of his ward Gamelyn. The boy is conscious of his wrongs and when Johan treats him as a menial once too often, flashes out at him: "'Thou shalt go bake þiself;    I will nouȝt be þy cook!'" (l. 92) and, stung by the taunt that he is base-born, seizes a pestle and beats off the servants sent to thrash him. To pacify him, Johan promises restitution and the innocent Gamelyn gives him the kiss of peace.

Discovery of his strength has, as with Havelok, given him self-respect and the means to help others oppressed by the abuse of power; at the wrestling, he avenges a poor franklin whose sons the champion had killed by crippling him at a single throw and celebrates by inviting all and sundry to feast with him at home. Johan bars the door, but Gamelyn kicks it in, tosses the porter into the well, and wastes his brother's substance in a week of unlimited hospitality. But he is as soft-hearted as he is generous and, when Johan tells him that he had taken an oath to bind him to avenge the porter's broken neck, allows himself to be fettered to a pillar in the hall rather than have his brother foresworn. Like Samson bound, he endures the insults of Johan's clerical guests, then turns the table with Adam's help, beating them out of the house and sitting down to feast before his brother fettered in his place. The assault and battery of ecclesiastics brings the sheriff against them; they drive off the first posse but as a second approaches they decamp to the wildwood – 'Tho fond þe sherreue    nest but non ay' (eggs) (l. 610).

While they live the fantasy of absolute freedom, the law takes its inexorable course: Gamelyn is declared a 'wolves-heed' and, as if he were legally dead, his lands pass into the hands of his brother as sheriff and his peasants pay fine to their new lord. To defend their interests he goes to the next shire court, is imprisoned, and released on Ote's surety, making his brother liable to his penalty should he break his bail. But the wildwood calls him back and he lingers there until Ote is in danger of being hanged by a packed jury bribed by Johan – no rarity in the period. As sentence is pronounced, Gamelyn strides into court, tosses the justice over the bar, empanels a jury from among his outlaw band, and executes sentence of hanging on sheriff, judge, and corrupt jurors. The tables have been turned by the kind of intimidation all too common in the period; when the law is corrupt, men must defend themselves by main force and mutual support. The institution itself is not under attack; the hero wins the King's personal pardon and is as loyal to him as his peasants are to Gamelyn. His experience is the contemporary reality that overlords are oppressive, clerical landlords grasping, judges venal; his remedy is a change of personnel not system, the substitution of poachers turned gamekeepers whose own experience of inequity is made to justify their use of the methods used against them in the name of justice.[28]

The solution is high romance, but the dubious morality is disguised by the vigour and self-conviction of the treatment just as the social bitterness is modified and ironized by the pervasive humour. The source of much of the humour is Gamelyn himself: as the yeoman hero turning the tables upon his oppressors by brute strength and commenting ironically on the justice of the reversal; and as an innocent in the ways of the world, simple-minded to the point of stupidity, allowing himself to be fettered rather than break his wicked brother's vow and exposing himself to arrest by going to protect his peasants. The ambivalent irony seems to arise from the dual perspective upon the hero – as a strong-arm champion of bourgeois values and as a parody of the aristocratic concept of the middle class as strong, crude, and inherently stupid – which may well have appealed to readers of both classes.[29] Thomas Lodge recognized the wider appeal of the central conflict when he made Gamelyn a King of France banished to the Forest of Arden by his usurping brother in his romance *Rosalynde* (1590), the source of Shakespeare's *As You Like It*.

In manner of presentation, *Gamelyn* is popular yet efficient and effective, resembling a series of six ballads, each introduced by a minstrel formula, 'Liþeth and lestneþ    and holdeþ your tonge' (l. 169), marking stages in the hero's maturation. The major episodes are established with the minimum of narration and the action is then played out in lively exchanges of colloquial dialogue and descriptions of physical violence in which the poet manifestly delights. The vividness of the verbal surface, the ironic commentary on events – such as the comment on Johan's fate when he is no longer able to bribe a corrupt judge: 'He was hanged by þe neck    and nouȝt by þe purs' (l. 885) – the exactness of legal references, all anchor the poem in the real world. The economy and simplicity of phrasing, the frequency of minstrel tags, the repetition of easy rhymes, the proverbial summations of popular wisdom – 'after bale cometh bote' – provide the distancing gloss of the ballads whose quatrains are vaguely echoed in the seven-stress lines of the couplets with their medial caesura and occasional alliteration. It is an archaic medium, though effective and oddly appropriate to the matter of the poem when read aloud, suggesting, like much in *Gamelyn*, an idiosyncratic creation deeply rooted in English tradition.

# The character of the Matter of England romances

Whatever fragment of the native narrative tradition is represented by this handful of texts, their homogeneity over some century and a half is remarkable. However pervasive the cultural influence of France before even the earliest was written, their dependence on the dominant tradition is far from slavish; from the radical abbreviation of *Horn* to the apparent independence of *Gamelyn* they seem to take from it only what they need for their particular creative purpose and, whatever the source of their material, to handle it confidently with particular effects in view. Their relationship to the romance mode is very variable, with a marked preference for the mimetic over the mythic element shown in a dim awareness of the ghost of native history hovering behind their tales, in consciousness of contemporary social conditions and legal procedures and fondness for the realistic evocation of everyday life. The mythic element projects with remarkable persistence the same basic folklore pattern of the exile of a charismatic hero who, through personal maturation and the development of powers of body and soul, returns to take possession of his birthright.

The codes such heroes seek to fulfil are not those of *roman courtois*; social aspirants like Bevis and Guy may know the conventions of chivalric deportment but share with their English compatriots an ideal of personal fulfilment and social service. The struggles in which they are caught up spring not from the internal contradictions of courtly codes but the oppressive forces of a wicked world. They take place at many levels, from the reconquest of a kingdom alienated by treachery and paganism when, as in *Horn* and *Havelok*, the struggle takes on epic overtones, to the recovery of a patrimony purloined by fraternal enmity and legal corruption when, as in *Gamelyn*, it is related to the outlaw tradition by the use of ballad techniques. But at their various social levels the Matter of England romances offer resolution rather than conflict of values – love supports and rewards rather than rivals chivalry – and even when, as in *Guy* and *Bevis*, they borrow the conventions of *roman courtois*, they divorce them from the class consciousness in which they are rooted there. Their heroes pass effortlessly from one social level to another, offering sympathetic figures for self-identification on the part of readers more socially diverse than the courtly audiences of French romance.[30] The result, thematically and expressively, is an amalgam less courtly and exclusive, more eclectic and broadly based than its Continental counterpart and, in the width of its appeal, a significant indicator of the future potential of English narrative literature.

# Notes

1. Jean Bodel, *Roman de Saisnes, Saxenlied*, edited by F. Menzel and E. Stengel (Marburg, 1906–09), ll. 6–7.

2. On the cultural effects of the Viking invasions see Margaret Schlauch, *English Medieval Literature and its Social Foundations* (Warsaw, 1956), pp. 75–84. On traces of Germanic and natives heroes in post-Conquest literature see R. M. Wilson, *Early Middle English Literature*, second edition, (London, 1951), pp. 196–98, and *The Lost Literature of Medieval England* (London, 1952), pp. 123–27; the example of Hereward is examined in Maurice Keen, *The Outlaws of Medieval Legend*, revised edition (London, 1979), pp. 9–38.

3. See H. G. Leach, *Angevin Britain and Scandinavia* (Cambridge, Massachusetts, 1921), pp. 328–31, and M. D. Legge, *Anglo-Norman Literature and its Background* (Oxford, 1963), pp. 96–104.

4. See Anne Wilson, *Traditional Romance and Tale* (Ipswich, 1976), pp. 59–62, and Derek Brewer, *Symbolic Stories* (Cambridge, 1980), pp. 64–65.

5. See Georgianna Ziegler, 'Structural Repetition in *King Horn*', *Neuphilologische Mitteilungen*, 81 (1980), 403–08.

6. Text from Cambridge University MS Gg.4.27 (II), normalized and modernized by D. B. Sands, *Middle English Verse Romances* (New York, 1966), pp. 15–54.

7. See Mary Hynes-Berry, 'Cohesion in *King Horn* and *Sir Orfeo*', *Speculum*, 50 (1975), 652–70.

8. H. L. Creek, 'Character in the Matter of England Romances', *Journal of English and Germanic Philology*, 10 (1911), 429–52, 585–609.

9. See, for example, George Kane, *Middle English Literature* (London, 1951), pp. 48–49: 'This story is loosely episodic, distorted by gratuitous duplication, inartistically expressed . . .'; 'absurdities . . . arise in it out of disregard for narrative structure and out of inadequate motivation. . . .'

10. On the historical background see Leach, pp. 324–28. Characteristic of *Havelok's* vague Norse associations are various attributes of Grim which connect him with Odin, notably the name of one of his sons, Hugh Raven, reminiscent of Huginn, one of the two ravens who are the god's familiars, suggesting that the story may have originated as a hero-myth in which the protagonist was aided by Odin in one of his many disguises (see Edmond Reiss, '*Havelok the Dane* and Norse Mythology', *Modern Language Quarterly*, 27 (1966), 115–24).

11. Text from Bodleian Library MS Laud Misc. 108, normalized and modernized by Sands, pp. 55–129.

12. See W. R. J. Barron, 'The Penalties for Treason in Medieval Life and Literature', *Journal of Medieval History*, 7 (1981), 187–202.

13. See Sheila Delany and V. Ishkanian, 'Theocratic and Contractual Kingship in *Havelok the Dane*', *Zeitschrift für Anglistik und Amerikanistik*, 22 (1974), 290–302; John Halverson, '*Havelok the Dane* and Society', *Chaucer Review*, 6 (1971), 142–51; David Staines, '*Havelok the Dane*: A Thirteenth-century Handbook for Princes', *Speculum*, 51 (1976), 602–23.

14. See Judith Weiss, 'Structure and Characterisation in *Havelok the Dane*', *Speculum*, 44 (1969), 247–57.

15. Comparison with cognate versions of the Helpful Fisherman story suggests that the English poet deliberately retained that part of the tradition which showed Grim as initially cruel and venial, providing narrative tension and a dramatic change in behaviour after he has seen the kingmark which are lacking in the more consistent characterization of the French version (see Maldwyn Mills, 'Havelok and the Brutal Fisherman', *Medium Aevum*, 36 (1967), 219–30).

16. The stylistic aspects of *Havelok* are particularly well treated in Dieter Mehl, *The Middle English Romances of the Thirteenth and Fourteenth Centuries* (London, 1968), pp. 161–72.

17. See J. C. Hirsh, '*Havelok* 2933: A Problem in Medieval Literary History', *Neuphilologische Mitteilungen*, 78 (1977), 339–47 (p. 343).

18. See J. M. Ganim, 'History and Consciousness in Middle English Romance', *The Literary Review*, 23 (1980), 481–96 (pp. 484–87).

19. See J. R. Hurt, 'The Texts of *King Horn*', *Journal of the Folklore Institut*, 7 (1970), 47–59 (p. 49).

20. See Legge, pp. 139–75, and Keen, pp. 39–52, 78–94.

21. See Derek Pearsall, *Old English and Middle English Poetry* (London, 1977), pp. 145–46.

22. See L. A. Hibbard, *Medieval Romance in England* (New York, 1924), pp. 137–38.

23. Text from National Library of Scotland Auchinleck MS edited by J. Zupitza, *The Romance of Guy of Warwick*, EETS, ES 42, 49, 59 (London, 1883, 1887, 1891, p. 379). Here as elsewhere texts taken from early editions have been regularized to conform to modern editorial practice.

24. On the influence of the legend of St Alexis on *Guy* see D. N. Klausner, 'Didacticism and Drama in *Guy of Warwick*', *Medievalia et Humanistica*, 6 (1975), 103–19. For a perceptive analysis of *Guy* see V. B. Richmond, *The Popularity of Middle English Romance* (Bowling Green, Ohio, 1975), pp. 149–93.

25. See Keen, pp. 95–190, and R. B. Dobson and J. Taylor, *Rymes of Robyn Hood* (London, 1976), pp. 1–36.

26. Text from British Library MS Harley 7334 edited by W. H. French and C. B. Hale, *Middle English Metrical Romances* (New York, 1930), pp. 209–35.

27. There is no reference to Robin Hood earlier than *c.* 1377 and the earliest ballad copies belong to the fifteenth century. *Gamelyn* is earlier, yet the hero is drawn into the ballads as Robin's rival and, later, lieutenant; it seems likely both were originally independent expressions of the outlaw tradition, born of the same social circumstances. See V. J. Scattergood, *Politics and Poetry in the Fifteenth Century* (London, 1971), pp. 362–67 and Keen, pp. 78–80.

28. See Keen, pp. 78–94, and E. F. Shannon, 'Medieval Law in the *Tale of Gamelyn*', *Speculum*, 26 (1951), 458–64.

29. See E. Z. Menkin, 'Comic Irony and the Sense of Two Audiences in the *Tale of Gamelyn*', *Thoth*, 10 (1969), 41–53.

30. The greater degree of political centralization in England, the absence of provincial counterparts to the court of Champagne where esoteric literature could be addressed to the known tastes of a defined audience, the linguistic exclusion of the ruling class may have required English poets to cater for a wider audience including the gentry if not the minor nobility. The assumption that the popular tone of these

romances, with their realism of detail and colloquial diction – often at odds with their serious themes – reflects a socially limited audience may be as misleading as the supposition, now modified, that the Robin Hood ballads reflected only the interests of the oppressed classes (see J. C. Holt, 'The Origins and Audience of the ballads of Robin Hood', *Past and Present*, 18 (1960), 89–110) or that the sexually explicit fabliaux could have appealed only to the vulgar bourgeoisie.

# Chapter 5

# The Matter of France

The dual effect of the Norman Conquest in severing the Germanic roots of English culture and importing a dialect of *romanz* which exposed England to the cultural influence of France in the age of its ascendancy was ultimately to have profound consequences. The Matter of England romances show how slow the roots were to wither and how readily they became entwined with elements of the imported culture to produce narrative literature equally appealing to English and Anglo-Norman audiences. Not all such elements were equally assimilable: the dominant form of secular literature in the century following the Conquest, the epics of the Matter of France, might have been expected to appeal to a society whose native tradition had long included heroic poetry of a similar character, yet they are represented in English by only a handful of texts, late in date and largely unrepresentative of the genre. There is evidence that the *chansons de geste* were popular with the French-speaking rulers of England, where three of the earliest texts have been preserved, but none that epics were ever composed in Anglo-Norman.[1] While the ruling class could understand the originals, there was no need for English adaptations; they came mostly in the fourteenth century when the form was already in decay and sufficiently adulterated with elements of romance to appeal to the tastes of ordinary men. As a result, the true epic of the *geste du roi*, of Charlemagne and his *douzepers*, the twelve peers of France, embattled against the forces of paganism for the defence of Christendom, is represented only by a single fragmentary text.

## The Song of Roland

This version of the *Chanson de Roland* (see above, pp. 15–19), made somewhere in the east Midlands about 1400, survives as a fragment of 1049 lines, about a quarter of the French original. It represents no known text of the *Roland*, combining details from the oldest manuscript with others from later rhymed versions, probably already conflated in its source. To this have been added some elements from the *Pseudo-Turpin Chronicle*, a Latin prose compilation of the first half of the twelfth century designed to do for the Matter of France what Geoffrey of Monmouth's *Historia* did for the Matter of Britain by weaving the material of the epics into a supposedly historical account attributed to Charlemagne's clerical lieutenant, Archbishop Turpin. The real clerical authorship of the *Pseudo-Turpin* is apparent in the occasional moral interpolations such as the incident with which the English fragment opens: Ganelon, returning from his mission to Saragossa, brings a present of wine and women from the Sultan with which Charlemagne's men indulge themselves on the journey back to France, suggesting a moral cause for the coming disaster, just as elsewhere Ganelon's greed is stressed as the motive for his betrayal. But if the English adapter too was a cleric, he made no thematic use of these importations; the morality of his version like the original is feudal and the root cause of the disaster is Ganelon's treason. How well he appreciated the underlying issues is difficult to judge from the surviving fragment, but the coverage of two key elements is sufficient to form some impression of his understanding.

In the original (ll. 737–73), when Ganelon nominates Roland to command the rearguard, Charles rages against him as a fiend of hell, but Roland first responds calmly that France will suffer no loss through him; then, in the variant *laisse*, with violence, mockingly reminding him how he let fall the Emperor's glove which was the emblem of his mission to Saragossa and claiming Charles's bow as the sign of his own charge. In the English version (ll. 134–77), the poet adds his own curses to Charlemagne's accusation that Ganelon desires Roland's death and Ganelon makes his self-interest more obvious by nominating himself to command the van, yet Roland accepts the charge eagerly without mentioning his stepfather, fear of whose treason is so widespread that no other *douzeper* will volunteer for the mission. By casting Ganelon so openly in the role of villain the redactor has removed the element of ambivalence from his character and much of the tension from the plot; substitution of simple malice on his part for the original conflict between his desire for chivalric reputation and his rivalry with his stepson has turned the mixture of open defiance and ironic acceptance of the implied challenge with which Roland originally responds into something like culpable blindness on his part. When, in the French (ll. 1017–90), the Saracen hordes fall upon the rearguard, Oliver immediately attributes the attack to Ganelon's treachery but Roland silences him, reminding him that he is speaking of his stepfather; the rebuke has gone from the English version (ll. 511–44) along with Oliver's triple call for the blowing of the horn, while Roland's repeated refusals for the sake of his own reputation, the fame of his kinsmen, the honour of France are reduced to a single denial that there is any need while they still remain uninjured. In fact the horn is never blown, though

Ganelon's assurance to Charles that Roland is merely hunting pointlessly survives; instead, Roland finally proposes to send a messenger to the Emperor to prevent further loss of life, to which Oliver angrily replies: "'Broder, let be all siche sawes!'" (*speeches*) (l. 1049).[2]

The English fragment ends at that point, leaving in doubt whether anything further was to have been made of the contrast between valiant Roland and prudent Oliver. There is no indication that the poet understood the original significance of Roland's *demesure* any more than Ganelon's ambivalent motivation; everyone seems wholly convinced of the latter's treachery and Charlemagne is criticized for not trusting those who tell him of it just as Roland is openly blamed (ll. 633–41) for his failure to blow the horn. In each case, the original supplies some warrant for what is said, but the redactor has not, apparently, appreciated the significance of the pattern of repetition with variation. What survives in his version are black and white issues of loyalty and treason, of Christian solidarity in resistance to overwhelming pagan forces. Two-thirds of the surviving section are concerned with battle, faithful to the original in general outline but largely independent in the detailed description of action.

Though the English changes scene with the French, moving from the battlefield to Charles's camp and back again, it does not reproduce the isolated tableaux of the original, moments of frozen action in which the variant *laisses* present different aspects of the same situation. The narrative moves swiftly and competently, with obvious pleasure in the description of violence effectively conveyed by the irregular but persistent alliteration in the four-stress line – though both alliteration and rhyme have obviously suffered in transmission. The poet lingers for a moment over some of the familiar topics of the alliterative tradition: wild and desolate scenery (ll. 305–09), a fierce storm among mountain peaks (ll. 845–62), speeches of battlefield defiance (ll. 570–77), the splendour of armour (ll. 702–11), above all, the violence of hand-to-hand fighting:

> Roulond rod furthe, he wold not rest, I wene;
> He sawe wher a Sairsyn seche hym wold,
> Kinge was of Criklond, crounyd with gold.
> In he ridithe ful fast hym againste;
> He smot throughe sheld and man almost,
> That man and horse on the hethe fell.
> Then he nemythe 'Mon joy!' full still,                    *cries 'Monjoie'*
> He drawithe out his swerd and swappithe hym about. – French war-cry
> Helmes and hedes he hewithe of stout,
> He hewithe doun hethy men full many.
> There ys no man alyf may say sothly
> That euer eny man sley so many.   (ll. 740–51)

Little of the alliterative tradition other than its rhetorical manner survives here. Even at this late date there were poets, such as the author of the alliterative *Morte Arthure* (see below, pp. 138–42), who inherited its epic spirit; had one of them undertaken this redaction, we might have had a version which showed more understanding of the *Roland* than this somewhat superficial, external account.

## The Matter of France as pious legend: *Otuel and Roland* and *The Sege of Melayne*

Whatever part churchmen may have played in the transmission of the legends which gathered round the names of Charlemagne and Roland and in the composition of the *chansons de geste*, once the Matter of France had established itself the Church was not slow to exploit its claim upon the imagination of the ruling class in the interests of faith and feudal solidarity. Propaganda was more to its purpose than poetry and what the early *chansons* demonstrated in action, without commentary, clerics made explicit in prose as well as verse. Characteristic is the Latin prose *Descriptio* which describes how the Emperor of Constantinople, finding himself unable to protect the Christian community in the East from a Saracen attack, calls for aid from Charlemagne as Emperor of the West and, when he has freed the Holy Land from their threat, rewards him with the only treasure he will accept, relics of Christ's passion to be revered in Western shrines. Sober historians recognized the improbability of such a campaign but, written early in the twelfth century, the chronicle caught the imagination of the age of the crusades by turning Charlemagne, whose struggle with Islam had been fought on his own doorstep, into a prototype crusader. The *Pseudo-Turpin Chronicle* (*c.* 1140) extended the same process to the Emperor's campaigns in Spain, using his legendary military exploits as a thread on which to hang numerous moral and didactic episodes in which Charles figures as a saint of the Church Militant. Both accounts were used in the *Vita Karoli Magni* compiled on the occasion of Charles's canonization in 1165, were translated into French in the early thirteenth century and finally conflated in 1206 as the *Estoire de Charlemagne* which proclaimed its academic respectability by denouncing the *chansons* as mendacious rhymes, with every success to judge from the numerous manuscripts which survive.[3] Now that the legends of Charlemagne had assumed the character of a saint's life, converts to the true faith were required to complete the analogy. Poets engaged on romanticizing the *chansons de geste* supplied them from among the Saracen ranks, converting them by force of arms or mystical experiences modelled on the Grail romances, and attaching them to the *geste du roi* in defiance of historical probability. The historicity of the Matter of France meant even less to fourteenth-century English audiences, but the flavour of the saint's life apparently appealed to them.

Two further fragments of the *geste du roi* in Middle English apparently represent detached portions of a lost tail-rhyme romance, referred to as *Charlemagne and Roland*, based on the *Estoire de Charlemagne* into which the redactor has inserted a version of *Otinel*, the romance of a Saracen convert which, in its Anglo-Norman version, was a popular source of other redactions in English, Welsh, and Icelandic. From *Charlemagne and Roland* the compilers of the Auchinleck MS (*c.* 1330) quarried the romance of *Roland and Vernagu* whose preoccupation with the miracles which demonstrate the genuineness of the relics of the Passion and assist Charles's triumphal conquest of Spain may have appealed to the pious tastes of the intended bourgeois readership. It ends with a combat between Roland and the giant Vernagu, who is so impressed by the courtesy of the Christian champion that he submits to instruction in his faith before resuming the fight to determine whether it is superior to his own Muslim code – and proves it by his death! The last lines announce that Vernagu's death was reported to his fellow-Saracen Otuel who vowed to avenge him, and the following item in the Auchinleck is a romance in short couplets headed *Otuel a Knight*; but, unexpectedly, it is not the continuation of the *Charlemagne and Roland* – that is found in another manuscript, the Fillingham (1475–1500), where *Otuel and Roland*, using a variation of its tail-rhyme stanza, gives a version of the *Otinel* and completes the *Estoire de Charlemagne* context. Neither *Otuel* text seems derived from the other, but there are sufficient verbal parallels between them to suggest that both derive from a lost English original presumably in couplet form. There is yet another version, *Duke Roland and Sir Otuel of Spain*, made in the North about 1400, using a tail- rhyme scheme so complicated that the poet has chosen to abbreviate and simplify the original story.[4]

What was there in this part of the Matter of France to appeal repeatedly to English tastes? *Otuel and Roland* begins with stanzas, apparently paraphrased from the original opening of *Charlemagne and Roland*, listing the overall content, divided between the pious legends of Charles's lightning conquest of the Holy Land and the parallel mission in Spain to which he was summoned by a vision of St James of Compostela who urged him to free his burial-place from pagan hands. The action opens as Otuel arrives at the court at St Denis demanding in the name of Garcy, Saracen King of Spain, that Charles turn

Muhammadan; Roland challenges him and, as they fight, the Holy Ghost as a dove alights on Otuel's helmet, he surrenders, is christened and betrothed to the Emperor's daughter Belisent, and joins her father in a campaign against Garcy's capital of Utaly in Lombardy. His fidelity to his new faith and allegiance is repeatedly demonstrated as he rescues Roland and Oliver from overpowering numbers, defeats the Saracen champion Clarel in single combat, and assists in the overthrow of Garcy who is led prisoner to Paris and baptized by Archbishop Turpin. The narrative then returns to the sequence of the *Estoire de Charlemagne*; the Emperor wins one Saracen kingdom after another in Spain, until the Sultan pretends submission, Ganelon turns traitor and events are set in train for the triumphant disaster of Roncevaux.

The poet's interests are indicated by the fact that, though he gives some 1700 lines to the adventures of Otuel, the whole Spanish campaign occupies him for only 1100. Many of them are taken up with the extraneous material, largely pietistic, of the *Pseudo-Turpin*: when Charles prays for a sign to distinguish those who will fall in the next day's battle and finds a thousand of his men marked with a red cross, he leaves them at home in his chapel but, returning after a bloodless victory, finds them all dead; Turpin, saying mass in Charles's camp, hears devils bearing the soul of a Saracen leader to hell and learns from them that Roland's soul is already in paradise; Charles is ruthless in hanging Saracen prisoners and christening the inhabitants of captured cities, but shows his piety by making Compostela the seat of an archbishopric and building a church at Roncevaux. Turpin is absent from the battle there, since he must survive to write the *Pseudo-Turpin*; so is Charles, yet he remains the focus of interest in this part of the poem, described in an elaborate set-piece portrait as of great size and strength, wearing the crown of thorns at the chief feasts of the Christian year and guarded as he sleeps by a hundred knights with drawn swords. Little is left for Roland to do but die; there is no personal conflict with Ganelon, no struggle over the command of the rearguard, no issue concerning the sounding of the horn. The pace is such that the poet has little time for theme, still less for ambivalence as he skips from one famous set piece to the next: the bursting of Roland's temples as he sounds the horn (which he has blown quite casually just before), his struggle to break his sword, his final prayer. The emphasis is upon sentiment which slips all too easily into bathos: Oliver, blinded by wounds, strikes out at Roland who asks him if he has become a paynim; Roland himself escapes from a tight corner by hiding in a ditch! The minstrel ineptitudes of the tail-rhyme stanza echo the degradation of the *Chanson de Roland*:

With dwele and muche crye,                    *lamentation*
Charlys went in hye,                          *haste*
Roulond for to se;
And fond hym there ded,
And thus to hym he sayde,
As y schal telle the:
'O Roulond, the good conqueror,
And the noblyst warryour,
That euermore schal be!
Now y haue the forlore,                       *lost*
Dey y wylle the before,
But God wyl saue!'   (ll. 2499–2510)[5]       *unless*

An even more complex variation of this stanza-form serves comparatively well for the Otuel section where only the superficial values of
the Matter of France are evoked, given an added interest by being
exemplified in a pagan convert. Initially, Otuel demonstrates all the
defects of the unenlightened: arrogance in boasting of Garcy's power
and demanding Charles's apostasy, anger at the celebration of mass
which delays his combat with Roland, obduracy in resisting conversion even when he is close to defeat. The French respond with
Christian magnanimity: Belisent arms him with her own hands, warns
him to beware of Roland's famous sword, and wishes him luck. Once
converted by divine intervention he displays the same Christian spirit,
refusing to marry Belisent until he has proved himself worthy, aiding
Roland and other *douzepers* when they are hard pressed, rescuing from
them a fellow-Saracen who responds with equal generosity of nature
until he learns of Otuel's conversion when his defiance forces Otuel to
remember where his Christian duty lies and he kills him – at which the
Saracens break their idols in bitterness.

Charlemagne's Lombardy campaign is no more than a backdrop to
this demonstration of the power of Christian chivalry to transform an
alien nature. But the romance is fractured at the heart; just when
Otuel's virtues might have found fuller expression in the Spanish
campaign he has to disappear from the action in order not to detract
from Roland's essential central role. Much of the spirit of the poem,
born of the poet's interest in his vigorous personality, exemplifying
Christianity in effective action without pietism, goes with him. The
fullness of the narration, allowing space for convincing detail, lively
exchanges of dialogue, and effective management of the minstrel
stanza, gives the character a chance to live, even, when he cleaves his
Saracen opponent to the teeth, for ironic humour:

| | |
|---|---|
| Tho lowe Otuel and sayd: | *laughed* |
| 'Y sawe neuer, so God me rede, | *guide* |
| Sythe that y was bore, | *since, born* |
| Neuer man in knyʒtys wede, | *dress* |
| Also fer as y haue rede, | |
| A berd so clene yshore. | *shorn* |
| So God me saue and Sent Sauour, | |
| Now ys Cursins a good rasour!'   (ll. 1464–71) | Otuel's sword |

Without Otuel the Roncevaux episode seems lifeless and perfunctory.

The tendency of the *chansons de geste*, after the earliest period of literary texts, to form themselves into cycles is not truly represented by the related versions of a limited range of subject-matter presented in the English romances. They seem designed for audiences whose attention span was strictly limited but who welcomed sequels from the same 'historical' context and dealing with similar themes. This is perhaps why the manuscript containing the abbreviated *Duke Roland and Sir Otuel* precedes it with a separate romance, also written in the North about 1400, *The Sege of Melayne* which, like *Otuel*, deals with the war against Garcy in Lombardy. No French origin for the episode is known, though references to 'the Cronekill', 'our rearguard', and 'our Bretons' imply such a source. Whether it can have served there as introduction to an *Otuel* version is uncertain. The text breaks off as the climactic battle is approaching; Garcy's death or baptism seem the inevitable conclusion to a detached romance, yet he is still at liberty to defy Christendom in the *Otuel* texts. Perhaps, like the carbon-copy movies made as sequels to a box-office success today, the compiler, French or English, was merely imitating a proven formula, reusing familiar situations and locations and an established hate-figure whose improbable survival need not be plausibly explained.

Certainly the well-tried motifs of the *Pseudo-Turpin* are apparent in the plot. When an angel in a dream warns Charles that the Lord of Milan has lost his city to the Saracen Arabas, Ganelon nominates Roland for the rescue mission which goes badly for him; he and other *douzepers* are imprisoned until their captors are blinded in a blasphemous attempt to set fire to a cross, when they escape, kill Arabas, and return to France as sole survivors. Turpin recruits 100,000 priestly warriors for a second mission, which Ganelon persuades Charles to ban until Turpin is forced to excommunicate the Emperor. Turpin then besieges Garcy, the new Sultan, in Milan, and by a combination of heroic feats and saintly fasts and self-sacrifice is about to overwhelm him when the poem breaks off. The vague outline of the *geste du roi* still supplies the background to action; Charles is still the champion to whom all Christendom turns for aid against the power of Islam, Roland his chief lieutenant in the field, Ganelon the traitor motivated by hatred of his stepson. But the focus of interest has shifted so that the religious theme of defence of the faith dominates almost to exclusion the feudal theme of conflicting loyalties, while the rare miraculous interventions of the early *chansons* now rival the military action in importance.

The established characters play out their formulaic roles, but much reduced in status and significance. Roland is still strong of arm, capable of killing sixty Saracens single-handed (statistically aided by a facile alliteration), but liable also to the humiliation of being captured and bound. He is now a missionary as much as a military figure, preaching conversion to his captors and being laughed at for his pains; he and his companions are rescued by divine intervention when the burning cross blinds their captors and provided with miraculous horses which vanish once they reach St Denis, where the bells ring of their own accord to greet them. He is still the object of Ganelon's malice, not from any conflict of feudal idealism but for the sake of the inheritance which his stepfather might gain by his death, and not to a greater degree than the rest of the French whose morale the traitor undermines, advising submission to the Sultan until Turpin publicly curses him. He shares that fate with the Emperor himself, excommunicated for his reluctance to renew the attack on Milan after the loss of an army of 40,000 men and finally goaded into laying violent hands on his archbishop. Charles's zeal is never sufficient for Turpin, and even when he takes the field in single combat against a Saracen leader, the Archbishop stands on the sidelines urging him on.

In Turpin the *geste du roi* has a new hero, moral and military, who dominates the action for the later two-thirds of the poem's 1600 lines. Faced with the massive defeat of Roland's mission, he reproaches the Virgin Mary for deserting the French, much as the Saracens abuse their gods when they suffer a reverse. But he immediately preaches a crusade, leads an army of militant clerics to Milan, and himself performs prodigies in the field. God shows himself on the side of the French – Roland sees a vision of his slaughtered companions led to paradise – and specifically on Turpin's side: when he celebrates mass for the dead, the bread and wine are sent down from heaven! On the battlefield he eclipses even Roland in skill and courage; with chivalric propriety he rebukes his squire for wishing to strip a fallen Saracen and when Charles hesitates to attack overwhelming numbers reproves him with: "'The more powers that they be,/The more honour wyn shall we'" (ll. 1510–11).[6] But there is as much of the saint as of the soldier in his nature: he vows not to eat or drink until Milan is captured and his example inspires the French to be satisfied with bloodstained water from a ditch; repeatedly wounded he three times refuses medical aid until the city falls; and if the spear-thrust and wound in his side suggest comparison with the sufferings of Christ, Turpin himself acknowledges the association:

> 'What! wenys þou, Charls,' he said, 'þat I faynte bee
> For a spere was in my thee,                                    *thigh*
>     A glace thorowte my syde.                                  *wound*
> Criste for me sufferde mare;
> He askede no salue to his sare,
>     No no more sall I this tyde.'   (ll. 1345–50)

His emphatic personality, domineering with men, demanding of God, gives coherence to a routine collection of incidents typical of the spiritualized Matter of France. The poet's interest in him may be reflected in the technical competence of the romance, forcefully narrated in short scenes whose point is chiefly made in dramatic dialogue. Despite its complex rhyme-scheme, the minstrel stanza is made to serve the various needs of the narrative with ease and occasionally with effective emphasis.

## The decadence of the Matter of France

The change in the relative importance of the twin concerns of the Matter of France, feudal and spiritual, was followed by a slow decline which was eventually to rob it of any real thematic interest and reduce the *chansons* to random sequences of stereotyped incidents often indistinguishable from those of the *roman d'aventure*. Their focus was most often external, concerned with the continuing Muslim threat which compelled the cohesion of feudal Christendom and overrode its internal tensions. They expressed an ambivalent attitude towards the Saracens who were made to represent the Islamic enemy in general: recognition of a social system and military ethos very similar to those of feudal Europe and rejection of pagan beliefs and practices which challenged the true faith. Constant commercial and military contacts with Islam in Spain and the Holy Land gave both poets and public every opportunity to know the true nature of that culture. In military matters the poets pay it grudging admiration; Saracens make excellent knights if only they can be won or forced to Christian conversion.

In two respects they traduce it with all the self-delusion of blind prejudice: the Muslim faith is polytheistic, idolatrous, its adherents superstitious, treacherous, polygamous; Muslim women are, in consequence, lascivious, seductive, irresistibly attracted to Christian knights, and, after willing conversion, faithful only to them. The adventures of the romanticized epic in which European readers could project themselves into such a fantasy of Islamic society allowed them both to indulge their prejudices and to father upon their traditional opponents an exotic version of their own idealism: Saracens who offended against their codes illustrated them by inversion like the various Black Knights of chivalric romance, those who adopted them upon conversion acknowledged their superiority, while the compliant Saracen maidens promised sensual fulfilment without the restraints imposed by Christian society. This was fertile ground for romance, combining a dominant preoccupation of contemporary reality, the Muslim threat, with the wish-fulfilment made possible by projecting ideals upon exotic but often chivalrous opponents in distant lands where forms of magic unknown in Christendom made possible the most fantastic adventures.[7]

## The *Firumbras* group: *The Sowdon of Babylon* and the Fillingham *Firumbras*

The degraded form of the *chanson de geste*, in which the original ideals were parodied and mocked, does not seem to have appealed to English audiences. But some compilations of exotic adventures largely devoid of thematic coherence which did were reworked in several versions, perhaps suggesting that the range of French texts available to those, such as the compilers of the Auchinleck MS, who catered for a popular readership, was not large. That the English texts which exemplify such random collections of adventures, those of the *Firumbras* group, were likely to appeal to such an audience is suggested by an odd detail which may connect them with the bookshop where the Auchinleck compilation was made. None of the French works dealing with Charlemagne's acquisition of relics from the Holy Land includes the lance of the Passion among them, but some English accounts of Athelstan, whose defeat of the Norsemen at the Battle of Brunanburh (937) led chroniclers to see him as the first true King of England, a national champion to rival Charlemagne, say that relics he received as a gift from France included the sacred lance once owned by the Emperor. The reference occurs twice in the Auchinleck MS, in its metrical *Shorter Chronicle* and again in the *Roland and Vernagu* account of the Passion relics. A similar reference figures in the Fillingham MS of *Firumbras*, though the lance is not among the relics mentioned in its French source. Just as the Fillingham *Otuel* may have derived from a version included in the Auchinleck MS, so its *Firumbras* text may originate from one of the thirteen items now lost from that compilation and have derived its knowledge of the lance from the reference to it there.[8] The persistence of this small detail, which other texts such as the alliterative *Morte Arthure* and Barbour's *Bruce* derived from their knowledge of the *Firumbras* tradition, shows the interest of English readers in anything which could associate the Matter of France with their own culture and the readiness of such popularizers as the Auchinleck editors to cater to that interest.

The *Firumbras* group derives from a lost twelfth-century *chanson* celebrating the role of the French in relieving Rome from the Saracen conquest of 846, the content of which is known from a summary in the *Chronique rimée* of Philippe Mouskés (*c.* 1243) who treated it as sober history. One of its romanticized episodes, dealing with Oliver's defeat of the Saracen champion Fierabras had been used already (*c.* 1170) as the starting-point of a compilation of stock motives and incidents by a poet who wished incidentally to explain how the relics of the Passion came to be in France. The mixture of elements in his *Fierabras* caught the interest of audiences all over Europe, and England produced at least four redactions based on various forms of the original. To replace the 'historical' context from which the Fierabras episode had been detached, a poet who knew the original *chanson* produced a prefatory poem, the *Destruction of Rome* which, in a Hanover manuscript, is followed by a copy of *Fierabras* not modified to take account of the introductory material. There is also an Anglo-Norman version in which the two components have been radically abbreviated and to some extent unified.

Of the English versions, *The Sowdon of Babylon* shares so many details with the Anglo-Norman text as to suggest that both derive from a common original now lost.[9] The triple division of the English poem, produced in the east Midlands about 1400–50, reflects the composite nature of the original. The opening section (ll. 1–938), derived from the *Destruction of Rome*, describes how the Sultan of Babylon and his son Ferumbras plunder the city and carry off the relics from St Peter's; Charlemagne, summoned by the Pope, arrives too late but pursues them to the Saracen capital in Spain. A linking passage (ll. 939–1050), compiled by the English redactor, makes apparent use of a passage from *Piers Plowman* in a conventional invocation to Spring, of Chaucer's 'Knight's Tale' in a Saracen prayer for victory adddressed to Mars, and of much information not found in the French texts on their pagan rites and the tribes of many origins who compose their army. In the third section (ll. 1051–3274), derived from *Fierabras*, the Sultan's son challenges Roland and his companions, fights all day with Oliver, and finally accepts baptism; Roland and Oliver, captured by the Sultan, are freed from prison by his daughter Floripas who, when the other *douzepers* arrive to rescue them, falls in love with their leader Guy of Burgundy; with her help they seize the Sultan's castle and hold him at bay until Charles, whom Ganelon has tried to persuade that they are already dead, comes to their aid; Floripas gives the relics to Charles who marries her to Guy, divides Spain between him and Ferumbras, and orders Ganelon's execution.

The redactor's additions in the linking passage, however derivative, suggest some wish to treat his material creatively; but it was not strong enough elsewhere to give him more than limited independence in paraphrasing the French, though with such loooseness and haphazard disregard for inconsistencies as to suggest that he was working, in part at least, from memory. He freely omits whole episodes in the siege of Rome, then, as if realizing that he has scamped an important event, tacks them on later, out of sequence and mingled with incidents of his own invention. His additions suggest a taste for grotesque comedy and a tendency to repeat effects: twice the curses of an insulting Saracen are cut off by an arrow and twice a pursuing infidel is cut in half by a falling portcullis! He shows as little regard for thematic consistency as for the factual contradictions introduced by his omissions and transpositions. Though his version opens with a blessing on all who read the tale, he virtually ignores the spiritual theme in the original. The relics are mentioned from time to time, but as trophies in the Christian–Muslim conflict rather than for their sacred significance. Christian knights may pray for aid in a tight corner, but it is the Muslim faith which receives most attention as a focus for prejudice and picturesque detail. Each time Saracen forces suffer a set-back the Sultan tries to destroy his gods and is only with difficulty dissuaded by the priests. Yet when finally captured and led to the font for baptism, he spits in it and is beheaded on the spot; his soul goes to hell to dance with the devils there. Ganelon still hovers in the background ready for any treason, but his feud with his stepson has gone and only a shadow of the old feudal tensions survives in Roland's resentment when Charles praises younger knights, which causes his uncle to strike him and call him traitor. Roland is little more than a cipher, robbed of the honour of defeating and converting Ferumbras by Oliver and unfitted by his 'historical' association to be loved by Floripas. Even her love for Guy, unexplained in origin, is a narrative convenience rather than a thematic element to be developed; the advances come from her, Guy can barely be persuaded by his companions to go through a kind of Saracen betrothal ceremony with her and thereafter she serves them all and the cause of France for his sake until, after her baptism, he accepts her from the Emperor's hands.

The real interest of the *Sowdon* is neither religion, love, nor even war, but adventure, a mass of incident, exotic in setting and varied in kind, to be enjoyed for its own sake. Like some minor epic of the modern cinema, made with the costumes, props, and surplus footage of an earlier success and a script which seems to have been extemporized during shooting, it capitalizes shamelessly on all the clichés of its kind: the band of companions holding out against superior numbers, the worthy foe whose defeat in fair fight converts him into a loyal partisan, the solitary woman who combines sexual promise with all the courage and resource of a good comrade, the massed cavalry riding to the rescue at the last moment. But just as such a film can succeed by sheer variety and rapidity of action, the clarity of its situations in which good and evil are opposed in black and white terms requiring only physical effort for their solution, the shamelessness with which it ignores manifest improbabilities of situation and motivation, so the *Sowdon* disarms criticism of its improbable events by the sweep of its narrative, the primary nature of its values – unabashed violence, crusading indignation, mutual loyalty between comrades in arms – the zest with which it piles up picturesque detail.

It revels in such exotic solutions to plot impasses as Floripas's magic girdle which quenches the hunger and thirst of her imprisoned companions while they wear it by turns, the dauntless spirit which leads her to push her duenna out of the window when she proves uncooperative and brain the prison warder with his own key, showing herself worthy of a Christian company whose wit and courage overcome such monsters as the giant Saracen bridge-guard and his scythe-wielding wife. The already abbreviated source is sometimes reduced to incoherence by the redactor, yet he finds space for such colourful incidentals as the giantess's twins, four feet tall at seven months old, the Sultan's treasure which Floripas uses to pelt his besieging forces much to his distress, and the feast with which the Saracens celebrate the fall of Rome:

> Thai blewe hornes of bras,
> Thai dronke beestes bloode.
> Milke and hony ther was,
> That was roial and goode.
> Serpentes in oyle were fryed
> To serve þe Sowdon with alle,
> 'Antrarian, Antrarian' thai lowde cryed
> That signyfied 'Ioye generalle'.    (ll. 683–90)[10]

Another treatment of the same scenario shows what a little art can do with indifferent material. *Fierabras* attracted at least two other English redactors: one whose version survives in the Ashmole MS worked in the Exeter district about 1380, producing a full if rather pedestrian account which changes metre at a point which may represent a switch from an abbreviated text of the original to one containing the fuller standard version; and one who, working apparently in the east Midlands about 1375–1400, left a fragmentary version of the standard text in the Fillingham MS.[11] Beginning about mid-point it completes the story in 1842 lines rhyming in couplets, each line of six stresses divided by a medial caesura. A more limited selection of episodes from a fuller version gives the redactor space to treat the narrative individually. The pace is still rapid but more coherent, with more of the spirit of epic in the numerous combats and a more genuine sense of the conflict of faiths: the Saracens still abuse their gods in moments of defeat but even Floripas, faint with hunger during the siege, thinks of praying to them for help and is only persuaded by the mockery of the French to admit that they are merely metal idols; the Saracens come to blows among themselves on the merits of the two faiths; when they set fire to the tower in which the Christians are besieged, Floripas uses her magic arts to turn the flames against them; the relics which she ultimately surrenders to Charles prove their authenticity by the miracles they perform.

It is not only this greater respect for the values of the original which distinguishes the Fillingham *Firumbras* from the *Sowdon*. Though equally fascinated by action, its author outlines the incidents with clarity and economy, setting scenes with a minimum of descriptive detail, allowing the characters to speak for themselves in a way which reveals them as youthful, impulsive, full of zest for life, largely independent of codes and conventions. A characteristic episode (ll. 554–732): when Guy, captured by the Saracens, is led to the gallows within sight of his besieged comrades, Floripas falls on her knees to Roland:

'The best knyʒt on lyue, y crye ʒow mercy!          *alive*
Schulde ʒe suffre my lord byfore ʒowre syʒt
To haue suche a deth – why wyl ʒe nouʒt fyʒt? –
Hit ne schal neuer be in no maner wyse,
But alle thys world schal speke of ʒowre cowrdyse.'

(ll. 578–82)[12]

The rescue is carried out in proper chivalric fashion: Roland kills one paynim to provide Guy with a horse and another for his armour and, while Floripas, rosy red and bathed in tears, watches from the tower, they cover the plain with Saracen dead. Then, seizing a passing supply train, they relieve the famished garrison. The incident has been given movement combining action and emotion resolved in victory and the lovers' reunion; the pedestrian but servicable verse caters adequately for a variety of moods.

## The late prose versions

As surprising as the repeated treatment in the verse romances of subjects from the same limited range is the absence of major categories of the Matter of France which might have been expected to appeal to English audiences. There is nothing from the *barons revoltés* tradition of the rebellion of his vassals against Charlemagne's autocracy, potentially attractive to a nation under foreign rule, or from the cycles of the crusades in which English forces had played a major role. But the surviving texts belong to an age when the rulers of England had long ceased to be regarded as foreign oppressors and were, to all appearances, intended for an audience beneath the social level at which feudal relationships or patriotic sentiment were likely to operate.[13]

Major treatments of those themes were to appear in English in the late fifteenth and early sixteenth century, but in prose and based on originals in which their true nature had already been radically altered. Caxton produced versions of the three major divisions of the Matter of France: of the *geste du roi* in his *Charles the Grete* (1485) in which the legendary history of France from the Trojan founding-father Francus to the Emperor's conquests in Spain is only a frame for the Fierabras story; of the *barons revoltés* in his *Foure Sonnes of Aymon* (1489) in which the epic struggle of Renaud de Montauban and his three brothers in resistance to their oppressive overlord Charlemagne, facing their father Aymon with a conflict of loyalties, has been elaborated by French prose redactors into a farrago of adventures involving their magician cousin, Renaud's marvellous horse who covers thirty feet at a stride, his pilgrimage to free Jerusalem from the Saracens and eventual 'martyrdom' while working as a labourer on the building of St Peter's at Cologne; and of the crusades in his *Siege of Jerusalem* (1481) whose history of how chance brought Godfrey of Bouillon, youngest son of an ancient but modest house, to the throne of Jerusalem at the end of the First Crusade (1099), reads like the stuff of romance. As his original prologues suggest, Caxton saw them all as chivalric propaganda expressing the belief of his noble patrons in the inspirational value of history, in the need to seek honour by emulating the positive code, uncomplicated by ambiguity, exemplified by his one-dimensional heroes, and to stem the tide of Turkish conquest after the fall of Constantinople in 1453. These ideas were current in the Burgundian courts which strongly influenced the England of Edward IV and from whose libraries many of Caxton's sources seem to have come. They were equally propagated by his manuals of courtesy and his versions of *romans courtois* on other matters; his full and faithful translation added little of his own except the gloss of his admirable style.[14]

He had his imitators in Robert Copeland, whose *Helyas, the Knight of the Swan*, printed by Wynkyn de Worde in 1512, also deals with Godfrey of Bouillon, but in a version which derives from the epic cycle where his crusade adventures are preceded by those of his legendary ancestor, the swan-knight; and in Lord Berners whose, *Duke Huon of Burdeux*, in which the hero, unjustly deprived of his lands by Charlemagne, rehabilitates himself by winning trophies from Babylon with the help of Oberon, King of the Fairies, was printed by de Worde about 1534. The romantic associations of Oberon in Shakespeare and in Weber's opera suggest how far the Matter of France has evolved from its roots in the *chansons de geste*. It was in these late prose redactions that it penetrated the imaginations of Spenser and the writers of Elizabethan romance, indistinguishable from other chivalric matters, largely devoid of nationalistic or religious significance. In an age when gunpowder was steadily devaluing individual initiative and courage in war, but when the nobility still wore the trappings of chivalry, played at jousting, mimicked the *douzepers* in their orders of knighthood, these unquestioning celebrations of the virtues of a golden age had all the allure of high romance.

## The character of the Matter of France romances

The process by which the ideals of one age, though originally presented as problematic, in conflict with each other or with contemporary reality, become, with the passage of time, the unquestioned achievements of heroes of old, is characteristic of the romance mode. The way in which it allows the imagination to project the ideal from the actual, conjuring what might be out of what is, often (as in science fiction) invoking powers beyond present possibility, makes it vulnerable to social change. Even in the age which produced it the relationship between ideal and reality may not have been precisely perceived, the element of wish-fulfilment in romance inhibiting objective judgement. The passage of time, obliterating knowledge of social circumstances and blurring the distinction between the real and the ideal, encourages the belief that once upon a time, in the age of gold, men were capable of heroism, idealism, fidelity to codes and values of which, in the age of iron, they seem incapable. If the golden age can be historically located and its heroes identified with revered ancestors, so much the more potent its romantic aura.

The age of Charlemagne, associated in men's minds with fundamental values of feudal solidity, individual heroism, and militant Christianity, exercised a fascination which gave the Matter of France currency throughout Europe and established its heroes in the order of the Nine Worthies, Ganelon as one of the archetypal villains of all time. Their charisma outlived precise memory of the qualities for which they were originally celebrated and their epoch served, like the Regency for modern romantic novelists or the two world wars for film-makers, as a highly coloured backdrop to adventures which had increasingly little to do with them or their values. It has become conventional to dignify the earliest treatment of the Matter of France as epic, distinguished by seriousness of purpose, solidarity, and worth of values from the fantasy and escapism of romance. The distinction may owe more to modern preconceptions than to any absolute difference of intention on the authors' part; the makers of the *chansons* may have been striving to subdefine and celebrate social codes already current, the *roman courtois* poets to project ideals to which their patrons might learn to aspire, but both acknowledged the challenge of reality in the characteristic manner of the romance mode. Since the values of the latter refined and supplemented rather than displaced those of the former, the Matter of France retained its general validity long after its specific idealism had faded to a romantic afterglow.[15]

In the English examples that process is already far advanced. The fascination of such key events as Roncevaux, the charisma of the archetypal figures linger still, lip-service is paid to the basic ethical values, but the ambiguities and internal conflicts to which they gave rise are no longer deeply felt, even in the surviving fragment of the *Roland*. They have been replaced by cruder, more generalized values – belief in might as right, comradeship rather than unique heroic virtues, a simplistic faith bordering on bigotry – celebrated not so much for their own sake than as a focus for martial adventure. Religion is treated with more commitment than chivalry, but it is a narrower, more prejudiced creed than the frank convictions of the *chansons de geste* that 'paien unt tort et chrestiens unt dreit'; love is a one-way process, loving women a prize or a battle trophy for successful warriors. Both are less significant in themselves than as furnishers of exotic incident, of warrior-priests, champion converts, and adoring girl Fridays. Action replaces theme, the remnants of history increasingly yield place to fantasy; Otuel disappears to leave the field clear for Roland at Roncevaux, but Ferumbras reduces him to one among many in the ranks of France. An occasional flicker of the old epic spirit recalls the origins of the legends, as when the *Foure Sonnes of Aymon* and *Huon of Burdeux* raise the old ghost of the tyrannous overlord; but when a rebellious vassal enlists the King of Fairy against his emperor the sun is setting for the Matter of France.

# Notes

1. See D. J. A. Ross, 'Old French' in *Traditions of Heroic and Epic Poetry*, I *The Traditions*, edited by A. T. Hatto, Publications of the Modern Humanities Research Association, IX (London, 1980), pp. 79–133 (p. 82), a useful introduction to the *chansons de geste* for non-specialists, and M. D. Legge, *Anglo-Norman Literature and its Background* (Oxford, 1963), pp. 3–5.

2. Text from British Library MS Lansdowne 388, edited by S. J. Herrtage, *The Sege off Melayne, The Romance of Duke Rowland and Sir Otuell of Spayne, together with a Fragment of the Song of Roland*, EETS, ES, 35 (London, 1880).

3. See R. N. Walpole, *Charlemagne and Roland: A Study of the Source of Two Middle English Metrical Romances, 'Roland and Vernagu' and 'Otuel and Roland'*, University of California Publications in Modern Philology, xxvi, No. 6 (Berkeley, California, 1944), pp. 387–400.

4. See Walpole, pp. 400–33.

5. Text from British Library MS Add. 37492, edited by M. I. O'Sullivan, *Firumbras and Otuel and Roland*, EETS, 198 (London, 1935).

6. Text from British Library MS Add. 31042, edited by S. J. Herrtage, *The Sege off Melayne*, EETS, ES, 35 (London, 1880).

7. See C. Meredith Jones, 'The Conventional Saracen of the Songs of Geste', *Speculum*, 17 (1942), 201–25, and Dorothee Metlitzki, *The Matter of Araby in Medieval England* (New Haven, Connecticut, 1977), pp. 160–210.

8. See L. H. Loomis, 'The Athelstan Gift Story: Its Influence on English Chronicles and Carolingian Romances', *PMLA*, 67 (1952), 521–37.

9. See H. M. Smyser, '*The Sowdon of Babylon* and its Author', *Harvard Studies and Notes in Philology and Literature*, 13 (1931), 185–218.

10. Text from MS Garrett 140 (formerly Phillips 8357) edited by E. Hausknecht, *The Sowdone of Babylone*, EETS, ES, 38 (London, 1881).

11. That yet another version once existed is indicated by the episode in John Barbour's *Bruce* in which Robert the Bruce reads a romance of Ferumbras to his men on the shores of Loch Lomond.

12. Text from British Library MS Add. 37492, edited by M. I. O'Sullivan, *Firumbras and Otuel and Roland*, EETS, 198 (London, 1935).

13. Poets occasionally selected from the traditional categories characteristic folk-tales which had been caught up in it or themselves attached such folk-tales to the Matter of France. This seems to have been so even from an early period; in 1287 Baron Bjarni Erlingsson took back to Norway an English romance, now referred to as *Olive and Landres*, which, judging from the version incorporated in the *Karlamagnussaga*, was on the old folklore theme of the caluminated wife and the cruel mother-in-law casually attached to the Matter of France (see R. M. Wilson, *Early Middle English Literature*, second edition (London, 1951), p. 201). These adventitious elements are to be treated separately (see below, pp. 181–82).

14. See Diane Bornstein, 'William Caxton's Chivalric Romances and the Burgundian Renaissance in England', *English Studies*, 57 (1976), 1–10.

15. On the changing perception of epic and romance as related expressions of the

romance mode see D. M. Hill, 'Romance as Epic', *English Studies*, 44 (1962), 95–107, and on the implications for the classification of English romances on the Matter of France see John Finlayson, 'Definitions of Middle English Romance', *Chaucer Review*, 15 (1980), 44–62, 168–81.

# Chapter 6
# The Matter of Rome

If the true nature of the Matter of France was gradually distorted by the instinct of the later Middle Ages to associate contemporary values with its ancient allure, the same impulse transformed no less drastically the epic narratives which they inherited from the ancient world. Societies recently emerged from the Dark Ages were inclined to interpret every document which gave them knowledge of the past as historically valid, as part of their own history. That instinct, coupled with the lack of historical perspective which made it difficult for them to realize the past except in terms of their own manners, morals, beliefs, and values, produced some strange hybrids in which a golden age that never was embodied an idealism that could never be. But the romance mode was not the product of the Middle Ages, and the process by which the epics of Greece and Rome were transformed was already far advanced in those Latin intermediaries which were part of Western Europe's classical heritage and, in an age when Greek was virtually unknown, made all knowledge of the ancient world part of the Matter of Rome (see above, pp. 20–22).

England did not have to wait for the Norman Conquest to participate in that heritage; it claimed its share directly through the Christian mission sent by Gregory the Great to Canterbury, in whose monastic school Latin and Greek were taught as well as anywhere in the Western world, and its northern outposts at Wearmouth, Jarrow, and York where the liberal monasticism of the Benedictine Order mingled with that of the Irish Church. Despite Gregory's instruction to limit the study of pagan authors to the minimum necessary for spiritual benefit, neither foundation made a rigid distinction between sacred and profane learning. The Canterbury curriculum included instruction in the liberal arts and the composition of religious verse upon classical models; the library at York contained not only classical grammarians and Christian poets but the works of Virgil, Statius, Lucan, Pliny, and Cicero. From the southern schools came Aldhelm (b. *c.* 650), author of abstruse and metrically complex Latin poetry but also of vernacular lays which he would perform as a minstrel to draw men to his teaching; from the northern, Bede (d. 735), historian, master of an admirable Latin prose style, and amateur of the earliest English poets. The work of both constantly echoes Virgil whose influence is also detectable in the native epic *Beowulf*. The northern tradition faded after the Danish invasions and the destruction at York of the largest library in Latin Christendom, but not before Alcuin (d. 804) had gone out from there to head the palace-school of Charlemagne and further his attempt to fuse Roman, Christian, and Germanic culture. The southern contributed to Alfred's revival of English learning in resistance to Danish barbarism and, stimulated by the monastic reforms of the tenth century and Continental contacts, served the needs of government and education rather than literature.

After the Conquest, when Greek studies had long withered, the return of Latin to official and administrative functions from which it had been displaced by Anglo-Saxon prose gave it added prestige as the language of history. By the end of the twelfth century, English historians, clerics now rather than monks, trained at the cathedral schools and nascent universities, moving freely between native and Continental centres as students and teachers, were unmatched in Europe. The best of them, John of Salisbury, Bishop of Chartres, believed the ethical teaching of Horace and Cicero compatible with the Christian faith and regarded Virgil as expressing, in allegorical form, the truth of all philosophy. Others, Walter Map and Giraldus Cambrensis, served the court of Henry II and, like Geoffrey of Monmouth, dignified with their Latinity matters of interest to laymen: pseudo-history, anecdote, and folklore. Inevitably they wrote poetry modelled on schoolroom classics, some with epic pretensions like Joseph of Exeter's *De bello Troiano*. Like similar classical matter which had already passed into English – Anglo-Saxon prose versions of *Apollonius of Tyre, Wonders of the East*, and *The Letter of Alexander to Aristotle* – Joseph's poem drew on partly romanticized forms of the Troy legends. The spirit of the age, with its glorification of the past, its fascination with heroic personalities, and its appreciation of Geoffrey of Monmouth's romanticized version of native history, demanded vernacular counterparts on classical subjects.[1]

# The Troy legends: *The Gest Historiale of the Destruction of Troy* and *The Seege of Troye*

The legends of the war of Troy, epitome of the heroic idealism of the ancient world, passed to the West not in Homer's *Iliad* and *Odyssey* but in debased Latin derivatives: the fourth-century prose *Ephemeris belli Trojani* attributed to Dictys, a Cretan who claims to have fought on the Greek side at Troy, and the *De excidio Trojae historia* of Dares the Phrygian, a Trojan ally. Both had Greek originals of the fourth to sixth centuries and breathe the spirit of Greek romance, ignoring the part which in Homer the gods play in the affairs of men, rationalizing the supernatural and romanticizing the roles of women. These 'eyewitness' accounts, however improbable, pleased the medieval penchant for fiction masquerading as fact and were received as sober history throughout the Middle Ages. Dares was particularly popular; Virgil's *Aeneid* having taught the nations of Western Europe to claim various Trojan refugees as their founding-fathers, they preferred the pro-Trojan account which was progressively elaborated and extended in various vernacular versions.

About 1165, a poet of northern France, Benoit de Sainte-Maure, conflated Dares and Dictys with much imaginative elaboration into the 30,000 lines of his *Roman de Troie*. On the bare foundation of their 'historical' record he erected a fantastic structure in which the war of Troy is treated as a feudal conflict of alliances, forays, truces, councils conducted from towered castles and donjon keeps, in helmets and hauberks, governed by the laws of chivalry and faith in one god. The divinities of classical mythology are scorned, the seer Calchas has become a bishop presiding over cloistered monks, but magic is rife – Hector is loved by Arthur's sister Morgan le fay and rides a magic horse she has given him! As the Trojan leader, he is presented as the flower of knighthood, courageous, patriotic, self-sacrificing, moderate in council and admired by women; Homer's hero Achilles is dismissed as a faithless coward. The action is interlarded with encyclopaedic information on the lands, beasts, tribes, and wonders of the East, the décor loaded with carved pillars of jasp and onyx, curtains of Indian silk, arrays of musical instruments, all designed for the luxurious tastes of Eleanor of Aquitaine, Benoit's dedicatee, the characters presented according to the best rhetorical principles by which a hundred lines may be spent on a heroine's face.

Among the endless battles, twenty-two of them, Benoit has found time for four famous love-affairs: the rape of Helen by Paris, modified from Dares and Dictys to soften their adultery into a loyal, marital relationship; Medea's desertion by Jason once she has helped him to win the golden fleece, an episode apparently elaborated from Ovid; Briseida parted from Troilus and seduced by Diomedes under the guise of *fine amor*; Polyxena wooed by Achilles the enemy of her country, torn like him by the conflict of love and duty. The new-found freedom of the romanticized epic to explore the interaction of love and war, to exalt personal devotion without shirking the social harm it can do, to convey feeling by Ovidian analyses gave Benoit enormous popularity and influence down to the seventeenth century. But disaster befell him when, in 1287, his poem was abridged into tedious Latin prose by Guido de Columnis, a judge of Messina whose academic respectability gave his *Historia Destructionis Troiae* even wider circulation than Benoit, including translation into all the European languages.[2]

Among its English derivatives is an alliterative poem of over fourteen thousand long lines, *The Gest Historiale of the Destruction of Troy*, probably composed in Lancashire in the second half of the fourteenth century. Neither the poet nor the patron for whom he evidently worked have been identified, but the unique manuscript was transcribed about 1540 by a country gentleman and left as an heirloom to his son, suggesting the continuing appeal of both matter and medium.[3] It is a patient, fluent, and competent paraphrase of Guido, remarkably faithful in view of the very different medium, omitting only a few of the many learned digressions and mythological explanations and adding little except summaries of the state of action to begin each book and some verbal elaboration in descriptive passages particularly suited to alliterative verse. Verse and diction apart – and they are a major part of the total effect – the result is to be judged less as an English creation than as an indication of the tastes and interests of an English audience.[4]

Though the poet opens by expressing a preference for 'sothe stories' of antiquity to some of the 'feynit' tales of modern writers, this need not imply any dislike for the romance mode to which Guido's *Historia* so clearly belongs.[5] The medieval view of history as a mirror providing a moral perspective on the contemporary world and the conviction that Western chivalric values derived from the ancient world lend weight and importance to his story-matter. The supposed Trojan ancestry of the British adds the romantic allure of a lost cause to the mixture of war and love characteristic of the matter of antiquity. The tragic outcome, familiar through tradition, gives an underlying tension of inevitability to the long, complex narrative. Jason, refused hospitality by the King of Troy on his quest for the golden fleece, destroys the city, kills the King and carries off his daughter Hesione. Her brother Priam rebuilds the city and sends an embassy demanding her return; it is led by his son Paris who has dreamt that, in reward for his judgement that Venus is the most beautiful of goddesses, she has promised him the loveliest woman in Greece. His prize is not Hesione but Helen, wife of Menelaus, King of

Greece, whose abduction precipitates the ten-year war in which the great heroes on either side slaughter each other in vengeful sequence, Troy is finally betrayed by two of her chief defenders, Aeneas and Antenor, and the Greeks who destroy her are themselves destroyed by vengeful gods, adulterous wives, illegitimate sons, and other blind instruments of Fortune.

In the bare bones of the Trojan legend something of its original significance survives: ideals of individual heroism in the service of a patriotic cause; supreme representatives of the military virtues pitted against each other, their charismatic powers heightened by divine parentage or patronage; male valour inspired or rewarded by women of surpassing beauty, often with their own charisma of magical powers; human aspiration defying the overmastering power of fate and the interference of divinities in the affairs of men. But underlying awareness of the folly of human resistance to superhuman powers, of the existence even in the most charismatic heroes of the Achilles' heel – self-confidence blind to its own limitations, overweening pride without regard for others' self-respect, self-interest avenging a private wrong under the cloak of patriotism – which makes them vulnerable to fate, of the ease with which heroism degenerates into arrogance or cruelty, love into infatuation or indifference, loyalty into treason rationally justified creates the ambivalent tension of the romance mode. The English poet evidently appreciated it to judge from the fullness with which he comments on Jason's betrayal of Medea who abandoned father and future kingdom on his promise of marriage (ll. 729–35). So also his prediction that many men will pay with their lives for the enslavement of Hesione (ll. 1393–1405), his endorsement of Cassandra's prophecy that entrusting Paris with the mission to Greece will bring Troy to ruin (ll. 2706–24), his careful reproduction of the catalogue of Greek and Trojan heroes in which, following rhetorical procedure, their physical traits are coupled with a moral itemization often far from favourable (ll. 3741–4024), his reminder that those who urge surrender to the Greeks had been most active in the abduction of Helen – who, despite her original complicity, now begs them to make her peace with Menelaus (ll. 11548–60) – and his bitter rendering of Hecuba's reproach to Aeneas:

> 'A! traytor vntrew, how toke þou on honde
> Þat trew to betray þat trist in þe euer –                    *trusted*
> Thy lege and þi lord þat the louet wele,
> And myche good hase þe gyffen of his gold red?
> Thou hase led to þi lord þat hym lothe was,
> His fomen full fele thurgh falshed of the;               *fierce*
> And done hym to dethe dolefully now,
> Þat thyselfe shuld haue socourd hade þou ben sad tru.'   *truly loyal*
>                                   (ll. 11975–82)[6]

All acknowledge realistically the human fallibility beneath the heroic surface.

But though his readers might share with those whose sensibilities first shaped the Troy legends a bitter-sweet awareness of the tragedy of human aspiration, the heroic achievements, personal fame, worldly glory which had absolute value for the Greeks were undermined by the Christian doctrine of eternity which gave all temporal values a relative and transitory significance. The medievalization of classical matter introduced a perspective which set heroic aspirations against the imperative need to achieve eternity through humility, charity, and a proper disregard for worldly values. True, chivalric aspirations raised a similar duality, theoretically resolved by treating the social aspects of the code as expressions of its religious basis, making knighthood subservient to celestial chivalry, but constantly at conflict in contemporary practice, creating that tension between ideal and reality which is at the heart of chivalric romance. The Matter of Rome provided the possibility of resolving that tension by allowing medieval poets to associate its heroic values with those of their own age while condemning their moral basis as pagan and temporal. The process of medievalization with its inherent critique is well developed in Guido and the alliterative poet approves and extends it. From the opening invocation of his 'Maistur in magesté, maker of alle' to his concluding prayer 'He bryng vs to the blisse, þat bled for our syn', the Christian faith is constantly evoked in references to God, bishops, saints, the sacraments and services of the Church, against which the classical pantheon, the supernatural intervention of deities in the affairs of men, the magic powers credited to mortals, the images whose protective powers they invoke are presented ostensibly as aspects of local colour, exotic but erroneous.

The pagan ethic underlying them is both implicitly and explicitly attacked. Implicitly in the evocation of such moral structures as the seven deadly sins to suggest the failings of heroes whose longing for glory is seen as pride of life, their military feats as violent outbursts of destructive anger, their plundering of each others' societies, snatching of women who serve as war-trophies and destruction of cities as envy, their readiness to turn traitor for personal gain as covetousness, their idolatry as refusal to know the true God, a form of spiritual sloth. Explicitly the poet condemns the pagan basis of Homer's fictions – 'How goddes foght in the filde, folke as þai were,/And other errours vnable (*impossible*) þat after were knowen' (ll. 45–46) – implies the mistaken nature of the Greek mission of revenge prompted by an ambiguous oracle of Apollo – 'For lacke of beleue þai light into errour,/And fellen vnto fals goddes' (ll. 4287–88) – and reveals the hopelessness of those who have no knowledge of eternal life in Ulysses's account of an island god from whom he sought guidance in his wanderings:

'There spird I full specially in spede for to here,          *asked, haste*
When dethe hade vs drepit and our day comyn,                     *killed*
And we went of this world, what worthe of our saules.        *becomes*
To all thing he answarit abilly me thoght,
But of our sawles, forsothe, said he me noght.'    (ll. 13263–67)

The medieval moral perspective is not only openly stated – the ceremony at Apollo's shrine is interrupted by a 164-line history of idolatry
(ll. 4295–4458), its origin in the pride of Lucifer, the many forms
assumed by Satan and the fall of all false gods at the coming of Christ –
but implied through the plot: Achilles taking the deceptive oracle at
Delos which will plunge the Greeks into a ten-year war meets Calchas
on the same mission for Troy and bribes him to commit the treason
which ultimately allows the prophecy of Greek victory to prove true (ll.
4488–4545).

The pro-Trojan bias of medieval authors has not spared her heroes
from critical evaluation. When, in Book xv, Hector, the model of
classical chivalry and one of the Nine Worthies, fails to press home his
advantage after killing Patroclus, throwing away final victory because
his cousin Telamon-Ajax among the hard-pressed Greeks asks for a
truce, the poet comments:

. . . he þat kepis not kyndly the course of his heale,          *earnestly,*
                                                                       *welfare*
But sodanly forsakes þat sent is of god,
Hit shal be gricchit hym þat grace in his grete nede.          *begrudged*
                                              (ll. 7070–72)

What might in a Christian knight have been a piece of quixotic chivalry
is judged as a rejection of divine grace, typical of that preoccupation
with the immediate present and with worldly values whose transience
exposes pagans to the vagaries of Fortune. So the Trojans are seen as
bringing their own destruction upon themselves, rejecting the wise
counsel of Hector and the prophecies of Cassandra to embrace their
'destiny', betrayed by the covetousness of two priests, Calchas and the
keeper of the Palladium who is bribed to surrender the protective image
to Ulysses, and by their own idolatry in bringing the brazen horse, filled
with Greeks, into the temple of Pallas.[7]

The women of both parties are doubly vulnerable to the critique of a
clerically trained poet. Their pagan faith in temporal and delusive
powers is illustrated by Medea's efforts to bind Jason to her by magic,
giving him, among other talismans, a charmed image to wear next his
heart; with their help he wins the golden fleece but does not keep his
promise to marry her sworn on a pagan idol. The poet mocks Medea's

art: 'What seruit it your sciense of the seuon artes,/That þou sogh not your sorow þat thee suet after?' (ll. 738–39). Her 'soden hote loue' suggests to him that emotional instability with which such anti-feminists charged all women; the equally sudden passion of Helen for Paris, the lamentations with which she bewails her abduction previously concerted with him and her overtures of reconciliation to her husband once she sees that Troy is doomed prove the case; the rapidity with which Briseis turns from tearing her hair on being parted from Troilus to encouraging Diomede's advances confirms the judgement on her sex: 'For yf the ton ee with teres trickell on hir chekes,/The tothur lurkes in lychernes and laghes ouerthwert' (*at the same time*) (ll. 8058–59). Like Achilles's love for Polyxena, these doomed liasions across the battle-lines of warring nations demonstrate the ability of romance to entertain conflicting ideals, celebrating the beauty of women and their power to inspire heroic conduct while admitting the ultimately destructive, anti-social effects of extra-marital relationships. But where Benoit, though ultimately favouring social above personal interests, encouraged understanding of the sufferings of women torn between love and duty, Guido and his English adapter illustrate the tendency of romance to degenerate into the literature of envy, encouraging readers to indulge in sexual fantasies – with sixty-six lip-smacking lines on a head-to-toe description of Helen (ll. 3019–84), for example – and one-sided, anti-feminist censure at the same time.

The moralistic viewpoint may be that of the medieval schoolmen, but the poet underlines it with stylistic enthusiasm, constantly intervening in the action to berate his characters on their shortcomings, particularly their blindness in the face of malign Fortune, or to lecture the listener on the significance of events, especially as they illustrate the power of fate. Often the long tirades, rhetorically developed, are capped with the proverbs for which he has a weakness. Some of his characters have the same sententious tendency and the action is constantly interrupted by set speeches of intrigue or counsel, battlefield defiance, or amorous persuasion which expound its meaning. The alliterative line, with its emphatic iteration and restatement of ideas in varied terms, is an ideal medium for the purpose. So also for the endless variation of details and cumulative richness of effect in his descriptions, some over a hundred lines in length, of cities, palaces, heroes arming, armies in battle array, navies assembling, storms at sea. Where Benoit has a single storm, Guido has added six more, all of which the alliterative poet enthusiastically reproduces with extra detail. A poet so conscious of the classical tradition may well have been directly influenced by the sea-passages in Virgil, Ovid, Lucan as well as by the topos which medieval rhetoricians modelled upon them. But he obviously enjoyed the opportunity to exploit the resonance and grandiloquence of his medium.[8]

In his determined attempt to remain faithful to Guido, he clearly found some difficulty in accommodating the alliterative line, particularly the rather rigid pattern (*aa/ax*) he almost invariably uses, to the very different syntax of the Latin. Having rendered the essential action of a phrase in the first half, he is often forced by the demands of alliteration to reduplicate the sense in the second or to improvise, not always successfully, using two terms instead of one to complete the metrical pattern or because they are traditionally associated in an alliterative tag. The general effect, occasionally lamely formulaic, often overloaded with verbal detail, is appropriate to the scale and significance of the subject if rather rhetorically overblown.[9] Read in full the *Gest Historiale* is somewhat indigestible, repetitive, over-rich; but a book at a time it is effective in the manner of some television series adapted from a historical classic with a large cast of familiar stereotypes, magnificently set and dressed, drenched in grandiloquent music and – in this case – provided with an authorial commentary on the vices of Claudius Caesar or the Borgias to heighten appreciation of the vivid detail in which they are being enacted.

The radical influence of the verse medium is apparent in another English version of the Troy legends, *The Seege of Troye*, composed in the north-west Midlands *c.* 1300–25. The ultimate source was Benoit's *Roman de Troie* whose 30,000 lines are represented by some 2060 four- stress couplets; yet the English version not only covers the whole history from Jason's search for the golden fleece to the fall of Troy (though omitting the wanderings of Ulysses) but adds additional details from Dares and elaborates several episodes with apparently original material. The source of the latter became apparent in 1934 with the publication of a hitherto unknown Latin prose *Excidium Troiae*, preserving elements of classical tradition still current early in the Christian era, from which the compiler of the *Seege* evidently drew fuller versions of the youth of Paris and Achilles.[10]

The use of such courtly and learned sources implies some sophistication and the compilation is attributed to a clerk (l. 22); but many egregious errors belie his learning – the 'goddesses' who rival Venus in the beauty competition judged by Paris are Jupiter, Saturn, and Mercury! The whole narrative procedure – opening reference to the Creation, concluding prayer and periodic cries of 'Listeneþ, lordyngis, er ʒe gange' introducing sequences of short episodes – speaks of the minstrel manner. The format and content of one of the four surviving copies, Lincoln's Inn MS 150, elongated like a pocket-book, modestly written without illumination and containing other verse romances, suggest that, whoever composed the *Seege*, some minstrel found it marketable and obtained a portable text. Each is independently related to the original, suggesting some popular interest; one is a handsome closet copy, beautifully illuminated, for private reading, and another, British Library, Harley 525, has been carefully edited to remove most of the minstrel mannerisms and lame rhymes while interpolating descriptions of female beauty, courtly feasts, gory combats, and scraps of classical lore as if to flatter more sophisticated tastes.

Even in this up-market version, the contrast with the vast scale, narrative complexity, and descriptive elaboration of Benoit is so extreme, errors in detail so frequent, and the intermixture of material from Dares and the *Excidium Troiae* so complete as to suggest that the *Seege* was composed from memory. If so, the process of recalling a corpus of legend, long familiar, current in many versions, and melding those available to the poet in such a way as to appeal to a popular audience with little learning and less time has clearly benefited by freedom from the written page. There are no signs of the loss of confidence which momentarily seizes the poet of the *Gest Historiale*. The *Seege* outlines the Troy legends with confident control and economy, plunging into an episode without preliminaries, establishing the situation in the sparsest terms, passing into direct speech at moments of dramatic or emotional interaction and gliding to the next scene of action in half a dozen verses. The whole episode of the golden fleece takes less than two hundred lines, but the poet was sufficiently conscious of its importance as the root of the Greek–Trojan conflict to summarize the outcome in emotional terms:

> Þeo forme bataile þis þenne was,    *first*
> Wherþoruȝ was mony child faderles.
> Þeo werre laste, ich vndurstonde,
> Þrytty wynter wiþ mukil wronge.
> Þeo children þat in heore modir wombe weoren
> Waxeden and vengede heore fadir þere.    (ll. 195–200)[11]

Thereafter the Trojan War is sketched in with lightning strokes: journeys between the rival countries occupy six lines (ll. 379–84), fleets are built in seven (ll. 425–31), a fallen hero ceremonially interred in eight (ll. 1513–20), and a whole campaign summarized in twelve (ll. 1102–13). The redactor's highly selective memory had no place for love-stories of unhappy women, for the rights and wrongs of the war, for any issues of morality personal or public. What it retained was the impression of an epic struggle which, reduced to a clear, bold narrative thread, might serve as an epitome of man's martial history.

Against this tapestry of old, unhappy, far-off things he has hung twin portraits of popular heroes, Paris and Achilles.[12] When he comes to tell how Hecuba dreamt that the son she was to bear would be a brand to burn Troy, the narrative scale broadens to provide more incident, longer speeches, a modicum of description. To forestall prophecy, Paris is sent to keep swine in 'Curtel and tabard and hod al whyt' (l. 268), but his martial spirit is roused whenever he sees bulls or boars fight, Priam recognizes him as his own son and gives him an earldom; he then demands to lead the mission against Greece, citing his dream of 'Foure ladies of eluene land' (l. 508) as proof that he is destined to win the fairest of women as his wife. Excited by his reputation and captivated by his beauty, Helen is swept away on her lover's horse, accompanied by a proper retinue of countesses. She dutifully laments, but marries Paris willingly, humbling herself for his sake: 'Furst heo was qwene and emperesse/And þo was heo bote a symple contasse' (ll. 797–98) – a union simply ignored when Menelaus takes her back with a kiss at the fall of Troy. The focus of the episode is not her love but Paris's career; the career of a folk-hero, a Horn or Havelok, rising from obscurity to prove his royal birth in combat and his supernatural destiny in the capture of a noble bride.

It is reduplicated in the career of Achilles, born of a 'wyche' (the goddess Thetis) and a centaur, made invulnerable by being dipped in 'þe water of helle' (l. 1463) so that he alone can kill Hector, given a hero's education by his father who teaches him to contend with the waves and rob the lioness of her cubs, but disguised as a girl by his mother who foresees his death in battle. He is eventually recruited by the Greeks who pierce his disguise by laying arms before him, confirms his heroic stature by the slaughter he makes at Troy, kills Hector, and, at his tomb, is stricken with love for his sister Polyxena. When the Greeks refuse to make a truce for her sake, Achilles sulks in his tent until Hecuba, to avenge her son, uses the prospect of marriage to Polyxena to lure him to the temple where he is set on by Paris and 100 knights and eventually killed through the vulnerable soles of his feet but which his mother had held him in Lethe. Both heroes end tragically by the flaws they display, reassuring to ordinary mortals, and are as much part of their popular appeal to those who envy their charismatic powers as the very human forms in which they sometimes express them – Achilles, disarmed, wrestles with his assassins like Havelok:

> Achilles sturede him, for nede him teches,
> Wiþ þe schuldres to heom he reches
> And slang heom abowte and lette heom gon
> Þat heo tobarsten aʒeyn þeo ston;
> And anoþir he slang aʒeyn a wal
> And þer he dyede among heom al;
> Þe þridde he tok in his armure stowt
> And kaste him at a wyndowe owt.
> As a hungry lyoun ferde he
> Þat hadde fast dayes þreo.    (ll. 1730–39)

The medievalization of classical matter here involves none of the moral judgements of the *Gest Historiale*. The author of the *Seege* has simply isolated from the *Excidium Troiae* – significantly closer to the Homeric form of the legends than the bogusly historical accounts of Dares and Dictys – two supreme examples of heroic aspiration romantically dogged by human fallibility, perhaps judging that they rather than a peerless Hector unjustly doomed by Fortune would appeal to modest men. His short couplets, occasionally rhyming too glibly or falling flatly into minstrel commonplaces, but swift in narrative outline, introducing new characters in familiar stereotypes, dutifully listing nouns and adjectives where description is unavoidable, accumulating verbs of action in battle passages, summarizing with the crispness of proverbs, are as characteristic of his view of the Troy legend as the alliterative medium of the more expansive, interpretative approach of the *Gest* poet.

The ability which the Troy story shares with other universal myths to mean different things to different men gave it currency at many cultural levels, of which the *Gest* and the *Seege* represent two extremes. Of other surviving versions, the *Laud Troy Book*, composed *c.* 1400 in four-stress couplets, paraphrases Guido at enormous length, but selects and expands with the clear intention of building a heroic romance round Hector. A Scottish poet of the fifteenth century also made a version of Guido in couplets which survives only in fragments used to fill gaps in Lydgate's *Troy Book* and too incomplete to show any distinctive interpretation. Lydgate's poem was itself epitomized in the brief fifteenth-century *Prose Siege of Troy* whose spare outline presents the legend as a tragedy of treason and bad faith in which neither side is truly victorious.

## Legends of Alexander the Great: *The Wars of Alexander* and *Kyng Alisaunder*

The ability of life to rival literature, even in the romance mode, is nowhere better demonstrated than in the career of Alexander (356–323 B.C.), son of Philip of Macedon: a pupil of Aristotle, successful general at sixteen, king at twenty, master of faction-ridden Greece, destroyer of the Persian Empire, conqueror of half the known world, founder of seventy cities, dead at the height of his triumphs in his thirty-third year. His career was known to the Middle Ages not only through historical tradition but in the many derivatives of a Greek prose biography written by an Alexandrian referred to as Pseudo-Callisthenes between 200 B.C. and A.D. 200, in which fact is already heavily adulterated with fantasy.

Various Latin translations, notably the *Historia de Preliis* of Leo, Archpresbyter of Naples (*c.* 950), gave the legendary version academic respectability and wide currency in a number of different recensions. Writers in *romanz* seized on it in the first years of the twelfth century, their early versions being ultimately amalgamated in the *Roman d'Alexander* where the hero is presented as the ideal courtly prince. The *Roman* in turn expanded to incorporate originally independent poems, such as the *Fuerre de Gadres*, an imaginative expansion of a passage on the siege of Tyre in the *Historia*, and the *Voeux du paon*, only superficially connected with Alexander but enormously popular. In the second half of the twelfth century, the Anglo-Norman poet Thomas of Kent went back to an epitome of the earliest Latin version of Pseudo-Callisthenes for the main source of his *Roman de Toute Chevalerie*. Other vernacular versions carried the legend of Alexander, already widespread in Asia and Africa, all over Europe.[13]

About 1450 an alliterative poet, possibly Northumbrian, translated a version of the *Historia de Preliis* into over 5600 long lines with great fidelity, though expanding some battle passages by verbal elaboration.[14] Apart from a brief prologue listing the topics suitable for literary entertainment, his own among them – 'Of kyngis at has conquirid and ouercomyn landis' (l. 10)[15] – and the division into books in the chronicle manner, the author of *The Wars of Alexander* has imposed no order on its endless sequence of incidents, defying geography and time. But there has survived from the Pseudo-Callisthenes an underlying structure of historical reality which is inherently dramatic: Alexander's precocity and his taming of Bucephalus; his visit, early in his Persian campaign, to the shrine of Ammon in the Libyan desert; his exchange of letters with the Emperor Darius and generosity to his captured family; the discovery of mutilated Greek captives which hardened his resolve to defeat the tyrant; his punishment of Darius's killers for their treason to their lord; repeated hints of resistance to his own authority lending colour to the suggestion that his premature death was due to poison. The bones of history have already begun to be covered with legends, some perhaps rooted in fact, which colour the charismatic personality of the world-conqueror: the Bucephalus he tames at the age of twelve is now a man-eater fed on criminals; at the shrine of Ammon his future fame is prophesied; he overtakes the assassinated Darius before rather than, as in fact, after his death and promises to avenge him; the democracy which he opposes to Persian tyranny makes him pour away the helmetful of water brought to him in the desert; he reaches the ocean at the world's end and turns back to Babylon and death triumphant. The fantastic nature of Alexander's achievements, the unbounded ambition and strength of personality which made them possible licensed the romantic imagination even of his own age to ignore the near disasters of the campaign, the drunken squabbles and murders among his closest companions, the ultimate frustration when their resistance forced him to turn back before reaching the encircling ocean which was his imagined goal.

The Pseudo-Callisthenes supplied the divine parentage appropriate to such a superman, incorporating Egyptian legends that the Pharaoh Nectanebo II, supposed incarnation of Ammon, in flight before the invading Persians, reached Macedon and sired Alexander on Philip's queen.[16] The boy, born amidst earth-shaking omens, with lion locks and eyes like blazing stars, grows up a rumbustious youth:

> In absens of Arystotill, if any of his feris            *fellow(-teachers)*
> Raged with him vnridly or rofe him with harme,         *harshly, hurt*
> Him wald he kenely on þe croune knok with his tablis,  *tablets*
> Þat al tobrest wald þe bordis and þe blode folowe.    (ll. 637–40)

Ignorant of his parenthood, he attempts to disprove Nectanebo's prophecy that he is to die by the hand of his son by pushing him into a ditch, so fulfilling it! Something of the folk-hero clings to Alexander throughout his career. When Philip takes a second wife, he defends his mother's interests – 'Out of þe hall be þe hare halis he þe bride' (l. 854); but he supports Philip in rejecting Darius's demand for tribute, telling the ambassadors that the hen who laid the golden eggs is barren now. His reconquest of Egypt from the Persians fulfils the prophecy made on Nectanebo's flight that a younger hero-god would avenge his nation's wrongs. Once embarked on his eastern campaign, the chronicle is largely concerned with war and wonders: strange beasts, birds defended by the flaming tree in which they perch, a phoenix, a desert river which freezes each night even in summer, armies of amazons, plagues of snakes, tigers, dragons. There are intervals for love – Alexander, at the request of the dying Darius, marries his daughter Roxana, but later Queen Candace lures him into a liaison and exposes him to the fury of her son – but they are brief and show Alexander as a wise emperor uniting East and West or craftily talking his way out of a tight corner rather than as a lover. The focus is constantly on him: as world-conqueror marking the limits of his conquest with memorial pillars, as philosopher corresponding with the Brahman Dindimus on materialism and the ascetic life, as scientist exploring the limits of the natural world in a griffin-powered airship and a crystal bathysphere, as hero-god penning behind the Caspian Gates the forces of Gog and Magog which threaten to overwhelm the civilized world.

Over all his triumphs hangs the shadow of an early death, the dissolution of an empire barely established, the end of an enterprise which, to the medieval mind, could have no rationale other than the pursuit of

worldly glory. Hence the ambivalence of the medieval view of
Alexander: admirable as conqueror, the type of the good king,
magnanimous and wise, master of the exotic and cultured East now
dominated by Islam; but contemptible as himself a pagan engaged in a
godless enterprise for vainglory, doomed to fall from Fortune's wheel
into limbo – the archetypal exemplar of tragedy.[17] In the flush of his first
triumph, the oracle of Ammon tells him that he will die by poison while
still young; again and again throughout his glorious career the omen is
repeated. In the moment of his own defeat, Darius warns him to avoid
the faults of Xerxes whom pride brought to disaster – '"Þinke þat
allanely of god þis ouirlaike (*supremacy*) þou haues"' (l. 3101) – and, dying
in Alexander's arms, urges him to learn from his fate:

'Me þink my lyfe as to þe lenȝth is like to þis werke
Þat þis coppis opon kell-wyse knytt in þe woȝes,                *spiders,*
                                                         *like a net, walls*
With þe lest winde of þe werd þat þe web touches            *world*
Þe note anentis ilk ane and all to noȝt worthis.'            *fabric,*
                                                  *becomes annihilated*
                                                         (ll. 3299–3302)

To the Brahmans' unfavourable contrast of his worldliness with their
own ascetic self-denial, Alexander replies that they exist like penned
beasts in their isolation while he is restlessly driven by a higher power,
fated to act as he does (ll. 4061–65). The underlying issue between a hero
predestined to aspire and the critical commentary of moralists preaching
free will and self-abnegation is unresolved in the *Historia de Preliis* with
its accretion of Christian commentary.

The English poet has not resolved it and adds no commentary of his
own, but he felt the underlying power of the legend with its unresolved
tension of heroic aspiration and human mortality and has exploited
every resource of his medium to give it life. He narrates when need be
with the directness of chronicle, building Alexandria in four lines
(ll. 1117–20) and capturing Babylon in one (l. 5611); but he also exploits
the exotic appeal of the subject in elaborate descriptions of Jerusalem
adorned for Alexander's entrance (ll. 1513–72), of the chief city of India
with its pillars of gold trailing golden vines with grapes of pearl
(ll. 3660–3703), of the many-tiered throne set up for the conqueror in
Babylon (ll. 5627–77). He provides outstanding examples of all the set
pieces beloved by alliterative poets: the violence of battle (ll. 1361–1445),
the formal rhetoric of letters (ll. 4211–4714), the tirade of an enraged
tyrant (ll. 1752–55). In his unremitting struggle with the bald Latin of
the *Historia* he vivifies even the flattest episodes, avoiding the risk of that
multiplication of crudely approximate terms which blurs and bloats so

much alliterative poetry by re-expressing the underlying idea rather than the verbal surface.[18] There is inevitably some verbal inflation – a single term used of the dying Darius (*semivivus*) becomes four lines (ll. 3230–33) – but there is also the constant imaginative stimulus of an enormous colloquial vocabulary employed with originality: an enemy is 'as wrath as a waspe' (l. 738), the Brahmans delight in the springtime woods 'Quen al is lokin (*roofed*) ouire with leuys as it ware littill heuen' (l. 4383), a bird of omen flies into Philip's arms:

> And þar hurkils and hydis as scho were hand-tame;    *crouches*
> Fast scho flekirs about his fete and fleȝtirs aboute,
> And þar it nestild in a noke as it a nest were.   (ll. 504–06)

Read aloud the alliterative version must have had an immediacy and vividness which allowed the audience to ignore its thematic imprecision.

The *Wars*, though all but complete in one of the two surviving manuscripts, is often associated with two other Alexander texts with which it was once thought to have formed part of a much larger alliterative romance. *Alexander A* (1247 lines) is genuinely fragmentary, covering the hero's early life in a version which supplements the *Historia* with material on his father's career from the Latin history of Orosius. *Alexander B* (1139 lines), interpolated in a sumptuous manuscript of the *Roman d'Alexander*, gives a self-contained account of Alexander's correspondence with Dindimus, suggesting the value which some cleric put on those philosophical interpolations which bore on the theme of the legend. Though both apparently originated in mid-fourteenth-century Gloucestershire, they were not necessarily parts of a single poem.[19]

That English authors could make the Alexander legend thematically as well as stylistically their own had already been demonstrated by Thomas of Kent's *Roman de Toute Chevalerie* and the version in the London dialect freely adapted from it at the beginning of the fourteenth century, *Kyng Alisaunder*. Thomas, working on an epitome of the Pseudo-Callisthenes, imposed his own interpretation on the outline, drawing on other Alexander material to emphasize its moral message. Thomas had had a clerical education; so too had his English adapter to judge from the rhetorical skill with which, in a generally abbreviated redaction, he interpolates passages from other Alexander texts, impressive lists of names of participants in battles and councils and an apparently independent version of the hero's last testament. Yet, despite this academic approach and the suggestion that the life of Alexander is to be read as an *exemplum* – 'For Caton seiþ, þe gode techer,/Oþere mannes lijf is oure shewer' (*preceptor*) (ll. 17–18)[20] – the manner throughout is that of a popular minstrel romance. The repeated calls for silence and attention, marking narrative divisions, and summaries of events show that it was intended for public recitation and addressed both 'To lewed men and to lerede' (l. 2). Three of the four surviving manuscripts confirm the impression: in MS Laud Misc. 622 it is the only secular item among religious and didactic poems; in the Auchinleck MS it forms part of a commercial compilation of popular romances and didactic pieces likely to appeal to aspiring middle-class readers; but it is also in the minstrel's pocket-book of Lincoln's Inn MS 150 along with the manifestly popular *Seege of Troye*. The source of this wide-ranging appeal is a shrewd mixture of entertainment and edification made appetizing by literary and stylistic devices of unexpected subtlety.

The nature and balance of the elements in *Kyng Alisaunder* remain much as in the *Wars*, the bulk of the 8000 lines dealing with the Persian Wars and the Indian campaign combining martial action and exotic wonders, comparatively limited sections at beginning and end with Alexander's mysterious birth and with his seduction by Candace and his death. The poet views them all with the same candid eye, describes everything with the same unblinking realism: Thebes destroyed with all its inhabitants in disgust at the crimes of Oedipus (ll. 2757–2896); Darius's murderers led in mounted procession as Alexander had promised – but facing the tail, on their way to a traitor's death (ll. 4681–4725); or an unfortunate occurrence while swimming a moat:

> Swiþe wiȝtlych hij bigynne,                                   *doughtily*
> Þe þriddendale and faire swymme                         *one-third*
> Of þe water þat hij were jnne,
> Vp berande faire chynne.
> Ac þoo hem aroos a vile meschaunce,
> Kyng Alisaunder to gret greuaunce!
> Ypotames comen flyngynge,                          *hippopotamuses*
> Out of roches, loude nayinge –
> Grete bestes and griselich,
> More þan olifaunz, sikerlich.                                 *larger, truly*
> Jn to þe water hij shoten onon,
> And freten þe kniȝttes euerychon.   (ll. 5151–62)         *devoured*

He narrates swiftly and efficiently in his admirably plain style, trying constantly to explain the nature of the wonders encountered and the significance of the tactical and political situations, vivifying the emotional impact, sometimes with no more than an unconventional adjective – 'Fair and foul, man and wijf,/Þere loren (*lost*)/her swete lijf!' (ll. 2837–38), a personal interjection – 'Þe deuel of helle hem mote stike, /Vche traitour þat his lorde biswike!' (*betrays*) (ll. 4717–18), or a concluding comment on the moral import of a scene (ll. 3880–85). The predominant effect is rhetorical rather than realistic: formulaic battle- scenes, alternating mass engagements with individual combats in a reduplicated pattern, stylized descriptions of armies massing, of embassies and feasts, whole episodes conducted as formal exchanges of letters or speeches. All the minstrel's efforts are directed to making this highly literary compound accessible to listeners sophisticated enough to be interested in Alexander but so unlettered as to need every assistance in following his adventures in unknown, exotic lands. This, the poet insists, 'Þis is nouȝth romaunce of skof (*frivolity*),/Ac storye ymade of maistres wyse' (ll. 668–69).

The master's chief contribution to understanding is the moral commentary which sets Alexander's triumphant career against the mutability of human life, from his opening announcement that this is a true tale of the vicissitudes which afflict all men, high and low (ll. 1–28), to his introduction to the hero's death-scene:

> Jn þis werlde falleþ many cas,         *chance event*
> Gydy blisse, short solas!
> Ypomodon, and Pallidamas,
> And Absolon, þat so fair was,
> Hij lyueden here a litel raas,         *while*
> Ac sone forȝeten vchon was.         *forgotten*
> Þe leuedyes shene als þe glas,         *bright*
> And þise maidens, wiþ rody faas,         *rosy*
> Passen sone als floure in gras.    (ll. 7820–28)

Alexander, his fate foreknown, undergoes no development and is subject to no spiritual conflicts, but the significance of his experience for lesser men is constantly underscored. His birth as a result of his mother's seduction draws the comment 'Gamen (*love sport*) is good whiles it wil last,/Ac it fareþ (*is ephemeral*) so wyndes blast' (ll. 235–36) and his father's death at his hand 'Of yuel lijf yuel endyng' (l. 752). His fate is prefigured in that of Darius, arrogant and tyrannical, who exploits the loyalty of a follower to have him assassinate Alexander and is himself traitorously killed by foundlings he had fostered. Faced with prophecies of the date and place of his own death, Alexander still hopes 'On sum manere forto askape' (l. 6971), forgetting that 'Noman þat lyues haþ borowe (*assurance*)/From euene libbe forto amorowe' (ll. 6986–87). On his deathbed, his thoughts are for the distribution of his conquered kingdoms among his barons who quarrel over them. 'God us lene (*grant*) wel to fyne!' (*end*) (l. 8009), comments the poet who constantly opposes Christian certainties to pagan blindness: in prayers interjected at moments of moral outrage (ll. 4313–18), in invocations of the Virgin's guidance against the perversity of human judgement (ll. 4739–46), above all in repeated evocations of seasons and times of the day which, by marking the progression of the divinely ordered universe, imply the transitoriness of human life and the transience of worldly achievements. Just after the illicit siring of Alexander, for example, the poet interjects:

| | |
|---|---|
| Yhereþ now hou selcouþe lijf | *(morally) irregular* |
| Comeþ to shame, sorouȝ, and strijf. | |
| Whan corne ripeþ in heruest-tyde, | |
| Mery it is in felde and hyde. | *open country* |
| Synne it is and shame to chide, | *utter recrimination* |
| For shameful dedes springeþ wyde. | *are noised abroad* |
| Kniȝttes willeþ on huntyng ride – | |
| Þe dere galpeþ by wode-syde. | *bell (in rut)* |
| He þat can his tyme abide | |
| Al his wille hym shal bityde.   (ll. 455–64) | *come about* |

The images suggesting sexual desire, pursuit (hunting is a common metaphor for the love chase) and seasonal fruition imply both the nature of the event alluded to and that in time the truth will out. When Alexander proves his supernatural origin by taming Bucephalus and is about to be crowned as Philip's heir, the same images recur (ll. 795–800), perhaps ironically reminding us of his real parentage. Then, as he is about to win his first victory, images of dawn (ll. 911–19) recall ideas of transience and mutability appropriate to his ultimate fate:

| | |
|---|---|
| Many ben jolyf in þe morowenyng | |
| And þolen deþ in þe euenyng. | *suffer* |
| Nis in þis werlde non so siker þing, | *secure* |
| Þe tyme neiȝeþ of her wendyng.   (ll. 916–19) | *approaches, passing* |

These seasonal headpieces, exploiting an imagery common to lyrics of love and of religion, were inherited from Latin models by the *chansons de geste* and, like other elements of epic style – similies and metaphors, ironic foreshadowing of events, hyperbole and understatement – seem to derive from the English poet's knowledge of the tradition rather than from his French source where they are limited. Used pervasively but without academic obtrusiveness, they underline the moral meaning of a narrative which is otherwise addressed to the unlearned in the plainest, most accessible terms.[21]

The wide appeal of the Alexander story is shown by the number and variety of surviving versions. The fifteenth-century, northern *Prose Alexander*, derived from the *Historia*, supplies a similar moral commentary much more directly than *Kyng Alisaunder*, evoking the Christian contrast in biblical echoes while exploiting the popular appeal of adventures and wonders in a matter-of-fact style which makes the mixture readily available to the common reader. Fifteenth-century Scotland produced, in Gilbert Hay's *Buik of King Alexander*, a vast compendium of all his adventures in short couplets, while the *Scottish Alexander Buik* (1438), also in couplets, gave over 11,000 lines to the Fuerre de Gadres and Voeux du paon episodes, chivalric and amorous exploits of followers of Alexander to which his own career merely supplies the framework. The fifteenth-century *Cambridge Alexander-Cassamus Fragment*, part of a *Voeux du paon* translation, gives further proof of the popularity of these adventitious elements which are quite foreign to the true nature of the Alexander legends.

## Chaucer, Lydgate and Caxton on the Matter of Rome

Such texts as these formed and reflected the common view of the Matter of Rome with its dual appeal of exotic adventure and moral meaning, allowing more self-consciously courtly writers to pitch their versions wherever they wished between the two poles. Chaucer, whose 'Knight's Tale' relates to the legends of Thebes as his *Troilus and Criseyde* to those of Troy, ignored their dynastic and heroic interest in favour of personal and social concerns. Significantly his sources are Boccaccio's *Teseida* and *Filostrato*, partial versions focused on individuals who exemplify the chivalric and amorous codes in a courtly but pagan context, radically rehandled by Chaucer in the light of Boethian concepts of Fortune and free will. The effect is neither to glorify exemplary types nor condemn blind victims of mutability. The 'Knight's Tale' reconciles the concept of benevolent government of human affairs with the arbitrary fates visited upon men; but somewhat uneasily, leaving a sense of tragedy rather than resolution. *Troilus* attempts no resolution, but through a narrator who affords varied and ambivalent views of the action – realistic, comic, and ironic – suggests multiple perspectives on its theme of the unstable, illusory nature of human love, leaving judgement to the individual reader.

Lydgate's treatment of the same legends in his *Siege of Thebes* (1420–22) and *Troy Book* (1412–20), though undertaken in emulation of what he saw as Chaucer's sententiousness, contradicts his oblique poetic method. The latter, for example, is based on Guido, reproduces his narrative unvaried and uninterpreted, but inflates it to over 30,000 lines by enormously expanding the moral commentary until it becomes a rhetorical exercise in its own right, the homily often irrelevant to the story, sometimes contradictory of its natural meaning. Caxton, responding to his patrons' wish to associate their revived chivalry with Roman military virtues published Ovid's *Metamorphoses, Aesop's Fables*, Chaucer's translation of Boethius, but also his own translations, begun under the patronage of the Burgundian court with its Order of the Golden Fleece, the *History of Jason, History of Troy* and *Eneydos*, all from thoroughly medievalized originals. He seems to have regarded both types of material as equally valid parts of practical knowledge and presents his classical heroes in their chivalric guise as exemplary figures rather than subjects for a moral critique.[22]

## The character of the Matter of Rome romances

In claiming their part in the classical heritage of Western Europe, English authors turned with significant frequency to Latin sources rather than accept the courtly gloss put upon the ancient world by French romance writers. Interest in the wonders of the East and romanticized versions of classical legend predated the Conquest; post-Conquest its status as history made it a mirror in which contemporary values could be viewed in moral perspective, sharpened in the case of the Troy legend by the sympathetic association of British audiences with the lost cause of their supposed ancestors. The range of inherent interests made possible a variety of approaches, from the academicism of the *Alliterative Alexander Fragments* supplementing a Latin source from Latin history (*A*) or abstracting a philosophical correspondence on brahmanic principles (*B*) to the popularization of the *Seege* with its use of the Troy legend as a backdrop to the adventures of swashbuckling heroes largely devoid of historical or chivalric associations; from Chaucer's elaboration of an episode as a magnifying glass for critical examination of the values of his own age to Lydgate's neglect of meaning in favour of an inflated rhetorical exercise. Often there is little trace of the romance mode except in the atmosphere of exotic lands, the conviction that the superhuman deeds recorded form part of the history of man.

Even those English versions which formally approximate to the romance genre are very various in their exploitation of the exoticism, the varied perspectives on heroic and chivalric values, the supreme examples of unbounded ambition brought to ruin by Fate or human folly. The alliterative poets of the *Gest Historiale* and the *Wars of Alexander*, despite their provincial medium, are academically dutiful in their somewhat heavy-handed efforts to reproduce their Latin sources fully, but leave unresolved the tension between their admiration for heroic idealism in the service of patriotic causes and the critical commentary of Christian moralists upon the fallibility of pagan aspirations inherited with their matter. By contrast, the popular poets of *Alisaunder* and the *Seege of Troye*, condensing with skill and confidence, concentrate attention upon the inherent meaning of the legends and when they wish to underline their exemplary function do so by rhetorical means which do not allow edification to obtrude upon entertainment. The number and variety of the surviving texts suggests their appeal was wider than that of more self-conscious, interpretative versions of the Matter of Rome.

# Notes

1. See F. B. Artz, *The Mind of the Middle Ages: A. D. 200–1500*, third edition (Chicago, Illinois, 1980), pp. 179–214, 305–19e; J. W. H. Atkins, *English Literary Criticism: The Medieval Phase* (Cambridge, 1943), pp. 36–90; F. J. E. Raby, *A History of Secular Latin Poetry in the Middle Ages*, 2 vols, revised edition (Oxford, 1957), I, 166–77; R. M. Wilson, *Early Middle English Literature* (London, 1951), pp. 23–54.

2. On the evolution of the Troy legends see A. M. Young, *Troy and her Legend*, reprint (Westport, Connecticut, 1971) or, more briefly, W. H. Schofield, *English Literature from the Norman Conquest to Chaucer*, reprint (Westport, Connecticut, 1970), pp. 282–94. On Benoit's treatment of love see R. M. Jones, *The Theme of Love in the Romans d'Antiquité* (London, 1972), pp. 43–59. On Guido see C. D. Benson, *The History of Troy in Middle English Literature* (Woodbridge, 1980), pp. 3–31.

3. See Thorlac Turville-Petre, *The Alliterative Revival* (Cambridge, 1977), pp. 58, 124; on the very uncertain dating see pp. 34, 51, 133, n. 14.

4. The poet seems slightly less at ease with love than war, though the appearance may simply be due to the effective vigour with which alliterative verse lends itself to violent action. His account of the love of Troilus and Briseida is, however, abbreviated in a way which suggests that he intended readers to refer to Chaucer's *Troilus* – and implies a date of composition after 1385 (see C. D. Benson, 'A Chaucerian Allusion and the Date of the Alliterative *Destruction of Troy*', *Notes and Queries*, 219 (1974), 206–07). For a contrary suggestion that the reference is to Lydgate's *Troy Book* and the composition of the alliterative poem consequently post-1420 see McKay Sundwall, 'The *Destruction of Troy*, Chaucer's *Troilus and Criseyde* and Lydgate's *Troy Book*', *Review of English Studies*, n.s. 26 (1975), 313–17.

5. Though elsewhere he refers to his source as 'the gest' (ll. 286, 12772, etc.), he is conscious that its subject-matter is 'aunter' (adventure) (ll. 5, 150, 153, etc.), the raw material of romance. Among the variety of generic terms by which English authors tried to distinguish varieties of narrative literature long after the emergence of the romance, others too tended to classify the Troy legends as

*historia* concerned with real events (*gestes*). See Paul Strohm. '*Storie, Spelle, Geste, Romaunce, Tragedie*: Generic Distinctions in the Middle English Troy Narratives', *Speculum*, 46 (1971), 348–59.

6. Text from the University of Glasgow Hunterian MS 388 edited by G. A. Panton and D. Donaldson, *The Gest Historiale of the Destruction of Troy*, EETS, 39, 56 (London, 1866, 1874).

7. The moral reinterpretation of the Troy legends in the *Gest* is helpfully discussed by V. B. Richmond, *The Popularity of Middle English Romance* (Bowling Green, Ohio, 1975), pp. 25–27, 29–34.

8. On the storm passages see Nicolas Jacobs, 'Alliterative Storms: A Topos in Middle English', *Speculum*, 47 (1972), 695–719.

9. See D. A. Lawton, '*The Destruction of Troy* as Translation from Latin Prose: Aspects of Form and Style', *Studia Neophilologica*, 52 (1980), 259–70.

10. See G. Hofstrand, *The Seege of Troye: A Study in the Intertextual Relations of the Middle English Romance* (Lund, 1936), and E. B. Atwood, 'The *Excidium Troie* and Medieval Troy Literature', *Modern Philology*, 35 (1938), 115–28.

11. Text from the Lincoln's Inn MS 150 edited by M. E. Barnicle, *The Seege or Batayle of Troye*, EETS, 172 (London, 1927).

12. On the poet's use of the *Excidium Troiae* in these episodes see E. B. Atwood, 'The Judgment of Paris in the *Seege of Troye*', *PMLA*, 57 (1942), 343–53 and 'The Story of Achilles in the *Seege of Troye*', *Studies in Philology*, 39 (1942), 489–501.

13. The astonishing diffusion of the Alexander legends is exhaustively documented by George Cary, *The Medieval Alexander*, edited by D. J. A. Ross (Cambridge, 1956).

14. Exact judgement of the redactive process is inhibited by the large, though no doubt incomplete, number of manuscripts of the popular I[3] recension of the *Historia*, none of which represents the exact source of the poem. It has been suggested that the poet interpolated a version of the *Fuerre de Gadres*, but his fuller account of that episode seems due to verbal inflation (see H. N. Duggan, 'The Source of the Middle English *The Wars of Alexander*', *Speculum*, 51 (1976), 624–36).

15. Text from the Bodleian Library MS Ashmole 61 edited by W. W. Skeat, *The Wars of Alexander*, EETS, ES, 47 (London, 1886).

16. See Betty Hill, 'Alexanderromance: The Egyptian Connection', *Leeds Studies in English*, n.s. 12 (1981), 185–94.

17. See William Matthews, *The Tragedy of Arthur* (Berkeley, California, 1960), pp. 68–95.

18. See D. A. Lawton, 'The Middle English Alliterative *Alexander A* and *C*: Form and Style in Translation from Latin Prose', *Studia Neophilologica*, 53 (1981), 259–68.

19. Fragments from a version of the *Voeux du paon* episode suggest the existence of a fourth alliterative text (see Thorlac Turville-Petre, 'A Lost Alliterative Alexander Romance', *Review of English Studies*, 30 (1979), 306–07).

20. Text from the Bodleian Library MS Laud Misc. 622 edited by C. V. Smithers, *Kyng Alisaunder*, EETS, 227, 237 (London, 1952, 1957).

21. See Richmond, pp. 35–42, and EETS, 237, pp. 28–40.

22. Limitations of space allow only summary treatment of these authors who are the subject of other volumes in this series.

# Chapter 7
# The Matter of Britain

Much that each of the other topics of romance individually had to offer English audiences was combined in the Matter of Britain: participation in world history through a flattering, if fictitious, chronicle of native dynasties rooted in antiquity and recorded in a learned language; affiliation through that dynastic fiction as well as political reality with the dominant contemporary culture which dignified the new matter with the courtly gloss of its values and its language; association with the native setting and access to the sources from which the legend was renewed and developed at a variety of cultural levels. The breadth of its appeal is reflected in the number and variety of the surviving English versions.

## Dynastic romance: Layamon's *Brut*

They fall broadly into two categories: those which present the supposed history of Britain in ways which echo political and dynastic concerns of their own age and those which use the Arthurian world as no more than a backdrop to the adventures of individual knights reflecting social and personal values of contemporary society. The formative impulse for the one was provided by Geoffrey of Monmouth's *Historia*, for the other by Chrétien's romances; the twin mirrors which they provided for feudal Europe were complementary and the vast Vulgate compilation united them in a world view which had wide currency (see above, pp. 43–45). In weaving Arthur into a chronicle which extended from the legendary Brutus to Cadwallader, last independent King of the British, Geoffrey invented freely; yet the shadows of earlier records lying behind his fiction lend it something of the depth and authority of myth. The Arthur glimpsed in early Welsh texts is a heroic if occasionally rumbustious figure; yet in the Latin Life of St Gildas he fails in his attack on Glastonbury to rescue Guinevere from her abductor (labelled Mardoc in the scene carved on an archivolt of Modena Cathedral) until the saint intervenes. This ambivalent view of him as powerful yet fallible, perceptible in Chrétien, is confirmed by Geoffrey even though he makes him the spiritual centre of his history, giving him the mysterious conception, upbringing in obscurity, and difficult accession to the throne which tradition prescribes for legendary heroes. Elaborating on the Latin historian Nennius, he makes Arthur a Christian patriot driving the pagan Saxon invaders out of his land, then credits him improbably with invading France and killing the Roman Viceroy, Frollo, in single combat, before marching on Rome itself. At this point tragedy, deep-rooted in tradition, strikes: Arthur's nephew Modred, left regent at home, usurps his crown and abducts his queen, falling into the role of Mardoc. The *Annales Cambriae* had recorded under the date 537 the deaths of Arthur and Medraut at the Battle of Camlann; the *Mirabilia* incorporated in Nennius mentions among the wonders of Wales the tomb of Arthur's son whom he himself killed. Now, in Geoffrey's version, Arthur returns, kills his nephew in battle, and, himself mortally wounded, is carried away to Avalon.[1]

The multiple appeal of this fiction dressed as fact for the mingled races of post-Conquest England explains its enormous popularity. For the Celts, including the numerous Bretons newly settled in Cornwall and Wales, there was the literary apotheosis of a national hero still potent in folk memory. For the English, psychological relief from the memory of their recent humiliation by identifying themselves with ancient tradition rather than Anglo-Saxon history, repeating the transmutation by which the Celts they once defeated had turned brutal fact into romantic fiction. For the Normans, legitimation of their conquest by putting it into historical perspective, showing Brutus as an invader bringing a superior culture, Cadwallader accepting the end of British rule as God-ordained, the Saxons as perfidious tyrants inviting overthrow, and the prophecies of Merlin predicting that the seed of Brutus shall once again rule Britain. There may be more specific reflection of Norman concerns in the recurrent theme of the seizure of thrones legitimized by an invitation to take power, in numerous instances of disputed inheritance echoing the quarrels between the Conqueror's sons, in the stress laid on the rights and powers of younger sons such as his eventual successor Henry I, in worries over dynastic continuity perhaps reflecting the loss of Henry's heir in the White Ship. Much more important is the *Historia*'s reproduction of the ideology of an age hovering between tyranny and anarchy, when the Conqueror's own example invited others to imitate him and the self-interested treachery of his feudal dependants threatened his *arriviste* dynasty from within. Geoffrey acknowledges its fears in a repeated pattern of realism tinged with optimism: traitors murder the ruler and turn on the deserving younger brother among his heirs, but he gains support from allies overseas or wins national support by his inherent qualities. Arthur provides the climactic example, justifying Norman rule by the rigour with which he imposes his will on domestic foes, and symbolizing their imperialist ambitions by his Continental conquests. But even he is not proof against what the age dreaded most: betrayal from within, civil war, and national collapse. There remains only the Hope of the British, vaguely expressed by Geoffrey, that Arthur may one day return from Avalon. Open endorsement of that legendary dream in a popular work given bogus authority by an elaborate display of academic apparatus might not have pleased the Norman magnates to whom the *Historia* was dedicated.[2]

The part played by the English in the history of Britain was known through the records, accurate by contemporary standards, of Bede and the *Anglo-Saxon Chronicle*. The very name of England refuted Geoffrey's fiction, yet sometime early in the thirteenth century, Layamon, parish priest of Areley Kings in Worcestershire, took enormous pains to reproduce and elaborate the story in over sixteen thousand long lines of alliterative verse. His unusually personal introduction describes the process of compounding various prestigious sources, including Bede, but effectively the poem is a version of Wace's *Roman de Brut* with a limited number of added incidents and a degree of imaginative expansion and verbal elaboration which doubles the original, increasing the Arthurian section to more than a third of the whole. Where Geoffrey chose to disguise the romantic fiction of his Arthuriad in the trappings of chronicle, and Wace to colour it faintly as *roman courtois*, the genre of Layamon's version is Old English epic.[3]

His medium is the loosely structured alliterative line of the post-Conquest survival, the half-line units often linked by rhyme or assonance; at times the stress patterns are so regular as to recall the classic types, at others they fall into syllabic couplets which seem to echo the octosyllabics of Wace. The alternation can be disconcerting, as if Layamon were hearing simultaneously the rhythms of past and present, but his medium is self-made not an archaic pastiche. Its stylistic means too are echoes of the past: the formulaic phrases, poetic vocabulary, word-compounds, variations of terms of Anglo-Saxon verse, sometimes, in battle passages, startlingly reminiscent of the original, yet remade rather than imitated. And there are innovations, such as the extended similes reminiscent of Virgil but perhaps imitated from Anglo-Norman epic; they too have fully absorbed any model they had and suggest first-hand observation of the beasts with whose behaviour, violent or cowardly, he compares that of his protagonists. Like his avoidance of French vocabulary, his archaic diction, and apparently bogus claims to learned antiquarian sources, they suggest a self-consciously literary effort to devise a medium appropriate to his view of his subject, a national chronicle breathing the spirit of a heroic age.[4]

In matter as in poetic manner Layamon's approach is eclectic yet conservative, a piecemeal originality which imports or develops whatever he finds appropriate to his subject. Major additions, such as the 'alven' (fays) who bestow gifts of strength, dominion, and long life on Arthur at his birth and the boat which bears him away, mortally wounded, to the care of the fay Argante in Avalon, Celtic in character but perhaps French in immediate provenance, are rare. More typical is Layamon's treatment of the Round Table: taking up the mention in Wace that Arthur had it made to prevent quarrels over precedence, he gives a long and violent account of the fracas which first suggested it; and his account of Arthur's armour where, to the Celtic names Wace gives for sword, shield, and spear, he adds the helmet Goswhit (Goose-white) and the coat of mail Wygar made by a son of Weland the legendary Germanic weapon-smith. The fusion of cultures seems entirely unconscious; whatever access Layamon had to Celtic and Anglo-Saxon traditions, written or oral, he clearly recognized what was germane to the heroic theme of his work.[5]

Narrative and theme remain essentially what they were in Geoffrey's *Historia*; the doubling in bulk arises from the methods which Layamon uses to make them vivid and imaginatively compelling in the interests of moral meaning and patriotic spirit. They are seen at their most effective in the 5000 lines given to Arthur's career, especially in his domestic wars against invaders and rebels where the extended similies crowd together. The even-paced outline of events in Wace is constantly interrupted whenever thematic significance or moral import tempt Layamon to dramatize an incident, showing violence in action and turning conflict into vigorous dialogue, multiplying the direct speech in his source many times over. He turns the 50 lines in which Wace narrates the murder of Arthur's father, King Uther, into a 100-line drama in which the murderers disguise themselves as citizens reduced to poverty by Saxon exactions, receive the royal charity, and then poison the well from which their benefactor drinks. There is no commentary; the action speaks directly to the medieval horror of treachery and ingratitude, underscored by the public expressions of gratitude and the private plotting of vengeance. Layamon adds to Merlin's promise to bring Uther to Ygerne magically disguised as her husband, his prophecy of the son she will bear:

'Al him scal abuȝe    þat wuneð inne Bruttene.
Of him scullen gleomen    godliche singen;
Of his breosten scullen æten    aðele scopes;
Scullen of his blode    beornes beon drunke.'    (ll. 9409–12)[6]

*(All who dwell in Britain shall obey him. Of him shall minstrels splendidly sing; of his breast noble bards shall eat; heroes shall be drunk upon his blood!)*

Coming to the throne at fifteen, Arthur immediately begins to display royal qualities, including the generosity in kind to his immediate retinue which was an essential attribute of Germanic kingship (ll. 9945–61), magnificence in his arming (ll. 10542–62, 11855–75), and personal prowess in single combat with Frollo (ll. 11904–69) and in the superhuman struggle with the giant of Mont St Michel (ll. 12974–13033). Once embarked upon the Roman Wars, Layamon's version becomes more and more independent: having used the argument that the conquest of Rome by Bren and Belin, legendary Britons, cancelled the Emperor's claim inherited from Julius Caesar on one occasion (ll. 12499–12519), he repeats it on another without warrant from Wace (ll. 13530–38, 13964–68), and constantly exalts Arthur through the praises of his own subjects (ll. 11327–44, 12081–96) and the grudging admiration of his enemies (ll. 12618–39). The King dominates the action as the active hero of a national epic, his lieutenants little more than shadowy instruments of his will.

It is the domestic struggle against the treacherous pagan Saxons and the traitor Modred which most excites Layamon's invention; the constant addition of minor details of direction and distance, times and seaons, names of places and persons, the fullness of description in scenes of pagentry and feasting, all suggest a desire to stimulate and convince. The battle-scenes abandon Wace in free invention, mingling formula – 'Breken braden speren,   brustleden sceldes' – and inventive detail – churls who fight with clubs and pitchforks – in a welter of bloodshed which the poet seems to relish, underlining the violence with an occasional ironic understatement or a telling image: 'Þer sunken to grunde   fif and twenti hundred;/Þa al wes Auene stram   mid stele ibrugged' *(bridged)* (ll. 10615–16). The effect is emotive rather than visual, rising at moments of climax to similies of Arthur as preying wolf and the enemies of Britain as hunted birds and beasts, to the incoherence of vision as Arthur gloats over the Avon choked with Saxon dead:

'Hu ligeð i þan stræme   stelene fisces,
Mid sweorde bigeorede,   heore sund is awemmed;
Heore scalen wleoteð   swulc gold-faȝe sceldes;
Þer fleoteð heore spiten,   swulc hit spæren weoren.'

(ll. 10641–44)

*('How steel fish lie in the stream, girt with swords so that their swimming is hindered; their scales float like gold-plated shields; their spines float as if they were spears!')*

Only the treachery at the heart of the Round Table excites his invention to the same degree. When Wace first mentions Gawain, Layamon adds a reference to his brother: 'Wale (*alas*) þat Modræd wes ibore! Muchel hærm com þerfore' (l. 11084). When Wace debates the truth of British history, Layamon adds a long confirmatory prophecy of Merlin, mingling forewarning of the downfall of the Round Table with hope of Arthur's eventual return to his kingdom (ll. 11465–75). As Modred enters the action the English version trebles the lines given to his characterization, stressing the dynastic implications of his treachery and making Guinevere equally complicit with him (ll. 12709–36). To Arthur's original dream of disaster, Layamon adds another in which he sees Modred and the Queen pulling down the royal hall, symbol of the state (ll. 13971–14051). The news of their rebellion excites bitter speeches of vengeance on Arthur's part and moral condemnation of his brother by Gawain (ll. 14052–85), neither in Wace. Modred invites the aid of the banished Saxons, retreats into Cornwall while Guinevere, conscious-stricken, takes the veil at Caerleon, and civil war wipes out the Round Table, symbol of concord. But the Hope of the British, doubted in Wace, lives on in Layamon:

> Bute while wes an witeʒe,   Mærlin ihate;
> He bodede mid worde   – his quides weoren soðe –
> Þat an Arður sculde ʒete cum   Anglen to fulste.   (ll. 14295–97)
> *(But once there was a sage called Merlin; he prophesied in words – his sayings were truthful – that an Arthur should yet come to help the English)*[7]

The extension of that hope to the English, Arthur's bitterest enemies, typifies the operation of the romance mode in Layamon's *Brut*, blurring historical identities to reconcile his readers to contemporary reality.[8] The fact that his vast work survives in two manuscripts, neither of which is the author's copy, suggests a remarkable degree of success. The later dating now proposed brings it into association with *Horn* and *Havelok* (see above, pp. 65–74) with which it shares an instinct for dramatic narration of action forwarded by speech; but its giant scale, deliberate archaism, and fascination with Old English epic suggest literary rather than minstrel preservation. The reviser whose modifications made it more accessible to the thirteenth century refers to Layamon living with 'the good knight' (as his chaplain?); if we knew who was the patron of such a massive effort of composition on so much expensive book-skin, we should know more of the audience for English literature as it struggled free from the dominance of Anglo-Norman.

## The alliterative *Morte Arthure*

*Layamon's Brut* may no longer seem such a cultural sport, but it suggests the end rather than the beginning of a tradition. Yet some hundred to a hundred and fifty years later a poet who, by routes still more untraceable, shared something of his Anglo-Saxon heritage, treated the dynastic theme in an even more uncompromising version of the alliterative long line. His *Morte Arthure*, composed somewhere in the north Midlands, probably in the last quarter of the fourteenth century, is so highly individual that its sources remain uncertain: rooted in some version of the chronicle tradition, most probably Wace, it shows an eclectic familiarity with other romance matters, the list of possible sources growing as research progresses. The dynastic theme dominates from the outset, reflected in many of the elements which Layamon used for the same purpose: the Trojan ancestry of the King (ll. 4342–46) and individual knights (ll. 1694–99), feasts and councils of the Round Table as demonstrations of his feudal power (ll. 52–77, 243–406, 636–92), repeated lists of names showing the wide involvement of its members in his wars (ll. 1601–08, 1738–45, 1993–2005, 2489–98) and the patriotic spirit in which the poet constantly refers to them as 'our knights'. But the linear sequence of chronicle has been replaced by something resembling the organized structure of epic: detached, highly dramatic scenes grouped into six major sections, five of which begin with messengers whose nature or news characterizes the following episode, giving it something of the nature of an *exemplum*.

The action is triggered, at a point four-fifths of the way through Layamon's history, by the arrival of ambassadors demanding that Arthur do homage to the Roman Emperor for his lands. But memories of his climactic place in British history have been evoked by an opening catalogue of his earlier conquests, ranging from Orkney to Provence, Ireland to Austria (ll. 26–47). Now, at the height of his powers, he defies the Emperor Lucius whose ambassadors, impressed by the splendour of Arthur's court, the magnificence with which they have been feasted, and the absolute refusal with which they were dismissed, warn him:

> 'He wyll werraye iwysse – be ware ȝif þe lykes;          *make war, wary*
> Wage many wyghtemen and wache thy marches,          *hire, warriors,*
>                                                                                                           *frontiers*
> That they be redye in araye and at areste foundyn;          *ready for battle*
> For ȝife he reche vnto Rome, he raunsouns it for euere!'          *will deliver*
>                                                                                          (ll. 546–49)[9]

Throughout some 4300 lines, Arthur is to remain the focus of the poem; but in a dual role as Christian king, conscious of dynastic duty to his nation and spiritual responsibility for the protection of Christendom, and as a knight, head of a chivalric order, vowed to personal prowess in defence of right, Charlemagne and Roland in one. At the opening council of the Round Table, subsidiary kings and knights in formal order vow vengeance against Rome for past wrongs, most probably imitated from the *Voeux du paon* which echoed the competitive boasting of the *chansons de geste*, but close in spirit to the *beot* (public declaration of intent) of the heroic age in England. The resultant campaign against Lucius is so structured that each in turn fulfils his vow against a vivid background of mass violence. Arthur outshines them all in knighthood, seeking out solitary adventures and killing the Emperor in single combat. The poet has made many minor changes in the episode at Mont St Michel to show the King as a David-like defender of his people against ungodly forces; the giant is a bestial creature, an eater of children who wears the beards of subject kings as trophies; Arthur encounters him alone, ordering his companions to stay behind, and is crushed beneath his monstrous body as he rolls down the mountain in his death-grip. The encounter exemplifies in miniature the whole struggle against a tyranny which allies itself with 'Sowdanes and Sarazenes' and makes war with giants, witches, and warlocks in its ranks. That Arthur's personal prowess is an instrument of Christian justice is constantly emphasized by his own manifest piety (ll. 1218–21, 2410–16, 3212–17), by the prophetic dream which promises him victory over Lucius (ll. 756–831), the prayers of the giant's victims at the moment when the struggle turns in Arthur's favour (ll. 1136–39), and his triumph 'thurghe þe crafte of Cryste' (l. 1107).[10]

Arthur's role as knight errant is illuminated by the way in which his nephew Gawain acts as his foil. The poet having eliminated his part in the initial council where, in Layamon, he praises peace against Cador's demands for war, he first appears as envoy to Lucius delivering Arthur's defiance with the arrogance and disregard for personal danger which are to be his hallmarks throughout. These qualities are exposed to critical evaluation in an episode (ll. 2501–2716) borrowed from the romanticized epic (either *Fierabras* or its English derivative *Ferumbras*): amid the bloody chaos of the Roman Wars, the poet isolates by a rhetorical evocation of the beauties of nature an encounter in which Gawain wins the adherence to Arthur's cause of the noble pagan Priamus by defeating him in a display of prowess bordering on the grotesque – flaming swords, helmets blazing fire, livers laid open to the light of day. Emerging from the dream world of high romance, he shows the same reckless courage in the chronicle context by overcoming, with the help of Priamus, vastly superior Roman forces, for which Arthur praises him where he had earlier censured Cador for endangering his followers under similar circumstances (ll. 1617–1949). By evoking the contrast between dynastic warfare and the self-vaunting chivalry of romantic knight-errantry the poet implies that courage and prowess are to be estimated by the validity of the cause they serve; by Arthur's approval of reckless bravery which he had previously condemned he marks a crucial change in the King's attitude to his own warfare. Just before the Priamus episode Arthur had held a council (ll. 2390–2415) announcing his intention to press on into Lombardy and Tuscany; the parallel with that initial meeting at which he had been urged by his knights to defend his lands against tyranny suggests that he has become greedy for the lands of others. Substitution of his announcement for the messengers who open other sections implies his growing self-isolation; hereafter the messengers announce the consequences of his decision. He presses on with increasing violence, warring against Pope and Church, threatening to kill his child hostages if Rome will not pay tribute, until, almost at the gates of the city, he is offered the imperial crown.[11]

This change from a just to an unjust war is marked by another prophetic dream (ll. 3218–3455) – almost certainly the poet's invention though rooted in tradition – in which Arthur sees himself raised upon Fortune's wheel in power and majesty only to be dashed down to destruction as it relentlessly turns. The philosophers who interpret it for him make explicit a moral commentary which has been implicit since the proem (ll. 1–25) in which the poet invokes divine grace for human misgovernment, promises a tale of the Round Table, 'How they whanne (won) wyth were wyrchippis (honours) many' (l. 22), but breaks off his outline at the height of Arthur's triumphs. From the outset war is linked with pilgrimage in a way which suggests ironic counterpointing of the aims of life: Arthur's knights vow war against Rome on Christ and the vernicle, reminders of the holy relics venerated there and the redemptive grace earned by his sacrifice which was the true object of such pilgrimages; he himself conceals his knight-errantry against the giant under the guise of a pilgrimage to the shrine of Mont St Michel; immediately after his dream of Fortune's wheel he meets one of his chamberlains on pilgrimage to Rome who tells him that Modred has usurped his kingdom, married Guinevere, and had a child by her (ll. 3468–3590). Now the philosophers tell him that, like the Nine Worthies he sees upon the wheel, he has misused his life in violent conquest for worldly glory:

> 'Thow arte at þe hegheste, I hette the forsothe;    *promise*
> Chalange nowe when thow will, thow cheuys no more.
>                                              *take up a challenge, will achieve*
> Thow has schedde myche blode and schalkes distroyede,    *men*
> Sakeles, in cirquytrie, in sere kynges landis.    *innocent, out of pride, many*
> Schryfe the of thy schame and schape for thyn ende.'    *shrive, prepare*
>                                              (ll. 3396–3400)

The immediate cause of Arthur's downfall, Modred's treason, is now seen as rooted in his imperial obsession; in his eagerness for conquest he had appointed Modred regent despite his protests at being deprived of his own chance of military glory, warning him against betrayal as he should answer for it at the Last Judgement (ll. 636–78). Now he turns upon his nephew with the ruthlessness which made him pay the tribute demanded by Rome in treasure-chests charged with the bodies of the Emperor and sixty senators (ll. 2290–2351), order a slaughter of prisoners in revenge for one of his own knights (ll. 2261–77), and swear to avenge Gawain who, as they invade their own country, is cut off in his reckless pursuit of glory by his cousin Modred (ll. 3712–3863). Stricken with remorse, Modred retreats and warns Guinevere to flee; she had wept at Arthur's departure, now she weeps at his vengeful return – 'And all for falsede and frawde and fere of hir louerde' (l. 3918) – and takes the veil at Caerleon. Too eager for vengeance to wait for reinforcements, Arthur is outnumbered in the final battle, but kills Modred with his own hand and orders the execution of the traitor's children. As death approaches, he recognizes the desolate end of worldly glory:

> 'I may helples one hethe house be myn one,    *dwell, all by myself*
> Alls a wafull wedowe þat wanttes hir beryn;    *is deprived of, man*
> I may werye and wepe and wrynge myn handys,    *curse*
> For my wytt and my wyrchipe awaye es for euer.'    *skill, honour*
> (ll. 4284–87)

Formal piety surrounds his death and burial at Winchester, but his all too human failings rule out any hope for his return.

The tragic outcome has led some critics to classify the *Morte Arthure* as epic rather than romance, but nothing dictates that the latter should end happily; if aspiring idealism is overmastered by reality the outcome may well be tragic. The poem is manifestly in the romance mode, its patriotic ideal of dynastic integrity undercut by the certainty of the death of kings and the possibility of their damnation should national defence turn to imperialist aggression. By evoking the various genres associated with military idealism the poet has infused chronicle material with the spirit of wish-fulfilment; but by using their conventions ironically and juxtaposing them with the moral and physical reality of war he has undermined their values to the point where he seems to be writing anti-romance. His presentation of Arthur's wars is uniquely and factually precise: geographical detail concrete enough to allow his campaigns to be plotted on a map (ll. 343–55, 419–42, 3092–3175), lists of place-names outlining territorial holdings (ll. 26–47, 2375–85); tactical details of a markedly non-chivalric kind: the effect of massed bowmen (ll. 2095–2110), mechanized warfare (ll. 3032–43), war at sea (ll. 3598–3711), grotesque

descriptions of wounds (ll. 2764–83), the disruption of everyday life
(ll. 3116–27) and the sufferings of non-combatants (ll. 3150–60). The
precision has led critics to identify episodes in the Continental campaigns of
Edward III, but to a nation exhausted by the endless cruelties and losses of
the Hundred Years War it was perhaps war itself which queried the validity
of Arthur's imperial ambitions – the poet's bitterness often blurs the
distinction between just and unjust warfare until he seems as anti- war as
anti-romance. His alliterative medium, iterative, emphatic, exploiting an
enormously varied vocabulary, reinforces the realistic approach, contrasting the sardonic humour with which Arthur comments on the
violence of battle (ll. 2123–29) with the passionate feeling of his outburst
over the dead Gawain (ll. 3955–68), and romantic evocation of pastoral
landscape (ll. 920–32, 2501–12) with realistic descriptions of scenery and
weather (ll. 2501–08), the pomp of military ceremony (ll. 900–19) with the
cruelty of war:

> Qwarells qwayntly swappez thorowe knyghtez,
> With iryn so wekyrly, that wynche they neuer:
> So they scherenken fore schotte of þe scharppe arowes,
> That all the scheltron schonte and schoderide at ones.
>
> (ll. 2103–06)
>
> (*Crossbow bolts whip smartly through knights, piercing them with iron so
> nimbly that they never wince. So, shrinking away from the sharp arrow
> shots, the whole troop shrank back and instantly scattered.*)

The gap between the mythic and the mimetic levels of the text is wide,
but from it comes the peculiar power of this romance.[12]

## The stanzaic *Morte Arthur*

The same desire to find meaning in the failure of an ideal marks
the work of another north-Midlands poet of the late fourteenth century
whose treatment of the dynastic theme is radically different in every
other respect. The medium and narrative manner of *Le Morte Arthur*
could scarcely be more strongly contrasted:

> Lordingis that ar leff and dere,                                *beloved*
> Lystenyth, and I shall you tell
> By olde dayes what aunturis were                          *adventures*
> Amonge oure eldris þat byfelle.   (ll. 1–4)[13]

The formulaic opening, the combination of the octosyllabic line of French romance with a stanza form compelling economy of statement, the limited vocabulary and terse diction reminiscent of ballad suggest a minstrel composition. But the stanza is unique in French or English and the casual ease with which the demanding rhyme-scheme (usually *ababbab* with some variations) is handled, the frequent alliterative tags, the linking of verse to verse at some points and the narrative hiatus between verses at others suggest a conscious artist at work. The paragraphs provided by individual stanzas are long enough to outline a situation, encapsulate a speech, describe a reaction; the natural breaks they provide allow for rapid changes of scene or speaker, dramatic shift of focus from an event to its consequence, vivid isolation of a significant detail. But they can also be linked in blocks to be balanced against other narrative divisions for thematic effect. The poet has exploited the facility with which the perspective can be changed to present action through the eyes of various characters; to show the arrival of a messenger watched from a tower then reported by the watchers to those who are to receive the message, creating a sense of tension; to allow the narrator to step into the background, leaving comment and evaluation to the actors and giving greater objectivity to the events. The effect of the minimal narration setting the scene for detached episodes introduced with a formulaic 'Than it felle uppon a day', speeches charged with suppressed passions and inner conflicts, snatches of dialogue which imply action not narrated, gestures vivified by their isolation is reminiscent of the ballad with its presentation of moments of startling intensity in a narrative too familiar for recapitulation.[14]

In outline the narrative is that of the *Mort Artu*, final branch of the vast Vulgate Cycle of prose romances (see above, pp. 43–45), but so freely adapted as to suggest that the source was a variant version for which there is no objective evidence. The characteristic interweaving of long-running narrative threads in the French has been unravelled to present only limited episodes whose thematic association is underlined by structural balance, strengthened by avoidance of digressions and the strict subordination of details to theme. The wholesale omission of material from the Vulgate version of the downfall of the Round Table, where the chronicle account of challenge from abroad and treason at home has been combined with the inherent conflict between feudal duty and chivalric aspiration, is thematically biased to shift the focus from Arthur, representative of the nation, to Lancelot the embodiment of knighthood. But the central concern is still that of dynastic romance: a troubled dream of the golden age of a nation brought to an end by inherent contradictions in the ideals on which it was built.

Returning to the adulterous love of Lancelot and Guinevere, whose socially beneficial effects are celebrated in Chrétien's *Lancelot* (see above, pp. 34–36), it takes up an issue tacitly ignored while the *roman courtois* was still in search of the most absolute statement of its personal idealism: is such a love compatible with the dynastic ideal which Arthur embodied for an age which condemned sexual relations with the wife of the ruler as treason? The English poet accepts that love, without approval or condemnation, as a 'historical' fact; so, it seems, does Arthur's court, for though '. . . men told in many a thede (*country*)/That Launcelot by the quene lay' (ll. 61–62), it has not been publicly exposed; but Agravain, Gawain's brother, spies upon the lovers. Suspicion breeds constraint between the couple: when the court goes to a tournament at Winchester, Lancelot pretends sickness to stay behind; but his meeting with the Queen lasts only two stanzas (ll. 65–80) before she abruptly dismisses him. Seeking renewed confirmation of his prowess, Lancelot goes to the tournament in disguise and fights on the weaker side; but his bearing instantly betrays him to Arthur, initiating the theme of identity and self-awareness which runs through the poem. Wounded, he is nursed at the castle of Ascolot by the lord's daughter who has fallen in love with him on sight; but he explains '"In another stede (*place*) myne hert is sette;/It is not at myne owne wille"' (ll. 203–04) and, out of compassion, leaves her his armour as a keepsake. Gawain, visiting Ascolot, is shown the armour as proof that Lancelot is her leman and boasts that his friend's chivalric qualities make him irresistible to all women (ll. 584–91). Without apparent malice he informs the King and Queen and when Lancelot returns to court Guinevere bitterly reproaches him, begging:

'That thou nevir more dyskere                          *disclose*
The love that hathe bene betwyxe us two,
Ne that she nevir be with the so dere
Dede of armys þat thou be fro.'    (ll. 754–57)        *cease from*

Acting, like others here, in response to his nature and the code which governs him, he bids her farewell for ever.

Then tragedy strikes: a poisoned apple, intended by a disaffected squire for Gawain, kills a Scottish knight at Guinevere's table and she is condemned to death – 'Thoughe Arthur were kynge þe land to weld,/He myght not be agayne the righte' (ll. 920–21) – unless she can find a champion to fight for her against the dead knight's kin. Meanwhile, a boat drifts down the river to Camelot with the body of the Maid of Ascolot and a letter in which she blames her death on Lancelot's refusal of her love, and Gawain apologizes for his earlier misinformation. Arthur can persuade none of his knights to defend the Queen, to whose desperate pleadings they coldly reply:

> 'The nobleste bodye of flesshe and blode
> That evyr was yete in erthe lente                        *remained*
> For thy wille and thy wykked mode                       *disposition*
> Out of oure companye is wente.'    (ll. 1352–55)

But Lancelot, learning of her distress, returns, defeats her accuser, and is reconciled to her. Challenged fortuitously from without, the unity of the Round Table has survived, though there are ominous factors in the destructive and divisive power of the love which makes Lancelot the glory of his society, Arthur's blind loyalty to all his knights and his inflexibility in administering seigneurial justice.

Now the challenge comes from within: Modred and Agravain, with Arthur's reluctant agreement, plot to trap Lancelot in the Queen's bedroom, against Gawain's protest: '"Yit were it better to hele (*hide*) and layne (*conceal*)/Than werre and wrake (*ruin*) thus to begynne"' (ll. 1694–95); though forewarned, Lancelot, overwhelmed by passion, is surprised in the Queen's bed but escapes by killing all his attackers save Modred. Guinevere is condemned to be burned and Lancelot, in snatching her from the stake, accidentally kills two more of Gawain's brothers. Gawain who had excused Lancelot's adultery as if love were a fate visited upon him, blamed Agravain as a trouble-maker, and absented himself from ambush and execution, undergoes a violent revulsion of feeling and swears:

> 'Betwixte me and Launcelóte du Lake,
> Nys man in erthe, for sothe to sayne,
> Shall trewes sette and pees make                         *truce*
> Er outher of us have other slayne.'    (ll. 2010–13)

The old Germanic law of kinship vengeance obsesses him, overriding the bond of chivalric brotherhood, and he draws Arthur into his blood-feud, besieging the lovers until, on the intervention of the Pope, Lancelot restores the Queen and retires to his lands in Brittany. The power of circumstance has forced both men from their true roles: Lancelot the lover-knight abandons love and war; Gawain the peacemaker becomes the avenger.

Events now mount to the disastrous climax in almost arithmetical progression. Arthur and Gawain, besieging Lancelot in his castle of Benwick, reject all the overtures he makes to spare his lands and kinsmen the horrors of war (ll. 2500–2715). Three times Gawain challenges him to single combat (ll. 2716–2945), abusing and baiting his former friend until his own companions call him mad and Arthur longs to abandon the siege; Lancelot, resisting his followers' wish to sally out *en masse*, shows endless restraint and courtesy and, knowing that

Gawain's strength increases with the mounting sun, postpones their encounter until noon and then lets him escape with a wound, increasing his chivalric stature as Gawain darkens his own reputation. The siege is finally abandoned when news comes that Modred has seized the throne and the fatal division of the Round Table culminates in civil war (ll. 2946–3565). Gawain, struck upon the wound Lancelot gave him, dies on the beach at Dover; warned by his ghost to postpone the final battle until Lancelot can come to his aid, Arthur makes a truce which is broken when an adder causes swords to be drawn, and he and Modred – in this version his illegitimate son – kill each other.[15]

There the *Mort Artu* effectively ends, but the English poem adds a last meeting between the lovers at Amesbury where Guinevere has taken the veil (ll. 3622–3723), echoing elements from the earlier treatment of their relationship. In the presence of the community she laments the disastrous consequences of their love and urges Lancelot to marry with the same generosity with which, at their earlier meeting (ll. 734–75) – another English addition – she steeled herself to surrender him to the Maid of Ascolot so that his chivalry should not be impaired; now as then he indignantly rejects the idea as deserving burning, the penalty for adultery, alluding to their love as a binding contract as she had done on that occasion (ll. 740–43) and vowing to follow her example in lifelong penance. To maintain her resolve she dare not give him a parting kiss but there is a sense that their love, beset as ever by doubts and insecurities, endures. It sustains them until death and leaves no sense of sin: Guinevere lies with Arthur at Glastonbury, the Hope of the British buried with them; but at Lancelot's death one of his order of hermit-knights dreams of him surrounded by an angelic host: "'Agaynste hym openyd the gatys of hevyn'" (l. 3879).[16]

His apotheosis and the penitential ending are not pious afterthoughts: throughout, the perfectionist codes he serves are implicitly set against the fallible nature of fallen man. Lancelot's intuitive understanding that self-glorification through the pursuit of chivalric perfection is not enough is shown in his unfailing self-control, courtesy, compassion, and tolerance towards others. To avoid offence to Arthur, shame for Guinevere, conflict with Gawain he is prepared to absent himself from court, to go to the Holy Land, to sacrifice everything except love and honour. But the absolute value of human love is questioned: the romantic passion of the Maid of Ascolot is shown to be egoistic, self-indulgent, and ultimately self-destructive; the love of Guinevere which inspires chivalry is adulterous, causing Lancelot to lie to Arthur, depriving the Queen of a legal defender and the Round Table of its best knight in the hour of need. It is the complacent, impetuous Guinevere who is shocked into recognizing the high cost of pursuing self-fulfilment: "'Oure wylle hathe be to sore bought sold'" (l. 3651); her example inspires Lancelot to abandon worldly glory in search of the greater self-knowledge which leads to grace. The poet does not preach but underscores his ironies of structure, balancing pairs of incidents against each other, and character, pairing contrasting personalities, with verbal ironies which imply comment. The compassionate narrator passes no judgements, but his repeated references to Lancelot's visits to the Queen taking place immediately after Arthur has gone out and his application to Agravain of the term 'traitor' which *he* had applied to Lancelot challenge opinion of the hero's behaviour. There is dramatic irony in the frequency with which characters act under a misapprehension apparent to the audience to whose judgement their credulity, hastiness, or lack of self-knowledge is exposed. The appearance of the adder at the Battle of Salisbury, precipitating the catastrophe already prepared, typifies the coincidence of accident and human error in this tragedy of consequence.[17]

## Malory's *Morte Darthur*

The theme of idealistic aspiration undermined by human fallibility, widened from the regnal focus of the alliterative *Morte* to the inner circle of the Round Table in the stanzaic version, is widened still further in Sir Thomas Malory's *Le Morte Darthur* to show the pursuit of worldly glory as the source both of greatness and of ruin in the whole history of the King's reign. The sole surviving manuscript runs to some 720 pages of prose in a modern edition, divided into eight tales whose *explicits* (closing words) show that the first was separately written without any thought of a continuation and that the last was finished in 1469–70; whether the others were also written piecemeal, in which order, and over what period is not clear. The first tale describes the author as 'a knyght presoner' and in the *explicit* to the last he asks his readers to pray for his 'good delyveraunce'; if he has been correctly identified, he was imprisoned on at least eight occasions in the course of a violent career. Born the son of an esquire with small estates centred on Newbold Revel in Warwickshire, he may have served in the French Wars under the Earl of Warwick, was later knighted and became a Member of Parliament. But in the growing civil unrest which led to the outbreak of the Wars of the Roses in 1453 the criminal records charge him with extortion, rape, church-robbery, cattle-raiding, horse-stealing, and lying in ambush to murder his patron the Duke of Buckingham. Some of the charges may be false, politically motivated as he changed sides in the civil war, imprisoned by one side, escaping by bribery or violence, only to be reimprisoned by the other.[18]

Such a career was by no means unique in a violent age when 100 years of exhausting, profitless foreign war were immediately followed by 30 of intermittent, divisive civil strife. But, paradoxically, it was this dubious character who produced the definitive summation of chivalric values in the service of a dynastic ideal which was to typify Arthurian romance through the ages until Tennyson gave it renewed life in his *Idylls of the King*. Its widespread influence began with Caxton who recommended his edition to his patrons, noble and mercantile:

> For herein may be seen noble chyvalrye, curtosye, humanyté, frendlynesse, hardynesse, love, frendshyp, cowardyse, murdre, hate, vertue, and synne. Doo after the good and leve the evyl, and it shal brynge you to good fame and renommee.[19]

The ambivalence of this publisher's blurb reflects the characteristically mixed mode in which Malory worked, providing for an age whose feudal polity, based on the ownership of land, was being rapidly transformed by the mercantile economy on which it now rested and whose idealization of the personal virtues of the mounted knight was contradicted by the increasingly tactical and mechanized nature of war, a display of chivalry so comprehensive as to contain its own critique of the code. Chivalry fascinated the fifteenth century as a historical ideal, but centuries of literary celebration had not resolved its inherent contradictions: the conflict between its absolutism and the principle of *mesure* (balance and moderation), its glorification of the individual, and the social service which was its professed aim. Whatever its continuing value as a personal code its limitations as a political model were as apparent to Malory in the failure of the dynastic dream of Arthurian Britain as in the chaotic nightmare of contemporary England.[20]

The implication of an overall interpretative approach raises the issue of the long-running controversy as to whether *Le Morte Darthur* was composed, as Caxton presented it, as a single book thematically and structurally unified or as eight separate tales individually conceived and self-contained in narrative. Growing thematic appreciation has tended to reduce its importance. Malory need not initially have planned the work as a coherent whole, but may have become increasingly conscious in the process of piecemeal composition of an inherent unity in his material arising from its long-established narrative tradition, the constant restatement and variation of its themes, and his own evolving response to both. Had unity been his first priority, he could have achieved it by passively accepting the structure of the Vulgate Cycle from which he drew most of his material. Instead, he has rejected content and structure at will, ranged widely for other matter, including such English texts as the alliterative and the stanzaic *Morte*, and supplied lengthy sections of his own invention – the characteristic medieval method of composition. The rarity and expensive format of some of his sources suggests the effort needed to collect them, some perhaps through his patron Warwick's connection with the court of Burgundy where many Arthurian texts had been assembled by Philip the Bold, whose compilers did for Charlemagne what Malory was to do for Arthur.

Whatever his overall structural conception, Malory's approach to individual tales shows an evident wish to simplify, unravelling the long-running sequences of the Vulgate in which the adventures of one knight are intertwined with those of others and knitting disjointed strands together end to end to resolve a theme within a single episode – his version of the Maid of Ascolot story compounds eight separate sections in the French. Traces of the original structure survive in occasional references to past events or anticipations of future incidents, but they are practical aids to narrative continuity rather than self-conscious indicators of structural complexity. The focus is now upon the events themselves, on patterns of human behaviour rather than patterns of composition, inherent meaning rather than the extrapolated significance provided in the commentary of the hermits who throng in the *Queste del Saint Graal*, largely eliminated by Malory. Each sequence, vivified by selection and concentration, the vague locations of French romance identified by English place-names and events dated by reference to incidents of Arthurian 'history', contributes to the underlying theme of the rise and fall of a society embodying ideals of individual conduct and social cohesion through its implicit reference to the dynastic tradition which centuries of celebration had given a powerful claim upon the imagination of Malory's contemporaries. At the core of that tradition for the authors of the Vulgate was Lancelot, a king of France; in restoring Arthur to his place at the heart of a national epic, Malory makes constant changes of content and emphasis, more and more frequent as the tragic climax approaches.[21]

The dynastic emphasis of Malory's version is apparent in the overall structure of his *Le Morte Darthur*. Ignoring the opening of the Vulgate, the *Estoire* whose apostolic prehistory of the Grail establishes the symbolism of the *Queste*, he begins with Arthur's rise to power and his imperial wars in Tales I and II, demonstrates in the middle books the great variety of chivalry on which his glory rests and, from the limitations of that chivalry shown in the Grail quest of Book VI, traces the downward turn of Fortune's wheel in the last two tales. Malory's source for his opening tale is the *Suite de Merlin*, a variant redaction and continuation of the Vulgate *Merlin*, which he takes up at the birth of Arthur who is brought up in secret during the anarchy after his father's

death, establishes his right to the throne by drawing his sword from a
stone, compels the recognition of his rebellious barons, and reorganizes
the Round Table, part of Guinevere's dowry, as an order of chivalry
dedicated to peace and justice.

The mingling of the mythic and the mimetic in this account of a
hero-king establishing his identity in domestic strife more reminiscent
of the Wars of the Roses than the Saxon invasion sets the framework of
dynastic romance which is expanded in Book II, derived from the
alliterative *Morte*, where the Roman Wars, coloured by memories of the
Continental campaigns of Henry V, end triumphantly in the crowning
of Arthur as emperor, Modred's treachery being postponed until the end
of the reign. Casual references to Lancelot have been expanded to show
him as the rising star of chivalry who, in Part III – selected episodes from
the French prose *Lancelot* – establishes his pre-eminence in one adventure
after another, championing the distressed, punishing the King's
enemies, triumphing against overwhelming odds, treachery, enchantment, false imprisonment; his aspiring idealism is shown as
effective in controlling the evils which just such competitive
assertiveness as his inflicted on Malory's England, and though his love
for Guinevere is not openly acknowledged he avoids all amorous en-
tanglements and sends defeated adversaries to submit to her. Chivalric
adventure dominates Part IV, invented by Malory or adapted from a lost
English romance, in which Gareth, an unknown youth, fights his way
to renown and recognition as Gawain's brother under the tutelage of
Lancelot, and Part V, selected from the French prose *Tristan*, dominated
by a hero whose ruthless reliance upon force, betrayal of Isolde with
other women, and breach of faith with fellow-knights parody Lancelot's
chivalry, yet make him a valued recruit to the Round Table.

The values observed by that society are embodied in the oath sworn
by Arthur's knights:

> . . . never to do outerage nothir mourthir, and allwayes to fle
> treson, and to gyff mercy unto hym that askith mercy . . . ; and
> allwayes to do ladyes, dameselis, and jantilwomen and wydowes
> socour: strengthe hem in hir ryghtes, and never to enforce them,
> uppon payne of dethe. Also, that no man take no batayles in a
> wrongefull quarell for no love ne for no worldis goodis.
>
> (ll. 38–44)

Yet the more they strive for 'worshyp' (*glory, honour*) the more often
those values are breached by chivalric excesses, the rivalry of Tristan and
Lancelot, the factions forming round Gawain and Lancelot as suspicion
grows of his adultery with the Queen, the trickery by which he is
deceived into sleeping with another woman believing her Guinevere.

Ironically, from that union, a blasphemy against the code of courtly love, is born Galahad who, combining his father's chivalry with a Christ-like purity and spirituality, is worthy to see the Grail clearly and comprehend the mystery of the Eucharist symbolized by it, where most of the Round Table fail abysmally and even Lancelot's knighthood proves fallible and he obtains only a limited vision. Malory's sixth tale, reducing the Vulgate *Queste* to one-third, dramatic rather than allegorical and expository, accepts the ambivalence of earthly chivalry exposed by the absolute values of celestial chivalry but praises it still as the finest human activity, Christianity in action, and criticizes Lancelot less for his adultery than the extent to which love led him to serve wrongful causes in self-confessed breach of his Round Table oath.

His new self-awareness is put to the test in Tales VII and VIII, based on the Vulgate *Mort Artu* and both the alliterative and the stanzaic *Morte* fundamentally restructured and supplemented by Malory. Striving to do God's will, he avoids Guinevere and champions defenceless women; her jealousy drives him from court leaving her defenceless when the incident of the poisoned apple unleashes the malice and enmity long gathering there. Their love endures through the misunderstandings of the Maid of Ascolot incident and the 'Knight of the Cart' episode (imported by Malory, probably from the version of Chrétien's story incorporated in the prose *Lancelot*), but its harmful effects are increasingly apparent: in the fatal passion of the Maid unthinkingly encouraged by Lancelot; in Meleagant's accusations of adultery against the Queen in which a legal quibble and Lancelot's assertion of might as right dubiously avoid exposure of their love; in his ultimate killing, on the Queen's instructions, of a fellow-knight of the Round Table as Meleagant is here. As the shadows gather, Malory strives to maintain chivalric idealism, inventing a great tournament in which the golden age of the Round Table is momentarily revived and an episode in which a wounded stranger who can only be cured by the best knight in the world is healed by Lancelot, 'and ever sir Launcelote wepte, as he had bene a chylde that had bene beatyn!' (p. 668, ll. 35–36) – in relief that he is still what he was or regret for what he might have been?

With the re-emergence of the dynastic theme in Part VIII the tragic clash of twin loyalties, of lover to lady and to her husband as his feudal lord, can no longer be avoided: from the entrapment of the lovers and the public proclamation of their adultery to their mutual separation in penance for the destruction of a noble society events follow the outline of the stanzaic *Morte*, but heightened by the whole history of that society, dynastic and chivalric. Under attack, all tension and suspicion between the lovers vanishes and each thinks only of the other; but in rescuing the Queen from the stake after what is here a legal condemnation Lancelot exemplifies anarchy and kills Gareth, his closest friend and protégé; surrendering Guinevere to Arthur he still blasphemously attests her innocence, citing the fellow-knights he killed in the Queen's chamber as God's testimony to the justness of his cause – 'worchyp' seems to have become unblushing defiance of shame. Increasing realism marks the closing pages at two different levels: the reflection of Malory's England in the division of the Round Table into warring factions, the usurpation of a regent, rebellion against a legitimate monarch, the chaos of a country sliding into civil war; the development of stereotypes embodying ideals into individuals motivated by instinct and emotion and torn by conflicting loyalties. Malory acknowledges in a form approaching the self-consciousness of the modern novel the power of idealism to make men aspire beyond their human limitations and the social reality of an age whose nostalgia was mingled with a sense of tragic loss.[22]

In addition to these highly literary, interpretative versions, fascination with the Arthurian legend as part of the nation's historical consciousness showed itself at many levels of social demand and artistic competence. In *Arthour and Merlin* (two versions: one Kentish, 1250–1300; the other a fifteenth-century abbreviation) the latter dominates a chronicle account of the reign of Uther, the illicit siring of Arthur and his early reign up to his coronation and betrothal to Guinevere, clearly outlined in some ten thousand lines in attractively handled four-stress couplets. The whole history of his reign is crammed into the 642 four-stress lines of *Arthur* (southern, second half of the fourteenth century), whose academic respectability, expressed in a tedious apparatus of names, lists, explanations, earned it insertion in a Latin chronicle. At the opposite pole of literary pretension are two ballads in the Percy Folio MS (*c.* 1650): *King Arthur's Death*, which covers his last battle in 155 lines, and *The Legend of King Arthur* in which he recounts his whole history in 100. The authoritative status of the Vulgate Cycle inspired numerous adaptations, though few English authors had the stamina for more than a single branch. About 1450, Henry Lovelich, a London skinner perhaps inspired by the translators employed in the commercial scriptoria, turned large parts of the *Estoire* and the *Merlin* into limping verse as a heavy-handed compliment to an admired lord mayor, and about the same time the *Merlin* was turned into English prose. One of the earliest poets of the alliterative revival had already mined the *Estoire* for the adventures of *Joseph of Arimathie* (Gloucestershire, *c.* 1340), a saint's life with the scale (709 lines) and much of the appeal of popular romance. The *Lancelot* produced at one extreme a Scottish verse romance, *Lancelot of the Laik* (1482–1500), ineptly disguised as a dream vision incorporating a critique of Arthur's regnal failings probably aimed at James III and, at the other, a ballad, *Sir Lancelot du Lake*, on one of the hero's many duels. There is no way of telling how representative these survivals may be; had Caxton not chosen to print Malory's *Morte Darthur*, the only comprehensive treatment of the dynastic theme would have been unknown but for the survival of a single manuscript not discovered until 1934.

## Chivalric romance and folk romance: *Sir Tristrem* and *Sir Perceval of Galles*

The variety and longevity of Arthurian romance reflects the range of interests inherent in the Matter of Britain. Once the monks of Glastonbury had 'discovered' the grave of Arthur and Guinevere in 1191, conveniently removing a possible focus of Welsh irridentism, English kings from Henry II to Henry VII could exploit the patriotic appeal of the legend and tacitly present themselves as the Hope of the British. The concept of the Round Table as an exemplar of the perfect feudal society, combining individual excellence in all aspects of chivalry with absolute fidelity to the overlord, served them as a model for the chivalric orders by which some of them sought to inspire a degree of idealism and loyalty in their own, increasingly independent, vassals – the Order of the Garter, founded by Edward III *c.* 1348, was originally to have been called 'The Order of the Round Table'. Once Chrétien had established as the proving-ground for chivalry the solitary quest through the wildwood in which adventure exposed the knight in search of his identity to all its inherent elements – the unknown and unexpected, the supernatural or providential – that became the pattern by which the individual might prove his worth to himself and his society.

Such archetypal heroes established their pre-eminence by defeating the various Black Knights who were their anti-types, their lesser companions of the Round Table whose flawed knighthood served as a foil to their own achievements, and eventually each other as the particular knightly quality in which one excelled was superseded by another in the gradual evolution and refinement of the chivalric code: the bold but arrogant Kay unfavourably contrasted with Gawain, perfect exponent of physical knighthood but fatally susceptible to women, and so surpassed in constancy by Lancelot inspired by a unique love, but besotted by passion and so outdone in the Grail quest by Galahad, devoted to spiritual chivalry in the service of divine love. The old-established among them had been Arthur's companions in the age of myth, before the evolution of knightly codes, when they aided youthful folk-heroes in impossible missions for the winning of giants' daughters or tested their own grotesque, superhuman powers in pursuit of self-fulfilment. The courage, quickwittedness, and physical strength which they displayed as popular heroes persisted in their chivalric adventures, giving them wide appeal once the literary trappings of courtly romance were stripped away. Such popularization took place very readily in England where vernacular romance was already at one remove from *roman courtois* and oral traditions of Arthurian heroes survived to become the subject of folk-romance, just as elements of chivalric romance were detached to become part of the literature of the folk.

One stage in the latter process is demonstrated by the only English treatment of the Tristan legend outside Malory, a late thirteenth-century version in closely rhymed stanzas preserved in that popular compilation the Auchinleck MS. *Sir Tristrem* derives from a text of the poem by Thomas (see above, pp. 23–25) which, to judge from the Old Norse version, was complete, and condenses the whole to some 3500 lines. The narrative outline is skeletal, uneven, and frequently inept, erratically summarizing episodes only to repeat them in some detail later, switching abruptly from scene to scene, omitting essential facts and reiterating others irrelevantly. Some of the blemishes in the Auchinleck text may be due to the unfamiliarity of its London scribe with the dialect of the original (perhaps northern) or to the fact that he was working from a version already damaged in transmission. Though the ultimate source was clearly a literary version, there are signs of oral transmission in the incoherence introduced by trying to condense a complicated plot without structural rearrangement, the erratic recollection of details out of context, and the minstrel style which is the most characteristic feature of the redaction.

The long pre-literary evolution of the Tristan legend provided mythic elements which should have allowed a popular redactor to re-create the career of a charismatic folk-hero, ignoring the courtly elaborations of Thomas's version. Initially that seems to be his intention: Tristan's childhood as an orphan, his abduction by sailors, abandonment on the shore of England, and ready reception at Mark's court because of his skill in music read like the story of Horn, incidents whose self-evident significance needs no literary commentary. One-third of the poem has passed before he meets Isolde, the episode of the love-potion is scamped in some eighty lines, little is made of their fugitive life in the wildwood, the debates and soliloquies which, in the original, express the nature of the passion binding them have disappeared. Theirs is no longer a love- story raising moral issues of adultery and feudal loyalty, but the tale of a good knight whose career is blighted by a fatal error, an adventure story robbed of its conventional ending in victory and marriage, slipping all too readily into burlesque. The rapid sequence of incidents might hold the attention of a popular audience, but little of their original meaning survives.

The inadequacy, or rather absence, of interpretation may be due to the form in which the story was transmitted, but the author of the extant version seems too preoccupied by the complexity of his chosen medium to have done much even to remedy the narrative defects. Understandably, since the eleven-line stanza with its exacting rhyme-scheme (*ababababcbc*), makes many other demands on him: the short ninth line, normally linked to the preceding one by syntax and often by alliteration also, rhymes with the last line, while the stanzas are frequently linked by verbal repetition or reuse of the same rhyme. It is a lyric medium well suited to moments of emotion such as the scene where Mark, discovering the lovers asleep in the forest with a naked sword between them, hangs his glove in a branch to shade Isolde's face:

> His gloue he put þerinne
> Þe sonne to were oway;                              *keep*
> Wreþe Mark gan winne.                          *anger, overcome*
> Þan seyd he, 'Wel ay!
> Ʒif þai weren in sinne,
> Nouʒt so þai no lay.
> Lo hou þai liue atvinne!                             *apart*
> Þai no hede nouʒt of swiche play,           *(love) sport*
> Y wis.'
> Þe kniʒtes seyden ay,
> 'For trewe loue it is.'    (ll. 2542–52)[23]

The summarizing effect of the last two lines is effective here, but elsewhere they often introduce an unrelated idea or begin the next narrative movement. The drawbacks of the medium are compounded by the frequency with which the poet falls back upon minstrel commonplaces or meaningless tags to achieve his rhyme. To Walter Scott, its first editor, who accepted at face value the minstrel's apparent confusion of 'Tomas' his author with the Borders poet Thomas of Ercildoun, it had all the rough appeal to be expected of folk romance. But the 'rym dogerel' of *Sir Thopas* is unworthy of such a subject.

What at first sight seems another case of a classic subject degraded by a minstrel medium provides an example of a chivalric romance genuinely reinterpreted as folk romance. *Sir Perceval of Galles*, the only English treatment of the Perceval legend, composed *c.* 1300–40 in the northern dialect, is in tail-rhyme stanzas of sixteen lines on only five rhymes each interlinked, as in some other romances found with it in the Thornton MS, by repetition in the first line of a key word in the last line of the preceding stanza or reduplication of the whole line. The stanza-linking is a literary device found in the more sophisticated Middle English lyrics, used here to modify the disruptive effect of a stanzaic medium on the narrative flow and to emphasize episodic divisions when the linking fails. Its choice may not be so much a reflection of minstrel authorship as of the popular interpretation deliberately put upon the matter of the romance. Chrétien's *Conte du Graal* flattered an age in which chivalry was increasingly associated with nobility by demonstrating that it sprang from nature as well as nurture in the story of Perceval who, well-born but brought up in ignorance of arms following the death of his father and brothers in tournaments, makes one blunder after another when he goes to Arthur's court, naïvely misunderstanding his mother's advice on conduct there. But his inborn instinct shows itself when he kills the Red Knight who has insulted Arthur and he is initiated into chivalry, love, and religion, growing in human, moral, and spiritual capacity until he seems destined to achieve the Grail, though his innocence is the subject of so much comedy and irony as to suggest that, in the incomplete text, his moral development still lags behind his worldly advancement. The English romance differs so radically in plot outline that it has been thought to have no connection with Chrétien's text: the Grail with its implications of spiritual enlightenment has disappeared entirely, so have the intercalated adventures in which Gawain sets chivalric standards to be surpassed by the hero, and many other episodes which contribute to the meaning of the original. Recent research, however, suggests that the English poet knew the *Conte du Graal* as well as its First Continuation and possibly some version of *Peredur*, a Welsh analogue of its ultimate source.[24]

Even that limited part of Chrétien's poem represented by *Sir Perceval of Galles* is abbreviated by half; many new episodes have been added and the whole radically reinterpreted to resemble the archetypal folk-tale of a naïve hero whose very innocence helps him to overcome all adversaries, marry a queen, and acquire a kingdom. The structure has been adapted to the new scale, tightened and simplified to produce a circular movement in which the hero, like Horn and Havelok, ultimately returns to his roots. His story, like theirs, belongs to the drama of family life, and the English poet sharpens awareness of relations between the generations by adding an account of Perceval's parents (ll. 1–160), naming them as he does other anonymous characters in the French, making the mother Arthur's sister so that his patronage of the boy becomes a natural familial act. He also attributes the father's death to the Red Knight, a piece of thematic economy which makes his later killing by Perceval a double act of kinship revenge. At fifteen, so untutored that he does not even know the God his mother invokes, he sets out in his suit of skins to find him and, meeting three of Arthur's knights, asks which one is God (ll. 161–432)! Inspired by them to seek knighthood, he sets off for court, on the way exchanging rings with a sleeping maiden in a wayside hall (ll. 433–80) – the English poet lets her sleep on through his kisses and so avoids offence to her and the vengeful pursuit of her lover. His comic irruption, on horseback, into Arthur's presence is abbreviated by the sudden entry of the Red Knight who snatches a gold cup from the table; Perceval pursues and kills him and, in his innocence, is trying to burn him out of his armour when Gawain arrives and teaches him how to arm himself in it (ll. 481–868). Tidying up that element with a finality which owes nothing to the French, he kills the Red Knight's mother, a witch, and burns her in the same fire as her son.

Seeking adventure, Perceval lodges by the way not with Gornemant, his chivalric tutor in Chrétien's poem, but with his own uncle, another of the Red Knight's victims, and only long enough to encounter a messenger hurrying to court with news that the Lady Lufamour is besieged by the Sultan (ll. 869–1060). The delivery of his message is the only survivor of several scenes in which the court eagerly anticipates Perceval's return (ll. 1061–1124) and Arthur is so uneasy about him that he excuses himself from the rescue mission until he learns that Perceval has already undertaken it. The siege, freed from the love interludes of Chrétien's version in which Perceval lies chastely all night in the lady's arms, becomes a demonstration of his inborn prowess as he repulses the Sultan, a popular substitute for the land-greedy seneschal of the original, and then fights to a draw against Gawain, arriving unrecognized with Arthur's forces. With the innocent ruthlessness of a boy, he beheads the defeated Sultan, is knighted by Arthur, and marries Lufamour (ll. 1125–1808).

The career of a folk-hero might end there, but Chrétien's hero is always haunted by the memory of his mother falling like one lifeless as he left her desolate in the wood where:

> Drynkes of welles, þer þay spryng,
> And gresse etys, withowt lesyng!
> Scho liffede with none othir thyng
>      In þe holtes hare;                                    *woods*
> Till if byfelle appon a day,
> Als he in his bedd lay,
> Till hymselfe gun he say,
>      Syghande full sare,
> 'The laste ȝole-day þat was,
> Wilde ways i chese;
> My modir all manles                                  *unprotected*
>      Leued i thare.'
> Þan righte sone saide he,
> 'Blythe sall i neuer be
> Or i may my modir see
>      And wete how scho fare.'    (ll. 1777–92)[25]

This sudden consciousness of filial duty sweeps away the many remaining episodes of Chrétien's text, with one exception: meeting the damsel with whom he had exchanged rings, he removes the suspicions of her cruel lover by restoring hers and, hearing that his had fallen into the hands of a giant, the Sultan's brother, fights him to the death, whereupon the ring leaps from his treasure-chest into its rightful owner's hands (ll. 1809–2192). Learning that the sight of his ring in the giant's possession had driven his mother insane, he forswears the use of arms and, clad in his boyhood suit of skins, journeys fasting seven days until, pausing to drink at a familiar fountain, he finds his mother there in her madness, restores her, and takes her to his kingdom before departing to die fighting in the Holy Land (ll. 2193–2285).[26]

Perceval returns to his roots as innocent as he left, the well water symbolizing his simplicity; the poet has exaggerated his naïvety throughout, calling him 'þe fole of þe felde', having him ask the name of every new object, while making his very ignorance the source of his success. He does not know that the Red Knight was his father's killer, attacks him for his armour, and hits him in the eye with a dart when he raises his visor in amazement. Even his victories are not wholly his; late in the poem we learn that his borrowed ring had made him invulnerable. Like a latter-day David the holy innocent is made the unconscious instrument of divine justice and the constant parody of conventional romance underscores the contrast with its self-vaunting chivalry. The effect culminates in the final episode when Perceval's search for his mother replaces the Grail quest of the original, where she actually dies when he first abandons her, emphasizing the recurrent theme of the primacy of instinct over instruction, nature over nurture, innocence over experience which runs through his career. The values of the folk romance, self-realization without rejection of the claims of kinship, override those of the chivalric code parodied in pursuit of that end.[27]

## Gawain romances: *Ywain and Gawain*

No member of the Round Table appealed more strongly to the English imagination than Sir Gawain, perhaps because he could be most readily identified with the archetypal folk-hero seeking self-knowledge through adventure. His mythic identity in Celtic tradition remains undefined though it seems to have left him with some of the characteristics of a sun-god. By the time he appears in Geoffrey of Monmouth's *Historia* he is already established as Arthur's sister's son, councillor and chief lieutenant in war, renowned for his military prowess. From Chrétien onwards no Arthurian romance is complete without him as the model of chivalry, courtesy, and skill in arms, against whom younger knights measure themselves in combat or in parallel quests. But increasingly his role as the exemplary foil robs him of personal development, they rather than he achieve the quest from which he is too readily distracted by incidental, if socially valid, missions, and they defeat him despite his mysterious solar might. Their prowess is often inspired by love of which Gawain knows nothing; women are drawn to his fame, but his relations with them are invariably superficial, physical, and fleeting. Slowly his static chivalry and the shallow *courtoisie* with which he loves and leaves undermines his reputation and French poets expose him to irony, treat him as a comic foil, reveal his spiritual inadequacy in the Grail quest, and hint that he stoops to treachery and murder.[28]

English poets reject the idea of a degenerate Gawain; with them he remains the loyal lieutenant of dynastic romance, the embodiment of the basic knightly virtues in accounts of his own chivalric adventures, but also as the most prominent protagonist in a group of folk romances in which Arthur and his companions are subjected to the kind of test by which popular heroes establish their identity. In *The Avowynge of King Arthur*, seventy-two sixteen-line stanzas written in the North *c.* 1425 tell how Gawain surpasses his companions in fulfilling the vows they had made to requite the boasts of their demonic host, King Cornwall, so allowing Arthur to behead him. Another Percy Folio fragment, *The Turke and Gowin*, a tail-rhyme romance originally of some six hundred lines, written in the North or the north-west Midlands *c.* 1500, tells how the Turk challenges the Round Table to an exchange of buffets, Gawain courteously accepts and, riding north for the return blow, succeeds in a contest of strength against the giant retainers of the King of Man by the help of the Turk whom he then beheads at his request, so releasing the knight Sir Gromer from his enchanted form. Two versions of *The Carle off Carlile* (Porkington MS: Shropshire, *c.* 1400; Percy Folio: Lancashire, early sixteenth century) represent variants of an original in which the giant Carl tests Arthur and his companions while they are his guests; only Gawain succeeds, obeying his commands to hurl a spear at his head and lie beside his wife, beheads his host, and so transforms him into a knight who joins the Round Table. There are analogues in French literature to many of the recurrent motifs here – tests imposed by a challenger, the fulfilment of vows or boasts, disenchantment by beheading; but they also have Celtic parallels suggesting that the authors drew upon common folk-motifs which, their localization hints, may have derived from Galloway, the bridge to Gaelic Scotland known in the twelfth century as 'the Kingdom of Gawain'. Their material had already been demythologized, the tests imposed during a visit to some

Otherworld being rationalized as the commands of an Imperious Host exacting obedience from his guests, giving them a rather half-hearted gloss as demonstrations of knightly qualities.

The process is exemplified in the way in which the motif of the Loathly Lady Transformed, widespread in European folkfore, has been associated with the Round Table. In *The Weddynge of Sir Gawen and Dame Ragnell*, a short tail-rhyme romance composed in the east Midlands *c.* 1450, and *The Marriage of Sir Gawaine*, a fragmentary ballad version from the Percy Folio, Arthur is threatened with death by Sir Gromer Somer Joure unless he can tell what it is that women love most; Gawain, by promising to marry the hideous Dame Ragnell, learns from her that they desire sovereignty above all and, in the marriage bed, reluctantly kisses her and finds that he has freed a beautiful young woman from the enchantment of a wicked stepmother. The story may be rooted in an Irish legend of a hero whose fitness for the kingship is tested by his willingness to kiss a faery woman in the form of a hag. Chaucer, in his 'Wife of Bath's Tale', used a version in which the roles of Arthur and Gawain were united in a young knight of the Round Table under sentence for the rape of a peasant girl and made it the vehicle, in the hag's pillow lecture to her unhappy bridegroom, for a noble re-statement of the nature of chivalry as gentle deeds rather than gentle birth. *The Weddynge*, in which the hag's disenchantment depends upon her marriage to the best man in England, celebrates Gawain's loyalty to Arthur as the other folk romances do those aspects of his reputation which made him a popular as well as a chivalric hero.[29]

Though he is not its hero, his reputation is vital to the theme of *Ywain and Gawain*, written in the North between 1300 and 1350, a radical abbreviation of one of Chrétien's romances in the same four-stress couplets as the original. Chrétien's *Yvain* follows the general pattern of his romances in narrating the heroic feats undertaken by one of Arthur's knights to redeem a breach of the courtly code: having, against all probability, won the love of Laudine whose husband he has killed, Yvain subsequently becomes so preoccupied in adventurous questing that he outstays the period set by her, runs mad on realizing his fault, then undertakes the defence of a series of distressed damsels to regain his lady's trust and love. As always, Chrétien is as much concerned with meaning as with matter and his narrative is interspersed with lengthy analyses of sentiment, rhetorical expositions of courtly values undercut by pervasive irony and humour, and a whole dialectic of thematic and verbal oppositions which direct the reader's response to events.

It is principally this extra-narrative material which has disappeared in the reduction of the 6800 lines of the original to some 4000. After the opening Whitsun feast, the lords and ladies of the Round Table discuss the pains and joys of love and lament its current decline (ll. 18–28); their English counterparts speak 'Of dedes of armes and of veneri (*hunting*)' and how honour may be won by doughtiness (ll. 25–36). When the hero first sees his lady, Chrétien gives some two hundred and forty lines to rhetorical analysis of his feelings in Ovidian terms and to the moral propriety of such feelings towards a woman whose husband he has just killed (ll. 1302–1541); the English poet states the dilemma in one line, 'His hert sho has þat es his fa', and after some forty summarizing the practical situation (ll. 869–908) concludes: 'He sayd he sold have hir to wive,/Or els he sold lose his lyve'.[30] Chrétien's heroine, with dubious logic, argues in an imaginary dialogue with her lover that since he acted in self-defence there can be no guilt in loving him (ll. 1760–75), ironically undermining her initial rejection of him when the dialogue actually takes place (ll. 1995–2004); the English poet ignores the dialectic in both places, bluntly recognizing the realities of widowhood: '". . . wemen may maintene no stowre (*combat*),/Þai most nedes have a governowre"' (ll. 1221–22). He also omits or greatly reduces descriptions of dress, ceremonial, combat, and much of the conversational fencing in which the original conveys the conflict between characters.

What survives is Chrétien's narrative, structurally unaltered but tightened and quickened by omission of minor incidents, helpfully paragraphed and recounted in a clear, swift-moving style unencumbered by verbiage. Where Chrétien's love of fantasy created complexities which offended his instinct for story-telling, the redactor has resolved them with a free hand. Chrétien, having trapped Yvain between inner and outer portcullises of Laudine's castle, improbably converts the place into a salon in which, with the aid of a ring of invisibility, he lies at ease while her retainers search for her husband's killer; the English poet has the helpful damsel who gave him the ring lead Ywain through a doorway into her own room, a more suitable place for him to observe the widow's distress – though it rules out the original confrontation with the funeral cortège of his victim, whose wounds bleed afresh in his invisible presence. Like the occasional identification of locations in the fantasy realm of the original with the real geography of Britain and comments on legal details in relation to contemporary English law, everything in the redaction is designed for clarity and concreteness and the ready comprehension by less courtly readers of a story whose manners and values were over one hundred and fifty years old.

The same concern for comprehension marks its thematic conduct. Chrétien constantly plays with his audience, praising Arthur's court in idealistic terms before showing it rent by dissension, seeming to resolve the conflicting claims of love and chivalry but in a narrative whose circular structure questions whether his characters really advance in understanding, stimulating judgement of the values they profess. The English poet rejects such ambivalence, establishing a single standard of values for both love and chivalry in his initial praise of Arthur's court:

Þai tald of more trewth þam bitwene
Þan now omang men here es sene,
For trowth and luf es al bylaft;                    *abandoned*
Men uses now anoþer craft.
With worde men makes it trew and stabil,
Bot in þaire faith es noght bot fabil;              *falsehood*
With þe mowth men makes it hale,                    *sure*
Bot trew trowth es nane in þe tale.   (ll. 33–40)

Ywain's early adventures ironically confirm this cynical judgement of
the real world rather than the values of the Arthurian golden age. He
rushes into the first, vowing to redeem the honour of his cousin who has
previously failed in it, but his real anxiety is to forestall his Round Table
companions in winning the glory. Having challenged Salados who, by
unexplained custom, guards a spring in the forest, he pursues him to his
castle, mortally wounded, with a ruthlessness which excites Chrétien's
irony but which draws no comment from the English poet. Not until,
helped by the persuasive arguments of the damsel Lunet, he has won the
widow Alundyne, a union which Chrétien characteristically implies
strengthens rather than replaces the mutual fidelity of courtly love, does
the redactor raise the issue of Ywain's *trowth*. As her new champion, he
answers the challenge when Arthur's court comes to the spring, defeats
the braggart Kay, but is persuaded by Gawain '"Þat knyght es nothing
to set by (*be esteemed*),/Þat leves al his chevalry"' (ll. 1457–58). When
chivalric adventure makes him outstay the period agreed by his wife,
Lunet denounces him in her name before the court as '"Traytur untrew
and trowthles"' (l. 1626), he loses his reason and sinks to the level of a
beast. Adherence to his sworn *trowth* initially brought him honour, love,
and a rich estate; but that such self-absorbed chivalry as Gawain's could
make him forget his pledged word to his mistress and liege lady suggests
how superficial has been his understanding of *trowth* in love and honour.

Rescued by a damsel whose magic ointment restores his sanity –
another of the compassionate women who blindly put their trust in him
– he shows a new understanding of duty and fidelity in a sequence of
adventures which demand increasing self-sacrifice and devotion to the
service of others. In rescuing the owner of the ointment from a wicked
earl he pursues her oppressor to his castle as he had done Salados, but
shows him mercy on promise of reparation to the injured lady. He next
saves a lion from a dragon, rescuing good from evil and gaining a
faithful companion whose strength proverbially was never used to harm
the humble. As if to identify his new chivalry with such service, Ywain
takes a new name as the Knight of the Lion and begins to repay old debts
by defending Lunet against a charge of treason in which she has been
failed by her sworn champion Gawain, absent in search of the Queen,

abducted yet again! Before the trial he undertakes another of Gawain's obligations, defending his niece from a giant whose stubborn resistance so delays him that he arrives only just in time to defeat Lunet's accuser and snatch her from the stake. Later he champions the younger of two sisters unjustly deprived of her inheritance by the elder whom Gawain champions; they fight to a standstill before recognizing each other, each confesses defeat to spare the other's honour and the sisters' case is referred to Arthur's arbitration. There is no apparent intention to denigrate Gawain's chivalry, but rather to extend and harmonize the lesson Ywain is learning from his own mistakes: that a verbal pledge may be made too lightly or in an unjust cause, but *trowth* lies in the service of others not self-glory. Often against Alundyne's wishes, Lunet strives to serve her real interests at her own risk; the lion, true to his nature, disobeys his master's commands and aids him in battle whenever he is faced with inhuman odds – *trowth* as justice overrides verbal *trowth*. In his new-learnt humility Ywain does not hope for Alundyne's forgiveness, yet she needs a champion to defend the spring; Lunet works upon her with the high repute of the Knight of the Lion and the lovers are reunited: 'Ful lely lufed he ever hys whyfe/And sho him als hyr owin life' (ll. 4011–12).[31]

## Golagrus and Gawain

English poets attracted to Gawain as representative of the fundamental knightly virtues largely exempt him from their critique of chivalry as a practical code. In *The Awntyrs Off Arthure*, probably written in the North-west *c.* 1400–30 and popular enough to have survived in four manuscripts, the ghost of Guinevere's mother rises from the Tarn Wadling near Carlisle to warn her daughter of the moral failings which will bring down the Round Table before Gawain demonstrates by defeating a challenger to right an injustice and win his submission to Arthur that knighthood is still socially valid. *Golagrus and Gawain*, composed in Middle Scots *c.* 1500 and extant only in an early print, shares with the *Awntyrs* a complex thirteen-line stanza combining alliteration with a close rhyme-scheme on four rhymes only. Its source has been identified in an episode of the First Continuation of Chrétien's *Perceval*, the Livre du Chastel Orguelleus, concerning a mission of the Round Table to rescue a member long imprisoned in the castle, during which Gawain's courtesy secures hospitality for them all in the house of Yder le Bel, his reconciliation to an old enemy, Bran de Lis, gains his support in the seige, and his own magnanimity in feigning defeat by the Riche Soudoier, Lord of Chastel Orguelleus, when he has actually won the encounter between them, brings his ultimate surrender to Arthur. It seems merely a conventional chapter in the hagiology of Gawain, but radical rehandling by the Scottish redactor makes it into a sincere demonstration of the basic chivalric virtues.[32]

His version retains the episodic structure of the original, but in some 1360 lines covers only two of them at very unequal length. The Yder le Bel episode (ll. 40–221), in which Kay's arrogant abuse of hospitality earns him a beating while Gawain's gentler approach brings a generous response from an equally courteous host, achieves its original effect with brevity. Omission of the Bran de Lis episode, unfinished business from an earlier part of the *Perceval* involving Gawain's seduction of Bran's sister, avoids that stain upon his reputation. The siege, narrated at length (ll. 248–1256), becomes the centre of interest, focused about Gawain's encounter with the Soudoier, here renamed Sir Golagrus, whose refusal to abandon his liberty on Arthur's imperious demand for allegiance initiates the action. During it representatives of the two parties meet in engagements which increase in violence and the numbers involved from the formality of judicial combat to the chaos of the mêlée with mounting fatalities on both sides. In the original the crescendo is interrupted by an interval for hunting during which Gawain comes upon an unknown knight lying in a swoon under a tree and later meets a distressed lady who, arriving late for a rendezvous with her lover, had found him apparently dead from grief and, reassured by Gawain, rushes off to join him. When, in the renewed fighting, Gawain encounters and overthrows Golagrus, he cannot refuse to surrender on the grounds given by his French counterpart, that shame would kill his *amie* watching from the walls. Golagrus prefers death to the dishonour which surrender would bring on his ancestors who had been no man's vassals, and Gawain magnanimously spares him public disgrace by pretending defeat and accompanying him to the castle until he can ensure himself of the continued loyalty of his followers once they learn the truth.

Excision of an admittedly somewhat artificial love-episode might seem no more than a provincial poet's distaste for courtly sentiment if it were not for the enormous pains taken by him to provide a substitute motivation appropriate to that aspect of the original which apparently attracted him. He has replaced a rather conventional conflict between the codes of chivalry and courtly love with a clash of personalities in which Gawain's self-sacrifice is based on respect for his opponent's honour and his personal estimate of the other's integrity and worth. His own reputation is restated in the familiar contrast with Kay in the Yder incident and the effect seems about to be repeated when Kay, who in the French had been humiliated in combat, rushes into the field just before

Gawain meets Golagrus – but here he wins his bout and leads his adversary to Arthur in submission (ll. 836–83). The alteration was presumably intended to increase the pressure upon Gawain when he feigns defeat by Golagrus knowing that, in the eyes of his companions, he will appear to have failed where Kay, his familiar foil, has just succeeded. His self-abnegation brings eventual praise from his opponent when he confesses the truth to his followers (ll. 1196–1219) and later before Gawain's Round Table companions (ll. 1315–23).

In making a worthy opponent out of the unknown Golagrus the redactor has gone to much greater lengths, transforming Bran de Lis as the original commentator on the usages of Chastel Orguelleus into Sir Spynagros an ardent partisan of its defender, interpreting his motives, describing his preparation for resistance – details almost wholly invented by the poet – and praising him openly before the Round Table. He accompanies Gawain on a mission to demand the surrender of the castle (ll. 320–457), another addition, warning him to approach Golagrus with the greatest respect, while he himself demonstrates his nature by the ceremonious and inflexible firmness with which he rejects the demand. Just before Golagrus enters the fight, Spynagros praises his courage and warns Gawain not to meet him (ll. 795–833) – yet another addition, while the original description of Gawain's armour as the outward expression of his prowess is replaced by the arming of his opponent (ll. 884–902). In the encounter Golagrus justifies his chivalric reputation by his stout resistance and the calmness with which he faces death rather than surrender in dishonour. Gawain surpasses him in magnanimity and their combat resembles one of those encounters in which two Round Table knights incognito battle to a standstill before recognizing each other. In such cases their names alone are the warrant of their chivalric standing; Golagrus owes both name and reputation to the Scottish poet who gave him the noble diction in which he rejects the embassy from Arthur (ll. 428–53), makes his apologia to his followers (ll. 1161–1245), and expounds his family honour:

> 'Wes I neuer yit defoullit, nor fylit in fame,     *disgraced, defiled*
> Nor nane of my eldaris, that euer I hard nevin;     *mention*
> Bot ilk berne has bene vnbundin with blame,     *man, free from*
> Ringand in rialte, and reullit thame self evin.     *ruling, royal power*
> Sall neuer sege vndir son se me with schame,     *man*
> Na luke on my lekame with light nor with levin,     *person, brightness*
> Na nane of the nynt degre haue noy of my name,
> I swere be suthfast God, that settis all on sevin!'
>         *true, ordains, in seven (days)*
>         (ll. 1038–45)[33]

The effective exploitation of this complex medium, detailing the violence of combat, elaborating the richness of feasts and ceremonies, constantly conveying the emotional import of the action in dramatic speech, places this among the chivalric romances which, even at such a late date, can express high idealism so emphatically without a trace of irony. The choice of medium was clearly primary; the independence which its complexity compels has been exploited to shift the balance in favour of the mimetic element, not at the level of surface realism but in fundamentals, substituting emotion for convention, human concerns for social forms, personal integrity for chivalric codes.[34]

## Sir Gawain and the Green Knight

As if to demonstrate that Gawain's ambivalent reputation made him acceptable to widely differing English audiences, it was precisely those episodes of the Livre du Chastel Orguelleus rejected by the author of Golagrus and Gawain as dishonourable, his seduction of the Damoisele de Lis and the inconclusive combat with her brother Bran, which a southern rhymster of the late fifteenth century made the subject of the short tail-rhyme romance The Jeaste of Syr Gawayne, little more than a bar-room anecdote. The illegitimate fruit of that affair, Gingelein, became the hero of Libeaus Desconus (southern, c. 1325), a tail-rhyme version of a widespread variant of the Perceval motif in which he turns up at Arthur's court ignorant even of his own name, demonstrates in the midst of much mockery that he has his father's prowess, wins a place at the Round Table, becomes the champion of distressed ladies, and marries one whom he has disenchanted from her serpent form – a chivalric gloss on the characteristic career of a folk-hero and, to judge from the six surviving manuscripts, highly popular with English audiences.

How closely folk romance coexisted with its chivalric counterpart is illustrated by The Grene Knight (south Midlands, c. 1500) which reduces to some five hundred lines in tail-rhyme stanzas the bare bones of the plot without the art of Sir Gawain and the Green Knight (north-west Midlands, late fourteenth century), perhaps the most sophisticated of all medieval romances, surpassing even Chrétien's works in complexity and concentration. The minstrel instinct of the adapter for what would interest a popular audience shows the plot to be compounded of the same motifs as other folk romances of which Gawain is the hero: a challenge to a beheading contest combined with a test to respond without discourtesy to the temptations of the wife of his wayside host. French literature provides comparatively close analogues to the Challenge, more remote parallels to the Temptation, nothing to correspond to the Exchange of Winnings motif which interlinks them thematically, making Gawain's survival of the beheading test dependent upon his behaviour under the lady's temptation. But close dependence upon a French original seems unlikely, less because of the structural complexity than the subtle verbal control on which the operation and meaning of the poem depend from line to line. It exploits a demanding variation of the alliterative medium, unrhymed long lines grouped in paragraphs of varying length punctuated, often at a narrative crisis, by a single-stress line rhyming with the quatrain which ends the *laisse*. Combining the ease of blank verse narration with the periodic pat summation of tail-rhyme, the medium, like so much else in *Sir Gawain*, combines traditional elements in a way unique to the poet.

Whoever the poet was – perhaps the domestic chaplain of some noble household – he was widely read, not least in French romance, and plays with its conventions with an ease and wit which require the co-operation of an equally informed audience for full appreciation, though even at the simplest level his narrative skill makes it a well-told tale. By repeatedly arousing familiar expectations only to disappoint them in the unexpected outcome, he keeps the reader constantly alert, unable to make any confident assumption from past experience, uncertain even whether he is dealing with myth or reality. The opening lines, for example, suggest chronicle by evoking the Trojan ancestry of Western chivalry; but ambivalently, reminding readers that the archetypal ancester Aeneas was famed for the trickery by which he saved Polyxena from the Greeks but also notorious for his treason in betraying Troy to them (ll. 1–12). The focus narrows to the dynastic romance of Geoffrey and Layamon whose Britain is equally ambivalently characterized as a place of 'blysse and blunder' (ll. 13–24), then again to announce the perennial theme of chivalric romance: 'an outtrage (*extraordinary*) awenture of Arthurez wonderez' (l. 29).[35] The word 'adventure' and variants which echo elements in its complex of meanings – chance, accident, risk, exploit, quest, miracle, a tale of adventures – cluster in the opening of the poem and will be echoed later: 'selly' (*marvel*), 'wonder', 'meruayle'. But the poet insists that this is to be 'an aunter in erde' (*an actual adventure*), a 'selly in siȝt' (*a manifest marvel*), evoking the twin components of the romance mode, fantasy, and reality.

The heightened reality of chivalric romance colours what seems at last the true beginning of the poem, a description of Arthur's court at its Christmas feasting in Camelot (ll. 37–129), the first of many elaborate set pieces in which a thorough mastery of rhetorical technique and deployment of the richest vocabulary of any alliterative poet in subtle variations of his emphatic medium serve any purpose to which the poet applies them with vivid brilliance. Here it is ceremonious assertion that 'Wyth all þe wele of þe worlde þay woned (*dwelt*) þer samen (*together*)' (l. 50), joining in games of love and war, jousting and kissing for forfeits, celebrating their corporate unity under Christ. But Arthur, by ancient custom, will not eat until he has heard 'Of sum auenturus þyng an vncouþe (*strange*) tale' (l. 93) or received a challenge to combat. The expectation of adventure brings adventure, not as romantic tale but as challenging reality, when there rides into the hall an 'aghlich mayster' (*fearsome figure*) described in an elaborate rhetorical portrait (ll. 136–220) as a fusion of the Knight Challenger of romance and the Wild Man of folk-tale, handsome, hairy, and green as the horse he rides, his ominous ambivalence symbolized by the massive axe in one hand and the holly bough, sign of peace, in the other. His challenge is equally ambivalent (ll. 250–300): an exchange of blows with the monstrous axe, a deadly duel yet he speaks of it as a game fit for the 'berdles chylder' of the Round Table. They sit in stunned silence while he mocks the renowned chivalry of Arthur's house – '"Where is now your sourquydrye (*pride*) and your conquestes?"' (l. 311) – until the King, famed for his 'ʒonge blod and his brayn wylde', seizes the axe to strike the first blow. At which point Gawain rises and with punctilious courtesy begs that, since his life would be the least loss to the Round Table, he might undertake the challenge (ll. 339–61). The court takes counsel and agrees 'To ryd (*exempt*) þe kyng wyth croun,/And gif Gawan þe game' (ll. 364–65).

A threat to the crown and the stability of the kingdom has been avoided, but the best of Arthur's followers is committed to a game of pluck-buffet whose terms, when repeated by the Green Knight, now have the formality of a legal contract (ll. 375–416). Undaunted, he severs the green head at a blow; but the knight picks it up, the eyes open and the mouth warns Gawain to be at the Green Chapel a year hence for the return blow (ll. 417–61). As he rides from the hall, Arthur who 'at hert hade wonder' laughingly dismisses the affair as a theatrical entertainment, 'a selly', fit sport for Christmas, and the laughter and feasting is renewed (ll. 462–86). Yet he had recognized the Green Knight at his entrance as an 'auenture' (l. 250) fulfilling the terms of his Christmas custom; is this attempt to dismiss him as fantasy self-deception or politic pretence? Gawain is silent; but the poet suggests what may be in his mind, warning him not to shrink from pursuing the adventure because of its danger.

Readers who have seen nothing in this first episode but familiar romance conventions are rudely challenged at the opening of the second (ll. 491–99) by a passage of incoherent syntax and ambivalent vocabulary suggesting that Arthur's yearning for adventure invoked the apparition of the Green Knight, that his Christmas game betokens ill for the year ahead, that the idle court is now concerned with serious business whose outcome may be grave; a year quickly passes and the beginning is seldom like the end. The year then passes in a lyrical evocation of growth and decay in nature (ll. 500–35) where death is a prelude to rebirth while the life of man is linear and his end very different from his beginning. On All Saints' Day the court feasts Gawain's departure, renewing the confident mood which opened the poem, surrounding him with ceremony as he dons the rich armour which symbolizes his chivalric status, emblazoned on shield and surcoat with the 'pure pentaungel', a perfect figure, emblem of his *trawþe*, absolute integrity in faith, deeds, and chivalric virtues (ll. 536–665). But the ceremonial mood is undermined by consciousness that no armour, perhaps no chivalric virtue, is proof against an undefended blow from the Green Knight's axe, by muttered regrets that Gawain should be beheaded by an 'aluisch mon' because of excessive pride, the court recognizing now the nature of the challenger yet blaming Arthur's pride for their corporate decision, and by the stiff-lipped reticence with which he bids farewell – 'He wende (*thought*) for euermore' (l. 669).

On his journey Gawain crosses and recrosses the borders of romance and reality (ll. 691–762), from Arthur's kingdom of Logres, through the wilds of north Wales and the Wirral into 'contrayez straunge' where he encounters all the perils of knight errantry:

> Sumwhyle wyth wormez he werrez, and with wolues als,     *dragons*
> Sumwhyle wyth wodwos, þat woned in þe knarrez,     *forest trolls,*
>      *dwelt, rocks*
> Boþe wyth bullez and berez, and borez oþerquyle,     *at times*
> And etaynez, þat hym anelede of þe heȝe felle;     *ogres, pursued*
>                         (ll. 720–24)

The real enemy is not the creatures of romance but the cruel winter of the North-west where the poem was written, where 'Ner slayn wyth þe slete he sleped in his yrnes/Mo nyȝtez þen innoghe in naked rokkez' (ll. 729–30), alone with his God, praying for a refuge where he might keep Christmas. As he crosses himself, it appears, a fairy-tale castle which 'schemered and schon þurȝ þe schyre (*lovely*) okez' (l. 772), an ambivalent place solid as a fortress yet insubstantial as the paper castles covering the dishes at a feast, another Camelot in the wilderness. It proves a place of courtesy and Christian observance ruled by a huge knight with a broad, beaver-hued beard, whose lovely wife is chaperoned by a hideous, wrinkled hag, youth ambiguously coupled with age (ll. 763–969). And it too is a place of games: the lord, Bertilak, proposes an equal exchange of what each gains over the next three days, he in the hunting field, Gawain at rest in the castle; courtesy requires obedience to his host and, as if unconscious that he is already bound by a similar compact, Gawain agrees (ll. 970–1125).

The third section follows an elaborate self-contained pattern which seems to isolate it from the rest of the action and Castle Hautdesert from the outside world. Each day, while the lord goes hunting, Gawain is visited in his bedroom by the lady who presses her attentions upon him; by exerting all his social skills he avoids offence either to her or her husband, to whom each evening he pays over the kisses she has pressed on him, receiving in return the spoils of the chase. The atmosphere throughout uneasily mingles comedy and menace. There is comedy in the spectacle of Gawain trapped naked in bed by his hostess whose conversation mingles sexual invitation with courtly love conventions as, reversing the usual roles, she declares herself his servant, reminds him of his reputation as the universal lover, and doubts his very identity as he struggles to maintain his *trawþe* and turn the affair into a game, a contest in 'luf-talkyng'; comedy too in the passivity with which he submits to her kisses and the jokes made about their value and their source when he passes them on to her husband. But it is undercut by uncertainty as to the lady's purpose, the variety of roles which tradition supplies for such wayside hostesses – the seductress bent on the moral entrapment of good knights, the wife of the Imperious Host who will resent rejection of his sexual hospitality – the implied association between the game of love in which she harries Gawain and the violence of her husband's hunting, the beheading, drawing, and quartering of the prey foreshadowing a traitor's death for Gawain should he break *trawþe* with his host, the vague resemblance to the Green Knight in Bertilak's size, hairiness, and animal vitality, the shadow of the old crone hovering in the background.

Whatever the nature of the game being played, Gawain maintains his integrity by skilful adherence to the pentangle virtues until, as the lady retires defeated on the third day, she offers him her green girdle, telling him that it will protect the wearer from violent death (ll. 1797–1869). Death has never been far from Gawain's mind, troubling his sleep with thoughts of what awaits him at the Green Chapel; he accepts the girdle, promising to conceal it from her husband and, in preparation for his departure, goes to confession and is absolved of all sins 'As domezday schulde haf ben diȝt (*due*) on þe morn' (l. 1884). Gawain has hitherto avoided the pattern of behaviour suggested for him by the beasts who are his counterparts in the hunting, the timid panic of the deer in the face of the lady's first assault, the brute force of the boar suggested by her virtual invitation to rape on the second day. Now (ll. 1893–1923), however, the prey is no longer noble game but vermin, a wily, thievish fox who, just when he thinks he has thrown off his pursuers, finds the lord in his path, shrinks back from his sword to fall into the mouths of the hounds and is instantly flayed – the punishment reserved for the worst forms of treason, including seduction of the wife of the seigneur, suggesting Gawain's fate should Bertilak so interpret his possession of the girdle given him as a 'drury' (*love-token*). But at that evening's exchange the girdle is not produced and Bertilak receives the kisses with his usual jokes on their value, the legal terminology of the exchange compact invaded by the language of commerce, a reminder that Gawain's 'prys' (*worth*) has been under test at Hautdesert.

New Year's Day, Gawain's doomsday, dawns wild and stormy, the cold reality of nature breaking in upon the seeming security of Hautdesert as the fourth section, in the linear structure of quest, breaks the hermetic Chinese-box structure of the third. The fourth parallels the second with the arming of the hero, his ceremonious departure, and moral testing in a wintry landscape on his way to an unknown destination and seemingly certain fate (ll. 1998–2159). But ironies are rife: in arming himself Gawain winds over his emblazoned surcoat the green girdle, which the poet persists in calling a 'luf-lace', juxtaposing the pentangle with a talisman which now seems a symbol of self-love; when his guide urges him to avoid an encounter with the Green Knight, offering to conceal his flight, he calmly rejects the temptation, declaring: "'To Goddez wylle I am full bayn (*obedient*),/And to hym I haf me tone (*committed*)'" (ll. 2158–59). What is the source of his confidence: *trawþe* or talisman, moral blindness to the means by which he obtained the 'luf-lace', or spiritual boldness rejecting any need for confession or divine grace? He receives a rude shock from the Green Chapel, a bubble of rock which seems to him 'a chapel of meschaunce' where the Devil has lured him to his destruction (ll. 2160–2212). But when the Green Knight appears he calmly bares his neck to the axe, flinching at the first feint, patiently suffering the mockery which precedes the second, and at the third receiving only a scratch from a glancing blow (ll. 2213–2314). As a drop of his blood gleams on the snow, joy leaps in his heart; challenge resolutely faced has proved a figment in the best manner of romance.

But the blow is still to fall. It comes in the Green Knight's explanation (ll. 2331–68) that the three feints related to the triple test of the Exchange of Winnings compact and the trifling wound was punishment for retaining the girdle, a failure in *trawþe* for "'Trwe mon trwe restore'" (l. 2354). Shame and self-disgust sweep away all Gawain's courtesy as, accusing himself of cowardice, covetousness, 'trecherye and vntrawþe', he throws the girdle at its owner's feet, recognizing in Bertilak, lord of misrule playing a festive game, the Green Knight, a force of nature challenging chivalric society to a life-and-death contest (ll. 2369–84). The uncourteous reaction and the terms of self-accusation seems excessive if all that is involved is petty theft; they are followed by a formal confession to which Bertilak jocularly responds with the formulae of absolution (ll. 2385–94). The confessional language suggests a sudden shattering realization on Gawain's part that his intention to retain the girdle, however unconsciously formed at the moment of acceptance, invalidated his confession at Hautdesert, that his failure to recognize his sin and claim the saving grace of the sacrament was a breach of *trawþe* with God, an act of spiritual treason associating him with the fox not only as sneak-thief but as the type of covetousness, pride, and hypocrisy. Sudden awareness of the spiritual peril into which he has fallen by his instinctive act of self-preservation in taking the 'luf-lace' inspires an equally instinctive impulse to confess, but he is not yet in a spiritual state to accept absolution. Bertilak's revelation that the Challenge had been contrived by the crone at Hautdesert, Morgan le Fay, to test the presumption of the Round Table and he himself planned the Temptation brings only a bitter outburst against the deceptive wiles of women and a refusal to be reconciled. Bertilak readily forgives a human failing – '"3e lufed your lyf; þe lasse I yow blame"' (l. 2368) and praises Gawain as the best of knights, a pearl above dried peas in worth. But the embittered idealist whose aim had been absolute rather than relative perfection is not yet ready for self-forgiveness.

He returns to Camelot like a penitent wearing the girdle slung baldric-wise across the pentangle on his chest as a bend sinister modifying his claim to *trawþe*, and in formal public confession before the Round Table proclaims: '"Þis is þe token of vntrawþe þat I am tan (*detected*) inne"' (l. 2509). He will wear it as long as he lives, 'for one may conceal one's offence, but cannot undo it, for once it has become fixed it will never leave one' (ll. 2511–12). The rejection of any remedy for sin suggests despair, itself a mortal sin; but his restitution of the stolen girdle, the penitential wound in his neck, the repeated impulse to confess promise eventual reconciliation to God. The gravity of such a possibility reflects the bitter realization of an idealist professing an absolute code that adventures do not come singly, that men cannot always distinguish game and earnest, that failure may result from a momentary impulse as instinctive as a natural reflex. The finality of his self-condemnation is immediately contrasted with the reaction of the Round Table whose members greet his confession with laughter and agree to wear the green lace as a badge of honour. Their response may seem mature acceptance of human limitations or, in the light of their formal agreement to the Challenge and subsequent criticism of Arthur for its outcome, super-ficial and escapist. The issue has divided the critics and the poet provides no resolution, inviting instead a rereading or reconsideration of all that has passed, gliding back through history to echo the Trojan opening, challenging experienced readers of romance – whose moral judgement has been as much under test as that of the hero – to detect the moment and the cause of his failure. For the first time he places the poem explicitly in the category of romance (ll. 2521–26), recalling his initial reminder of the ambivalence of adventure, suggesting that in a world whose history is a record of 'blysse and blunder' the ultimate reality is human fallibility against which aspiring idealism must appear profoundly comic. Then, beyond the hermetic structure of historical experience, he offers, under the guise of the tritest of terminal conventions in minstrel romance, an escape from the inevitable failure of human idealism: 'Now þat bere þe croun of þorne,/He bryng vus to his blysse! AMEN' (ll. 2529–30).[36]

# Notes

1. Though Geoffrey's claim to a single unified source in 'a very old book in the British language' is not generally credited, it seems increasingly likely that, in addition to modelling invented episodes on incidents in ancient history, he had written sources for British history lost to us. On such a source for Arthur's campaign in France see Geoffrey Ashe, '"A Certain very Ancient Book": Traces of an Arthurian Source in Geoffrey of Monmouth's *History*', *Speculum*, 56 (1981), 301–23.

2. See Stephen Knight, *Arthurian Literature and Society* (London, 1983), pp. 38–67.

3. The date and incidental sources of the *Brut* remain undetermined. Bede may have supplied a single incident and correct spellings of Anglo-Saxon names; additional details of faery intervention in Arthur's career suggest Celtic origins, but in what form they reached Layamon is uncertain (see J. S. P. Tatlock, *The Legendary History of Britain* (Berkeley, California, 1950), pp. 483–531). A recent suggestion that two details derive from Old English homilies qualifies the redating of the poem from *c.* 1200 to 'some time not very early in the second half of the thirteenth century' (E. G. Stanley, 'The Date of Layamon's *Brut*', *Notes and Queries*, 213 (1968), 85–88), since it implies that to read the twelfth-century copies Layamon must have been educated late in that century (see P. J. Frankis, 'Layamon's English Sources', in *J. R. R. Tolkien, Scholar and Storyteller: Essays in Memoriam*, edited by M. Salu and R. T. Farrell (London, 1979), pp. 64–75). The general effect is of a lively imagination exploiting whatever it found relevant in French, Germanic, and Celtic tradition.

4. See Derek Pearsall, *Old English and Middle English Poetry* (London, 1977), pp. 80–81, 108–13. Now that the two surviving texts are thought to be of roughly the same date, it would seem that the archaisms stripped away by the reviser of the Otho MS must have appeared to the Caligula scribes who faithfully preserved them as uncharacteristic of their age as he found them (see E. G. Stanley, 'Layamon's Antiquarian Sentiments', *Medium Aevum*, 38 (1969), 23–37).

5. See R. S. Loomis in *Arthurian Literature in the Middle Ages*, edited by R. S. Loomis (Oxford, 1959), pp. 104–111.

6. Text from British Library MS Cotton Caligula A. ix, edited by G. L. Brook and R. F. Leslie, EETS, 250, 277 (London, 1963, 1978).

7. The limited critical discussion of the *Brut* includes helpful contributions by Dorothy Everett, *Essays on Middle English Literature*, edited by P. Kean (Oxford, 1955), pp. 28–45, and C. S. Lewis, *Studies in Medieval and Renaissance Literature*, edited by W. Hooper (Cambridge, 1966), pp. 18–33.

8. Commentators have explained the process by suggesting that Layamon distinguished between the Saxons as evil and the Angles as guiltless and true successors of the ancient British (see I. J. Kirby, 'Angles and Saxons in Layamon's *Brut*', *Studia Neophilologica*, 36 (1964), 51–62) or that his pejorative account of his English ancestors was intended to suggest the moral cause of the Norman Conquest (see Stanley, 'Layamon's Antiquarian Sentiments', pp. 31–34). But Englishmen in later ages, with greater opportunities for historical perspective, were no less ready to accept the Arthurian fiction, unifying and flattering, in preference to the reality of disunity at home and conquest from abroad.

9. Text from Lincoln Cathedral MS 91 (Thornton MS), edited by Valerie Krishna, *The Alliterative Mort Arthure* (New York, 1976).

10. See Maureen Fries in *The Alliterative 'Morte Arthur': A Reassessment of the Poem*, edited by K. H. Göller (Cambridge, 1981), pp. 30–43, and John Finlayson, 'The Concept of the Hero in *Morte Arthure*' in *Chaucer und seine Zeit*, edited by A. Esch (Tübingen, 1968), pp. 249–74.

11. See J. L. Boren, 'Narrative Design in the Alliterative *Morte Arthure*', *Philological Quarterly*, 56 (1977), 310–19.

12. Many aspects of this complex poem remain controversial; a useful summary of our present understanding is supplied in *The Alliterative 'Morte Arthure'*, edited by Göller.

13. Text from British Library MS Harleian 2252, edited by P. F. Hissiger, *Le Morte Arthur* (The Hague, 1975).

14. See S. E. Knopp, 'Artistic Design in the Stanzaic *Morte Arthur*', *ELH*, 45 (1978), 563–82, and Dieter Mehl, *The Middle English Romances of the Thirteenth and Fourteenth Centuries* (London, 1968), pp. 190–93.

15. See R. A. Wertine, 'The Theme and Structure of the Stanzaic *Morte Arthure*', *PMLA*, 87 (1972), 1075–82.

16. Though the need for a final meeting of the lovers also occurred to the redactor of one text of the *Mort Artu* (Vatican MS Palatinus Latinus 1967), the scene in the English version seems independently conceived in relation to its overall interpretation (see J. Beston and R. M. Beston, 'The Parting of Lancelot and Guinevere in the Stanzaic *Le Morte Arthur*', *AUMLA*, 40 (1973), 249–59).

17. On the moral interpretation see V. B. Richmond, *The Popularity of Middle English Romance* (Bowling Green, Ohio, 1975), pp. 129–42, and on the interpretative function of irony F. M. Alexander, '"The Treson of Launcelote du Lake": Irony in the Stanzaic *Morte Arthur*' in *The Legend of Arthur in the Middle Ages*, edited by P. B. Grout *et al.* (Cambridge, 1983), pp. 15–27.

18. Malory's criminal career is conveniently summarized in William Matthews, *The Ill-framed Knight* (Berkeley, California, 1966), pp. 14–34.

19. Text from the preface to Caxton's edition cited in Malory's *Works*, edited by Eugène Vinaver, second edition (London, 1971), from the Winchester MS (now British Library, Additional MS 59678).

20. For contrasting views of Malory's work as a conscious critique of the flaws inherent in chivalry and as an attempt to present it as a valid historical ideal of life unconsciously undermined by the failure inherent in Arthurian tradition see Charles Moorman, *The Book of Kyng Arthur: the Unity of Malory's 'Morte Darthur'* (Lexington, Kentucky, 1965), and E. T. Pochoda, *Arthurian Propaganda: 'Le Morte Darthur' as an Historical Ideal of Life* (Chapel Hill, North Carolina, 1971).

21. See Eugène Vinaver, *The Rise of Romance* (Oxford, 1971), pp. 123–39.

22. For two views on the coexistence of mythical and historical elements in the *Morte Darthur* see Knight, pp. 105–48, and Muriel Whitaker, *Arthur's Kingdom of Adventure: The World of Malory's 'Morte Darthur'* (Cambridge, 1984). The contribution of Malory's remarkable prose style to the character of his work, too complex to exemplify briefly, is demonstrated in P. J. C. Field, *Romance and Chronicle: A Study of Malory's Prose Style* (London, 1974), and Mark Lambert, *Malory: Style and Vision in 'Le Morte Darthur'* (New Haven, Connecticut, 1975).

23. Text from National Library of Scotland MS 19.2.1 (Auchinleck), edited by G. P. McNeill, *Sir Tristrem*, STS, 8 (Edinburgh, 1885–86).

24. See Keith Busby, '*Sir Perceval of Galles, Le Conte du Graal* and *La Continuation-Gauvain*: The Methods of an English Adaptor', *Etudes Anglaises*, 31 (1978), 198–202.

25. Text from a transcript of the Thornton MS, edited by W. H. French and C. B. Hale, *Middle English Metrical Romances* (New York, 1930), pp. 531–603.

26. See C. D. Eckhardt, 'Arthurian Comedy: The Simpleton-Hero in *Sir Perceval of Galles*', *The Chaucer Review*, 8 (1974), 205–20, and D. C. Fowler, '*Le Conte du Graal* and *Sir Perceval of Galles*', *Comparative Literature Studies*, 12 (1975), 5–20.

27. See F. X. Baron, 'Mother and Son in *Sir Perceval of Galles*', *Papers in Language and Literature*, 8 (1972), 3–14.

28. See Keith Busby, *Gauvain in Old French Literature* (Amsterdam, 1980).

29. See R. W. Ackerman in *Arthurian Literature in the Middle Ages*, pp. 493–505.

30. Text from British Library MS Cotton Galba E.ix, edited by A. B. Friedman and N. T. Harrington, EETS, 254 (London, 1964).

31. For helpful literary analysis see J. Finlayson, '*Ywain and Gawain* and the Meaning of Adventure', *Anglia*, 86 (1969), 312–37, and G. K. Hamilton, 'The Breaking of the Troth in *Ywain and Gawain*', *Mediaevalia*, 2 (1976), 111–35.

32. See P. J. Ketrick, *The Relation of 'Golagros and Gawane' to the Old French 'Perceval' of Chrétien de Troyes* (Washington, D.C., 1931).

33. Text from the Chepman and Miller Print (Edinburgh, 1508) edited by F. J. Amours, *Scottish Alliterative Poems in Riming Stanzas*, STS, 27, 38 (Edinburgh, 1892–97).

34. For a more detailed literary analysis see W. R. J. Barron, '*Golagrus and Gawain*: A Creative Redaction', *Bibliographical Bulletin of the International Arthurian Society*, 26 (Nottingham, 1974), 173–85.

35. Text from British Library MS Cotton Nero A.x, Art. 3, edited by J. R. R. Tolkien and E. V. Gordon, revised N. Davis (Oxford, 1967).

36. Such a summary treatment of an enormously complex text cannot adequately acknowledge its debts to published scholarship, key items of which are listed in the Bibliography. An aspect of its verbal complexity, suggesting the poet's

exploitation of the ambivalent nature of romance, is treated in W. R. J. Barron, 'The Ambivalence of Adventure: Verbal Ambiguity in *Sir Gawain and the Green Knight*, Fitt I', in *The Legend of Arthur in the Middle Ages,* pp. 28–40, 228–30.

# Chapter 8

# The Matter of Romance

The preceding survey of the recognized Matters of medieval romance does not constitute a coherent history of the mode. Whether or not one believes that it is rooted in the human temperament, the universal instinct to project from experience of existence an imaginative concept of how life might be or might once have been not wholly contradicted by life as it is guarantees that as a narrative mode it was re-created not invented in the Middle Ages. The emergence of literature in the vernacular, providing a medium in which the ideals and social concerns of the secular aristocracy could find expression, allowed the evolution of a genre which ultimately pre-empted the description 'romance', implying formal distinction under what was originally and for long remained primarily a linguistic label.

## From mode to genre

Each of the Matters made its distinctive contribution to the formation of the genre, but they did so by virtue of their common adherence to the romance mode. The Matters of France and Rome, by providing a powerful focus – national, dynastic, religious – for ideals of individual heroism, demonstrated how heroes in search of personal fulfilment might serve and yet, by the very extremism of their aspiration, endanger the interests of their society. The ambivalence inherent in the mode may be less apparent in the *Chanson de Roland* than in Chrétien's works, but it finds open expression in epics of the *barons revoltés* tradition dealing with divided loyalties within the feudal system. In *Roland*, structure, narrative repetition, and verse form recall the oral affiliations of the *chansons*, but its distinctive combination of matter and manner did not long resist the literary influence of the emergent romance which expressed its central ideal of military valour by very different formal means. By stressing the formal contrast, by comparing *Roland* with the works of Chrétien, it has been possible to establish distinctive genres of epic and romance. But in evolutionary terms the distinction is far from absolute either in predominant concerns or expressive means. If passionate commitment between man and woman, within marriage or outside it, is an essential characteristic of romance, it predates Chrétien in the epic context of the Matter of Rome, expressed through a formalized analysis of emotion which the romance is to exploit for similar purposes. If the essential distinction is the elevation of an individual relationship above duty or social convention, that is already the centre of interest in Marie's *lais* and the Tristan texts. Both owe obvious debts to folk-tale, just as the narrative motifs which seem most characteristic of Chrétien's romances – the challenge, the solitary quest, the wayside ordeal, the combat against superhuman odds, the winning of a bride – closely resemble the experiences of folk-heroes, the patterning of whose adventures by repetition and variation, parallelism, inversion seems to be mirrored in his narrative structures. What is truly distinctive in Chrétien's work is not the assemblage of conventions but the skill with which they are employed, the high art which made his romances into archetypes of the genre. Yet after him as before him the genre went on evolving, changing in scale, medium, structure, in the relationship of the adventures of individuals to the dynastic theme, in the development of allegorical undercurrents expressing religious as well as chivalric values. New themes evoke new combinations of conventions, the romantic perspective remains constant, veering now towards fantasy now towards realism, always maintaining a balance however precarious between myth and mimesis. The conventions of the genre are the accidents of the mode; its essence is the romantic perspective.

The evolution of the Matter of Britain, in which the values and aspirations of a few, highly evolved, feudal courts were projected upon narrative material whose specific meaning had been largely obliterated leaving only the underlying patterns of folk-tale, exemplifies the process by which story-matter can be recast in the romance mode. Reassured by Geoffrey of Monmouth's *Historia* of the 'reality' of Arthur's realm, Chrétien and his contemporaries made it a crucible for the idealism of their own age, all the more readily because other Arthurian material available to them expressed the basic human aspirations of folk-heroes in which they could identify the basis of their more specialized social codes. The folk-tales most likely to survive are those which best express awareness of the human condition and how it might be mastered, the literary romance is an extension of the same function by more conscious means.

Once the mode had found an expressive pattern appropriate to the

Middle Ages, there was almost no story-matter which could not be reinterpreted to fit it. The Matter of Rome shows that the heroic values of the ancient world were not devalued by their pagan basis which both licensed extreme aspiration and accounted for its failure; the Matter of France that historical respectability could not defend fact from reinterpretation in the image of desire. Chrétien's interpretation is not escapist fantasy but exploration, demonstration of values important to him and his patrons. But once the genre had been established a narrative could be fitted to its conventions without any serious intention of exploring its meaning. Just as the modern novel of incident is often superficially indistinguishable from the novel of ideas, so the *roman d'aventure* may imitate the format and techniques of the *roman courtois* without any interpretative intention, seeking merely to entertain through variety of incident recounted for its own sake. The established patterns of the romances on the various Matters made them natural subjects for imitation by hack poets in search of a viable model.

## A derivative of the Matter of England: *Richard Coer de Lyon*

The self-conscious nature of the process is well illustrated by *Richard Coer de Lyon* (London area, *c.* 1300), not a late literary crystallization of the folk-tales gathered round some Germanic hero or legendary ancestor but a composite formed on well-tried models to exploit the patriotic sentiment associated with Richard I (1157–99), second son of Henry II and Eleanor of Aquitaine. Heir to his mother's duchy, brought up largely in her court at Poitiers, constantly embroiled with his father and brothers and the kings of France who claimed his allegiance, he threw himself on his accession into the Third Crusade, captured Acre, fought Saladin to a standstill, was imprisoned by the Duke of Austria on his return overland and ransomed by his subjects for a vast sum, only to die pointlessly besieging the castle of a petty vassal. Though he spoke no English and spent only a few months of his reign in the island, this vigorous, ruthless man of action appealed enormously to the national love of adventure, a Guy of Warwick operating in the mysterious East of Alexander the Great.

Like Alexander, his charismatic personality and improbable achievements made him the focus of legend even in his own lifetime. The chroniclers, French as well as English, shamelessly interpolated his actual deeds, often grossly exaggerated, into the stereotype heroic career: mysterious birth from a demon-mother, a precocious adolescence in chivalry, public proof of prowess at his coronation in a tournament where Richard incognito is said to have defeated the best knights of his realm, numinous experiences in the appearance of St George, St Thomas à Becket, and various angels in moments of peril on his crusade; incredible deeds of personal valour in the Holy Land, recovery from fever after a meal of roast Saracen substituted for the pork unavailable in that Muslim land, massive slaughter of Saracen prisoners on the advice of an angelic voice, humiliation of Saladin in personal combat followed by mass baptism of his followers; then imprisonment on the return journey by Modred, King of Almain, illicit liaison with his daughter resulting in exposure to a lion whose heart he tears out and eats, eventual discovery by his minstrel Blondel, return home to right the misrule of his brother John and recruit the outlaw Robin Hood among his loyal followers.[1]

Despite much greater accessibility to the process by which a legendary hero is created out of an ambivalent historical figure than in the cases of Charlemagne and Arthur, this blend of fact and fiction has proved almost impenetrable to the discrimination of historians, but it kept Richard alive in the popular imagination into the seventeenth century. The romantic career of the King mingled with many motifs, characters, and trappings borrowed from romance – Modred as villain, Excalibur as the hero's sword, his triumph at a tournament in arms of different colours, the game of pluck-buffet in which he kills Modred's son, the Sultan's gift of a magic horse – left the compiler of *Richard Coer de Lyon*, or the Anglo-Norman poet who may have preceded him in the process, little to do but clothe it in the commonplaces of the genre. His use of the linear sequence of episodes, the stereotyped characters sustained in their unvarying poses is competent, the easy couplets echoing the texts which served as his models:

> Fele romaunses mon maken newe,                    *many*
> Off goode knyȝtes, stronge and trewe;
> Off here dedys men rede romance,
> Boþe in Engeland and in Ffraunce:
> Off Rowelond, and off Olyuer,
> And of euery Doseper;
> Off Alisaundre, and Charlemayn;
> Off Kyng Arthour, and off Gawayn,
> How þey were knyȝtes goode and curteys;
> Off Turpyn, and of Oger Daneys;
> Off Troye men rede in ryme,
> What werre þer was in olde tyme;
> Off Ector, and off Achylles,
> What folk þey slowe in þat pres.   (ll. 7–20)[2]

The mixed company in which Richard is placed reflects a composite conception of romance drawing on all the Matters. The melange was popular to judge from the seven surviving manuscripts and two Wynkyn de Worde prints, some of which are markedly more fabulous than historical in tone.[3]

## Derivatives of the Matter of France: *Rauf Coilyear* and *Chevalere Assigne*

The power of the established Matters to attract material originally unconnected with their ethnic themes is strikingly illustrated by *The Taill of Rauf Coilyear* (Scottish, late fifteenth century), based on a widespread folk-tale of a king entertained incognito by a commoner who teaches him, in the terms of a French variant, that 'charbonnier est maître chez soi' (even a collier is master in his own house) and exacts compliance from his royal guest. Charlemagne is unexpectedly cast in the role of the King and the theme is reduplicated by an original extension in which Ralph, invited to court to be rewarded for his honesty, challenges Roland to a duel but encounters instead the Saracen Magog and proves himself worthy of the knighthood received from Charlemagne by fighting him to a standstill, when Roland arrives to bribe him to convert by the promise of a Christian bride. The second episode parodies the Christian–Muslim combats of *Otuel* and *Firumbras* in the mocking spirit of the folk-tale opening, both given life by the skill with which the colloquial diction is fitted to the demanding thirteen-line stanza, closely rhymed and heavily alliterative, of *Golagrus* and the *Awntyrs*. The medium prevents the mindless reproduction of conventions, producing what is technically and creatively the best of the English texts on the Matter of France with which its connection, as a popular fantasy of high life set against the reality of peasant Scotland, is purely adventitious.

The opposite process is represented by *Chevalere Assigne* (north-west Midlands, late fourteenth century) in which a folk-tale caught up in the opening, *Naissance* section of the vast Crusade Cycle to lend mystery to the ancestry of its hero Godfrey of Bouillon is restored to independence in a brief alliterative version. It is a composite of folklore motifs telling how seven children borne by a queen at one birth are abandoned in a forest by her jealous mother-in-law, brought up by a hermit, and later, when the chains they wore at birth are cut off, transformed into swans, with the exception of the boy Enyas who defeats the old Queen's champion in combat and restores the others to human form, though one, whose chain had been melted down, remains a swan drawing the boat in which Enyas departs on adventures, eventually to become the *chevalere assigne*, ancestor of Godfrey. Only the hero's chivalric title reveals his association with the *Naissance du Chevalier au Cygne*; the radical abbreviation, less than one-fifth of the original, largely ignores the courtly detail to show a folk-tale hero rising through inherent prowess to the rank in which he was born, a Perceval figure whose ignorance of arms is both a source of amusement and proof of the divine protection which allows him to defeat the forces of evil. The opening and closing lines suggest presentation as an *exemplum*, but no didactic theme is developed in the narration which strives for clarity of action and exploits the naïvety of the boy hero like some latter-day Sunday-school prize advancing piety through formulaic adventures.

## The Matter of the Orient: *Floris and Blancheflur*

The readiness with which English redactors catering for popular audiences detected elements of folk-tale which could be freed from their context in courtly literature suggests the frequency with which the authors of epic and romance had drawn upon sub-literary sources often undetectable by scholarship. The *roman d'aventure* required incident of almost any nature or origin; the *roman courtois* episodes expressing basic human aspirations upon which its more specialized codes could be moulded. The origin of a particular incident or motif is often untraceable since its occurrence in more than one culture may result from mutual reflection of common social factors rather than oral transmission or literary borrowing. So, though there are European romances with oriental settings, with incidents paralleled in the *Arabian Nights*, direct derivation has not been clearly established. The issue is complicated by the multiple lines of communication: in the warring contact of the crusades, through Byzantium where there was a mutual exchange between Greek and Arab cultures, in Spain and in particular in Norman Sicily where, as the tide of Islamic conquest retreated, its influence could be absorbed without enmity. Where the Matter of France projected fantasies of Christian victory and Muslim conversion against the underlying reality of the threat still represented by the power of Islam, the Matter of the Orient allowed the exploration through an admired if imperfectly known culture of personal issues seemingly insoluble in the reality of European society.[4]

*Floris and Blancheflur* (south-east Midlands, *c*. 1250) deals with the triumph of young love over parental opposition and tyrannical authority. The contribution of various oriental analogues to the French original adapted into many European languages is unclear, but the extant texts represent a courtly version, idyllic and sentimental in tone, and a popular account replacing emotion with action, the power of love with force of arms. The English, following the former, tells how Blancheflur, a Christian slave, is loved by Floris, Prince of Spain, whose parents sell her into Babylon where he eventually finds her in the Emir's harem; detected, they are sentenced to death but melt the Emir's heart by their fidelity and mutual self-sacrifice, are married, and rule Spain together. The composition of the original somewhere in western France about 1160 associates it with the application of the rhetorical art of the schoolmen to pre-existing story-matter; their influence is apparent in the implication of a learned source for *Floire et Blancheflor*, its attachment to the national epic by making the young lovers the parents of Charlemagne's mother, and the descriptive set pieces on settings, properties, and portraits of the protagonists quite out of proportion to the narrative context. The narrative itself is simple, chronologically structured with numerous repetitions reminiscent of the patterning of the *chansons de geste*.

The English version is a radical abbreviation, perhaps one-third of the original, reducing in particular the descriptive passages from rhetorical ornament to practical function, and selecting a pattern of scenes dramatized by exchanges of dialogue in a way which must have made it highly effective in minstrel performance. Numerous discrepancies between the four existing manuscripts suggest a complex textual history testifying to its popularity. The narrative focuses upon the young people, not with the French version's interest in their precocious sexuality but as paragons of fidelity proving that love can endure through time and distance, override separation, self-interest, and difference of faith to triumph in the face of death, a Tristan and Isolde without need of magic potions or offence to feudal values. Born in the same hour, Floris the son of a Saracen queen, Blancheflur the daughter of a Christian captive who nurses both, named for the flowers whose festival marks their birth, they are inseparable even when Floris is put to school:

> All weeping saide he,
> 'Ne shall not Blancheflour lerne with me?
> Ne can I noght to scole goon
> Without Blauncheflour,' he saide than,
> 'Ne can I in no scole sing ne rede
> Without Blauncheflour,' he saide.
> The King saide to his soon,
> 'She shall lerne, for thy love.'   (ll. 17–24)[5]

Their love has no rationale, needs no psychological explanation; it exists from the beginning and everything else must give way to it. So that Floris may make a suitable marriage, his parents think of killing Blancheflur, but instead send the boy to stay with relatives where he pines away:

> Love is at his hert roote,
> That no thing is so soote.                         *sweet*
> Galingale ne licoris                        *spice, licorice*
> Is not so soote as hur love is,
> Ne no thing ne non other.   (ll. 117–21)      *other (person)*

Told that she has died for love in his absence, he cannot be dissuaded from suicide until the tomb that bears her name is opened and shown to be empty. As in Marie's *lais* such concrete objects, elaborately described, serve as symbols round which episodes are focused.

As in Marie, too, the theme of *amor vincit omnia* justifies every form of deceit, trickery, and sleight of hand to ensure the triumph of love; the English author, like his contemporary the *Horn*-poet, takes an obvious interest in the skill with which the hero uses his wit to surmount obstacles, observing youth overcome age with malicious pleasure. Once he has won his parents' support, they supply Floris with equipage and treasure, including the rich cup carved with Paris's abduction of Helen for which they had sold Blancheflur to Babylonian merchants and a ring which can protect the wearer from death, and he sets out on a quest for his own stolen bride: "'Hur to seken I woll wende,/Thaugh it were to the worldes ende'" (ll. 329–30). By his own ingenuity and the good counsel of those he wins to his cause, he eventually traces his beloved to the Emir's harem where she waits with forty others to become his bride for a year should she be elected by a blossom falling upon her in the springtime ritual of that *paradeisos*:

> About the orchard is a walle;
> The foulest stone is cristall;
> And a well springeth therinne
> That is made with muche ginne.                    *skill*
> The well is of muche pris;                         *worth*
> The stremes com fo Paradise;
> The gravel of the ground is precious stoones
> And all of vertu for the noones.   (ll. 609–16)   *(magic) power*

Winning the porter's good will by losing to him at chess and bribing him with the precious cup – the price of his bride's slavery for her freedom now – he has himself smuggled into the harem tower in a basket of flowers where he is discovered by the maiden Claris who shows him to Blancheflur as if he were the blossom of the Emir's choice:

> 'Fellow, come and see a faire flour!                    *comrade*
> Suche a flour thee shall well like,
> Have thou it sene a lyte.'                              *little*
> 'Away, Claris!' quod Blauncheflour;
> 'To scorne me, it is none honoure.
> I here, Claris, without gabbe,                          *a lie*
> That the Amiral will me to wif habbe;                   *Emir*
> But that day shall never be
> That he shall ever have me –
> That I shall be of love so untrewe,
> Ne chaunge my love for no newe.'   (ll. 780–90)

No rhapsodies mark the reunion of the lovers; instead they go immediately to bed – 'There was no man that might radde (*estimate*)/The joye that they two madde' (ll. 825–26) – and Floris, the heathen Prince, gives thanks to Christ! Discovered and brought to trial before the Emir, their love endures in the face of death. Floris tries to give his life-saving ring to Blancheflur, she resists and each strives to be first to offer his neck to the Emir's sword. He, with a magnanimity which the Matter of France denies in Saracens, requires only an explanation of how his harem was penetrated, a recapitulation of the hero's ingenuity, before knighting him and leading the lovers to be married in church. The fairy-tale ending, the Christian wedding in a pagan land, the lack of comment on the hero's conversion seem unsurprising in the amoral context of a romance whose tenuous relationship with reality must be seen in the light of contemporary concepts of love and marriage. Comparison with its contemporary, Layamon's *Brut*, indicates the range of the romance mode at the beginning of the English tradition; but it also suggests that the range was no less wide in terms of genre.[6]

How little the origin of the story-matter determined the relation of a romance to the wide-ranging mode is illustrated by the contrast between *Floris and Blancheflur* and *The King of Tars* (London area, early fourteenth century) whose theme reflects chronicle accounts of the marriage of a princess of Christian Armenia to the brother of the Tartar Khan, Ghazan, who expelled the Saracens from Jerusalem and raised hopes in the West that conversion of the pagan hordes might counterbalance Muslim power in the Middle East. Even in the chronicles this historical event is associated with the widespread motif of a monstrous birth miraculously transformed by baptism. In the romance, when his child is born a formless lump of flesh, the Tartar

Prince's pleas to his pagan deities prove vain, but when the Princess arranges baptism it becomes a handsome boy. Moved to accept baptism himself, the Prince turns from black to white in the font, then joins his wife's father in the forced conversion of his Tartar subjects. The mode may be romance, a fantasy of an ultimate solution to the Muslim threat rooted in a grain of fact, but the incidents are more characteristic of pious legend, *exemplum*, or saint's life.[7]

In other romances of oriental origin the intermixture of Byzantine, Greek, and Arabic matter is so thorough and of such ancient date that individual motifs cannot be traced to their source with any certainty. A classic example is provided by the story of Apollonius of Tyre which circulated for a thousand years in hundreds of Latin versions before passing into the vernacular literature of every European country. It compounds folklore motifs of the Incestuous Father, Faithful Servitor, evil stepmother, suitor tests, perilous riddle, etc. into a story which ranges widely over the eastern Mediterranean telling how the hero, set to answer a riddle for the hand of a princess, divines her incestuous father's plot to destroy her suitors, marries elsewhere, loses wife and child at sea, and after many trials recovers both. Already translated into Old English, only a fragment of the Middle English *Apollonius of Tyre* (Dorset, 1376–81) survives; but the story was used by Gower in his *Confessio Amantis*, was widely popular in the sixteenth century and provided the subject for Shakespeare's *Pericles*.

# A derivative of the Matter of Rome: *Sir Orfeo*

English versions of the Matter of Rome, even when ultimately derived from classical literary texts, reflect the degree of romanticization introduced in intermediate treatments. In the case of *Sir Orfeo* (Southeast, possibly London area, c. 1300) the transformation has been so fundamental as to affect its relationship to the romance mode. The Greek myth of the Thracian musician and poet who journeyed to the underworld to win back his wife but, unable to maintain his undertaking not to look at her on the return journey, loses her for ever, was known to the Middle Ages not primarily in the versions of Ovid and Virgil, but through the Christian allegory of Boethius's vastly influential *Consolation of Philosophy*. In the hands of a Breton poet it absorbed elements of Celtic tradition, took the form of a *lai*, and, passing most probably through a lost French *Lai d'Orphey*, became one of the most complex and highly integrated compositions in Middle

English. The accretions at each stage in its evolution cannot be absolutely determined, but it seems likely that King Alfred's Old English translation of Boethius suggested the long period of self-exile in which Orpheus expresses his grief and the repeated effect of his music in charming wild beasts; Celtic elements already incorporated in Walter Map's *De Nugis Curialium* may account for his chance discovery of his wife among a group of ladies during his grief-stricken wanderings and the sense of the otherworld as a fairy place; while the Irish *Wooing of Etain* perhaps supplied the identification of the protagonists as king and queen, the replacement of her death by an abduction preceded by a dream of the abductor, and the rash promise by which the Fairy King is tricked into releasing her. The localization of the English version in which Thrace is identified with Winchester, Parliament is summoned to appoint a successor to Orpheus, and the wintry landscape suggests a local setting, was no doubt due to the redactor. So also, perhaps, the final episode in which Orpheus recovers his kingdom, a logical addition required by earlier changes which made him a king and exiled him for ten years – though it may have been the French poet who first felt its thematic necessity.[8]

The result is a balanced structure of double loss and recovery demonstrating a dual ideal of love and loyalty, of husband to wife and subjects to their king. In the initial introduction of characters, Orfeo is established as a king of noble ancestry – 'His fader was comen of King Pluto,/And his moder of King Juno' (ll. 43–44) – whose largess is extended to all harpers, and himself a harper of miraculous skill, and his queen, Dame Heurodis, as 'Ful of loue and of godenisse;/Ac no man may telle hir fairnise' (ll. 55–56). The action begins in May, season of renewal with its reminder of human love in harmony with nature but also of man's mortality, when Heurodis lies sleeping under an 'ympe-tre' (that mystery in nature, a grafted tree) and wakens in frenzy – 'Sche froted (*wrung*) hir honden and hir fet,/And crached (*tore*) hir visage – it bled wete' (ll. 79–80) – inconsolable by all the love that surrounds her:

> In þe orchard to þe quene hye come,
> And her vp in her armes nome,                          took
> And brouʒt hir to bed atte last,
> And held hir þere fine fast:                          very firmly
> Ac euer sche held in o cri,                            persisted
> And wold vp, and owy.   (ll. 91–96)[9]              away

In Orpheus's arms she recounts a dream in which knights summoned her before their lord who, on her refusal, came himself and warned her to be ready next day to join him for ever in the kingdom he has just shown her:

> 'And ȝif þou makest ous ylet,                          *cause, hindrance*
> Whar þou be, þou worst yfet,                            *will be fetched*
> And totorn þine limes al,                              *torn asunder*
> Þat noþing help þe no schal;
> And þei þou best so totorn                             *though*
> Ȝete þou worst wiþ ous yborn.'   (ll. 169–74)          *carried*

On the morrow, a thousand knights surround the 'ympe-tre', but the Queen is taken from their midst: 'Men wist neuer wher sche was bicome (*gone*)' (l. 194). Orpheus, faithful to his pledge to her, '"Whider þou gost ichil (*I will go*) wiþ þe,/And whider y go þou schalt wiþ me"' (ll. 129–30), with its marital and religious implications,[10] commends his kingdom to the high steward and, barefoot, in pilgrim garb with harp on shoulder, wanders ten long years in the wilderness where only the beasts come to his playing:

> He þat had yhad kniȝtes of priis                       *worth*
> Bifor him kneland, and leuedis
> – Now seþ he noþing þat him likeþ,                     *sees*
> Bot wilde wormes bi him strikeþ.   (ll. 249–52)        *serpents, glide*

But the act of will involved in his self-exile begins the process of restoration, penetrating the paper-thin barrier between this world and that other which so resembles it:

> He miȝt se him bisides
> (Oft in hot vnder-tides)
> Þe king o fairy wiþ his rout                           *noontides*
> Com to hunt him al about                               *company*
> Wiþ dim cri and bloweing.   (ll. 281–85)

Among the marching fairy troops, the dancers to trump and tabour, the bands of ladies hawking, he one day catches sight of Heurodis: 'Ȝern (*eagerly*) he biheld hir, and sche him eke (*too*),/Ac noiþer to oþer a word no speke' (ll. 323–24); putting fear of death out of his mind, he follows them through a rock into a country 'As briȝt so sonne on somers day' (l. 352). Entering a castle of fantastic richness which seems to him 'Þe proude court of Paradis' (l. 376), he finds it littered with the undead, some headless, some witless, as they were taken on battlefield or childbed, and among them Heurodis sleeping still under the 'ympe-tre'. *He* was not so summoned, the Fairy King protests; but Orpheus replies that minstrels are accustomed to go where they are not welcome, and so delights him with his harping that he is promised a boon and chooses Heurodis. The King objects that one withered by

age and hardship is an unfit match for her beauty, untouched by time
in that timeless world, but Orpheus dares him to break his given
word. Once back in their own land, Orpheus goes in his rags to spy
out the state of the kingdom and, meeting the steward, asks alms of
him:

> 'Of þat ichaue þou schalt haue some.        *I have*
> Euerich gode harpour is welcom me to
> For mi lordes loue, Sir Orfeo.'   (ll. 516–18)

When he plays, the steward recognizes the harp but not the player;
Orpheus tells him that he found it by the body of a man torn by wild
beasts and his faithful lieutenant falls in a swoon, lamenting the death
of a good lord:

> King Orfeo knewe wele bi þan        *that*
> His steward was a trewe man
> And loued him as he auȝt to do.   (ll. 553–55)        *ought*

Orpheus rewards his loyalty with a promise of the succession and,
bathed, shaved, and crowned, goes in procession to bring home the
Queen: 'Þus com Sir Orfeo out of his care:/God graunt ous alle wele to
fare! Amen!' (ll. 603–04).

The minstrel platitude, the simplicity of diction, the naïvety in
matters of classical knowledge are deceptive; the English poet, even if
he did no more than fit the verbal skin to a borrowed *lai*, evidently
respected the integrity of a subtle composition. The seemingly casual
linear narrative is tightly structured in relation to the underlying
pattern of dual loss and recovery whose turning-point comes at mid-
point (l. 303) when his first sight of the hawking ladies changes
Orpheus's negative will, shown in his attempt to prevent the abduction
and self-exile, to a positive resolution leading to the recovery of both
wife and kingdom and with them his chivalric identity reflected in the
qualities he evokes in others: honour in the Fairy King, loyalty in the
steward. The sparse narrative, highlighting what it chooses to dwell
upon, creating mystery by what it leaves unsaid; the directness and
passion of the language picturing this world and the other with the
same unblinking realism; the congruity and contrast between the two,
suggesting the goodness and security of a courtly society menaced by
its shadowy counterpart in which beauty and ugliness, courtliness and
motiveless violence mingle; the tensions created by such unexplained
mysteries as the manner of Heurodis's taking and the presence of the
'ympe-tre' in both realms – all underscore the theme of the power of
human will inspired by love to resist malign Fortune. The complete

absence of commentary and the substitution of passionate gesture – the silent glance exchanged between lovers, the mirroring of her frenzy of fear in his reaction to her taking (ll. 196–200), the steward's swooning at news of the dead harper in the wood (ll. 549–52) – reinforce it by affective rather than didactic means. The power of the work lies in the antithesis between this complexity and the simple narrative surface.[11]

An equal complexity of meaning invites the multiple interpretation which the Middle Ages applied even to secular texts. The courtly overtones of a narrative rooted in human feeling imply association with the archetypal romance motif of the abducted lady rescued by her lover which projects the classic struggle of mankind against the undefined powers which oppose his idealism. At the mythic level those powers might be seen as embodying the nature of a world governed by Fortune in which a happy prince may be suddenly overwhelmed by loss, fall from prosperity to adversity, wander the world as a barefoot pilgrim, reminded by the repeated contrast of present and past of the illusory nature of worldly well-being. Unlike the saints who tread similar paths of exile, Orpheus learns not contempt for the world but the enduring power of love, loyalty, and honour. As a king who has proved powerless to prevent the abduction of his wife, he acknowledges his presumption by exiling himself and the fidelity of the steward by yielding the succession to him, suggesting that in this parable of power he has recognized his own failings in that other kingdom, 'Þe proude court of Paradis'. His pilgrim's progress through expiation in the wilderness to ultimate redemption acknowledges the sin of pride, without giving Christian allegory or *exemplum* priority over the mythic or human levels of meaning in a complex poem.[12]

## The Breton lay in English: *Sir Launfal*

The cultural fusion of *Sir Orfeo*, whose adherence to the romance mode is expressed in terms of fundamental human values rather than the social codes of any particular culture, demonstrates the primacy of the meaning which a narrative could have for a medieval audience over its origins or literary affiliations. The character of the poem has been determined by the poet's concept of it as a Breton lay (see above, pp. 22–23), declared in prologue and epilogue (ll. 1–20, 597–602). The prologue is shared by *Lai le Freine*, a free version of one of Marie's *lais*, whose plot is a mosaic of familiar motifs on the theme of twins parted at birth and reunited through the magnanimity of one, who has become the mistress of a knight, when he unwittingly marries her sister. These apart, the Middle English texts which announce themselves as 'a lay of Bretayn' or claim such a derivation have little to distinguish them from other romances, especially those comparatively brief examples with which they share the twelve-line tail-rhyme stanza rather than the four-stress couplet characteristic of the *lai*. Love and the supernatural feature in them, but they are exemplary and sensational rather than primarily celebrations of the power of love like Marie's *lais*.

*Emaré*, for example, tells the story of a virtuous woman cast adrift at sea for rejecting the incestuous love of her father, then again when the King who marries her is falsely persuaded that she has given birth to a devil, only to be finally reconciled to husband and father by the noble behaviour of her son. In *Sir Gowther*, a youth actually fathered by the Devil redeems his paternity by virtuous deeds which ultimately earn him the hand of a princess. The central motifs in both – typified by the story of Constance falsely accused of a monstrous birth and by that of Robert the Devil – were widely used in other genres, including the *exemplum*, and one manuscript of *Sir Gowther* recognizes its similarity to a saint's legend by ending *Explicit vita sancti*. In *Sir Degaré*, the supernatural father is a fairy knight who leaves behind a pointless sword by which he is ultimately reunited with wife and child, but not before the boy has married his own mother and met his father in combat. *The Earl of Toulous*, vaguely based on a scandal involving Charlemagne's son Louis I, tells how a knight unjustly treated by the Emperor none the less vindicates the honour of his empress by fighting as her champion and succeeds him on the throne. A vague romantic core of heroism in the service of the distressed, in self-regeneration, in the righting of ancient wrongs is perceptible in each, but their predominant appeal is that of bizarre incidents and exotic locations.

The contrast with the classic lay may be rooted in treatment as much as in theme, witness the various English versions of Marie's *Lanval*. Three texts in couplets (*Sir Landeval, Sir Lambewell,* and *Sir Lamwell*) probably derive from the same Middle English translation giving a faithful if briefer and less courtly version of Marie's *lai*. Thomas Chestre's *Sir Launfal* (South-east, late fourteenth century) conflates the *Landeval* text with the more primitive, non-Arthurian, version of *Graelent* and two episodes from a lost source known only through surviving analogues. Much of the sophistication of Marie's treatment, with its Arthurian setting, courtly detail, focus on the power of love and interest in legal technicalities, is absent from his story of a knight of Brittany driven from court by the enmity of the Queen but rewarded by the love of a *fée* who vindicates him when he later praises her beauty above the Queen's by proving his boast and forgiving his breach of secrecy. It shares with the tail-rhyme romances their brevity

(1044 lines), their twelve-line stanza on five rhymes, and their emphasis on adventure, uncovering the bones of a folk-tale on which the more courtly *lai* was based.

The hero, Sir Launfal, is that popular figure the just steward, honoured by all for his generosity: 'He gaf gyftys largelyche,/Gold and syluer and clodes ryche,/To squyer and to knyȝt' (ll. 28–30).[13] But when his master marries Guinevere, whose bad reputation has already reached Launfal's ears – 'sche hadde lemmannys (*lovers*) vnþer (*in addition to*) her lord,/So fele (*many*) þer nas noon ende' (ll. 47–48) – she snubs him by omitting him from her gift-giving and he leaves court. At Caerleon he is reluctantly lodged by the mayor, once his servant, but wastes his substance with accustomed prodigality until Arthur's nephews, his faithful companions, are forced to leave him: 'Þey seyd, "Syr, our robes beþ torent,/And your tresour ys all yspent,/And we goþ ewyll ydyȝt (*ill clad*)"' (ll. 139–41). On Trinity Sunday, too ragged to go to church, he borrows saddle and bridle from the mayor's daughter and rides out alone. As he lies under a tree, not having eaten for three days, two beautiful maidens summon him to the pavilion of their mistress, Dame Tryamour:

> For hete her cloþes down sche dede
> Almest to her gerdylstede:                                    *waist*
> Þan lay sche vncouert.
> Sche was as whyt as lylye yn May,
> Or snow þat sneweþ yn wynterys day –
> He seygh neuer non so pert.                                   *lovely*
> Þe rede rose, whan sche ys newe,
> Aȝens her rode nes nauȝt of hewe,                             *complexion*
> J dar well say, yn sert.                                      *in truth*
> Her here schon as gold wyre.   (ll. 289–98)

She immediately declares her love: '"Yf þou wylt truly to me take, /And all wemen for me forsake,/Ryche J wyll make þe"' (ll. 316–18), promising him a never-empty purse, a servant, horse, and a banner ensuring victory in any tournament. They spend the night together – 'For play lytyll þey sclepte þat nyȝt' (l. 349) – and next day she dismisses him with a warning never to boast of her on pain of losing her love.

When the promised gifts are brought to him at his lodging by a troop of finely dressed young men, the mayor grows suddenly gracious and Launfal, splendid in purple and ermine, entertains all and sundry from his bottomless purse and overthrows one noble after another at a tournament given in his honour: 'And euery day, Dame Triamour,/Sche com to Syr Launfal bour (*room*)/Aday whan hyt was nyȝt' (ll. 499–501). When Sir Valentine, a giant knight of Lombardy, challenges him to a duel, he defeats him with the help of his invisible servant Gyfre. His renown causes him to be summoned back to court where, at a dance, Guinevere makes him an avowal of love which he indignantly rejects as treason to Arthur and, when she hints at homosexuality, bursts out: '"J haue loued a fayryr woman/Þan þou euer leydest þyn ey vpon,/Þys seuen yer and more!"' (ll. 694–96). Falsely denounced by the Queen, deprived of his fairy gifts for his breach of faith, Launfal is condemned by his peers to produce the lady of whom he boasted or die on the gallows. When he fails to do so by the stated day, some judges plead for exile rather than death, declaring: '"Greet schame hyt wer vs alle vpon/Forto dampny þat gantylman, /Þat haþ be hende (gracious) and fre (noble)"' (ll. 841–43). At that moment ten maidens announce the coming of their mistress, then as the legal wrangles continue, ten more and, as Guinevere demands that Arthur override the partiality of the judges towards Launfal, Tryamour herself appears in regal splendour, stuns them all by her beauty and wins the King's acknowledgement: '"Ech man may yse þat ys soþe ,/Bryȝtere þat ye be"' (ll. 1004–05). She goes to Guinevere who had wagered her grey eyes upon her superior beauty, breathes upon them and blinds her for life. Gyfre appears with Launfal's horse and together they ride away 'ynto Fayrye'.

*Sir Launfal* has generally disappointed those who read it as a Breton lay by its lack of charm, matter-of-fact treatment of the supernatural, preoccupation with wealth and possessions, unscrupulous and ruthless use of violence. But Marie too can be ruthless in the interests of her lovers, just as with her possessions have symbolic as well as material value, characters, natural and supernatural, embody primary qualities rather than human ambivalences. The virtues of the English version are those of folk-tale: rapid narration unencumbered by detail which does not serve a thematic purpose, episodes following each other with the detached clarity of panels in a strip cartoon, a one-dimensional presentation of the world, natural and supernatural, merely as a backdrop to action, all in the service of a conflict of black and white values embodied in stereotyped characters. Launfal, steward of a king 'Þat held Engelond yn good lawes' (l. 2), whose first thought on being restored to fortune by his lover is to feast 'pouere gestes', clothe knights, reward religious (his charity mirroring her love), whose benevolence sways judges in his favour, represents order, generosity, justice. Guinevere, whose shameless avowal of her passion for the hero is a perversion of Tryamour's frankness, expresses her enmity by withholding her gifts, sows disorder in the court, and abuses justice by false accusation and improper influence. The personal conflict between them is reflected at the social level in those who share their values: the mayor with his grudging hospitality, Arthur moved to override justice by Guinevere's suasion (ll. 835–37), the urchin who greets the procession bringing gifts to Launfal with: "'Nys he but a wrecche!/What þar (*need*) any man of hym recche?'" (ll. 394–95); the generosity of the mayor's daughter, the resistance of his barons to Arthur's injustice (ll. 838–46), the magnanimity of his nephews, finally forced to leave the impoverished Launfal, who explain their old clothes as worn only for hunting with him on a rainy day (ll. 154–80). Such concrete details constitute the realism of *Launfal*; its romance is rooted in its values – in the conviction that the hero's qualities deserve to be rewarded by a love more honourable and more socially valid than that of Guinevere, focus of adulterous passion and feudal chaos – rather than in the trappings of the genre which barely disguise its folklore frame.[14]

## The dominance of genre: *William of Palerne*

The ease with which a shift of emphasis reveals the patterns of folk-tale underlying romance is a reminder that both are deeply formulaic in nature. The romance mode, in search of appropriate narrative forms, not only borrowed many of the expressive means of folk-tale but itself evolved formal conventions which gradually assumed an independent existence of their own, constituting a grammar of romance which could be individually and creatively used to explore conflicting aspects of contemporary codes, of individual idealism in breach of social code, or of ideal at odds with reality, or mechanically manipulated to illustrate comfortable truisms of a vaguely idealistic or escapist kind. The genre so established is formulaic from its linguistic surface to its underlying plot structure, often a dual pattern of exile and return or love and marriage embodying a number of conventional episodes, freely interchangeable, each of which may in turn be composed of motifs conventionally associated with them. Under the dominance of genre the compositional process may become largely automatic: as with folk-tale, the episodes and motifs which become conventionalized are those which have acquired associations which make them particularly appropriate in relation to others, so the author's initial choice of deep narrative structure largely determines his choice of components at other levels if the work is to fulfil established expectations. So with the modern genres of film, television, and pulp literature, much of the audience's pleasure may come from the fulfilment of expectations, the ritualistic working out of formulae, with the comforting assurance that this is how the world works and the vague approval of some generalized value of individual freedom, social justice, or defence of democracy. Just as intellectuals, though they may work with or against the genre conventions to demonstrate their own more self-conscious conception of the mode, are probably ill-fitted to appreciate the meaning which such clichés hold for a popular audience, so modern readers cannot with confidence judge the satisfaction originally provided by what seem to them mechanical compilations of genre conventions. The persistence of such story-patterns as the career of a male Cinderella suggests that it encodes a message of the inevitable success of humble ability coupled with the implication that such ability is rooted in nobility of nature reassuring to all classes in any age of social stratification. A genre exploiting such conventionalized codes at many levels was assured of widespread and long-lasting appeal.[15]

Between the late fourteenth century and the beginning of the sixteenth England produced a number of such composites of genre conventions, some translated from French, some apparently original compilations. Some are parasitical upon the established Matters: such as Lord Berner's *Arthur of Little Britain* translated from a French fantasy of adventures and wonders; John Metham's *Amoryus and Cleopes* which borrows many features of the Alexander romances to create an exotic setting for a version of the Pyramus and Thisbe story which ends with the resurrection of the lovers by a miracle of the Virgin, their conversion and that of the Persian hosts; and *The Siege of Jerusalem* and *Titus and Vespasian*, twin English representatives of a widespread fusion of legend and romance in which the Emperor and his son, cured of disease by Christian relics, destroy Jerusalem and take a terrible revenge for the death of Christ. Others are widely eclectic, drawing adventures from every kind of source, set in the highest society regal and noble, ranging widely in locations but with a preference for the exotic Middle East, vaguely focused upon love of every kind from divine love to incest.

Many are characteristically romantic in their double standard of morality, climaxing the violent careers of their heroes with pious retirement to hermitage or Holy Land. The twin heroes of *Valentine and Orson*, born to an empress of Constantinople falsely banished for adultery, meet after long separation when the latter, nursed by a bear, is tamed by his brother who has been brought up as a perfect knight, and joins him in endless adventures, slaughtering Saracens and fighting dragons, before Valentine unwittingly kills his father and retires to live in abject humility under the palace steps while Orson becomes a hermit. The hero of *Generides*, born of a casual union between a king of Ynde and a princess of Syria, later goes to his father's court where he rejects the Queen's advances and is beaten by the steward who is her lover; falling in love with a princess of Persia, he commutes between her service and the restoration of his father, dethroned by his wife and her lover, and after numerous adventures marries his princess and reigns in both kingdoms. Where the settings are more domestic the emotions seem even more violent. In *Melusine* and *The Romauns of Partenay*, two versions of a family legend of the house of Lusignan, the Duke breaks a vow never to visit his fairy wife at time of childbirth and is imprisoned in a mountain by his three daughters whom she in turn punishes, condemning Melusine to become a serpent from the waist down every Saturday; married to Raymond, Count of Lusignan, he breaks his vow never to visit her on that day, forcing her to wander the world as a spectre. The grotesque dominates in *The Squyr of Lowe Degre* whose humble hero must prove his fidelity to a princess of Hungary over seven years in the course of which their love is betrayed by a steward whom the squire kills and dresses in his own clothes; the Princess, mistaking the disfigured body for her lover's, keeps it by her bed until the King, convinced of her fidelity, allows her to marry the exiled squire. There are constant echoes of other texts, barely detectable among the common stock of romance conventions – secret love of a superior lady, exchange of rings, father–son, brother–brother combats, marriage of mortal and *fée*, pursuit of a magic hart, three-day tournaments – themselves not absolutely distinguishable from inherited folklore motifs: twin brothers as heroes, faithful companion, false steward, credulous king, exiled queen, children stolen by a wild animal. Convincing or incredible according to the talents of the compiler, these widely popular composites left to following ages the dominant impression of romance as fantastic, exotic, fictitious, divorced from real life yet irresistibly fascinating.

The composite nature of such romances allowed English redactors to discriminate between their components and so alter the balance of genre characteristics without radically affecting its relationship to the mode. There is an interesting if indeterminate example in *William of Palerne* (south-west Midlands, *c.* 1350), a version in alliterative long lines of *Guillaume de Palerne*, composed in the late twelfth century for Yolande, daughter of Baldwin IV, Count of Hainaut. Exceptionally, the English poet too acknowledges a patron, Humphrey de Bohun, Earl of Hereford who commissioned it 'For hem þat knowe no Frensche' (l. 5533), possibly the households of his two manors near Gloucester rather than his own courtly circle.[16] The redaction might be expected to reflect this contrast of audiences in fundamental alterations to the original, but both versions tell essentially the same story. William, Prince of Apulia, is stolen in infancy by a werewolf who, to protect him from the murderous designs of his uncle, carries him from Sicily to a wood near Rome where he is brought up by a cowherd until the Emperor, struck by the lad's promising appearance, appoints him page to his daughter Melior who inevitably falls in love with him. William, knighted for his valour against invading Saxons, elopes with the Princess just as she is about to be married to a prince of Greece and, aided by the werewolf, crosses to Sicily where he finds his mother besieged in Palermo by the King of Spain, defeats him in combat and forces his queen to disenchant the werewolf, her stepson Alphouns, whom she had hoped to replace in the succession with her own son. William becomes emperor, Alphouns King of Spain, and multiple marriages reward the virtuous.

The mixture of elements suggests a folk-tale of the male-Cinderella type incorporating the motif of the helpful beast and much popular lore on werewolves. Its relationship to the romance mode is evident in the basic pattern of young love frustrated by social barriers fighting its way to happiness by mutual loyalty, courage and ingenuity, largely freed from the restraints of reality by folk-tale optimism and the exotic setting. In genre terms the French version is usually classed as a *roman d'aventure* on the basis of its close-packed incident and characteristic plot-machinery of mistaken identities, disguises, enchantments, and prophetic dreams. But just as the Sicilian setting probably reflects the fact that the Count of Saint-Pol, Yolande's husband, spent the winter of 1190–91 there on his way to the Holy Land, so the influence of the patroness may account for the extent to which the folk-tale has been impregnated with the doctrines of *amour courtois* expressed in repeated analyses of emotion emphasizing the agonies of love-sickness and the joys of lovers in each other's company.[17]

In a faithful, if somewhat plodding redaction in which, despite omissions, the French octosyllabic couplets are bloated by alliterative grandiloquence to greater bulk than the original, the adventures survive at full length but the courtly elaboration of the love-scenes is more cavalierly treated. They form a self-contained episode in which Melior's dawning love for William leads her to examine her feelings in a long monologue and confide in her companion Alisaundrine who promises her a herb which will bring relief. Meanwhile William dreams that Melior offers herself to him and reflects on his unworthiness but, questioned by her confidante, describes his sufferings in which Melior recognizes her own, leading her to reflect again on the nature of her feelings before Alisaundrine brings them together in mutual confession of their love.

The English poet reproduces the classic *amour courtois* pattern, but shows his impatience with its conventions by fusing the heroine's two soliloquies into one extended monologue (ll. 433–570), switching at a point in the first when she accuses her heart of betraying her into feelings for which others will blame her to her own rejection of such a liaison in the second. Love now speaks in her heart warning her that he prefers nobility of nature to noble birth, an argument which the compressed English version places within a few lines of the doubts it is intended to dispel, but loosely paraphrased, the persuasive voice of Love being replaced by Melior's own deduction from the rich clothes in which the infant William had been found, her observation of his gallant behaviour and the regard in which others hold him. The effect is forthright and explicit, leading to Melior's determination to give herself to William, allowing the redaction to return to the sequence of her first soliloquy where she reflects on the practical problem of how to inform him. The result is more effective dramatically and more convincing in human terms, giving point to Melior's soul-searching by allowing her to reason away objections to her love so that the action need not be delayed when the opportunity to declare it occurs, though there are occasional lapses in the pruning process leading to unnecess- ary repetition of ideas and over-emphatic translation which turns fantasy into comedy, as when William, clasping his pillow, dreams that Melior is in his arms:

> Þat puluere clept he curteisly and kust it ful ofte,                 *pillow*
> And made þerwiþ þe most merþe þat ani man schold;
> But þan in his saddest solas softili he awaked.     *deepest pleasure*
> Ak so liked him his layk wiþ þe ladi to pleie,                    *sport*
> Þat after he was awaked a ful long þrowe,                          *time*
> He wende ful witerly sche were in is armes;                     *surely*
> Ac Peter! it nas but is puluere, to proue þe soþe.   (ll. 675–81)[18]

Once rhetorical convention gives way to mutual confessions of love, the English author pays close attention to the practical problems facing the young lovers. Far from providing a herb to end their love, Alisaundrine forwards it in every way; but the herb may have suggested to the redactor that she has magic powers since he inde- pendently credits her with causing the dreams in which William's passion is first roused by a vision of Melior and then calmed by her gift of a rose. It is she who provides the disguise, two white bearskins, in which they escape from the Emperor's palace, fascinating the redactor who doubles the account given by a terrified servant who sees them (ll. 1764–85), virtually creates a scene in which the Emperor is given a graphic report (ll. 2154–73), and turns a single speech into a lively colloquial exchange between workmen who find the bears asleep in a quarry (ll. 2241–77). His only substantial invention of incident comes in a similar context: to help the lovers, disguised now as deer, to land in Sicily, the werewolf creates a diversion by leaping ashore pursued by the crew (ll. 2713–66); the English author adds a scene in which a shipboy strikes down the hind and is surprised to see her caught up and carried ashore by the hart (ll. 2767–91), an account of which he later gives to his shipmates (ll. 2805–29). Such human reactions seem to interest him more than the conventional values of romance. He doubles the original account of how the Emperor discovers the foundling William in the forest (ll. 170–383), emphasizing the boy's good heart and simple nature, his generosity in killing game for his playmates, in protecting his foster-parents from the Emperor's enquiries and thanking them for their care on leaving for the court. When he finally recovers his patrimony, the rewards he heaps on his foster-parents are detailed at twice the original length (ll. 5859–97).

The effect is to present William as a folk-hero rather than a chivalric figure. By contrast, two long battle sequences, the Saxon invasion in which William wins his spurs and shows himself worthy of Melior (ll. 1067–1310) and the Siege of Palermo in which he wins back his heritage (ll. 3261–3934), are cut to less than half the original length, concentrating on the hero's personal exploits and such exotic details as the respect shown by his horse in kneeling before him. Surprisingly, he shows little of the alliterative poets' usual fondness for description of conflict, ceremonial, and feasting, preferring the beauty of nature in the garden where the lovers meet (ll. 816–24) and the scene where the cowherd sits 'clouʒtand (*mending*) kyndely his schon' with his dog beside him until William is tempted out of the werewolf's lair by the beauty of the place (ll. 21–27). The naïvety of tone suits well the elements of *roman idyllique*, of young lovers united against a hostile world and their boy and girl adventures in the wildwood; less well the courtly and chivalric trappings in which the tastes of the Countess Yolande had clothed them and from which one of the earliest alliterative romance writers lacked the independence to free the original folk-tale.

## Romance as a didactic genre: *Amis and Amiloun*

The romance mode, by its projection of an ideal in defiance of reality, is inherently revolutionary and reformist, though comparatively oblique in its didactic means. The association, however diluted, gave the flexible conventions of the genre particular expressive value for didactic writers in an age when didacticism was the dominant mode. The result was romances like *Roberd of Cisyle* in which a proud king who derides the idea that God can put down the mighty and exalt the humble, finds himself transformed into a beggar mocked and abused in his own court until the angel who has taken his place as king appoints him court fool before restoring him, humbled, to his throne. The hero of *Sir Amadace*, who has exhausted his estates in largess, spends his last coin to bury a knight who had died in debt but is directed by a White Knight to a rich wreck from which he equips himself for jousting in which he is so successful that he wins the hand of a princess; when the White Knight reappears, demanding that the half-share promised to him should include wife and child, Amadace is about to cut them in half when his benefactor reveals himself as the spirit of the buried debtor and praises his honour in fulfilling his pledge. Pious legend comes even closer to a secular saint's legend in *Sir Cleges* for whose hero, similarly impoverished, a cherry tree bears fruit at Christmas, earning him royal favour through which to avenge himself on royal officers who mocked his poverty.

The popularity and flexibility of such ambivalent material is illustrated by the four surviving texts of *Amis and Amiloun* (east Midlands, late thirteenth century), independently derived from a lost Anglo-Norman original and none directly derived from another, implying considerable popularity, and at more than twice the length (2500 lines) of existing analogues of the supposed source, suggesting expansion apparent in a number of additional scenes. The medium is the twelve-line tail-rhyme stanza on four rhymes only whose technical demands have not inhibited the poet's creation of vivid dramatic scenes and lively dialogue. The story, found in every European literature from Norse to Hungarian and every genre from ballad to drama, tells of two friends, knights of Lombardy, born on the same day to neighbouring barons, who grow up together indistinguishable in beauty, strength, and courtesy. When the death of his parents calls Amiloun away from the ducal court they serve, he presents Amis with one of a pair of golden cups symbolizing their friendship, renewed in a parting oath:

> 'Broþer, as we er trewþe-pliȝt                       *contracted*
> Boþe wiþ word and dede,
> Fro þis day forward neuer mo
> To faily oþer for wele no wo,
> To help him at his nede,
> Broþer, be now trewe to me,
> And y schal ben as trewe to þe,
> Also god me spede!' (ll. 293–300)[19]

But already it is under threat from a steward who, jealous that his

proposal to replace the absent Amiloun as his friend is rejected by
Amis – "'Y no schal neuer mi treuþe breke'" (l. 371) – spies on him
when the Duke's daughter Belisaunt begs him to plight her his troth.
He refuses out of loyalty to her father – "'And y ded mi lord þis
deshonour,/Þan were ich an iuel traitour'" (ll. 607–08) – but reluctantly
consents when she threatens to play Potiphar's wife; the false steward
denounces him to the Duke as a traitor and undertakes to prove the
charge in trial by combat.

This brings the first crisis of the story: Amis cannot in honour refuse
the challenge and yet cannot meet the steward since his charge is true.
He sets out to seek the aid of his sworn brother who meanwhile
dreams of Amis being attacked by a bear and goes to find him only to
learn: "'Bot þou help me at þis nede,/Certes, y can no noþer rede (*other
course*),/Mi liif, it is forlorn!'" (ll. 1078–80). They exchange clothes and
Amiloun goes to take up the steward's challenge while Amis imper-
sonates him in his domain and, on his insistence, in his marriage bed
where he lays a naked sword between himself and his friend's wife –
much to her annoyance! Amiloun, meanwhile, arrives at the Duke's
court just in time to prevent Belisaunt and her mother, as sureties for
the missing Amis, being burnt alive. But as he rides to the lists, a voice
from heaven warns him that if he fights in his friend's name he will be
a leper within the year.

> 'Þo þat be þine best frende
> Schal be þi most fon,                                    *greatest foes*
> And þi wiif and alle þi kinne
> Schul fle þe stede þatow art inne,                       *place*
> And forsake þe ichon.'   (ll. 1268–72)

But Amiloun will not abandon his brother – "'To hold mi treuþe schal
y nouȝt spare,/Lete god don alle his wille'" (ll. 1283–84) – and, calling
on God to justify his oath of Amis's innocence, engages the steward,
kills him, and, having vindicated his friend's honour, is awarded
Belisaunt in Amis's name. Returning to marry her, Amis promises
Amiloun his help in any necessity; with his own wife, accounting for
the absence of the sword from their bed, he explains what he has done
and answers her reproaches with:

> 'Y no ded it for non oþer þing
> Bot to saue mi broþer fro wo,
> And ich hope, ȝif ich hadde nede,
> His owhen liif to lesse to mede,                         *lose, in consequence*
> He wald help me also.'   (ll. 1496–1500)

Fortune now favours Amis, who fathers two children and succeeds the Duke, while Amiloun, stricken with leprosy, is driven from home by his wife, taking only his golden cup and a young nephew who is finally forced to push him about in a little cart. One day, as they beg before Amis's court, he sends them wine in his cup which Amiloun receives in his; Amis, thinking the leper must have stolen it, attacks him, but the boy reproaches him with ingratitude to one who had rescued him. He and Belisaunt nurse the leper tenderly and, when an angel promises a cure if he is washed in the blood of their children, agonize over where their duty lies:

> 'O lef liif,' sche seyd þo,                              *dear*
> 'God may sende ous childer mo,
> Of hem haue þou no care.
> ȝif it ware at min hert rote,
> For to bring þi broþer bote,                         *cure*
> My lyf y wold not spare.'     (ll. 2392–97)

The sacrifice is made, but when they go to bury the bodies the children are found playing happily together. Returning home, cured, Amiloun finds his wife about to marry again; the two friends imprison her on bread and water, take revenge on her disloyal supporters, bestow the estate on his faithful nephew and, after a happy life together, die on the same day and lie together in an abbey they had built.

The celebration of a friendship which defies Fate and human malice is diagrammatically clear-cut, the pattern of major scenes connected by brief narrative links providing thematic emphasis in the absence of any commentary. The English poet seems, so far as his treatment of the original can be judged, to have reordered and elaborated elements with that end in view: the emphatic form of the initial vow on which the lifelong commitment rests; the twin cups which symbolize it, introduced earlier and at greater length; the heavenly voice warning of retribution, transferred from after the trial by combat when Amiloun is about to marry Belisaunt to just before it so that it warns not of bigamy but of his frustration of divine justice by personating Amis, making his decision to put friendship above self-interest a fully informed and conscious one.

The very thoroughness with which the theme is stated and restated has alienated some modern readers, not by such improbabilities as the identity of the two friends even in bed but because the absolute value given to friendship seems to be at the expense of other values – feudal loyalty, truthfulness, and justice. More recently, however, their mutual fidelity has been seen as part of a wider principle operative in all of these, that universal *treuþe* which binds man to God, to his fellow

men in the bonds of feudalism, and which constitutes his own integrity. This is the frame within which their friendship is tested: the
extremity of Amiloun's self-sacrifice is to be judged against his conscious breach of *treupe* to God; his patient acceptance of his leprosy
acknowledges the contemporary view of it as divine retribution for sin;
the corresponding sacrifice of his children by Amis, a monstrous
breach of the laws of God and man and of familial loyalty, is none the
less prompted by an angelic messenger. The theme is harmonized by
the behaviour of others: Belisaunt, who begins by trying to seduce
Amis into a breach of trust to her father, his liege lord, and forces him
to plight his troth to her, learns to value above such an empty form the
spirit of *treupe* in her husband's readiness to sacrifice their children for
his friend's sake and acquiesces in it; Amiloun's wife, by contrast, is
justified by the letter of medieval law in driving her leper husband
from his home but not by the spirit of Christian charity which informs
*treupe*. His nephew is true to 'the law of kinde', which unites natural
feeling and family loyalty, in refusing to desert him, even when a
knight of Amis's court, unable to comprehend such disinterested
behaviour, offers him an office if he will leave the leper (ll. 1909–2004).
The boy's fidelity moves Amis to send his cup to the leper and, once
recognized as his friend, to take him in his arms without thought of
personal risk. Without knowing that the leprosy was due to the
sacrifice made on their behalf, he and his wife sacrifice their children in
blind faith as Abraham would have Isaac. *Treupe* is not mere technical
fidelity to a vow but a universal quality uniting brotherhood and
Christian charity.[20]

*Amis and Amiloun* is exemplary by virtue of the model of fidelity
which it presents, but the manner of presentation is not didactic.
Generalization of that quality as an aspect of *treupe* gives it a specifically
Christian framework; but that need not, as some critics have supposed,
make it a secular saint's life. Tacitly or explicitly, the Christian faith is
the ultimate frame of reference for all medieval romances and the
miraculous revival of the sacrificed children, like the cure which their
blood has effected, are signs of God's grace to sinful men rather than
rewards for saintly endurance under spiritual tests. True, the basic
story-pattern of fidelity tested to extremity invited pietistic treatment;
already in the twelfth century the *Vita Sanctorum Amici et Amelii*
attaches the two friends to the court of Charlemagne in whose wars
against an enemy of the Pope they die as martyrs, when their tombs
are miraculously united in the same church. But the English version
derives from a different branch lacking these hagiographic embellishments. So the saint-like patience with which Amiloun endures his
leprosy need not imply that, as in the *Vita*, he recognizes it as God's
chastisement of his beloved. Having supplied a specific cause, Christian

but also feudal, for his illness, the author of the chivalric version has simply exploited a narrative pattern familiar in saint's lives as the appropriate response to divine affliction.[21]

## The diffusion of genre

It would have been strange if the romance mode which gradually invaded the epic, coloured past history and contemporary chronicles, lent charismatic overtones to royal biographies should not also have influenced sacred narrative in an age of pietism. England produced a number of texts which cling to romance by their social setting, reshuffling the familiar genre motifs while exalting the spiritual values of Christian legend. The hero of *Sir Isumbras*, absorbed in happy family life, forgets his duty to God until visited with misfortune, Saracens carrying off his wife, wild beasts his children, an eagle his gold; all this he bears patiently, labouring as a smith until, after many years, an angel announces his forgiveness and good fortune returns, he finds his gold in the eagle's nest, recovers his queen, and is joined by three knights, who prove to be his sons, in forced conversion of his pagan subjects. In *Octavian*, the Emperor's mother accuses his wife of infidelity, she is driven out into the forest where wild beasts carry off her twin sons; one is found and raised by a Paris butcher, becomes a popular hero for his skill in rough sports, defeats the Sultan's giant champion, and marries his daughter; when he, the Emperor, and the King of France are captured by the Sultan, they are rescued by the other son and his companion lion, do great slaughter on the Saracens, are reunited with the Empress, and take revenge on her wicked mother-in-law. The dual appeal to popular and chivalric values, the repeated pattern of rejection or exile, trial, constancy and reward, the overtone of piety, defence of the weak, and defiance of God's enemies are characteristic. The passive endurance of abused women who serve as the object of active male idealism is the most persistent motif. In *Sir Triamour*, a false steward, repulsed in his advances to the Queen of Aragon, accuses her of infidelity, she is driven into exile, bears a boy in the forest who grows up to triumph in tournaments, unwittingly defeating his own father, then serving as his champion in a trial by combat, defeating three giants to win the hand of a princess and reunite his parents at his own wedding.

These distressed queens are sisters to a trio of saintly women: Constance who, fleeing from an unnatural father, marries in a foreign land only to be accused in her husband's absence of giving birth to monstrous offspring, endures endless sufferings with patient meekness to be eventually reunited with her forgiving husband (as in Chaucer's 'Man of Law's Tale'); Florence who, in the absence of her husband, is persecuted by one of her rejected suitors, assaulted, and abandoned in a forest, betrayed by those who befriend her, sold overseas, ship-wrecked, finds refuge in a nunnery, acquires fame as a healer, and cures her former persecutors before being reunited with her husband (as in *Le Bone Florence of Rome*); and Griselda, subjected by her husband to endless tests of her devotion in adventures which echo theirs (as in Chaucer's 'Clerk's Tale'). They, in turn, are near kin to Eustace, a worldly officer to the Emperor Trajan who, in his hunting, is con-verted by the appearance of Christ between the antlers of a hart, bears with fortitude the loss of his wealth, the abduction of his wife, the inevitable carrying off of his sons by wild animals, before fighting his way back to fortune and voluntary acceptance of martyrdom for his faith. And St Eustace is a blood-brother of Sir Isumbras.

Modern critics, embarrassed by the association of sacred and secular, have sought criteria by which such texts could be classified either as romances or as sacred legends. Distinctions have been found in the nature of the hero's powers, inherent and personal in the romance, manifestations of divine power through a mortal in the saint's life; in the forms of supernatural intervention, magical or miraculous; and in the hero's moral character as chivalric idealist or sinful man in need of regeneration.[22] They may serve to distinguish clear-cut examples at the extremes of each genre, but those considered above vacillate not only from text to text but from one episode to another between folk-tale, romance, and sacred legend. Others familiarly classified as romances blur these distinctions: the derivatives of the *Pseudo-Turpin* extend the charisma of epic heroes by characteristic attributes of militant saints; in *Chevalere Assigne* divine intervention allows the boy hero a victory beyond his personal prowess; the hero of *Sir Gawain and the Green Knight* is both chivalric idealist and sinner. Just as chivalric values are rooted in Christian faith, so the romance genre was a valid idiom for the expression of saintly charisma and motifs from the lives of saints could express the spiritual aspirations of chivalric heroes, giving some Guy of Warwick a second career as a champion of God.

## Notes

1. See B. B. Broughton, *The Legends of King Richard I Coeur de Lion: A Study of Sources and Variations to the year 1600* (The Hague, 1966).

2. Text from Cambridge, Gonville and Caius College MS 175/96, edited by Karl Brunner, *Der Mittelenglische Versroman Über Richard Löwenherz* (Leipzig, 1913).

3. Some leaves of an eighth manuscript have been identified by Norman Davis, 'Another Fragment of *Richard Coer de Lyon*', *Notes and Queries*, n.s., 16 (1969), 447–52.

4. See Dorothee Metlitzki, *The Matter of Araby in Medieval England* (New Haven, Connecticut, 1977), pp. 240–50.

5. Text from British Library MS Egerton 2862, edited by D. B. Sands, *Middle English Verse Romances* (New York, 1966).

6. See Geraldine Barnes, 'Cunning and Ingenuity in the Middle English *Floris and Blauncheflur*', *Medium Aevum*, 53 (1984), 10–23.

7. See Metlitzki, pp. 136–40, and L. H. Hornstein, 'The Historical Background of the *King of Tars*', *Speculum*, 16 (1941), 404–14.

8. See J. B. Friedman, *Orpheus in the Middle Ages* (Cambridge, Massachusetts, 1970), pp. 146–210, and J. Burke Severs, 'The Antecedents of Sir Orfeo', in *Studies in Medieval Literature in Honour of Professor Albert Croll Baugh*, edited by MacEdward Leach (Philadelphia, Pennsylvania, 1961), pp. 187–207.

9. Text from the National Library of Scotland MS 19.2.1 (Auchinleck MS), edited by A. J. Bliss, *Sir Orfeo*, second edition (Oxford, 1966).

10. H. Bergner ('*Sir Orfeo* and the Sacred Bonds of Matrimony', *Review of English Studies*, n.s., 30 (1979), 432–34) suggests that the formula echoes both Ruth 1. 6 and the medieval vow of matrimonial consent.

11. See P. J. Lucas, 'An Interpretation of *Sir Orfeo*', *Leeds Studies in English*, n.s., 6 (1972), 1–9, and Mary Hynes-Berry, 'Cohesion in *King Horn* and *Sir Orfeo*', *Speculum*, 50 (1975), 652–70.

12. See J. K. Knapp, 'The Meaning of *Sir Orfeo*', *Modern Language Quarterly*, 29 (1968), 263–73, and Patrizia Grimaldi, '*Sir Orfeo* as Celtic Folk Hero, Christian Pilgrim, and Medieval King', in *Allegory, Myth and Symbol*, edited by M. W. Bloomfield (Cambridge, Massachusetts, 1981), pp. 147–61.

13. Text from Btitish Library MS Cotton Caligula A.ii, edited by A. J. Bliss, *Thomas Chestre: Sir Launfal* (London, 1960).

14. See B. K. Martin, '*Sir Launfal* and the Folktale', *Medium Aevum*, 35 (1966), 199–210, and D. F. Lane, 'Conflict in *Sir Launfal*', *Neuphilologische Mitteilungen*, 74 (1973), 283–87.

15. See Susan Wittig, *Stylistic and Narrative Structures in the Middle English Romance* (Austin, Texas, 1978), pp. 179–90.

16. See Thorlac Turville-Petre, 'Humphrey de Bohun and *William of Palerne*', *Neuphilologische Mitteilungen*, 75 (1974), 250–52.

17. See C. W. Dunn, *The Foundling and the Werewolf: A Literary-Historical Study of 'Guillaume de Palerne'* (Toronto, 1960).

18. Text from Cambridge, Kings College MS 13, edited by W. W. Skeat, *The Romance of William of Palerne*, EETS, ES, 1 (London, 1867).

19. Text from the National Library of Scotland MS 19.2.1 (Auchinleck MS), edited by MacEdward Leach, *Amis and Amiloun*, EETS, 203 (London, 1937).

20. See Dale Kramer, 'Structural Artistry in *Amis and Amiloun*', *Annuale Medievale*, 9 (1968), 103–22, V. B. Richmond, *The Popularity of Middle English Romance* (Bowling Green, Ohio, 1975), pp. 92–105, and D. R. Baldwin, '*Amis and Amiloun*: The Testing of *Treuþe*', *Papers on Language and Literature*, 16 (1980), 353–65.

21. For a hagiological interpretation see Ojars Kratins, 'The Middle English *Amis and Amiloun*: Chivalric Romance or Secular Hagiography?', *PMLA*, 81 (1966), 347–54; in the Introduction to the Leach edition of *Amis and Amiloun* it is seen as a romance with didactic tendencies.

22. See D. T. Childress, 'Between Romance and Legend: "Secular Hagiography" in Middle English Literature', *Philological Quarterly*, 57 (1978), 311–22.

## Chapter 9
# Conclusion

It is evident that neither the critical basis of this study, definition by mode rather than genre, nor its structural independence of preconceived theories of genre categorization has provided any universal key to the understanding of medieval romance; it was not to be expected that it should. What it has perhaps done is to clarify some of the issues which have confused understanding and limited appreciation of the distinctive character of the English examples. The disparate nature of the corpus has perplexed and irritated critics, leading them either to reject large parts of it as displaying, upon a strict definition, only the superficial accidents rather than the essence of the genre, or to adopt a genre definition so imprecise as to include almost any example of vernacular narrative.[1] Both attitudes are inherent in English criticism from the earliest surveys and compilations in which scholars still under the influence of nineteenth-century Romanticism, expecting a quality of imagination obsessed by the mystery of the remote and unattainable, found disappointingly little of it in those texts which best reproduced the superficial characteristics of the genre. What they regarded as essential characteristics – marvellous adventures motivated by passionate love in a combination of chivalric action and courtly sentiment – they found only in the most sophisticated examples. With the *roman courtois* as their model they inevitably judged much of the English corpus too variable in kind and quality to be conveniently included under any definition of romance. Their critical heritage has left more recent commentators with a half-conscious conviction of the inferiority of English medieval romance in relation to a concept of the genre as incorporating particular values and literary motifs never precisely defined.[2]

That concept was supposedly embodied in the narrative fiction of France, the most innovative culture in medieval Europe, yet the outline survey presented in Chapter 2 scarcely suggests a monolithic genre even of *roman courtois*. Within the space of little more than a century – brief time when the cultural climate changed so slowly – courtly fiction changed radically in scale, structure, story-matter, and social values despite the relative uniformity of its audience and the common literary inheritance of its authors. The period of evolution can be shortened by over fifty years if the *Chanson de Roland* is omitted. It is certainly not essential to a demonstration of the variety of courtly narrative in this formative period. But it seems perverse to exclude from the history of romance a text which so perfectly exemplifies its archetypal characteristic of reality transformed in the image of desire, the unpalatable facts of history glossed as a golden age when feudal solidarity in the service of a strong monarch defied internal and external threats to nationhood and faith, presenting the empire of Charlemagne not as it was but as the feuding barons of *c.* 1100 might have wished their fragmented France to be. For literary historians there is an obvious convenience in presenting the epic in stark contrast with the romance; when the *Roland* is set against the works of Chrétien de Troyes the effect is compelling and informative. But it is particularly so in terms of their values and the means by which they are expressed, those genre characteristics which were to be rapidly blurred as the military and feudal concerns of one age gave way to the wider social issues of the next, and expressive means shaped by oral performance were rapidly intermingled with those suited to reading and reflection. Later treatments of the Matter of France do not afford the sharp contrast provided by the *Roland* from whose epic purity they may be seen as degenerating. But that contrast has been exaggerated by the very uniqueness of the *Roland*, in its apparent crystallization of a lost oral tradition, its exclusively masculine concerns, and the marks of individual genius in its composition. It has been compounded by the preoccupation of literary historians with the promising concreteness of definition by genre, with the modern conception that the values of epic are more worthy, more 'real' than those of romance, even perhaps by the preference of patriotic sentiment for 'history' rather than fantasy. The effect has been unfortunate in so far as it has distracted attention from the fact that fundamentally both are in the same mode, two among the many specialized genres in which it has expressed itself through the ages.

In terms of mode the history of narrative literature from 1100 onwards appears coherent and progressive, changing in interests and values, rapidly evolving the expressive means of a new genre, but consistent in its ambivalent balance of ideal and reality, individual and social concerns, and its inherent challenge to the reader to measure them against his own values and experience. In those terms the first treatments of the Matter of Rome seem rather a shift of emphasis than the creation of a new genre; in the revamped epics love is added to war as a further test of heroic powers, but somewhat extraneously, the subject of rhetorical elaboration rather than moral analysis, coexisting with rather than challenging older values. Only in *Narcisus* and *Piramus et Tisbé*, epic neither in scale nor in values, does passionate love emerge as the thematic focus, and there it is female-centred, tragic in its outcome and implicitly disapproved as well as admired; and they, of course, are echoes of Greek romance, reminders of the persistence of the mode. Of the twin ideals of war and love which the Matter of Rome had to offer twelfth-century France, one was familiar and welcomed for its continuing relevance to contemporary life, the other stimulated awareness of an element in human relations which social conditions had hitherto suppressed. The Ovidian sentiment and rhetorical techniques it brought with it may have been welcome to the schoolmen who evolved the new genre, but they might not have gone beyond the schoolroom if both elements in the new-found matter had not appealed to something in contemporary situations and sensibilities.

If proof were needed that the emergent genre was now a living medium largely independent of literary tradition, ready to use whatever material could best express the interests of the age, it is provided by the *lais* of Marie de France, varied in scale and narrative source, but consistent in their presentation of the right of women to love and be loved as a positive value. The determined single-mindedness of her heroines and the frequency with which they are allowed to eat their cake and have it in the best manner of romance may owe something to the preferences of the authoress, but they testify to the existence of an audience not hitherto clearly identified and interests not openly expressed in the restricting context of the Matter of Rome. Despite the intrusion of the supernatural, the freedom of the story-matter from historical associations gives it greater contemporaneity and wider social reference than the distanced, aristocratic, male-centred epic. Fiction has begun to impose its own relevance, its own form of truth.

It is true that in Marie's *lais* the sole value on which their idealism is based does not openly meet the challenge of reality; the power of husbands and fathers is acknowledged, fate may bring lovers to a tragic end, but mutual love ignores or overrides marital duty, feudal obligation, moral law, and church doctrine – which is not to deny the thrill which contemporary readers may have derived from the silent defiance of forces omnipresent in their minds. That challenge, unresolved but constantly acknowledged, is at the heart of the various versions of the Tristan legend. Its perennial fascination is rooted in the idea of love as an overmastering passion whose supernatural source in the love-potion tacitly admits the might of the inhibiting forces marshalled against an ideal which would value personal feeling above feudal obligation, marital fidelity, social duty. The irremovable objection of contemporary reality to the irresistible force of such a love provided a tension which informed a myriad illustrative episodes ranging in motivation from romantic daring to low trickery, in outcome from exaltation of selfless devotion to mockery at the impotence of a feudal cuckold, in atmosphere from high tragedy to low farce. All testify to the power of an ideal which defies ridicule, legal and moral sanction, death itself – though its chemical inspiration clearly worried some who would have preferred it to originate spontaneously in the human heart. A characteristic piece of romance machinery has made it possible to imagine the unimaginable, a mutual, selfless love which refines and ennobles; but the conscience of the age insists that it must also be degrading, socially destructive, and finally fatal.

It was left for Chrétien to attempt a reconciliation between ideal and reality, using the ideologically uncommitted Matter of Britain to suggest a variety of forms in which the old idealism of arms and the new one of love might harmonize in the service of a society more complex than that reflected in the *chansons de geste*, acknowledging the internal life of the individual as well as his relationship to others. If *Erec et Enide* suggests that married love, once its true nature is understood as mutual trust and self-abnegation, can inspire chivalry in the service of society more effectively than the tyranny of courtly love, *Lancelot* seems to imply that willing and absolute acceptance of that bond brings freedom from such forms of self-interest as concern for reputation to serve others instinctively and without expectation of reward. The apparent conflict of values need not reflect the preference of his patroness for adultery over Chrétien's for love within marriage; his purpose was not primarily didactic and the irony, ambivalence, and other methods by which he makes the reader conscious of the fictional process leave discrimination and moral judgement to him. In the best manner of romance, he provides for a wide range of temperaments, from the uncritical day-dreaming of the idealist to the ironic detachment of the realist. His fictions offer each a detached perspective on himself, his relations to others of both sexes and to society as a whole. Some critics have preferred the personal focus, contrasting the fantasy realm of Arthur unfavourably with the concrete political setting of the *Roland*; but the Round Table provided a valid, if ambivalent, model for a more settled age in which the personal ties of feudalism, loosened by the easing of external pressures, were slowly being replaced by the rule of law. At both levels, personal and social, the ambivalent relationship between the real and the ideal, inherent in the romance mode, seemed to have found perfect expression in Chrétien's conception of the genre.

Yet the genre went on evolving, Chrétien's *Perceval* foreshadowing the vast scale, interlaced structure, and thematic complexity of the Vulgate Cycle. In terms of mode the perspective is now dynastic, the personal idealism of the *roman courtois* set in the context of the history of a race and a faith, and the values cosmic, representatives of all the courtly virtues tested in the spiritual mission of the Grail and the inadequacy of worldly chivalry demonstrated against the ultimate reality of the downfall of a society. Set against the domestic miniatures of Marie's *lais*, this mammoth with its multiple levels of meaning, complex symbolism, and overt didacticism strains the concept of a uniform genre to the limit. Such contrasts were to multiply in the following centuries as French romance diversified in matter, form, and theme, the genre gradually assuming a life of its own so that its conventions could be applied to subjects at one extreme or other of the essentially mixed mode of romance, mystical, idealistic, didactic, or realistic, or to compilations of adventures to be enjoyed for their own sake without any thematic core. With the growth of a bourgeois audience inclined to affect the tastes of its betters, works were produced which imitated the fashionable externals of the genre without any real understanding of the aristocratic ideals by which the medieval mode had originally been formed. Liberated from the need to serve a code, incident became an end in itself and folklore, history, sacred legend, even contemporary life were plundered to produce hybrid compilations in which the aristocratic mode of *roman courtois* seemed to become lost. To those for whom Chrétien's romances represent the perfect embodiment of mode by genre all this must suggest degeneration. But even the early history of French romance illustrates the evolutionary nature of the mode, always searching for a more nearly perfect formulation of the aspirations of an age even while changing social circumstances are gradually remoulding them. The stimulus of some new social concept, such as courtly love, or the individual genius of such a poet as Chrétien may produce a perfect mating of mode and genre; but as its social references become outdated and its ideals fade into the romantic afterglow of the already-imagined and, in theory, already-achieved, its very classic status makes it unfit to express the new idealism of a new age. Artistically Chrétien's romances represent a high point of achievement in the genre but not the ultimate expression of the mode.

The extent to which English medieval romance participated in the evolutionary process may in one respect be judged by whether its handling of the various Matters which represent stages in it shows understanding of their related values or merely reproduces the associated genre characteristics. Any estimate of national appreciation of the mode which is based only on the surviving English corpus must be distorted by beginning so late in the evolutionary process. Quite apart from any inherent tendency towards romance in its pre-Conquest literature, England had been culturally involved in that process from the beginning as both producer and consumer and only the linguistic barrier, highly pervious in those trilingual centuries, prevented her from assuming that the *roman courtois* was part of her national heritage.[3] It is therefore natural that the versions of the Matter of France included in the corpus show no particular national consciousness; the campaigns of Charlemagne have become the general cause of Christendom versus Islam and the epic values once associated with them have faded to generalized truisms. By the familiar process by which ideals projected by the wish-fulfilment of one age in defiance of reality and their own ambivalence are seen in retrospect as glorious achievements of that golden age, the tension between aim and achievement has been very largely resolved in a romantic aura affirming feudal solidarity and Christian militancy. The *chanson de geste* has dwindled to what the *roman courtois* was to become for the Renaissance, a source of dramatic incident featuring charismatic heroes and coloured by the afterglow of an age of idealism. In the English versions action dominates, the charismatic figures have been pushed into the background by secondary or parvenu heroes observing generalized male codes in the service of common prejudices bordering on racism and bigotry.

But the degeneration of the original values of the *chansons* is not primarily due to the obtuseness of English redactors or the vulgarity of English audiences; it is part of the general degradation of the Matter of France once the social and military circumstances which both formed and challenged its central ideals had passed. Working for audiences at an even greater remove from those circumstances it is scarcely surprising that they were commonly attracted to such material and that they carried still further its neglect of meaning in favour of action. Where their discrimination can fairly be judged, as in the version of the *Roland*, their preference for black and white values over the ambivalences of the original has removed much of the narrative tension, though the partial nature of the surviving text may have weakened coherence as its martial episodes strengthen the impression of action predominating over meaning. But to generalize from this failure to a universal blindness to epic values in the romance mode would be to ignore the very variety of the English corpus and the part played by time and chance in the random process by which it grew; if the *Roland* had fallen into the hands of Layamon or the author of the alliterative *Morte Arthure* its values might have received more understanding treatment from poets who appreciated the tensions which could develop within a heroic society and the conflicting claims of personal reputation and feudal duty. The contrast can scarcely be due to any chauvinistic preference for native 'history'; identification with the French heroes is no less enthusiastic in these rough-and-ready redactions apparently intended for popular audiences than in the elaborate courtly productions of Caxton and Lord Berners who equally exploited their romantic aura and oversimplified their codes in the interests of chivalric propaganda.

There was equally little reason why the Matter of Rome should not have been welcome to a wide range of English readers. Coming to it as part of their own classical heritage, English authors were not compelled to accept any particular genre categorization imposed upon it by intermediate cultures. It could be seen as history, in part as their own history, as epic or romance, as a subject for philosophical and moral commentary, or exercises in rhetorical elaboration. Its evolution over many centuries had implanted a variety of values between which redactors could discriminate in emphasis if not absolutely. At one stage or another in the transmission its historical core had been overlain by legend and exotic lore, romanticized by the influence of Greek and later French romance, medievalized, Christianized, and given academic and literary respectability by the Latin paraphrases and rhetorical exercises of the schoolmen. It could therefore provide, in terms of mode, a vague romantic aura of momentous events in distanced and exotic settings; the careers of charismatic heroes exemplifying timeless male virtues with whose triumphs contemporary readers could associate themselves while attributing their failures to pagan vulnerability to fate and human folly; a historical perspective on contemporary values, including romantic love, clarified by distancing yet exposed to moral judgement.

All are exploited, in varying proportions, in the English versions. The clerics who abstracted the historical and philosophical material of *Alexander A* and *B* were capitalizing upon its romantic associations; exotic settings and the wonders of the East were made much of in the more academic redactions; the charisma of the heroes made them fit subjects for rhetorical celebration into the Renaissance. The alliterative redactors, though dutiful in their admiration of heroic idealism in the service of patriotic causes, comment critically on the inevitable failure of pagan aspirations, relishing the indulgence of wishful thinking and muffled moral doubts without resolving the characteristic tension of the mode which they inherited with their material. Their more popular counterparts, whose radical abbreviations discriminate in favour of adventure rather than codes, nevertheless reveal in it the romance of heroes grappling with fate, measuring them against human fallibility and the mutability of life rather than censoring them on the basis of Christian morality. In both love is incidental to the heroic career, women are inspirers or rewards of male virtue, pitied for the ill-usage they receive, but regarded as emotionally unstable and socially destructive. The serious interest of the French versions in emotional relations and their sporadic attempts to reconcile them with male values have left little trace.

It would seem that English redactors were not fully aware of the central focus of the romance mode in the Matters of France and Rome, valuing them more for their incidental appeal rather than for the particular ideals they had once expressed, now blurred by the passing of the social circumstances which formed them. In the Matter of Britain, however, they seem to have found a sharper relevance to their own age, helped perhaps by conviction of its historical truth, the variety of literary forms in which it was available, and the deep roots it had struck in native folklore, overriding distinctions of class and degrees of literacy. The range of meanings they found in it is indicated in the triple structure of Chapter 7, though individual texts treated there show how elements of the dominant mode can be combined in varying proportions. In those designated dynastic romances the central ideal is the triumph of a society unified round a hero-king and the opposing reality is the historical awareness that regal ambition, external resistance, and internal treachery have so often undermined such achievements. Established by Geoffrey of Monmouth as a necessary fiction dressed as fact, it provided a corporate racial memory for multiracial Britain in which post-Conquest tensions could be acknowledged yet glossed with an optimism which surmounted inevitable disaster with the Hope of the British. Layamon strengthened its claim upon the English imagination by recasting it, dramatically and in diction, in terms likely to evoke racial memories and associations.

Ambivalence enters with the alliterative *Morte Arthure*, adding the possibility that the vaunting ambition underlying the dynastic ideal, regal judgement unbalanced by the chivalric urge to personal prowess, may contribute fatally to its failure. The stanzaic *Morte Arthur* confronts the dynastic ideal embodied in Arthur with the central ideal of the *roman courtois*, that selfless love inspires perfect chivalry, embodied in his wife and loyal lieutenant, suggesting in the fatal exposure of the Round Table to divisive forces the limitations of idealism in the face of the conflicting demands which it makes upon men. The comprehensive view presented in Malory's *Morte Darthur*, though it cannot avoid the fatal outcome, celebrates the triumphs of worldly chivalry as well as its failures, admits its limitations in comparison with spiritual chivalry, yet leaves a lingering sense of the nobility of human aspiration to build a better society. The persistence of that aspiration beyond the failure of the dynastic ideal typifies the bitter-sweet ambivalence of the romance mode which, while acknowledging a world unchanged, can still imagine what a better world might be.

Ambivalence is not lacking in the chivalric romances as they strive to define the most absolute form of male idealism and its most perfect accomodation to the ideal of love and service, but the English versions suggest a preference for uncomplicated and positive statements of the romance mode. In them loss of ambivalence may involve loss of meaning, as with *Sir Tristrem* where the fated passion is looked on merely as an unfortunate accident, reducing the conflict of love and duty to a series of motiveless incidents. The opposite process is exemplified in

*Golagrus and Gawain* where conventional genre episodes are elaborately reinterpreted to express an ideal of self-abnegation and respect for another's integrity which, against normal chivalric experience, achieves its purpose without loss of honour on either side. Elsewhere it is Gawain's reputation as exemplar of the basic chivalric virtues, formalized and outdated by the gradual development of more specialized codes, which serves as a foil to an organic concept of chivalry as harmonizing rather than opposing personal, social, and moral qualities, perhaps the most original contribution of English romance to the evolution of the mode. In *Ywain and Gawain* his self-absorbed chivalry is set against the hero's gradual realization of the organic unity of qualities which constitute *trowth*, that integrity which lies in duties not forms, the service of others rather than self-glory. *Sir Gawain and the Green Knight*, most complex of all in its exploration of the romance mode, uses the same concept of *trowth*, combining that ideal of integrity to self, society and the chivalric code which the hero, haunted by his established reputation, strives to maintain with such absolute absorption that he momentarily, unconsciously neglects those inseparable aspects of *trowth*, integrity of soul, fidelity to God, which constitute the ultimate reality against which his idealism must be judged, forgetting in the bitterness of his self-condemnation the saving grace provided for fallible mankind. No romance acknowledges more clearly the dual roots of the mode in man's aspirations and his limitations.

Despite the complexity of the moral and chivalric oppositions in *Sir Gawain*, the underlying motif resembles that of the youthful hero who through trial and temptation gains greater understanding of himself and his values, a basic formulation of the romance mode commonly found in folk-tale. It seems to have appealed particularly to English authors who sometimes identified and emphasized it in more sophisticated narratives. In the radical reinterpretation of *Sir Perceval of Galles*, Chrétien's concern with the opposition of courtly nurture and innate nobility has largely been ignored in favour of the underlying ideal of a naïve hero made the instrument of divine justice by virtue of his very innocence. Many of the short romances classed as part of the Matter of Britain because they feature Arthurian personages and locations are merely compilations of folklore motifs in which the hero, most frequently Gawain, submits to trial by supernatural powers, winning honour for and new adherents to the society he represents. Despite occasional patches of courtly colour and chivalric morality they adhere to the romance mode in its basic folk-tale form: facing the forces of a harsh and evil world with courage and innate ability wins maturity and self-mastery. Whether the English authors of these folk romances compiled the traditional motifs personally or inherited ready-made composites, they apparently felt no need to reinterpret the thematic core in terms of specific codes and values.

Equally in the selection of narrative matter springing from English tradition they seem to have been attracted by basic expressions of the romance mode rather than complex social codes or conflicting values. The surviving examples of their treatment of the Matter of England are remarkably homogeneous. In basic terms each concerns the exile of a charismatic hero who, by personal maturation and the development of exceptional physical and moral powers, regains his heritage and wins a bride. Though in submitting their heroes to supreme tests they do not hesitate to deploy an occasional dragon, in general they prefer the mimetic to the mythic extreme of the romance mode, sketching a faint background of national history, acknowledging contemporary social conditions, evoking law in confirmation of the values they express. Individually they may enter, temporarily at least, the social sphere of *roman courtois* and pay lip-service to its values: *Horn* and *Havelok* at the regal level, though their polity is that of fairyland expressed in basic terms of firm rule and stern justice; *Guy of Warwick* and *Bevis of Hampton*, rooted in the need of the Anglo-Norman nobility to establish a native ancestry, none the less endow those ancestors with the basic virtues of folk-heroes who, though they may practise chivalry both worldly and spiritual, adopt them, like their fashionable armour, as the heroic manner of the age rather than codes to be expounded and demonstrated; their aspirations, expressed in basic terms of the struggle for equity and justice within and beyond the law, are shared by the yeoman hero of *Gamelyn*, as by Robin Hood, Ned Kelly, and millions of readers through the ages. For these English heroes love supports and rewards their manhood; the pressures of life leave no time for the internal conflicts of chivalry and courtly love.

The same basic formulation of the romance mode underlay much of what has here been called the Matter of Romance, often apparently of folklore origin, though in its adaptation to the expressive conventions of the genre it may have acquired some gloss of the associated courtly codes. English redactors had little difficulty in discriminating in favour of its basic values or in detecting and freeing folk-tales from courtly contexts in which they had been made to carry more specific ideals. Where there was little of the genre involved other than its association with adventure, as in *Richard Coer de Lyon*, the poet could happily accept the thin thread of patriotic sentiment on which the formulaic episodes are hung as a sufficient gesture to the spirit of romance. Elsewhere the enthusiasm with which he identified the original folk-tale meaning of an episode, as in the *Chevalere Assigne* version of the innocent regaining his patrimony through inherent prowess, might conflict comically with the lingering associations of the heroic context from which he took it. Equally in fitting the folk-tale of natural manly qualities triumphing over courtly pretensions to the genre conventions in *Rauf Coilyear*, juxtaposing two extremes of the romance mode, he ran the risk of parodying one or the other. Where he lacked sufficient discrimination or courage for a radical redaction the result might be, as in *William of Palerne*, a hybrid in which the original folk-tale of young love resisting repression is still so embedded in the expressive conventions of *roman courtois* as to expose its more specialized codes to ridicule by comparison with the spontaneous expression of natural feeling.

But, since the evolution of the medieval genre involved the shaping of basic romance values to the specific codes of a particular society, the effect springs from the juxtaposing of extremes rather than from anything mutually inimical in them. An early stage in that process is represented by *Floris and Blancheflur* where the English poet accepted the romantic aura of the distanced and exotic as appropriate to the story of young lovers under trial, triumphing over self-interest, bigotry, separation, and the threat of death out of natural feeling unsupported by codes. A later stage is exemplified by the Breton *lais* whose English adapters appreciated the amalgam sufficiently to reproduce it – somewhat starkly in *Sir Launfal* where an honourable and socially valid love is presented as the crowning reward of those innate qualities by which the hero wins back his patrimony, and with enormous complexity in *Sir Orfeo* which harmonizes at mythic, courtly, and moral levels a dual idealism of love and loyalty as fundamental human values rather than as the courtly codes of an aristocratic society. So also the ideal of male friendship defying fate and human malice in *Amis and Amiloun* is seen as part of the universal principle of *trowth* comprising the brotherhood of men and Christian charity as well as personal integrity and chivalric loyalty. To rank the lifelong fidelity of Floris and Blancheflur as a fit subject for romance because the *roman courtois* idealizes love between the sexes and the eternal friendship of Amis and Amiloun as bordering on hagiology, despite the many instances of self-sacrifice for a brother knight in chivalric literature, is to ignore their common frame of reference, moral as well as social in the characteristic medieval fashion.

The variety of expression given to the romance mode in the English corpus is wide, ranging from the inherent contradiction between a perfectionist code and the nature of fallen man in *Sir Gawain and the Green Knight* to those Jack-the-Giant-killer analogues in which Gawain escapes the malignity of some Imperious Host by using all the wit and muscle of a folk-hero; from the comprehensive view of Malory's *Morte Darthur* relating the triumphs and failings of chivalry to the fate of a dynasty to Gamelyn's growth to manhood through family squabbles over a yeoman's will; from the implicit mockery of chivalry in *Rauf Coilyear* to its exaltation in the reinterpretation of *Golagrus and Gawain*.

These limited signs of coherence are more evident now than they were when the corpus was first surveyed and characterized; they may strengthen as individual texts and groups of texts are more closely studied and as they gradually teach us the terms in which they should be read. In so far as the English corpus continues to disappoint critics it is because the texts do not constitute a tradition or follow an obvious evolutionary process, do not in themselves define the kind to which they belong or constitute sub-categories within it, indicate the readership or even the social class for which they were intended, or maintain consistent expressive means which would allow their quality to be judged in relation to each other. Failing that, they have most often been judged in relation to their French counterparts and in general found inferior to the relatively consistent, progressive, aristocratic, self-consciously literary tradition of twelfth-century France. Yet the very variety of French sources upon which English redactors drew indicates that that tradition was only part of a larger whole, more varied in nature, social reference, and quality of achievement. The tacit assumption that the French tradition can be equated with the *roman courtois*, that Chrétien's work represents the climax of an evolutionary process in which other texts are either rudimentary or decadent, ignores the tendency which that tradition so well illustrates for the romance mode to refine and redefine the ideals with which it is concerned and to match new expressive means to each new formulation. Chrétien's romances represent a particularly subtle and influential mating of mode and genre, but they could no more determine the future development of the form than the success of Defoe or Dickens or Joyce could fix for all time the form in which the novel was to express the mimetic mode. The generally unfavourable comparison of English romances with the French corpus, rooted in the assumption that they were trying merely to reproduce a genre, ignores the possibility that they were actually seeking, however ineptly, to express their own conception of the mode.

Attention has been distracted from that possibility by the manifest, widespread derivation of English romance from French sources, comparison with which has tended to suggest either slavish dependence or perverse deviation from originals whose superiority is assumed from their membership of the classic canon. But generalizations are particularly dangerous in this field; in many instances the exact original cannot be identified, in others the textual complexity on both sides inhibits judgement and sufficiently detailed comparisons have not yet been undertaken. Where they have, they may reveal changes for which there were positive and creative reasons in a different appreciation of the nature of the material or the genre characteristics appropriate to it, and the reinterpretation deserves to be judged as such. There are, of course, among the English corpus, routine, commonplace, incompetent redactions. But there are also many which display varying degrees of independence and creativity. There are versions of clearly conservative intent, such as *William of Palerne* which copes manfully with a detailed narrative of action in its somewhat cumbersome alliterative long line and, faced with elaborate monologues of courtly love reflection and self-analysis, resorts to painstaking and quite skilful elision and abbreviation rather than take the radical step of freeing the original folk-tale entirely from the literary conventions in which some French court poet had clothed it. There are some which seem equally ill at ease with French rhetorical art but appreciative of the values it expressed, such as *Ywain and Gawain* whose radical abbreviation of *Yvain* omits many elements of Chrétien's *conjointure* but strives to make his *sens*, somewhat simplified, self-evident through the story-line, tightened and quickened by the excision of minor episodes. There are others, such as *The Seege of Troye* and *Kyng Alisaunder*, which treat prestigious sources with the cavalier freedom of simple popularizers yet take pains to make clear both narrative and heroic values, drawing on additional materials with the confidence of original authors. The limitations of such confidence, even after centuries of practice in the genre, is illustrated by *Golagrus and Gawain* which radically alters the context, structure, plot, motivation, and values of its French original when it would have been simpler for the poet to have invented a new narrative to express the theme, different but still chivalric, for which he had been at pains to invent an expressive rhetoric. *Sir Perceval of Galles*, on the other hand, shows how far confidence could carry an author already freed from the chivalric ethos as, rejecting the structure, most of the plot, the theme of spiritual chivalry and its Grail symbol, he created many new episodes to express a familial drama centred round a folk-hero. Each of these redactors claimed his own degree of creative independence as it was generally understood in the Middle Ages, reusing established narratives, characters, conventions for his own purposes.

In the adaptative process French was not necessarily always the donor and English the receiver. There are some signs that, in the trilingual centuries after the Conquest, the raw material of romance might pass in either direction. The Anglo-Norman *Waldef* implies an English source; the lost Anglo-Norman romance on Fulk Fitzwarin also existed in an alliterative English version. *Horn* and *Havelok* exist in both languages, but in versions indirectly related as part of a complex textual tradition at different social and literary levels; the primacy of the Anglo-Norman texts has not been proven and the English are radically different in scale. In the equally complex textual tradition derived from Marie's *Lanval*, Thomas Chestre's *Sir Launfal* conflates an English version with the more rudimentary *lai Graelent* and adds episodes not in either. The richness and comparative coherence of the French tradition has operated to the disadvantage of the relatively disjointed English one in source studies. Layamon's dependence upon Wace has inhibited appreciation of his originality; yet the distinction of his *Brut* lies not in the comparatively few additional episodes but in the imaginative expansion and dramatization of Wace's narrative and the transformation of atmosphere wrought by the alliterative diction. The alliterative *Morte Arthure* was underrated for much the same reason until advancing source study showed how eclectic the compositional process had been. The rich manuscript tradition of the Vulgate Cycle still limits appreciation of the stanzaic *Morte*, with its radical restructuring of the *Mort Artu* and apparently independent invention of the thematically vital final episode.

Wace's dependence upon Geoffrey's *Historia* is a reminder of the Latin tradition common to medieval Europe on which English writers on the Matter of Rome drew quite naturally, though admittedly rather academically and on the historical periphery of the romance genre. At the opposite extreme of literary respectability were those who made the folk romances on the Matter of Britain. Some were no more than crude popularizers, pillaging the chivalric romances for anything they thought likely to appeal to an ale-house audience, like *The Grene Knight* which reduces *Sir Gawain* to a sensational plot robbed not only of its ambiguities and therefore its meaning but even of its suspense by egregious explanations often offered before the event. Others were ballad-makers relying on the established significance of the familiar romance motifs on which they drew to supply a thread of meaning in their skeletal narratives. Both illustrate the readiness of the English tradition to feed upon itself at this sub-literate level. The extent to which such texts fortuitously preserved in literary form drew upon native oral tradition cannot be determined; medieval folk-tales are available to us only when transposed into literary form, identifiable as such by the archetypal patterns they share with their counterparts in other ages and societies, and many of the motifs found in English folk romances also occur in French texts. The development of a native folk-tale into an integrated romance is inherently improbable, though *Athelston* and *Gamelyn* which have no known sources may have been compounded from elements of native oral tradition. More characteristic, perhaps, was the process by which *Rauf Coilyear* seems to have been produced, skilfully combining elements from two versions, one English one Continental, of a widespread folk-tale with the personnel of the Charlemagne romances and conscious imitation of episodes in other Matter of France texts. Other English romance writers may have felt equally at liberty to combine literary and sub-literary materials, but the process is usually beyond our examination.

The key instance is, of course, *Sir Gawain and the Green Knight*, so thoroughly steeped in *roman courtois* tradition, with comparatively close French analogues for one of its main plot components, more distant ones for another, none whatsoever for the vital motif which unites them thematically, and echoes of its themes of compact, trial, and disenchantment in English ballads and popular romances which also have Gawain as their hero. Early source-studies, forced to reconstruct an elaborate process of derivation to connect the rudimentary analogues with the complexities of the poem, assumed, with the natural prejudice of the period, that only a French author could have been equal to it. They were prepared to credit the English poet with such 'ornamental' passages as the passing of the seasons, the arming of the hero, the hunting scenes, without apparently noticing their organic function. As thematic understanding has increased and its dependence upon verbal detail almost from line to line has made clear that whoever contrived the outer skin of the poem thoroughly understood its inner structures, the source issue has gradually diminished in importance.[4] That it involved the compounding of traditional elements, literary and sub-literary, is beyond doubt; but at whatever stage he entered that process the alliterative poet had ultimate control over the smallest detail of expression and therefore of meaning. The implication for other composites in equally distinctive verse forms – both alliterative and stanzaic *Morte Arthur*, for example – should be that their literary integrity is at least as significant as the origin of their components.

Their example raises the issue as to why redactors working in a derivative tradition should have gone to so much trouble to replace the medium commonly used in their models with far more demanding verse forms. The octosyllabic couplet of *roman courtois* has its counterpart in the four-stress line of the earliest English romances and continues into the fourteenth century, competing there with numerous varieties of tail-rhyme stanza, while prose versions characterize the fifteenth century. Alliterative verse runs through the whole period, growing in frequency and in ever more complex combination with rhymed stanzas. The four-stress line rhyming in couplets showed that English could be painlessly fitted to the flexible, minimally poetic medium, undemanding of poet or audience, which had already served French poets for the better part of a century. There seemed no reason why it should not become equally firmly associated with vernacular narrative in England, providing a ready line-by-line correspondence in translation. But medieval translation was rarely of such a slavish kind and English redactors, abbreviating, elaborating, often apparently rendering lengthy sections from a cursory reading, composed freely in a preferred medium rather than attempt the tedious reproduction of the diction of a very different language.

The results are variable: at worst couplet versions achieve rapid and easy narration at the price of excessive reliance on rhyming tags, as in *The Seege of Troye*; but when handled with the smooth competence of *Arthour and Merlin* or the graceful fluency of *Kyng Alisaunder* couplets make a positive contribution to understanding. As early as *Havelok* there are poets who show the skill of a trained rhetorician in exploiting their effectiveness in colloquial speech, emotive tirade, and the succinct summation of proverb; as late as *Ywain and Gawain* others who sacrifice all literary effects to the clarity of a medium which makes itself invisible in the interests of the narrative and its meaning. But from the very beginning there are signs that the French model was not found wholly satisfactory. The couplets in *King Horn* are of three stresses only, apparently derived from the six-syllable line used in some Anglo-Norman poems, an innovation which contributes largely to the swift, ballad-like narration. The same three-stress line recurs frequently among the predominantly four-stress lines of *The Sowdon of Babylon* to produce, in association with an *abab* rhyme-scheme, something approaching the ballad quatrain. *Gamelyn* achieves a similar effect by rhyming in couplets seven-stress lines with a medial caesura, often ending the resultant quatrain with some ironic summation expressed with the crispness of proverb. In *The Song of Roland* the four-stress line is combined with irregular rhyme and persistent if unsystematic alliteration to produce something like an echo of the alliterative epic, particularly in the many battle-scenes. The Auchinleck text of *Guy of Warwick* switches from couplets to a tail-rhyme stanza just before the hero embarks on his spiritual mission, creating an appropriately lyrical tone. It would seem that, in medium as in matter, English authors saw no objection to hybrid compounds of native and imported elements.

Metrical experimentation did not originate with the writers of romance; the thirteenth-century miscellanies which were didactic storehouses for the teaching and preaching friars contain poems, many of them from the previous century, variously compounding the Latin seven-foot line with alexandrines in the manner of some Anglo-Norman poets but with repeated occurrences of the alliterative long line. Rhyming in *laisses* of varying length in imitation of Anglo-Norman poems, or in the shorter lines of a tail-rhyme stanza (*³aabaab*) derived from Latin models, or in a complex ten-line stanza originally designed for singing, these metres provided a basis for further experimentation.[5] The romance writers who chose to use various forms of tail-rhyme stanza may have been influenced by a minstrel tradition preserving the type of sung narrative which is said to have preceded the literary *lai*. If so, the tradition must have been powerful to overcome the practical difficulties of story-telling in a medium so technically demanding and the temptation presented by the simpler form usually offered by the source. The result can be deplorable, limping from tag to tag in search of an easy rhyme and mangling sense in the jingling doggerel of *Sir Thopas*, the inept effect often magnified by careless copying to total incoherence. But where the stanzas are used to encapsulate scenes, speeches, or narrative summaries, link episodes by running rhyme or separate them by its failure, using traditional formulae for their evocative associations rather than merely as rhyming tags, the effect can be positive. The independence which its technical complexity thrust upon redactors evidently meant little to those who, like the authors of *Otuel and Roland, The Sege of Melayne*, and *Sir Tristrem*, used it merely to amass adventures in simplistic outline. But for the author of *Sir Perceval of Galles* the particularly demanding sixteen-line variant he chose seems part of his distinctive approach to the Perceval story, the element of incoherence it induces suggesting the inconsequence of folk-tale, its simple diction the naïvety of the boy hero, and its occasional lyricism the magical atmosphere of the *lai*. In *Sir Launfal*, on the other hand, Chestre appears to be imitating a metre and diction associated with his kind of tale rather than evoking a mood appropriate to the love of fairy and mortal, so that it seems merely an episode in the career of a folk-hero raised to chivalric status. The conviction with which verse is handled in *Amis and Amiloun* allows the narrative to operate dramatically but also, aided by the richness of the closely rhymed stanza, emotively. How such effects may have been heightened in performance by a skilled reader or minstrel can only be guessed at; but a purely literary judgement must be incomplete.[6]

The frequency with which ornamental alliteration occurs among the conventional formulae of the tail-rhyme romances suggests their long-standing debt to the alliterative tradition. The rigidity of the alliterative line may make it seem as ill-suited to romance as the complexity of tail-rhyme, but its native associations were with narrative and, having survived as a living tradition, it underwent continual modification to meet changing needs. Already in Layamon's *Brut* its formal and stylistic means mingle past and present: Anglo-Saxon stress patterns in occasional lines of battle poetry, but elsewhere half-lines which rhyme aphoristically, brief moments of lyricism, grandiloquent speeches, and a surprisingly long-breathed syntax which narrates emphatically yet with ease. Just as Layamon's archaism seems less a retrograde instinct than an attempt to draw strength from native roots, so the use of the alliterative long line in *The Gest Historiale* and *The Wars of Alexander* may reflect not the preference of pedants for an archaic medium but their wish to match the dignity of their subjects and the verbal intricacy of their Latin sources. Though all their technical skill cannot avoid some tedium and rigidity in narration, they exploit the iterative power of the medium in storms and battles, its rhetorical formality in letters and speeches, its verbal richness in descriptive catalogues. Stylistic magnificence sometimes swamps the meaning, but at least never trivializes it as couplets might have done.

Any idea of alliterative verse as an obsolescent medium is given the lie by the *Morte Arthure* where it is used in a most uncompromising form, emphatic in the regularity of its stress patterns, adding a wide range of consonant-groups to the established alliterations often carried on over three or four lines, employing a fantastically varied vocabulary as rich in verbs as in adjectives, flaunting technical terms and playing upon exotic words. The battles are more violent, the descriptive catalogues more crowded then ever, but it is the complex narration, phrase balanced against phrase, one half-line paralleling another in long-running, tightly controlled sentences, which makes the medium not an ornamental but an essential adjunct to meaning. The addition to a scarcely less regular and demanding line of the formal requirements of a thirteen-line stanza rhyming $abababc^4ddd^3c^2$ in *Golagrus and Gawain* creates a medium seemingly only fit for an exhibitionist or a masochist, constricting its rhythmic vigour and verbal richness with the end-stopping effect of rhyme. A medium whose complexities encumber narration seems particularly ill-suited to a radical redaction, but the reinterpretation makes use of its particular merits: descriptive richness in the arming of the unknown adversary establishing his chivalric reputation, formal rhetoric in the speeches of those who praise him and his courteous exchanges with Gawain, rhythmic emphasis in the hand-to-hand struggles between them. This technical *tour de force* is surpassed in *Sir Gawain and the Green Knight* where every technical resource is exploited with an art that conceals art: the stress patterns of the long line skilfully varied to provide rapid narration, concrete visualization in descriptive passages, courtly or colloquial speech, moments of lyricism, and, in the irregular pauses supplied by the bob and wheel, summary, anticipation, ironic comment, and shock development sometimes defused as the next *laisse* opens. Most subtle of all is the poet's exploitation of the traditional verbal imprecision of a formally demanding medium in employing patterns of related terms seemingly imprecise in their immediate context whose relationship to each other and the theme suddenly becomes apparent when one or other is used in an unacceptable context, making the verbal surface of the poem a key to its meaning.

Such community of medium and message is unique, yet it is evident that for most English authors romance implies some form of verse. In many cases it is no more than a formal gesture, mechanical rhyming in the minstrel manner often at the expense of coherent meaning. But in others, to varying degrees, verse is an expressive means to clarity, emphasis, grandiloquence, charm, evoking epic grandeur, courtly ease, the naïvety of folk-tale or moments of mystery or magic. Redactors struggle with restrictive verse forms which make literal reproduction of their sources impossible, sometimes with disastrous, often with creative, results. Had meaning been their primary concern, French romances had provided a model of prose narrative early in the thirteenth century, English had a functional prose from long before; yet it remained for Malory to create a variety truly compatible with the needs of English romance, composed of familiar stylistic elements but as unique in its way as the verse of *Sir Gawain*. Meanwhile English authors largely rejected French models, striving to evolve verse forms, hybrids of native and foreign, literary and sub-literary elements, which they felt appropriate to their concept of romance.

The resultant amalgam reflects their approach to other aspects of the genre; made heirs to the expressive means evolved in the French tradition they evidently felt free to pick and choose at will, compounding its literary formats with elements provided by the native tradition, written and oral. Recognizing similar hybrids among their French models and unwilling or incapable of reproducing the 'pure' examples admired by modern critics, they produced composites as various as their view of the romance mode. The genre models most likely to have been available to the earliest English romance writers included such examples of *roman courtois* as may have filtered down from courtly circles, the Anglo-Norman romances largely of the 'ancestral' tradition produced for the aristocracy and, no doubt, some form of popular folk-tale. The general affiliation of *King Horn* is with the Anglo-Norman texts, yet its most obvious genre characteristics are those of the multi-move folk-tale repeating in schematic outline a pattern of events in which, step by step, the exiled hero regains his patrimony. Yet the fact that the fate of nations is caught up with his, that events relate symbolically to both, that law and just government are the fundamental realities invoked, and that the reader's involvement in the narrative is direct without any consciousness of a narrator, without irony, all distantly evoke the epic. *Havelok* clothes the same folk-tale skeleton with a greater degree of surface realism, similarly structured to demonstrate both personal and regal virtues in the hero, evoking concepts of good and bad government as the reality against which the myth is to be seen. The coexistence in both of elements from genres of such disparate prestige is a reminder that genre classification is the product of literary history and that poets celebrating both basic human qualities and their social specialization may have seen no need to discriminate between the expressive means associated with them. The ease with which the 'Horn' story was later turned into a didactic French romance and the 'Havelok' story given courtly gloss in a *lai* suggests how readily the balance of genre characteristics could be changed to meet changing expectations.

The ease with which that balance could be altered in the redactive process, the generally derivative and hybrid nature of English romance, and the possibility that modern perceptions of genre may differ from those of contemporaries make classification on that basis an uncertain process. There is obvious danger in the too ready identification of elements of folk-tale since the originals are not accessible to us, only the most persistent are now perceptible and others caught up in the early evolution of romance may no longer be apparent as such. The presence of a folklore theme in an English romance need not imply that the means by which it was expressed in folk-tale have also been incorporated there. *Gamelyn* is clearly based on that period of the folk-hero's career in which his struggle for maturity and identity is still within the family, but as in *Horn* and *Havelok* the theme has been replicated at the social level, expressing the underdog's struggle for justice. The sparse, direct narrative, the sequence of self-contained episodes, the terse acknowledgement of the brutality of life, occasional flashes of malice and aphoristic comments suggest ballad as the genre model. The coherence of genre and theme suggests that *Gamelyn* developed organically in the hands of those who thoroughly appreciated how the one could express the other. The author of *Chevalere Assigne*, who disinterred a folk-tale from the *enfances* section of an epic cycle, seemingly knew no conventions appropriate to the career of his boy- David hero, exposing him to ridicule as he repeats the chivalric gestures of his French counterpart in a simplified folk-tale context. By contrast, the redactor of *Sir Perceval of Galles*, faced with a similar problem, imaginatively re-creates a feasible folk-tale setting for Chrétien's holy innocent by a circular structure which brings him back triumphant to the family for whose vindication he has fought throughout, by emphasis on the natural qualities in which his charisma lies, by the symbolic value given to certain objects and the distancing effect of the semi-lyrical stanza.

When the career of a folk-hero supplied the human basis for more specialized social codes it might be expressed through the genre conventions associated with them. The authors of the popular folk romances of the Matter of Britain evidently felt little need for the literary apparatus of their chivalric counterparts beyond the Arthurian milieu and personnel; the characteristic structure of challenge, quest, and trial was part of their folklore inheritance. In *Guy of Warwick*, however, the redactor has respected the influence of the epic cycles which gave his hero a secular career in love and war, a spiritual one in the service of God, and a like-father-like-son heir whose heroic adventures are in the same vein. He reproduces the parallelism by which Guy's spiritual career mirrors his chivalric one and in both the chain of adventures characteristic of romance, but mechanically without interpretative commentary – and the addition of the didactic *Speculum Guy* suggests that he valued function above purity of genre. In *Rauf Coilyear*, on the other hand, the admixture of genre characteristics seems deliberate, the conventions of chivalric combat burlesqued by the natural pugnacity of the folk-hero, mirroring the underlying contrast of natural and courtly behaviour. The redactive process in *William of Palerne* distinguishes between the major components of an obvious composite, curtailing the courtly love conventions with understanding of their function and impatience at their elaboration, discriminating in favour of those adventures of the hero which demonstrate natural rather than chivalric qualities. In all three adventure dominates; the elements of genre involved seem to be tolerated because of their association with valued material rather than exploited for their expressive value.

The *roman d'aventure* is an accepted sub-genre of French romance distinguished by the narration of events for their inherent interest rather than for any specific meaning to be extrapolated from them by literary means. They exploit any action-packed material and the classic Matters are liable to be so treated once their associated ideals are no longer novel and problematic. The versions of the Matter of France selected by English redactors had already reached that stage and their abbreviations discriminate still further in favour of action, omitting episodes too freely to have any regard for epic structure, depriving the Saracen enemy of the occasional chivalric gesture which in the original matched him with the Christian heroes, and retaining only a flicker of heroic spirit in the indiscriminate violence of their battle descriptions. Even the *Roland* abandons the pattern of repetition with variation, the isolated tableaux, the detached narration in favour of headlong action and violent intrusions on the part of the narrator.

Yet there is evidence elsewhere that English authors appreciated at least some elements of epic narration. Not, in Layamon's case, its overall structure but the unvarying focus upon a hero-king embodying faith and nation, the repeated pattern of challenge, council, march, battle, victory feast, the use of speech to dramatize moments of thematic crisis, of description to stimulate emotion, simile to evoke the meaning of key events. His chronicle structure was also that inherited by English redactors of the Matter of Rome who, in the case of the alliterative *Gest Historiale* and *Wars of Alexander*, found its episodic movement convenient for sporadic moral commentary, display of erudition on exotic wonders, of rhetorical skill in letters and speeches, of poetic art in set-piece descriptions of storms and battles; the underlying spirit is encyclopaedic rather than epic. In both the hero's legendary charisma bonds together a variety of materials which the poets elaborated with their didactic, rhetorical, poetic art. In the popular abbreviation of *The Seege of Troye*, on the other hand, the Matter of Rome becomes merely an exotic backdrop to the adventures of folk-heroes sketched in the minstrel manner with considerable competence but without defined genre characteristics. *Kyng Alisaunder*, though basically similar, seeks to edify as well as entertain and mingles swift narration with explanatory commentary and some stylistic devices from the *chansons* such as the seasonal transitions which underscore the theme of mutability. Both lack consistency of genre, but seek to make their material accessible and appetizing by literary and stylistic means. The consistency of the alliterative *Morte Arthure* is startling by comparison; despite being in-debted to the chronicle tradition for its narrative outline and to various forms of romance for incidental components, it more closely resembles the *chansons de geste* than anything else in the English post-Conquest tradition. Its thematic emphasis on the fate of a society as conditioned by the character and personal conduct of the hero-king, the structural pattern of detached, highly dramatized scenes organized in sections marked by the recurrence of pilgrimage references implying a basis of moral judgement, the use of formal vows, prophetic dreams, and the fulfilment of both, the pervasive realism heightened by an emphatic medium exploited for rhetorical effect suggest the aims and techniques of epic. The native medium and the absolute mastery with which it is controlled for thematic purposes rule out any suggestion of an imitative amalgam; the dynastic theme, the epic vows, the episode of self-vaunting chivalry contrasted with the just use of imperial might are deliberately employed in the service of a distinctive view of human aspiration as both admirable and tragic.

Evidence that English redactors were capable of an independent approach to genre is most apparent where they worked upon clear-cut originals exemplifying specific varieties of *roman courtois*. Of those who in treating the downfall of the Round Table gave a dynastic focus to chronicle material, the author of the stanzaic *Morte Arthur* radically recast his chosen section of the Vulgate in terms of the classic chivalric romance, while Malory accepted its cyclic scope yet rejected its long-running interlace in favour of thematic concentration within isolated episodes. But in both appearances are deceptive. The linear narrative, the brief, self-contained scenes, the shifting perspective from one to the next of the stanzaic poem only vaguely imitate the *roman courtois*; the real expressive means of the redaction, the sequence of spare episodes with-out commentary, the narrative elisions, flashes of dialogue, and drama-tic gestures suggest the dominant influence of the ballad, like the skilful, seemingly naïve stanza itself. Malory's apparent rejection of long-term coherence none the less achieves through the vividness of individual episodes, the addition of others, the repeated patterns of human behaviour a mosaic effect which, particularly in the last books of the *Morte Darthur*, creates its own kind of dramatic and thematic coherence.

In terms of sub-categories *Floris and Blancheflur* represents the *roman idyllique*, a courtly, sentimental treatment of youthful love, but simplifies and selects among the patterned repetitions of the original, favouring action over sentiment and ingenuity above courtly qualities. Of the two derivatives of the *lai*, *Sir Orfeo* announces its affiliation in the characteristic prologue and, despite its deceptively simple verbal surface, structures the seemingly casual, linear narrative in relation to the thematic pattern of loss and recovery, highlighting what it momentarily dwells upon, creating mystery and tension by what it leaves unsaid, a sense of two worlds existing simultaneously by the sparse, vivid detail with which it evokes them both. *Sir Launfal*, by contrast, seems bent on denying its associations, defusing the mystery of the *lai* by its matter-of-fact treatment of supernatural elements, eliminating courtly detail to uncover the original folk-tale in an appropriately spare narrative divided into a cartoon-like sequence of detached episodes illustrating its black and white values. The didactic value of established genre conventions is evident in *Amis and Amiloun* whose diagrammatically clear-cut pattern of major scenes linked by brief narrative passages allows multiple illustrations of its friendship theme, unified without intrusive commentary as manifestations of the underlying principle of *trowth*. Like *Sir Launfal* it relies on basic principles of good tale-telling rather than the ready-made conventions of any specific genre.

The eclectic instinct of many English authors in creating their own expressive means, whatever genre models they had before them, is illustrated by three romances closely related to the *roman courtois* tradition. *Ywain and Gawain*, while accepting the basic theme and narrative pattern of *Yvain*, omits almost entirely the dialectic by which Chrétien adduces meaning, relying instead on the simplified story-line to convey a clear, if less sophisticated, sense of chivalric values. The author of *Golagrus and Gawain*, to whom neither the values nor the structure of his source, a long-running interlaced prose sequence, was acceptable, returned instead to a rudimentary version of Chrétien's procedure: clear-cut linear narrative, episodes patterned in relation to each other for thematic purposes including one of his characteristic inversions, meaning adduced not by authorial comment but by interaction, speech, and commentary within the narrative. As so often, *Sir Gawain and the Green Knight* presents the issue in a form so heightened as to constitute a difference of kind. Clearly at ease with a wide range of *roman courtois* conventions and aware of the motifs which romance shares with folk-tale, the poet plays upon both in a unique amalgam evoking often contradictory expectations. The narrative pattern of challenge, departure, test, and return is both that of folk-heroes in search of their identity and that of knights errant bent on giving proof of the qualities symbolized on their emblazoned shields. The structure implies adventures between initial challenge and return–match, but the unexpected stasis which occurs presents a more subtle challenge in a complex box-within-box arrangement which makes the outcome of the one depend upon the outcome of the other. The interval at Hautdesert, with its repeated triple patterns, evokes the folk-tale tests imposed by wayside hosts and their seductive wives, yet its events seem no more than courtly games of love and wagering, irrelevant to the life-and-death mission on which the hero is bound. The ultimate invasion of its dualism by the triple blow incurred by the wager brings startled realization that every facet of Gawain's pentangular *trowth* had been under test, that the seemingly trifling games were more dangerous than the manifest, familiar chivalric ordeal, that the internal threat of human fallibility was greater than the external enmity roused by knightly aspiration, that idealism has been undermined by natural instinct. The complexity of structure implies thematic conclusions but leaves the ultimate implications to the judgement of readers. So also does the ambivalent presentation of the hero as the supreme example of natural man in accordance with English tradition and as the courtly exemplar haunted by his amorous reputation in French tradition, of his adversary as the Knight Challenger of romance and, at the same time, some personified force of nature from folk-tale, of his wayside temptress as the bait laid by some Imperious Host and as the seductive hostess of *roman courtois*. The seemingly candid narrative appears to offer no guidance to meaning but the rare authorial interventions challenge understanding, the decorative descriptions create ambivalent atmosphere, the shifting dialectic requires reinterpretation of key terms and their associated values. The juggling with genre conventions, the guessing games to which the reader is invited, the pervasive humour and irony query the nature of romance as fantasy or projection of truth beyond the limitations of reality.

What audience in the rural England of the late fourteenth century was equal to such sophistication? What audience had found pleasure in the archaism of Layamon's *Brut* some two centuries earlier? Despite hypotheses the enigma remains in both cases; and no consistent picture has emerged of those for whom English romances were written in the years between, only isolated, fleeting glimpses liable to misinterpretation. Among the modern preconceptions which may bias judgement are a too-ready equation of social class and artistic appreciation, of literacy and literary discrimination, of literature with private reading rather than the performing arts. But before meritocracy had creamed off the ability of the humbly born, when aristocracy need not imply literacy, when poetry courtly and popular was still largely addressed to ears rather than eyes, social differences were not an absolute bar to enjoyment of a lively narrative packed with action. Folk-heroes might win a princess as their bride or be rewarded with half a kingdom; their borrowed adventures might serve as testing-ground for the prowess of some chivalric hero. The variety of genres often intermingled, the extremes of sophistication and vulgarity in Chaucer's poetry suggest the range of tastes which a court poet might expect in his audience. A courtly audience which could enjoy the 'Miller's Tale' with its mocking use of romance conventions could scarcely have objected to the yeoman values of *Gamelyn* incorporated in many manuscripts of *The Canterbury Tales*; and the large number of surviving texts indicate the widespread popularity of the *Tales* far beyond the court. Variant versions of romance texts show how they might be modified even by the carelessness or good taste of a scribe. The relationship of *The Grene Knight* to *Sir Gawain* indicates the debasement which the search for sensational incident could inflict on the most subtle text. By contrast, the manuscripts of *The Seege of Troye*, varying in format and textual modification, suggest that a competent popularization might appeal to audiences at many social levels. *Gamelyn* continued to rise in the world, becoming the subject of courtly romance and romantic drama in the age of Elizabeth; his knightly brethren Guy of Warwick and Bevis of Hampton sank to be chap-book heroes in the nineteenth century. The minor modifications of *William of Palerne* indicate that the folk-tale at its heart might appeal to modest members of Humphrey de Bohun's household 'þat knowe no Frensche' despite the courtly love conventions foisted upon it by the court poet who composed the original for the Countess Yolande. Each text carries some indication of its intended audience, but the collective impression is too complex to support generalizations.

The enigma of Layamon's *Brut*, vast, linguistically difficult, harking back in style and spirit to a vanished culture, has been explained on the grounds that he lived only ten miles from Worcester where much of that culture's learning was kept alive by St Wulfstan, the last surviving Anglo-Saxon bishop; but the *Brut* is not learned or pious and many of its literary means, like its source, are French, suggesting that it may have been meant for some household of minor gentry already abandoning bilingualism for the old vernacular. The aristocratic households for which the Anglo-Norman 'ancestral' romances were composed may well have been bilingual to judge from the readiness with which they drew on English sources written and oral. The serious, legalistic epic *Horn* may have come from a modest household of the kind which, fifty years earlier, would have welcomed its Anglo-Norman analogues while the ladies would probably have enjoyed the sentimental *Floris and*

*Blancheflur,* recited in the hall both could have been appreciated below as well as above the salt. Neither romance was designed for peasant tastes; the *Floris* redactor chose to follow the courtly rather than the popular version of his French source; one text of *Horn* (British Library MS Harley 2253) occurs as the sole romance in a distinctly highbrow compendium of Latin and French material, largely religious, and English verse, including sophisticated love-lyrics – suggesting the intellectual value placed on it.[7] Despite the popular appeal of its realistic surface, *Havelok* is coupled with *Horn* in another manuscript, due recognition of its moral and political seriousness while its historical interest is attested by its inclusion in chronicles. The quality of these early romances does not suggest a literature painfully struggling to rise from folk-tale; they challenge comparison with their Anglo-Norman counterparts which they displaced in bilingual households as the balance swung towards the mother tongue.

The fundamentals with which they dealt earned them respectful treatment not extended to the Anglo-Norman 'ancestral' romances whose familial roots had been obscured by the passage of time. The English versions of *Bevis* and *Guy* are competent but somewhat vulgarized, given to the reduplication of striking effects, paying lip-service to the heroes' values while almost wholly preoccupied by their adventures. In *Gamelyn*, by contrast, the values seem heartfelt and they are those of yeomen, the rural gentry whose social position in the post-Conquest centuries is difficult to define. With the fourteenth century comes evidence of dramatic growth in the audience for vernacular literature assumed, largely on the evidence of the Auchinleck MS, to be due to the rising bourgeoisie. But though the London bookshop where it was compiled may have calculated the commercial success of its combination of pious didacticism and sensational romances – *Guy of Warwick, Sir Tristrem, Richard Coer de Lyon*, the Matter of France vulgarizations – on the social aspirations of city merchants, not all the material translated, abbreviated, and subdivided by its hacks came from the capital still less the court. Some of the redactions from French and Anglo-Norman were not specifically produced for the volume; surviving traces of the dialect of composition show that they were drawn from a wider region of the South-east. It would seem that the London merchants were content to be secondary consumers of material prepared for others whether or not it had a superior social cachet for them. The general character of English romance makes clear that its primary audience was not aristocratic, just as its literary stamp shows that it was not a minstrel product fortuitously rescued from oral oblivion. The range of regional dialects represented in the corpus and its readiness to acknowledge chivalric values without being preoccupied by the inherent contradictions of courtly codes suggest a provincial audience of less than the highest rank.

Precise definition of such an audience is not possible; but in an age whose social structure was rooted in the ownership of land provincial origin need not imply rustic tastes, and in the evolving feudalism of medieval England sons of modest landowners might rise in the world. For landless younger sons the Church, the law, the developing administrative structure of the nation offered ladders to education, independence, and affluence. For them as for their mercantile counterparts the hallmark of success was the purchase of country estates; and in their new-built or renovated manor-houses the addition of a family parlour away from the public hall provided a place of comfort where literature could be a private thing. Its provision was often no doubt a casual function of resident chaplains, domestic tutors, or stewards and, perhaps, members of local monastic houses under the patronage of the landowner, ensuring a degree of literary sophistication without absolute divorce from the oral entertainment of the humbler folk who were their servants and neighbours. Not only London but the major provincial cities provided centres where merchants and rural gentry met; the fuller social records of the fifteenth century show them exchanging literary texts to be read and copied. If, as seems likely, a similar relationship already existed in the previous century, the provinces apparently gave as much as they received.[8]

Such a community of audiences might help to explain the combination of literary sophistication and provincial medium in the alliterative romances whose serious, ethical treatment of chivalric values seen in historical perspective has puzzled critics in works written far from court and capital. A possible continuity of audience is suggested by the fact that the Anglo-Norman 'ancestral' romances, with their projection of feudal ideals upon a backdrop of English 'history', were also written for a cultured but non-courtly audience. Long after the extinction of the regional nobility they celebrated, the texts continued to be circulated and popularized into the fourteenth century while their heroes passed into English romance. Their influence may account for certain technical features, notably the persistence in Anglo-Norman of the old epic *laisse*, grouping variable numbers of ten- or twelve-syllable lines by monorhyme or assonance, paralleling the persistence of the alliterative medium and the grouping of the long line into blank-verse paragraphs punctuated by sense or marked by the rhyming quatrains of *Sir Gawain*. But it is the continued existence of their audience rather than any direct literary influence which may explain the confidence with which alliterative poets, working upon Latin sources or freely combining French materials, at medium or extended length, could critically reinterpret them in expectation of being understood and appreciated. The evident interest and skill of poets too diverse to constitute a school in exploiting a complex, weighty medium, creating not translating, implies the existence of a public capable of more than adventures in jingling tail-rhyme. The probability is that it was an audience of the middle and upper classes, still partly at least bilingual like the poets who served it, appreciative of the historical perspective upon contemporary values provided by *The Gest Historiale* and *The Wars of Alexander*, thoroughly familiar with the French tradition but sympathetic to the critical detachment from its codes shown in the *Morte Arthure, Golagrus and Gawain*, and *Sir Gawain and the Green Knight*.[9]

The audience for romance was probably never more than a minority; most survive in limited copies which contrast with the multiple manuscripts of didactic and homiletic treatises. Readers fully alert to all the subtleties of *Sir Gawain*, then as now, must have been fewer still. But *Sir Gawain* is a characteristic, if supreme, example of alliterative romance; and it is rooted both in the tradition of *roman courtois* and that of the English folk-tale. No doubt the audience of English romance was as much a hybrid as the corpus itself. A court poet like Chaucer might mock its absurdities of convention and diction; but he explored the mode, played with the conventions, and his own diction is thoroughly permeated by the language of romances read in youth.[10] He typifies the means by which its influence was to be diffused long after romance had come to mean 'lying tale' and the adventures of knights errant had been displaced by those of the rogues who were to be the first heroes of the realist tradition. The golden-age nostalgia of Caxton and Lord Berners created the ambience of Sidney's *Arcadia* and Spenser's *The Faerie Queene* and the décor of many masques and pageants. The motifs of exile, trial, endurance and triumphant return, of bitter experience transformed by wish-fulfilment, became the machinery of romantic drama. The detached irony of high romance, reaching a perfect balance of ambivalence in the *Don Quixote* of Cervantes, lived on in the novelists to whom he taught the power of the imagination to create its own version of reality, to question values and attitudes without self-delusion. The mockery of *Sir Thopas* was matched by that of Beaumont and Fletcher's *Knight of the Burning Pestle*, with the same oblique compliment to the power of romance. The *roman d'aventure* sank to the penny chap-books, waiting for cinema and television to raise motiveless derring-do to a lucrative industry once more. The fantasy and escapism which licensed the imagination to create the unimaginable lay dormant through the age of rationalism, waiting to provide medieval mystery for the Romantics to conjure with. Most pervasive of all because most invisible, the telling of tales as a literary art lost itself in manifold forms of English narrative.

# Notes

1. John Finlayson ('Definitions of Middle English Romance', *Chaucer Review*, 15 (1980), 44–62, 168–81), for example, would exclude at least half the texts listed in J. Burke Severs, *A Manual of the Writings in Middle English 1050–1500: I Romances* (New Haven, Connecticut, 1967) on the grounds that though they exhibit incidental characterisics of the genre they lack its essential concern with knightly adventures in pursuit of personal reputation without social, political, or religious motivation and divorced from contemporary reality (p. 178).

2. Finlayson (p. 48) summarizes the situation aptly: 'It is this curious mingling of a recognition of the difference between the actuality of medieval romance and the nineteenth century's vision and expectations of it and a regret that it is not something other than it is, which seems to have bedevilled discussion of the Middle English romance.'

3. Whether or not the native epic *Beowulf*, with its ironic awareness of the personal and social conflicts inherent in the practice of a heroic code when beset by fate and bad faith, already embodies the romance mode, the Anglo-Saxon version of *Apollonius of Tyre* suggests that the genre would have been welcomed from classical sources irrespective of the French cultural influence which preceded the Conquest.

4. For an outline treatment of the source issue see W. R. J. Barron, 'French Romance and the Structure of *Sir Gawain and the Green Knight*', in *Studies in Medieval Literature and Languages*, edited by W. Rothwell, W. R. J. Barron, D. Blamires, and L. Thorpe (Manchester, 1973), pp. 7–25.

5. On the friars' miscellanies see Derek Pearsall, *Old English and Middle English Poetry* (London, 1977), pp. 94–102.

6. A detailed survey is supplied by A. M. Trounce, 'The English Tail-Rhyme Romances', *Medium Aevum*, 1 (1932), 87–108; 168–82; 2 (1933), 34–57, 189–98; 3 (1934), 30–50; his idea of a distinct school of tail-rhyme poets is no longer accepted.

7. On the contents of MS Harley 2253 see Pearsall, pp. 120–32.

8. The limited evidence on the audience for English romance has most recently been assessed by P. R. Coss, 'Aspects of Cultural Diffusion in Medieval England: The Early Romances, Local Society and Robin Hood', *Past and Present*, 108 (1985), 35–79.

9. See Rosalind Field, 'The Anglo-Norman Background to Alliterative Romance', in *Middle English Alliterative Poetry and its Literary Background*, edited by D. Lawton (Cambridge, 1982), pp. 54–69, 136–40.

10. See D. S. Brewer, 'The Relationship of Chaucer to the English and European Traditions', in *Chaucer and Chaucerians*, edited by D. S. Brewer (London, 1966), pp. 1–38.

# Chronology

*Note: Despite the apparent precision of chronological listing, many of the English romances can only be uncertainly and imprecisely dated.*

| DATE | ENGLISH ROMANCES | OTHER WORKS | HISTORICAL/CULTURAL EVENTS |
|---|---|---|---|
| 1066 | | | Norman Conquest of England under William I |
| 1096–99 | | | First Crusade; capture of Jerusalem |
| | | *Chanson de Roland* (c. 1100); poetry of William IX, first troubadour (1100–20) | |
| 1135 | | | Accession of Stephen |
| | | Geoffrey of Monmouth *Historia Regum Britanniae* (c. 1136) | |
| 1135–54 | | | Civil War of Stephen and Matilda |
| 1154 | | | Accession of Henry II |
| | | Robert Wace's *Roman de Brut* (1155); *Roman d'Eneas* (c. 1160); Benoit de Sainte-Maure's *Roman de Troie*; *Tristan* of Thomas (c. 1165); romances of Chrétien de Troyes (1170–90); *lais* of Marie de France (c. 1184–86); Andreas Capellanus's *De Amore* (c. 1185) | |
| 1189 | | | Accession of Richard I |
| | | *Tristan* of Béroul (c. 1190); Wolfram von Eschenbach's *Parzival* (c. 1200) | |

| DATE | ENGLISH ROMANCES | OTHER WORKS | HISTORICAL/CULTURAL EVENTS |
|---|---|---|---|
| 1199 | | | Accession of John |
| | | *Poema de Mio Cid* (late 12th–early 13th century) | |
| 1204 | | | Loss of Normandy; division of the Angevin kingdom |
| | | Gottfried von Strassburg's *Tristan und Isolde* (c. 1210) | |
| 1216 | | | Accession of Henry III |
| | c. 1220: Layamon's *Brut* c. 1225: *King Horn* | | |
| | | Development of the Vulgate Cycle of Arthurian romances (first third of 13th century) | |
| | | Guillaume de Lorris's *Roman de la Rose* (c. 1235) | |
| | c. 1250: *Floris and Blancheflur* 1250–1300: *Arthour and Merlin* | | |
| 1272 | | | Accession of Edward I |
| | Late 13th century: *Amis and Amiloun* *Sir Tristrem* | | |
| | | Jean de Meun's *Roman de la Rose* (c. 1275) | |
| | c. 1290: *Havelok the Dane* c. 1300: *Bevis of Hampton*; *Guy of Warwick*; *Kyng Alisaunder*; *Lai le Freine*; *Richard Coer de Lyon*; *Sir Orfeo* | | |
| 1307 | | | Accession of Edward II |
| | | Dante's *Divina Commedia* (c. 1307–21) | |
| | 1300–25: *Seege of Troye*; *Sir Degaré* 1300–40: *Sir Perceval of Galles* 1300–50: *Sir Landeval*; *Ywain and Gawain* | | |
| 1314 | | | English defeat at Bannockburn |
| | c. 1320: *Horn Child* | | |
| 1321 | | | Death of Dante |
| | c. 1325: *Libeaus Desconus* | | |

| DATE | ENGLISH ROMANCES | OTHER WORKS | HISTORICAL/CULTURAL EVENTS |
|---|---|---|---|
| 1327 | | | Accession of Edward III |
| | Early 14th century: *King of Tars; Sir Isumbras* | | |
| | *c.* 1330: *Otuel a Knight; Otuel and Roland; Roland and Vernagu* | | |
| | | Giovanni Boccaccio's *Filostrato* (*c.* 1335) | |
| 1337 | | | Beginning of the Hundred Years War |
| | *c.* 1340: *Joseph of Arimathie* | | |
| | 1340–70: alliterative *Alexander Fragments A and B* | | |
| *c.* 1343 | | Juan Ruiz's *Libro de Buen Amor* | Birth of Chaucer |
| 1346 | | | English victory at Crécy |
| 1348 –49 | | Giovanni Boccaccio's *Decameron* (1349–51) | The Black Death |
| | *c.* 1350: *Octavian; Sir Eglamour of Artois; William of Palerne* | | |
| | 1350–70: *Tale of Gamelyn* | | |
| | 1355–80: *Athelston* | | |
| | 1350–1400: alliterative *Morte Arthure; Chevalere Assigne; Gest Historiale of the Destruction of Troy* | | |
| 1356 | | | English victory at Poitiers |
| | | *Piers Plowman*, A-text (*c.* 1362); Chaucer's *Book of the Duchess* (*c.* 1370) | |
| 1374 | | | Death of Petrarch |
| 1375 | | John Barbour's *Bruce* | Death of Boccaccio |
| | 1375–1400: Fillingham *Firumbras; Sir Gawain and the Green Knight; Titus and Vespasian* | | |
| | 1376–81: *Apollonius of Tyre* | | |
| 1377 | | *Piers Plowman*, B-text (*c.* 1377) | Accession of Richard II |
| | *c.* 1380: Ashmole *Firumbras* | | |

| DATE | ENGLISH ROMANCES | OTHER WORKS | HISTORICAL/CULTURAL EVENTS |
|------|------------------|-------------|----------------------------|
| 1381 | | | Peasants' Revolt |
| | | Chaucer's *Parlement of Foules* (*c.* 1382); Chaucer's *Troilus and Criseyde* (*c.* 1382–85); Chaucer begins *The Canterbury Tales* (*c.* 1387) | |
| | Late 14th century: *Arthur*; *Bone Florence of Rome*; *Generides*; *Ipomadon*; *Knight of Curtesy and the Fair Lady of Faguell*; *Roberd of Cisyle*; *Sir Amadace*; *Sir Cleges*; *Sir Degrevant*; *Sir Triamour*; Thomas Chestre's *Sir Launfal* | | |
| | | *Piers Plowman*, C-text (*c.* 1390) | |
| | 1390–1400: *Siege of Jerusalem* | | |
| 1399 | | | Accession of Henry IV |
| 1400 | *c.* 1400: *Duke Roland and Sir Otuel of Spain*; *Earl of Toulous*; *Emaré*; *Laud Troy Book*; *Marriage of Sir Gawaine*; *Sege of Melayne*; *Sir Gowther*; *Sir Torrent of Portyngale*; *Song of Roland*; stanzaic *Morte Arthur*; *Syre Gawene and the Carle of Carelyle* | | Death of Chaucer |
| | 1400–30: *Awntyrs off Arthure* | | |
| 1413 | | | Accession of Henry V |
| | 1412–20: Lydgate's *Troy Book* | | |
| 1415 | | | Battle of Agincourt |
| | 1420–22: Lydgate's *Siege of Thebes* | | |
| 1422 | | | Accession of Henry VI |
| | | James I (of Scotland)'s *Kingis Quair* | |
| | *c.* 1425: *Avowynge of King Arthur*; Henry Lovelich's *History of the Holy Grail* | | |
| | 1425–50: prose *Siege of Troy* | | |

| DATE | ENGLISH ROMANCES | OTHER WORKS | HISTORICAL/CULTURAL EVENTS |
|---|---|---|---|
| 1431 | | | Burning of Joan of Arc |
| | | Lydgate's *Fall of Princes* (1431–38) | |
| | 1438: *Scottish Alexander Buik* | | |
| | 1400–50; Cambridge *Alexander-Cassamus Fragment*; Gilbert Hay's *Buik of King Alexander*; *King Ponthus*; Henry Lovelich's *Merlin*; John Metham's *Amoryus and Cleopes*; prose *Alexander*; *Sowdon of Babylon* | | |
| 1450 | | | Jack Cade's Rebellion; Gutenberg prints the Bible |
| | *c.* 1450: *Eger and Grime*; prose *Merlin*; prose *Siege of Thebes*; *Wars of Alexander*; *Weddynge of Sir Gawen and Dame Ragnell* | | |
| 1453 | | | Turks take Constantinople; end of the Hundred Years War |
| 1455 | | | First battle of the Wars of the Roses |
| | *c.* 1460: *Ipomedon* | | |
| | *c.* 1470: Sir Thomas Malory's *Le Morte Darthur* | | |
| 1471 | | | Accession of Edward IV |
| | 1473(?): Caxton's *History of Troy* | | |
| | 1477(?): Caxton's *History of Jason* | | |
| | Late 15th century: Dublin *Alexander Epitome*; *Jeaste of Syr Gawayne*; *King Arthur and King Cornwall*; *Roswall and Lillian*; *Taill of Rauf Coilyear* | | |
| 1476 | | | Caxton introduces printing into England |
| 1478 | | Caxton's first printing of *The Canterbury Tales* | |
| | 1481: Caxton's *Siege of Jerusalem* | | |
| | 1482–1500: *Lancelot of the Laik* | | |

| DATE | ENGLISH ROMANCES | OTHER WORKS | HISTORICAL/CULTURAL EVENTS |
|---|---|---|---|
| 1483 | | | Accession of Richard III |
| 1485 | Caxton's Malory and *Charles the Grete* | | Accession of Henry VII |
| 1488 | Caxton's *Foure Sonnes of Aymon* | | |
| 1490 | Caxton's *Eneydos* | | |
| 1492 | | | Columbus lands in the West Indies |
| | *c.* 1500: *Grene Knight; Golagrus and Gawain; Melusine; Romauns of Partenay; Squyr of Lowe Degre; Three Kings' Sons; Turke and Gowin* | | |
| | Late 15th–early 16th century: *Clariodus* | | |
| | *c.* 1502: *Valentine and Orson* | | |
| | 16th century: Lord Berners's *Arthur of Little Britain; Carle off Carlile; King Arthur's Death; Legend of King Arthur; Sir Lambewell; Sir Lamwell; Sir Lancelot du Lake* | | |
| 1509 | | | Accession of Henry VIII |
| 1512 | Wynkyn de Worde prints Copeland's *Helyas, the Knight of the Swan* | | |
| 1513 | | *Niccolò Machiavelli's Il principe* | Battle of Flodden |
| 1516 | | More's *Utopia* | |
| 1517 | | | Luther's Wittenberg theses |
| 1528 | | Baldassare Castiglione's *Il cortegiano* | |
| 1532–34 | | François Rabelais's *Pantagruel* (1532); *Gargantua* (1534) | |
| | *c.* 1534: Wynkyn de Worde prints Lord Berners's *Duke Huon of Burdeux* | | |
| 1536 –40 | | | Dissolution of the Monasteries |
| 1547 | | | Accession of Edward VI |

# Bibliography

## Bibliographies

### General

*New Cambridge Bibliography of English Literature*, 1 (600–1600), ed. G. Watson
    (Cambridge, 1974). (Comprehensive cumulative bibliography,
    covering historical, cultural, and literary material; 2.1: Middle
    English Romances; 3.III: Caxton, Malory.)
*A Manual of the Writings in Middle English: 1050–1400*, and *Supplements I–IX*,
    ed. J. E. Wells (New Haven, Conn., 1916–52). (Covers all extant
    texts in print, grouped by genres, summarizes gist of critical
    writings, and lists all relevant publications to 1945.)
*A Manual of the Writings in Middle English: 1050–1500*, 1: *Romances*, ed. J. B.
    Severs; III: *Malory and Caxton*, ed. A. E. Hartung (New Haven,
    Conn., 1967, 1972). (On same principle as Wells above, revising
    critical summaries and extending bibliographies to press date.)
*The Index of Middle English Verse*, ed. C. Brown and R. H. Robbins (New
    York, 1943); supplement by R. H. Robbins and J. L. Cutler
    (Lexington, Ky., 1965).
*Bibliography of English Translations from Medieval Sources*, ed. C. P. Farrar and
    A. P. Evans (New York, 1946). (Lists and evaluates translations
    of medieval writings from fourth to fifteenth centuries.)

### Selective

*A Concise Bibliography for Students of English*, ed. A. G. Kennedy and D. G.
    Sands, 4th edn (Oxford, 1960).
*The Beginnings of English Literature to Skelton, 1509*, by W. L. Renwick and H.
    Orton, 3rd edn rev. by M. F. Wakelin (London, 1966). (General
    introduction to the culture and literature of the period, brief
    summaries on individual texts; bibliographies on both not fully
    revised since first edition (1939).)
*Guide to English Literature, from 'Beowulf' through Chaucer and Medieval Drama*,
    by D. M. Zesmer with bibliographies by S. B. Greenfield, 8th
    printing (New York, 1969). (Introductory survey with related

annotated bibliography on the period, genres, and individual
texts.)

*The Arthurian Bibliography*, ɪ: *Author Listing*; ɪɪ: *Index*, ed. C. E. Pickford and R.
Last (Cambridge, 1981, 1983). (Compilation of earlier Arthurian
bibliographies to 1977 including many general studies and other
non-Arthurian material.)

*The New Pelican Guide to English Literature*, ɪ, Part One: *Medieval Literature:
Chaucer and the Alliterative Tradition*, ed. B. Ford with
bibliography by B. Windeatt (Harmondsworth, 1982).
(Introductory survey of culture and literature, with representative
texts and selective bibliographies on period, genres, and individual
authors and texts.)

*Arthurian Legend and Literature: An Annotated Bibliography*, ɪ: *The Middle Ages*, ed.
E. Reiss, L. H. Reiss, and B. Taylor (New York, 1984).
(Comprehensive listing of Arthurian material in all languages,
elaborately sub-categorized.)

*Middle English Romance: An Annotated Bibliography, 1955–1983*, ed. J. A. Rice
(New York, forthcoming). (Comprehensive, annotated listing of
editions, translations, secondary scholarship, reviews, unpublished
dissertations.)

(Specialist bibliographies on individual fields, authors and texts are listed at
relevant points below.)

# Annual

*Annual Bibliography of English Language and Literature*, ed. for the Modern
Humanities Research Association (Cambridge, 1921–   ).
(Particularly useful for tracing reviews and individual items in
collections, memorial volumes, etc.)

*Bibliographical Bulletin of the International Arthurian Society* (Paris, 1949–66;
Nottingham, 1967–75; Paris, 1976–84). (Analytical summary of
publications of the preceding year, mainly Arthurian, organized
on basis of national origin.)

*International Bibliography of Books and Articles on the Modern Languages and
Literatures*, ed. for the Modern Language Association of America
(New York, 1956–   ). (Comprehensive listing with limited
annotation.)

*The Year's Work in English Studies*, ed. for the English Association (London,
1921–   ). (Analytical summary with some evaluation.)

# The nature of romance

## Romance as genre or mode

Auerbach, E.,   *Mimesis: The Representation of Reality in Western Literature*, tr., W. Trask, paperback (New York, 1957). (Chapter 6 considers the balance of the real and the ideal in courtly romance.)

Beer, G.,   *The Romance* (London, 1970). (Definition, history of evolution, brief and readable outline of later development of the genre.)

Bloomfield, M.,   'Episodic Motivation and Marvels in Epic and Romance', in *Essays and Explorations* (Cambridge, Mass., 1970). (Contrasts structure of epic and romance in relation to motivation, in the latter reflecting the influence of fairy-tale and saint's life.)

Brewer, D.,   'The Nature of Romance', *Poetica*, 10 (1978), 9–48. *Symbolic Stories: Traditional Narratives of the Family Drama in English Literature* (Cambridge, 1980). (On symbolic significance underlying improbable narratives of folk-tale and romance seen as *rites de passage* to maturity and self-knowledge.)

Childress, D. T.,   'Between Romance and Legend: "Secular Hagiography" in Middle English Literature', *Philological Quarterly*, 57 (1978), 311–22. (Despite many common features, distinguishes romance from saint's life on basis of protagonists' character and power of action.)

Everett, D.,   'A Characterisation of the English Medieval Romances', in *Essays on Middle English*, ed. P. Kean (Oxford, 1955), pp. 1–22. (Seminal attempt to differentiate romance by formal characteristics, now somewhat dated.)

Finlayson, J.,   'Definitions of Middle English Romance', *Chaucer Review*, 15 (1980), 44–62, 168–81. (In light of recent scholarship, usefully modifies concept of romance form in relation to epic on basis of hero's motivation, types of the supernatural, etc.)

Frye, N.,   *Anatomy of Criticism* (Princeton, N.J., 1957). (Fundamental attempt to redefine literary genres on the basis of essential concerns rather than formal characteristics.)
*The Secular Scripture: A Study of the Structure of Romance* (London, 1976). (Wide-ranging reconsideration of the forms of fiction, distinguishing literary romance from myth, folk-tale, etc.)

Gibbs, A. C. (ed.),    *Middle English Romances* (London, 1966).
(Introduction briefly reviews formal definitions,
seeing romance as variant form of epic.)

Gradon, P.,    *Form and Style in Early English Literature* (London,
1974). (Chapter 4 surveys variety of English
romance, noting persistence of epic matter, and
prefers definition by mode rather than genre.)

Griffin, N. E.,    'The Definition of Romance', *PMLA*, 38 (1923),
50–70. (Attempts to distinguish romance from epic
on basis of social values.)

Hill, D. M.,    'Romance as Epic', *English Studies*, 44 (1963), 95–107.
(Criticizes W. P. Ker's definitions on basis of value
judgements inherent in them; romance seen as
development of epic.)

Hume, K.,    'Romance: A Perdurable Pattern', *College English*, 36
(1974), 129–46. (On the psychological basis of
romance as reflected in the treatment of the hero.)
'The Formal Nature of Middle English Romance',
*Philological Quarterly*, 53 (1974), 158–80. (Categorizes
romances according to a spectrum of narrative types
distinguished by varying relationship of hero to
social context.)

Ker, W. P.,    *Epic and Romance*, reprint (London, 1908). (Classic
characterization of both genres on wide-ranging
descriptive and analytical basis.)

Kratins, O.,    'The Middle English Romance *Amis and Amiloun*:
Chivalric Romance or Secular Hagiography?',
*PMLA*, 81 (1966), 347–54. (Attempts, through a
specific example, to define sub-categories within
romance.)

Pearsall, D.,    'Understanding Middle English Romance', *Review*, 2
(1980).

Stevens, J.,    *Medieval Romance: Themes and Approaches* (London,
1973). (Introduction distinguishes between
characteristic experiences of romance and the
expressive conventions which typify the genre.)

Strohm, P.,    '*Storie, Spelle, Geste, Romaunce, Tragedie*: Generic
Distinctions in the Middle English Troy Narrative',
*Speculum*, 46 (1971), 348–59. (Problem of definition
illustrated through contemporary terms applied to
narrative types.)
'The Origin and Meaning of Middle English
*Romaunce*', *Genre*, 10 (1977), 1–20.

Tuve, R.,    *Allegorical Imagery: Some Medieval Books and their Posterity* (Princeton, N.J., 1966). (Chapter 5 considers the extent to which allegory forms part of the distinctive character of romance.)

Wilson, A.,    *Traditional Romance and Tale: How Stories Mean* (Ipswich, 1976). (Considers how wish-fulfilment shapes the superficially illogical and unrealistic narrative of folk-tale and popular romance.)

# Technical aspects of English romance

Barron, W. R. J.,    'Arthurian Romance: Traces of an English Tradition', *English Studies*, 61 (1980), 2–23. (On problems of classification and the identification of a sub-category on homogeneity of theme and treatment.)

Baugh, A. C.,    'The Authorship of the Middle English Romances', *Bulletin of the Modern Humanities Research Association*, 22 (1950), 13–28. (Queries the part played by minstrels in the composition of romances.)
'Improvisation in the Middle English Romance', *Proceedings of the American Philosophical Society*, 103 (1959), 418–54. (Significance of the numerous instances of oral formulaic technique in romances.)
'The Middle English Romance: Some Questions of Creation, Presentation, and Preservation', *Speculum*, 42 (1967), 1–31.
'Convention and Individuality in the Middle English Romance' in *Medieval Literature and Folklore*, ed. J. Mandel and B. A. Rosenberg (New Brunswick, N.J., 1970). (Analysis of *Bevis* and *Octavian* demonstrates creative originality in the treatment of romance conventions.)

Bennett, M. J.,    '*Sir Gawain and the Green Knight* and the Literary Achievement of the North-west Midlands: the Historical Background', *Journal of Medieval History*, 5 (1979), 63–88. (Political and social circumstances relevant to production of alliterative romance in the fourteenth century.)
'Courtly Literature and Northwest England in the Later Middle Ages' in *Court and Poet*, ed. G. S. Burgess *et al.* (Liverpool, 1981), pp. 69–78. (Suggests that courtiers from the North-west may have provided the audience for alliterative poetry at the court of Richard II.)

Bennett, H. S., *English Books and Readers: 1475 to 1557* (Cambridge, 1952). (Literacy, patronage, translation, and the press from Caxton onwards.)

Bornstein, D., 'William Caxton's Chivalric Romances and the Burgundian Renaissance in England', *English Studies*, 57 (1976), 1–10. (Influence of the Burgundian court on Caxton's choice of romances for his press.)

Brunner, K., 'Middle English Metrical Romances and their Audience', in *Studies in Medieval Literature in Honour of Professor A. C. Baugh*, ed. M. Leach (Philadelphia, Pa., 1961), pp. 219–27. (Implications of MSS contents for social class and tastes of readership.)

Chaytor, H. J., *From Script to Print*, reprint (London, 1966). (Conditions governing authorship and publication in the Middle Ages.)

Crosby, R., 'Oral Delivery in the Middle Ages', *Speculum*, 11 (1936), 88–110. (Characteristics of texts intended for oral recital.)

Girvan, R., 'The Medieval Poet and his Public', in *English Studies Today*, ed. C. L. Wrenn and G. Bullough (London, 1951). (Influence on nature and preservation of medieval literature of growth of literate public.)

Loomis, L. H., 'The Auchinleck MS and a Possible London Bookshop of 1330–1340', *PMLA*, 57 (1942), 595–627. (Implications of the make-up of the MS for the audience and commercial production of romance texts.)

Olson, C. C., 'The Minstrels at the Court of Edward III', *PMLA*, 56 (1941), 601–12. (Status and duties of royal minstrels.)

Pearsall, D., 'The Development of Middle English Romance', *Medieval Studies*, 27 (1965), 91–116. (Identification of the corpus of romance on formal and stylistic grounds.)
'The English Romance in the Fifteenth Century', *Essays and Studies*, n.s. 29 (1976), 56–83.
'The Alliterative Revival: Origins and Social Backgrounds', in *Middle English Alliterative Poetry and its Literary Background*, ed. D. Lawton (Cambridge, 1982), pp. 34–53, 132–36. (Re-examines existence, identity, transmission, nature of authors and audiences.)

Salter, E., 'The Alliterative Revival', *Modern Philology*, 64 (1967), 146–50, 233–37. (Attempts to define the audience.)
'Alliterative Modes and Affiliations in the Fourteenth Century', *Neuphilologische Mitteilungen*, 79 (1978), 25–35. (Suggests the influence of rhythmical prose on evolution of alliterative medium.)

Trounce, A. M.,    'The English Tail-Rhyme Romances', *Medium Aevum*, 1 (1932), 87–108, 168–82; 2 (1933), 34–57, 189–98; 3 (1934), 30–50. (Analysis of common characteristics of group suggesting association with East Anglia.)

Wittig, S.,    'Formulaic Style in the Middle English romance', *Neuphilologische Mitteilungen*, 78 (1977), 250–55. (Applies the concept of formulaic analysis to show the extent to which the style is composed of stereotypes.)

Wurster, J.,    'The Audience', in *The Alliterative 'Morte Arthure': A Reassessment of the Poem*, ed. K. H. Göller (Cambridge, 1981), pp. 44–56. (Suggests the sophistication of the audience for one alliterative romance.)

# The social context of Romance

## General history

*A Bibliography of English History to 1485*, ed. E. B. Graves (Oxford, 1975).
*Writings on British History*, ed. for the Institute for Historical Research (London, 1901–   ). (Originally periodic, latterly biennial, volumes.)
*Annual Bulletin of Historical Literature*, ed. for the Historical Association (London, 1911–   ).

Artz, F. B.,    *The Mind of the Middle Ages*, 3rd edn (Chicago, Ill., 1980).

Barlow, F.,    *The Feudal Kingdom of England, 1042–1216*, 3rd edn (London, 1980).

Clanchy, M. T.,    *England and Its Rulers, 1066–1272* (London, 1983).

Fowler, K.,    *The Age of Plantagenet and Valois* (London, 1967).

Gillingham, J. B.,    *Richard the Lionheart* (London, 1978).

Harriss, G. L.,    *King, Parliament, and Public Finance in Medieval England to 1369* (Oxford, 1975).

Harvey, J.,    *The Black Prince and His Age* (London, 1976).

| Heer, F., | *The Medieval World: Europe 1100–1350*, tr. J. Sondheimer, reprint (London, 1969). |
|---|---|
| Jacob, E. F., | *The Fifteenth Century, 1399–1485*, Oxford History of England, Vol. VI (Oxford, 1961). |
| Jolliffe, J. E. A., | *Angevin Kingship*, 2nd edn (London, 1970). |
| Keen, M. H., | *The Pelican History of Medieval Europe*, Penguin Books, reprint (Harmondsworth, 1979). *England in the Later Middle Ages* (London, 1973). |
| McFarlane, K. B., | *Lancastrian Kings and Lollard Knights* (Oxford, 1972). |
| McKisack, M., | *The Fourteenth Century, 1307–1399*, The Oxford History of England, Vol. V (Oxford, 1959). |
| Matthew, D. J. A., | *The Norman Conquest* (London, 1966). |
| Myers, A. R., | *England in the Late Middle Ages*, Penguin Books (Harmondsworth, 1952). |
| Painter, S., | *The Reign of King John*, (Baltimore, Md., 1949). |
| Poole, A. L., | *From Domesday Book to Magna Carta, 1087–1216*, Oxford History of England, Vol. III (Oxford, 1955). |
| Powicke, F. M., | *The Thirteenth Century, 1216–1307*, Oxford History of England, Vol. IV (Oxford, 1953). |
| Previté-Orton, C. W., | *The Shorter Cambridge Medieval History*, 2 vols, reprint (Cambridge, 1978). |
| Ross, C. D., | *Richard III* (London, 1981). |
| Sayles, G. O., | *The King's Parliament of England* (London, 1975). |
| Stenton, F. M., | *The First Century of English Feudalism, 1066–1166*, 2nd edn (Oxford, 1961). |
| Thomson, J. A. F., | *The Transformation of England, 1370–1529* (London, 1983). |
| Warren, W. L., | *Henry II* (London, 1973). *King John*, reprint (London, 1961). |

# Social history

Bellamy, J. G.,    *Crime and Public Order in England in the Later Middle Ages* (London, 1973). (Illustrates the disruptive forces within the chivalric society and development of law as an instrument of control.)

Bloch, M.,    *Feudal Society*, tr. L. A. Manyon (London, 1962). (Classic study, in parts now somewhat outdated, including consideration of literary conditions.)

Brooke, C.,    *The Structure of Medieval Society*, reprint (London, 1978). (Introductory sketch, readable and well illustrated, of social hierarchy.)

Coulton, G. G.,    *Life in the Middle Ages*, 2 vols, paperback (Cambridge, 1967). (Annotated extracts from contemporary social documents; pleasantly anecdotal.)

Duby, G.,    *Medieval Marriage*, tr., E. Forster (Baltimore, Md., 1977). (On conflicting views of Church and nobility on marriage in twelfth-century France.)

Ganshof, F. L.,    *Feudalism*, tr. P. Grierson, 3rd edn (London, 1964). (Survey of classic form from origins; limited treatment of English feudalism.)

Goody, J.,    *The Development of the Family and Marriage in Europe* (Cambridge, 1983).

Hilton, R. H.,    *The English Peasantry in the Later Middle Ages* (Oxford, 1975). (Specialist essays illustrating aspects of peasant economy and culture.)

Le Goff, J.,    *Time, Work, and Culture in the Middle Ages*, tr. A. Goldhammer (Chicago, Ill., 1980). (Collection of articles on trade, workers, and academics, popular, clerical, and literary culture.)

Little, L. K.,    *Religious Poverty and the Profit Economy in Medieval Europe* (Ithaca, N.Y., 1978). (Survey of place of the religious orders in the economy of the Middle Ages.)

McFarlane, K. B.,    *The Nobility of Later Medieval England* (Oxford, 1978). (Specialist essays giving comprehensive view of dominant class, 1290–1536.)

Mathew, G.,    *The Court of Richard II* (London, 1968). (Detailed, illustrated treatment of court as a cultural centre.)

Murray, A.,    *Reason and Society in the Middle Ages* (Oxford, 1978). (Stimulating study of social attitudes on arithmetic, aristocracy, miracles, avarice, ambition, etc.)

Myers, A. R.,    *England in the Late Middle Ages, 1307–1536*, Pelican History of England, Vol. IV, Penguin Books, rev. edn (Harmondsworth, 1961). (Valuable survey including chapters on literature, art, and education continuing pattern of Stenton below.)

Newton, S. M.,    *Fashion in the Age of the Black Prince* (Woodbridge, 1980). (Dress as an element of courtly display in mid-fourteenth century.)

Platt, C.,    *Medieval England: A Social History and Archaeology from the Conquest to 1600* (London, 1978). (Relates archaeological evidence to historical interpretation of period.)

Pollock, F., and F. W. Maitland,    *History of English Law Before the Time of Edward I*, 2 vols, 2nd edn (Cambridge, 1968). (Extremely detailed, very readable account of evolution of law, illuminating underlying social conditions.)

Poole, A. L.,    ed., *Medieval England*, 2 vols, rev. edn (Oxford, 1958). (Sound, wide-ranging, survey by various scholars on landscape, war, trade, heraldry, learning, science, etc.)

Power, E.,    *Medieval People*, Penguin Books, 10th edn (Harmondsworth, 1963). (Highly readable studies of individuals illustrating various aspects of society.)

Reynolds, S.,    *An Introduction to the History of English Medieval Towns*, reprint (Oxford, 1982).

Rickert, E.,    *et al.*, *Chaucer's World*, ed. C. G. Olson and M. M. Crow (Oxford, 1949). (Anthology of documentary excerpts illustrating life of typical fourteenth-century person.)

Robertson, D. W.,    *Chaucer's London* (New York, 1968). (Portrait of the city as a political and cultural centre.)

Shahar, S.,    *The Fourth Estate: A History of Women in the Middle Ages*, tr. C. Galai (London, 1983).

Southern, R. W.,    *The Making of the Middle Ages*, reprint (London, 1959). (Valuable study of structure and evolution of society and culture; Ch. 5: 'From Epic to Romance'.)

Stenton, D. M.,    *English Society in the Early Middle Ages, 1066–1307*, Pelican History of England, Vol. III, Penguin Books, 2nd edn (Harmondsworth, 1959). (Uses contemporary sources to show development of monarchy, Church, Commons, education, art, and literature.)

Trevelyan, G. M.,    *Illustrated English Social History*, I: *Chaucer's England and the Early Tudors* (London, 1949). (Illustrated, highly readable outline of social life.)

Ullmann, W.,    *The Individual and Society in the Middle Ages* (London, 1967).

Ziegler, P.,    *The Black Death*, reprint (London, 1969). (Popular survey of effects of plague on English life.)

# Chivalry and courtly love

Batty, J.,    *The Spirit and Influence of Chivalry* (London, 1980).

Boase, R.,    *The Origin and Meaning of Courtly Love* (Manchester, 1977). (Up-to-date, critical review of scholarly opinion on social and literary aspects.)

Duby, G.,    *The Chivalrous Society*, tr. C. Postan (London, 1977). (Specialist studies on aspects of feudal society: nobility, chivalry, justice, youth, kinship, value systems.)

Ferguson, A. B.,    *The Indian Summer of English Chivalry: Studies in the Decline and Transformation of Chivalric Idealism* (Durham, N.C., 1960).

Keen, M.,    *Chivalry* (New Haven, Conn., 1984). (Comprehensive up-to-date survey of all aspects; includes useful bibliography.)

Kelly, D.,    *Medieval Imagination: Rhetoric and the Poetry of Courtly Love*. (On the function in medieval poetry of imagination, rhetoric, and courtly love allegory.)

Lewis, C. S.,    *The Allegory of Love: A Study in Medieval Tradition* (Oxford, 1936). (Seminal study, now much queried, on function of allegory in literary expression of courtly love.)

Moorman, C.,    *A Knyght Ther Was: The Evolution of the Knight in Literature* (Lexington, Ky., 1967). (Analyses literary expressions of chivalry in *Roland*, Chrétien, Malory, etc.)

O'Donoghue, B.,    *The Courtly Love Tradition* (Manchester, 1982). (Selected texts with translation on facing page and helpful commentary.)

Painter, S.,    *French Chivalry: Chivalric Ideas and Practices in Medieval France*, reprint (Ithaca, N.Y., 1962).

Parry, J. J. (tr.),    *The Art of Courtly Love by Andreas Capellanus* (New York, 1941). (Classic courtly love treatise in translation with valuable introduction.)

Shapiro, N. R.,    *The Comedy of Eros: Medieval French Guides to the Art of Love* (Chicago, Ill., 1971). (Verse translations of thirteenth-century French courtly love texts.)

Topsfield, L. T.,    *Troubadours and Love* (Cambridge, 1975). (Study of troubadour poetry in the work of representative poets.)

Vale, M.,    *War and Chivalry* (London, 1981). (On effects on chivalric concept of increasingly mechanized fifteenth-century warfare.)

Weigand, H. J.,    *Three Chapters on Courtly Love in Arthurian France and Germany* (Chapel Hill, N.C., 1956). (Studies of Chrétien's *Lancelot*, Andreas Capellanus and Wolfram von Eschenbach's *Parzival*.)

## Literature and society

Alford, J. A., and D. P. Seniff, (eds),    *Literature and Law in the Middle Ages: A Bibliography of Scholarship* (New York, 1984). (Comprehensive listing of studies on law and justice as reflected in vernacular literature European-wide.)

Badel, P. Y.,    *Introduction à la vie littéraire du moyen âge* (Paris, 1969). (On social and intellectual factors governing literary production in medieval France.)

Barber, R.,    *The Knight and Chivalry* (New York, 1970). (Detailed study of chivalry in relation to religious and social ideas and literary treatment.)

Barnie, J. E.,    *War in Medieval English Society: Social Values in the Hundred Years War, 1337–99* (London, 1974). (Deals with chivalry and the romance as expressions of contemporary social conditions.)

Bloch, R. H.,    *Medieval French Literature and Law* (Berkeley, Cal., 1977). (Legal procedure as a formative influence on and a mimetic element in romance.)

Burrow, J.,    *Medieval Writers and their Work: Middle English Literature and its Background, 1100–1500* (Oxford, 1982). (On social and professional circumstances of medieval writers and nature of major genres.)

Clanchy, M. T.,    *From Memory to Written Record: England 1066–1307* (London, 1979). (On the extent and use of literacy, including sporadic references to minstrels and romances.)

Coleman, J.,    *Medieval Readers and Writers*, English Literature in History, I: 1350–1400, ed. R. Williams (London, 1981). (On influence of social and historical circumstances upon the literature of the age.)

Gist, M. A.,    *Love and War in the Middle English Romances* (Philadelphia, Pa., 1947). (Considers the extent to which romances idealized or reflected the reality of contemporary life.)

Green, R. F.,    *Poets and Princepleasers: Literature and the English Court in the Late Middle Ages* (Toronto, 1980). (Demonstrates the persistence of courtly interests in an age of emergent bourgeois literary audience.)

Hanning, R. W.,    *The Individual in Twelfth-Century Romance* (New Haven, Conn., 1977). (On emergence of concept of individuality and its reflection in French courtly romances.)

Huizinga, J.,    *The Waning of the MiddleAges*, tr. F. Hopman, Penguin Books (Harmondsworth, 1965). (First published 1924; classic treatment of social concepts as reflected in Continental art and literature of late Middle Ages.)

Jackson, W. H. (ed.),    *Knighthood in Medieval Literature* (Woodbridge, 1981). (Six original essays on the social reality and the literary reflection of knighthood.)

Knight, S.,    *Arthurian Literature and Society* (London, 1983). (Analyses works of Geoffrey of Monmouth, Chrétien, Malory, Tennyson, and Twain as they reflect dominant social concerns of contemporary society.)

Köhler, E., *L'Aventure chevaleresque: Idéal et réalité dans le roman courtois*, tr. E. Kaufholz (Paris, 1974). (Sees writers of courtly romance, especially Chrétien, as idealizing political, moral, and social concepts of the age.)

Medcalf, S. (ed.), *The Later Middle Ages* (London, 1981). (Studies of the political and cultural context of literature, including Arthurian legend in chapter on 'The Ideal, the Real, and the Quest for Perfection'.)

Norbert, M., *The Reflection of Religion in English Medieval Verse Romances* (Bryn Mawr, Pa., 1941).

Owings, M. A., *The Arts in the Middle English Romances* (New York, 1952). (Includes architecture, furnishings, supernatural objects, and the element of realism in romance.)

Owst, G. R., *Literature and Pulpit in Medieval England* (Cambridge, 1933). (On interrelations of vernacular literature and popular preaching.)

Scattergood, V. J., *Politics and Poetry in the Fifteenth Century* (London, 1971). (On literary reflection of contemporary political and social attitudes.)

Van de Voort, D., *Love and Marriage in the English Medieval Romances* (Nashville, Tenn., 1938).

# French romance

## Bibliographies

*A Critical Bibliography of French Literature*, I: *The Medieval Period*, ed. U. T. Holmes, Jr (Syracuse, N.Y., 1947; enlarged edition, 1952). (Selective, but critical, coverage.)

*Manuel bibliographique de la littérature française du moyen âge*, ed. R. Bossuat (Melun, 1951); *Supplément*, in collaboration with J. Monfrin (Paris, 1955); *Second Supplément* (Paris, 1961). (Comprehensive coverage of European material; less so on transatlantic publications.)

*Bibliographie der französischen Literaturwissenschaft: Bibliographie d'histoire littéraire française*, ed., O. Klapp (Frankfurt, 1960– ) (Annual; comprehensive listing of books, articles, reviews, theses.)

*A Concise Bibliography of French Literature* ed. D. Mahaffey (London, 1975).

*Bibliographie de la littérature française du moyen âge à nos jours*, ed. R. Rancœur (Paris, 1966– ). (Annual; bias towards material in French.)

# Literary histories

Bezzola, R. R., *Les Origines et la formation de la littérature courtoise en Occident*, (500–1200), 3 vols in 5 parts (Paris, 1944–63). (Vast survey on European basis stressing clerical influence on courtly literature.)

Bossuat, R., *Histoire de la littérature française*, I: *Le Moyen Age*, ed. J. Calvet, 2nd edn (Paris, 1955). (Sound, somewhat dated, outline.)

Cohen, G., *La Vie littéraire en France au moyen âge* (Paris, 1949). (Lively, somewhat sketchy, outline from origins to fifteenth century.)

Crosland, J., *Medieval French Literature* (Oxford, 1956; reprint Westport, Conn., 1976). (Surveys development of various genres from 1100.)

Ford, B., ed., *The New Pelican Guide to English Literature*, I, Part 2: *Medieval Literature: The European Inheritance* (Harmondsworth, 1983). (Convenient compendium of European vernacular literature (in translation) with introductory cultural outline, literary essays and bibliographies.)

Fox, J., *Literary History of France*, I, Part 1: *The Middle Ages*, ed. P. Charvet (London, 1974). (Outline survey giving useful narrative abstracts as well as critical analysis.)

Legge, M. D., *Anglo-Norman Literature and its Background* (Oxford, 1963). (Detailed treatment of courtly literature in Norman England, including Marie's *lais* and the origins of the 'Ancestral Romance'.)

Le Gentil, P., *La Littérature française du moyen âge*, 3rd edn (Paris, 1969). (Outline survey from earliest times to fifteenth century.)

Holmes, U. T., Jr, *A History of Old French Literature from the Origins to 1300*, rev. edn (New York, 1962). (Helpful introductory survey, now somewhat dated.)

Payen, J. C., *Littérature française: Le moyen âge, I: Des origines à 1300*, ed. C. Pichois (Paris, 1970). (Particular attention to the social context; useful bibliographical section.)

Poirion, D., *Littérature française: Le moyen âge, II: 1300–1480*, ed. C. Pichois (Paris, 1971). (Similar format to Payen above.)

Wilmotte, M.,     *Origines du roman en France: L'évolution du sentiment romanesque jusqu'en 1240* (Paris, 1941). (Classical and Christian influences on the evolution of the romance.)

Zumthor, P.,     *Essai de poétique médiévale* (Paris, 1972). (On material circumstances of medieval authorship and the evolution of genres.)

## Studies of romance

Dorfman, E.,     *The Narreme in the Medieval Romance Epic: An Introduction to Narrative Structures* (Manchester, 1969). (On analysis of literary structures on linguistic principles.)

Doutrepont, G.,     *Les Mises en prose des épopeés et des romans chevaleresques du XIVe au XVIe siècle* (Brussels, 1939). (Survey, with critical study and bibliography, of prose versions of epics and romances.)

Fourrier, A.,     *Le Courant réaliste dans le roman courtois en France au moyen âge, i: Les Débuts (XIIe siècle)* (Paris, 1960). (Traces development of mimetic elements in *roman courtois*.)

Frappier, J., and R. R. Grimm (eds),     *Le Roman jusqu'à la fin du XIIIe siècle*, Grundriss der romanischen Literaturen des Mittelalters, iv (Heidelberg, 1978). (Comprehensive survey, mainly on Arthurian romance, by eminent French and German scholars.)

Green, D. H.,     *Irony in the Medieval Romance* (Cambridge, 1979). (On the nature and function of irony in German, French, and English romance.)

Payen, J. C., and F. N. M. Diekstra *et al.*,     *Le Roman*, Typologie des sources du moyen âge occidental, fasicule 12 (Turnhout, 1975). (Outline survey of European romance on national basis, with bibliographies.)

Rossman, V. R.,     *Perspectives of Irony in Medieval French Literature* (The Hague, 1975). (Structural, dramatic and verbal irony in narrative literature, including Béroul and Chrétien.)

Ryding, W. W.,   *Structure in Medieval Narrative* (Paris, 1971).
                 (Evolution of narrative forms in the vernacular
                 tradition to the sixteenth century.)

Vinaver, E.,   *The Rise of Romance* (Oxford, 1971). (Evolution of
               romance form and narrative method from *Roland* to
               Malory.)

## La Chanson de Roland

Earliest and greatest of the Old French *chansons de geste*, composed in its
existing form in north-western France about 1100, but utilizing much older
material. Preserved in several manuscript copies of which the oldest was made
in England *c.* 1125–50. Remotely based on events of 778 when the army of
Charlemagne returning from a Spanish campaign was attacked in the rear by
Pyrenean mountaineers with the loss of eminent members of his court
including Roland, Count of the Breton Marches. Transformed into a glorious
episode in the struggle of Christendom against Islam, it provided a model of
heroic behaviour for the age of feudalism and as such was sung by the Norman
minstrel Taillefer at the Battle of Hastings in 1066.

*A Guide to Studies on the 'Chanson de Roland'*, ed. J. F. Duggan (London, 1976).
                 (Annotated bibliography listing annual bibliographies, editions,
                 studies.)

Brault, G. J. (ed.),   *The Song of Roland: An Analytical Edition*, 2 vols
                       (University Park, Pa. 1978). (With translation.)

Calin, W. (ed.),   *La Chanson de Roland* (New York, 1968). (Student
                   edition; difficult words translated in footnotes.)

Owen, D. D. R. (tr.),   *The Song of Roland* (London, 1972) (Blank verse
                        version.)

Sayers, D. L. (tr.),   *The Song of Roland*, Penguin Books
                       (Harmondsworth, 1957).

Whitehead, F. (ed.),   *La Chanson de Roland* (Oxford, 1970). (First
                       published 1942; student edition with introduction,
                       notes, vocabulary, and bibliography.)

See:   Crosland, J.,   *The Old French Epic* (Oxford, 1951). (Somewhat
                       dated survey useful to those without French.)

Faral, E.,   *La Chanson de Roland: Etude et analyse* (Paris, 1934).
             (Comprehensive literary study which still provides a
             sound introduction.)

Jones, G. F.,   *The Ethos of the Song of Roland* (Baltimore, 1963).
                (Analysis of ethical values and personal relationships
                on the basis of vocabulary.)

Le Gentil, P.,     *The Chanson de Roland* (Cambridge, Mass., 1969).
(Most comprehensive literary analysis available.)

Lejeune, R., and J.     *The Legend of Roland in the Middle Ages*, 2 vols, tr.
Stiennon,     C. Trollope (New York, 1971). (Splendidly
illustrated survey of the influence of the legend on
medieval art.)

Owen, D. D. R.     *The Legend of Roland: A Pageant of the Middle Ages*
(London, 1973). (Lavishly illustrated popularization,
paraphrasing poem, summarizing scholarly
opinion.)

Riquer, M. de,     *Les Chansons de geste françaises*, 2nd edn, tr. I. M.
Cluzel (Paris, 1957). (Original Spanish; only modern
study of *Roland* in the context of epic genre.)

Ross, D. J. A.,     'Old French', in *Traditions of Heroic and Epic Poetry,
I: The Traditions*, ed. A. T. Hatto (London, 1980).
(Useful introductory survey of epic tradition and
conventions for English readers.)

Rychner, J.,     *La Chanson de geste: Essai sur l'art épique des jongleurs*,
reprint (Geneva, 1968). (Stylistic study of *Roland*
and other epics.)

Vance, E.,     *Reading the Song of Roland* (Englewood Cliffs, N. J.,
1970). (Basic study of language, heroic society,
literary conventions.)

## The Matter of Rome romances

The work of poets of northern France serving a feudal aristocracy convinced that
its social values derived from its supposed Trojan ancestry through Rome. Related,
directly or indirectly, to the classical epics, they met the contemporary need to
believe that the record of antiquity formed part of European history, that chivalry
was rooted in ancient and honourable military values, that women might play valid
roles as inspirers and rewarders of male virtue. Between 1150 and 1165 were
produced the *Roman d'Eneas*, derived from Virgil's *Aeneid*, the *Roman de Thèbes*,
based on the *Thebaid* of Statius, and Benoit de Sainte-Maure's vast *Roman de Troie*
elaborated from post-Homeric accounts of the Trojan war. Various versions of the
*Roman d'Alexandre* provided a chivalric context for the wonders of the East and
adaptations of Ovid in *Narcisus* and *Piramus et Tisbé* examples of the frustration of
youthful love.

Armstrong, D. L. *et al.*     *The Medieval French 'Roman d'Alexandre'*, Elliott
(eds),     Monographs, 37, 38, 39, 41 (Princeton, 1937–55).

Boer, C. de (ed.),     *Piramus et Tisbé* (Paris, 1921).

Constans, L. (ed.),     Benoit de Sainte-Maure, *Le Roman de Troie*, 5 vols
(Paris, 1904–12).

| | | |
|---|---|---|
| Pelan, M. M., and N. C. W. Spence, | | *Narcisus* (Paris, 1964). |
| Raynaud de Lage, G., | | *Le Roman de Thèbes*, 2 vols (Paris, 1966–68). |
| Salverda de Grave, J. J., | | *Le Roman d'Eneas*, 2 vols (Paris, 1964–68). |

See:

| | | |
|---|---|---|
| Bolgar, R. R., | *The Classical Heritage and its Beneficiaries*, reprint (Cambridge, 1963). (On influence of classical literature and learning on vernacular European literature.) |
| Cary, G., | *The Medieval Alexander*, ed. D. J. A. Ross (Cambridge, 1956). (Exhaustive survey of all medieval versions of Alexander legend.) |
| Cormier, R. J., | *One Heart One Mind: The Rebirth of Virgil's Hero in Medieval French Romance* (University, Miss., 1973). (Detailed analysis of *Roman d'Eneas* as example of medieval transformation of classical matter and values.) |
| Curtius, E. R., | *European Literature and the Latin Middle Ages*, tr. W. Trask, reprint (Princeton N.J., 1967). (Massive survey of contribution of classical culture to Latin literature of the Middle Ages.) |
| Faral, E., | *Recherches sur les sources latines des contes et romans courtois du moyen âge* (Paris, 1913). (Standard treatment of Ovidian influence on courtly narrative and evolution of Matter of Rome romances.) |
| Jones, R., | *The Theme of Love in the Romans d'Antiquité* (London, 1972). (Study of the common characteristics of group in treatment of love.) |
| Raby, F. J. E., | *A History of Secular Latin Poetry in the Middle Ages*, 2 vols (Oxford, 1934, 1957). (Comprehensive analytical and critical survey, European-wide, to end of twelfth century.) |
| Reynolds, L. D., and N. G. Wilson, | *Scribes and Scholars*, 2nd edn (Oxford, 1974). (On the survival and transmission of classical literature.) |
| Roulleau, G., | *Etude chronologique de quelques thèmes narratifs des romans courtois* (Paris, 1966). (Traces themes from classical literature.) |

## The *lais* of Marie de France

The work of a poetess of whom nothing is certainly known but who probably wrote in England in the last quarter of the twelfth century, using themes from folklore, some of them Celtic. Their persistent concern is with love between the sexes, particularly the struggle of young lovers against contemporary social restrictions. Marie is also credited with a collection of Aesopian fables, *Ysopet*, said to have originated with King Alfred as a repository of traditional wisdom.

*Marie de France: An Analytical Bibliography*, ed. G. Burgess (London, 1977; supplement no. I, 1986). (Annotated bibliography listing manuscripts, editions, translations, studies.)

| | |
|---|---|
| Burgess, G., and K. Busby (tr.), | *The Lais of Marie de France*, Penguin Books (Harmondsworth, 1986). |
| Ewert, A. (ed.), | *Marie de France: Lais*, reprint (Oxford, 1978). (First published 1944; sound edition with good glossary.) |
| Hanning R., and J. Ferrante (tr.), | *The Lais of Marie de France* (New York, 1978). (Translation based on Ewert edition.) |
| Jonin, P. (tr.), | *Les Lais de Marie de France* (Paris, 1972). (Excellent translation into modern French.) |
| Mason, E. (tr.), | *Lays of Marie de France and other French Legends*, Everyman's Library (London, 1954). (English prose translation, first published 1911.) |
| Rychner, J. (ed.), | *Les Lais de Marie de France* (Paris, 1966). (Classic edition, useful notes, bibliography.) |

| | | |
|---|---|---|
| See: | Baum, R., | *Recherches sur les œuvres attribuées à Marie de France* (Heidelberg, 1968). (Major historical, biographical study; questions the attribution of the *lais* to Marie.) |
| | Hoepffner, E., | *Les Lais de Marie de France* (Paris, 1966). (First published 1935; major study, but literary analysis now somewhat outdated.) |
| | Mickel, E. J., Jr, | *Marie de France* (New York, 1974). (Very readable general study of intellectual background, sources, concept of love.) |
| | Payen, J. C., | *Le Lai narratif*, Typologie des sources du moyen âge occidental, fascicule 13 (Turnhout, 1975). (General survey of genre, evolution, audience, historical context; useful bibliography.) |
| | Rothschild, J. R., | *Narrative Technique in the Lais of Marie de France*: *Themes and Variations*: I (Chapel Hill, N.C., 1974). (Extended analyses, literary, structural and thematic.) |

# The Tristan legend

Legend of uncertain origin but largely compounded of Celtic elements whose earliest surviving versions are in French: that by Thomas of Britain (variously dated 1155–70) probably composed at, or for, the court of Henry II and Eleanor of Aquitaine; and that by Béroul (*c.* 1190), both of them fragments of a much larger whole. The story of Tristan bound by the unbreakable bond of the love-potion to Iseult, his uncle Mark's bride, torn between feudal duty and infatuation, is most powerfully told by Gottfried von Strassburg (1205–15), but appears in almost every European language throughout the Middle Ages.

*The Old French Tristan Poems: A Bibliographical Guide*, ed. D. J. Shirt (London, 1980). (Comprehensive listing of publications on French verse texts, development of the legend and reconstructed versions.)

Ewert, A. (ed.),        *The Romance of Tristan by Béroul*, 2 vols (Oxford, ɪ: 1939, ɪɪ: 1970).

Fedrick, A. S. (tr.),   *The Romance of Tristan by Béroul and the Tale of Tristan's Madness*, Penguin Books (Harmondsworth, 1970).

Loomis, R. S. (tr.),    *The Romance of Tristan and Ysolt by Thomas of Britain*, 3rd edn (New York, 1951).

Payen, J. C. (ed. & tr.),   *Tristan et Yseut: Les Tristan en vers* (Paris, 1974). (Versions of Béroul and Thomas with modern French translation.)

Roberts, V. (ed. & tr.),    *Thomas of Britain: Tristan*, Garland Library of Medieval Literature (New York, forthcoming).

See:    Barteau, F.,    *Les Romans de Tristan et Iseut: Introduction à une lecture plurielle* (Paris, 1972). (Parallel analyses of both versions.)

        Eisner, S.,     *The Tristan Legend: A Study in Sources* (Evanston, Ill., 1969). (On origins and mingling of classical mythology and north British traditions in the legend.)

        Ferrante, J. M.,    *The Conflict of Love and Honour: The Medieval Tristan Legend in France, Germany and Italy* (The Hague, 1973). (Compares early and later versions to show development of different interpretations.)

        Gallais, P.,    *Genèse du roman occidentale: Essais sur Tristan et Iseut et son modèle persan* (Paris, 1974). (On Eastern analogues to the legend and possible means of transmission to the West.)

        Rougemont, D. de,   *Passion and Society* (London, 1956). (First published (Paris, 1939) as *L'amour et l'occident*; general survey of love-theme.)

## Evolution of the Matter of Britain

### In legend

*The Arthurian Encyclopedia* ed. N. J. Lacy (New York, 1984). (Comprehensive coverage of the legend in literature, art, history, music, folklore from the Middle Ages to the present.)

*The Romance of Arthur: An Anthology*, ed. J. J. Wilhelm and L. Z. Gross (New York, 1984). (Translations of Arthurian material in Latin chronicles, early Welsh poetry and prose, Geoffrey of Monmouth's *Historia*; complete versions of Chrétien's *Lancelot*, *Sir Gawain and the Green Knight*, and selections from the alliterative *Morte Arthure* and Malory's *Le Morte Darthur*.)

Alcock, L.,   *Arthur's Britain: History and Archaeology A.D. 367–634*, Penguin Books (London, 1971). (Study of period of the historical Arthur.)
*'By South Cadbury is That Camelot . . .': Excavations at Cadbury Castle 1966–70* (London, 1972). (Discusses evidence for Arthurian connections.)

Ashe, G.,   *From Caesar to Arthur* (London, 1960). (On historical basis of legend.)
(*et al.*) *The Quest for Arthur's Britain*, reprint (London, 1971). (Illustrated survey of associated archaeological and natural sites.)
*Camelot and the Vision of Albion*, reprint (London, 1975). (On Camelot and the excavations at Cadbury Castle.)

Barber, R. W.,   *King Arthur in Legend and History*, rev. edn (Ipswich, 1973). (Popular introduction to the historical Arthur and survey of English Arthurian literature to the nineteenth century.)

Bullock-Davies, C.,   *Professional Interpreters and the Matter of Britain* (Cardiff, 1966). (On the transmission of the legend in twelfth-century bilingual communities.)

Chambers, E. K.,   *Arthur of Britain: The Story of King Arthur in History and Legend*, reprint (New York, 1966). (First published, 1927; still useful, especially on early traditions.)

Darrah, J.,   *The Real Camelot: Paganism and the Arthurian Romances* (London, 1981). (Sees legend as rooted in Bronze Age traditions and romances as orally transmitted memories of pagan rituals.)

Loomis, R. S.,   *Celtic Myth and Arthurian Romance* (New York, 1927). (On transformation of Celtic legend into Arthurian romance.)

Loomis, R. S. and L. H. Loomis   *Arthurian Legends in Art*, reprint (New York, 1970). (Illustrated study of Arthurian subjects in medieval art.)

Morris, J.,     *The Age of Arthur: A History of the British Isles from 350–650* (London, 1973). (Arthur as a key figure in post-Roman Britain.)

Treharne, R. F.,     *The Glastonbury Legends: Joseph of Arimathea, The Holy Grail and King Arthur*, reprint (London, 1971). (General introduction to the historical basis of the legend.)

**In literature**

Bruce, J. D.,     *The Evolution of Arthurian Romance: From the Beginnings Down to the Year 1300*, 2 vols, reprint (Geneva, 1974). (First published 1923; still valuable for clear historical outline and plot abstracts.)

Cavendish, R.,     *King Arthur and the Grail: The Arthurian Legends and Their Meaning*, reprint (London, 1980). (General survey focusing on theme of individual's search for integrity.)

Frappier, J.,     *Le Roman breton: Introduction; des origines à Chrétien de Troyes* (Paris, 1950). (General survey of origins of Arthurian romance.)

Grout, P. B.,     et al., *The Legend of Arthur in the Middle Ages: Studies Presented to A. H. Diverres* (Cambridge, 1983). (Primarily literary studies on Celtic, French, German, Spanish, and English texts.)

Jenkins, E.,     *The Mystery of King Arthur* (London, 1975). (General survey of influence of Arthurian texts, mainly English, to twentieth century.)

Loomis, R. S. (ed.),     *Arthurian Literature in the Middle Ages: A Collaborative History* (Oxford, 1959). (Fullest available study of origins of legend, literary evolution, interrelation of texts, versions, etc.)
*The Development of Arthurian Romance*, reprint (New York, 1970). (First published 1963; general survey of versions up to Malory.)

Owen, D. D. R. (ed.),     *Arthurian Romance: Seven Essays* (Edinburgh, 1970). (Literary subjects, French, German, English from Chrétien to Malory.)

Varty, K. (ed.),     *An Arthurian Tapestry: Essays in Memory of Lewis Thorpe* (Glasgow, 1981). (Twenty-nine literary studies, largely on Chrétien.)

## Geoffrey of Monmouth's *Historia*

One of the most seminal works of medieval literature, the *Historia Regum Britanniae* (*c.* 1136) gives an account of the legendary history of Britain from its founding by Brutus, supposed great-grandson of Aeneas, to the late sixth century, including a full version of the reign of King Arthur, his defeat of the Saxons, Continental conquests, betrayal by Mordred, and departure to Avallon. Geoffrey, a Welsh cleric teaching in Oxford, claims as source 'a very old book in the British language' whose existence is doubted, but uses all his academic skill to lend historical conviction to matter which, though it may incorporate sources now lost, he seems largely to have invented.

Griscom, A. (ed.),　　The 'Historia Regum Britanniae' of Geoffrey of Monmouth, reprint (Geneva, 1977). (Edition of Cambridge, University College MS with variants; first published 1929.)

Hammer, J. (ed.),　　'Historia Regum Britanniae': A Variant Version (Cambridge, Mass., 1951). (Edition of manuscripts comprising the Variant version.)

Thorpe, L. (tr.),　　The History of the Kings of Britain, Penguin Books, 4th edn (Harmondsworth, 1976). (Based on Griscom's edition.)

See:　Tatlock, J. S. P.,　　The Legendary History of Britain: Geoffrey of Monmouth's 'Historia Regum Britanniae' and Its Early Vernacular Versions (Berkeley, Cal., 1950). (Very detailed study of function, details, motifs, and relation to versions of Wace and Layamon.)

## Wace's *Roman de Brut*

Robert Wace, a native of Jersey, dedicated to Eleanor of Aquitaine his French verse translation of Geoffrey of Monmouth's *Historia*, completed in 1155. His limited additions, such as the first mention of the Round Table, the courtly gloss which he gave to Geoffrey's chronicle, and the elegance of his verse gave added impetus to the rapid dissemination of the Arthurian story throughout Europe.

Arnold, I. (ed.),　　Le 'Roman de Brut' de Wace, 2 vols (Paris, 1938, 1940).

Arnold I. and M. Pelan (eds),　　La Partie arthurienne du 'Roman de Brut' de Wace (Paris, 1962).

Mason, E. (tr.),　　Arthurian Chronicles by Wace and Layamon, Everyman's Library, reprint (London, 1976). (Translations of Arthurian sections of both.)

See:　Pelan, M.,　　L'Influence du 'Brut' de Wace sur les romanciers français de l'époque (Paris, 1931). (Assesses influence of Wace on Chrétien, Thomas, Marie de France, etc.)

## The romances of Chrétien de Troyes

A poet of northern France of whose life nothing certain is known, Chrétien worked under the patronage of Marie, Countess of Champagne, *c*. 1160–80, and then for Philip of Alsace, *c*. 1180–90. Though as a leading figure in the literary renaissance of the twelfth century he shared in the dissemination of motifs from Latin literature, translating Ovid and showing the rhetorical influence of Cicero, his claim to fame rests on his romances in which folklore narratives, chiefly Celtic in origin, are made the vehicle of sophisticated analysis of contemporary social values. In apparent order of composition they are: *Erec et Enide c.* 1170; *Cligés, c.* 1176; *Yvain* or *Le Chevalier au lion, c.* 1177; *Lancelot* or *Le Chevalier de la charrette, c.* 1177–81; *Perceval* or *Le Conte du Graal, c.* 1180 – there has been a recent tendency to date the romances as much as a decade later than originally proposed.

*Chrétien de Troyes: An Analytic Bibliography*, ed. D. Kelly (London, 1976).
(Unannotated listing under subjects and topics as well as works.)

Carroll, C. (ed. and tr.),   *Erec and Enide*, Garland Library of Medieval Literature (New York, forthcoming).

Cline, R. H. (tr.),   *Yvain, or the Knight of the Lion* (Athens, Ga., 1975). (Verse translation.)

Comfort, W. W. (tr.),   *Chrétien de Troyes, Arthurian Romances*, Everyman's Library, reprint (London, 1975). (First published 1914.)

Kibler, W. W. (ed. and tr.),   *Lancelot, or The Knight of the Cart* (New York, 1981).

Kibler, W. W. (ed. and tr.),   *Ywain, or The Knight with the Lion* (New York, 1985).

Linker, R. W. (tr.),   *The Story of the Grail*, 2nd edn (Chapel Hill, N.C., 1960). (Prose translation.)

Nelson, J., and C. W. Carroll (eds),   *Yvain, ou le Chevalier au lion* (New York, 1968).

Reid, T. B. W. (ed.),   *Yvain*, 2nd edn (Manchester, 1948).

Roach, W. (ed.),   *Le Roman de Perceval ou le Cont du graal*, 2nd edn (Geneva, 1959).

Roques, M. (ed.),   *Les Romans de Chrétien de Troyes*, Classiques français du moyen âge (Paris, 1952–75). (*Erec et Enide*, 1952; *Cligés*, ed. A. Micha, 1957; *Le Chevalier de la charrette*, 1958; *Le Chevalier au lion*, 1960; *Le Conte du graal*, ed. F. Lecoy, 2 vols, 1973, 1975.)

See:   Artin, T.,   *The Allegory of Adventure: Reading Chrétien's 'Erec' and 'Yvain'* (London, 1974). (Sees narratives as allegorically related to sacred history.)

Bednar, J.,    *La Spiritualité et le symbolisme dans les œuvres de Chrétien de Troyes* (Paris, 1974). (Relates Chrétien's concern with conjugal love and spiritual development of characters to contemporary religious developments.)

Bezzola, R. R.,    *Le Sens de l'aventure et de l'amour* (Paris, 1947). (On the symbolism inherent in love and adventure, chiefly in *Erec*.)

Carasso-Bulow, L.,    *The "Merveilleux" in Chrétien de Troyes' Romances* (Geneva, 1976). (Chrétien's mingling of realism and fantasy gives ironic detachment to his statement of ideas.)

Cross, T. P., and W. A. Nitze,    *Lancelot and Guenevere: A Study on the Origins of Courtly Love* (Chicago, Ill., 1930). (Chrétien's adaptation of Celtic story of abduction of woman by Otherworld figure, and use of Ovid in development of courtly love theme.)

Frappier, J., tr. R. T. Cormier,    *Chrétien de Troyes: The Man and His Work* (Athens, Ohio., 1982). (Original published 1957; general study emphasizing nature of *conjointure*.)
*Chrétien de Troyes et le mythe du Graal: Etude sur 'Perceval' ou le 'Conte du Graal'* (Paris, 1972). (General introduction stressing psychology of the age of composition.)
*Autour du Graal* (Geneva, 1977). (Collected articles, mostly on *Perceval* and other Grail narratives.)
*Etude sur 'Yvain' ou le 'Chevalier au lion' de Chrétien de Troyes* (Paris, 1969). (Detailed analysis of all aspects of poem.)

Haidu, P.,    *Lion-queue-coupée: l'écart symbolique chez Chrétien de Troyes* (Geneva, 1972). (On varieties of symbolism, particularly Yvain's lion.)
*Aesthetic Distance in Chrétien de Troyes: Irony and Comedy in 'Cligés' and 'Perceval'* (Geneva, 1968). (Irony as the basis of compositional method in *Cligés*; function of incongruity in *Perceval*.)

Kelly, F. D.,    *'Sens' and 'Conjointure' in the 'Chevalier de la Charrette'* (The Hague, 1966). (Problems of interpretation, especially function of structure and characterization.)

Lacy, N. J.,    *The Craft of Chrétien de Troyes: An Essay in Narrative Technique* (Leiden, 1980). (On use of structural repetition, symmetry, interlacing, analogical patterning in composition.)

Loomis, R. S.,    *Arthurian Tradition and Chrétien de Troyes* (New York, 1949). (Celtic background and motifs.)

Luttrell, C.,    *The Creation of the First Arthurian Romance: A Quest* (London, 1974). (Creative method, largely exemplified in *Erec*.)

Pickens, R. T.,    *The Welsh Knight: Paradoxicality in Chrétien's 'Conte del Graal'* (Lexington, Ky., 1977). (Irony and paradox as means of extending romance conventions to express relation of Grail vision to worldly chivalry.)

Reason, J. H.,    *An Inquiry into the Structural Style and Originality of Chrestien's 'Yvain'*, reprint (New York, 1968). (On tripartite structure.)

Ribard, J.,    *Chrétien de Troyes, 'Le Chevalier de la Charrette': Essai d'interprétation symbolique* (Paris, 1972). (Christian allegorical interpretation with Lancelot as the saviour figure.)

Rider, P.,    *Le chevalier dans le 'Conte du Graal' de Chrétien de Troyes* (Paris, 1978). (Gawain–Perceval contrast viewed in folklore terms.)

Topsfield, L. T.,    *Chrétien de Troyes: A Study of the Arthurian Romances* (Cambridge, 1981). (General study of literary method, concepts of love and chivalry, relationship of man to God, etc.)

## Continuations of Chrétien's *Perceval*

Roach, W. (ed.),    *The Continuations of the Old French 'Perceval' of Chrétien de Troyes: The First Continuation*, 3 vols (Philadelphia, Pa., 1949–52); *The Second Continuation* (1971).

Potvin, C. (ed.),    *Perceval le Gallois ou le Conte du Graal* (Mons, 1866–71; reprinted Geneva, 1977): iii: *First Continuation*; iv: *Second Continuation*; v: *Third Continuation*; vi: *Fourth Continuation*.

See:    Greenhill, E. S.,    'The Child in the Tree: A Study of the Cosmological Tree in Christian Literature', *Traditio*, 10 (1954), 323–71. (Two episodes in Second Continuation related to traditions of cross as tree.)

Larmat, J.,    'Le péché de Perceval dans la Continuation de Gerbert', *Mélanges d'histoire littéraire, de linguistique et de philologie romanes offerts à Charles Rostaing* (Liège, 1974), i, 541–57 (Sees hero's sin as associated with pride of knightly class and Fourth Continuation as designed to persuade knights to serve Church.)

Marx, J.,    *Nouvelles Recherches sur la littérature arthurienne* (Paris, 1965). (On interrelations of the Third Continuation and the *Queste*.)

Roach, W.,     'Transformations of the Grail Theme in the First Two Continuations of the Old French *Perceval*', *Proceedings of the American Philosophical Society*, 110 (1966), 160–64. (Grail, seen as pagan cauldron of plenty in First Continuation, is associated with Chrétien's eucharistic conception in the Second.)

## The Vulgate Cycle

The thirteenth century, with its encyclopaedic impulse to collect and harmonize knowledge, saw the appearance of the vast prose compilation of Arthurian romances which scholars came to regard as the Vulgate, the basic text in which the accumulated matter of the tradition had been interrelated and reconciled into a universal history. The branches are: *L'Estoire del Saint Graal*, *c.* 1230; *L'Estoire de Merlin*, *c.* 1215; *Lancelot du Lac* (or *Lancelot* Proper), *c.* 1215; *La Queste del Saint Graal*, *c.* 1215; *La Mort le Roi Artu*, *c.* 1215.

Cable, J. (tr.),     *The Death of King Arthur*, Penguin Books (Harmondsworth, 1971). (Translation of the last book of the cycle, *La Mort Artu*.)

Carman, J. N. (tr.),     *From Camelot to Joyous Guard: The Old French 'La Mort le Roi Artu'* (Lawrence, Kans., 1974).

Comfort, W. W. (tr.),     *The Quest of the Holy Grail*, Everyman's Library (London, 1926).

Frappier, J. (ed.),     *La Mort le Roi Artu: Roman du XIIIe siècle*, 3rd edn (Geneva, 1959).

Matarasso, P. M. (tr.),     *The Quest of the Holy Grail*, Penguin Books (Harmondsworth, 1969).

Micha, A. (ed.),     *Lancelot: Roman en prose du XIIIe siécle*, 7 vols (Paris, 1978–80).

Patton, L. A. (tr.),     *Sir Lancelot of the Lake: A French Prose Romance of the Thirteenth Century* (London, 1929). (With parts of the *Queste del Saint Graal* and *La Mort Artu*.)

Pauphilet, A. (tr.),     *La Queste del Saint Graal*, reprint (Paris, 1949).

Sommer, H. O. (ed.),     *The Vulgate Version of the Arthurian Romances*, 8 vols, reprint (New York, 1969). (First published 1908–16.)

See:   Briel, H. de, and M. Herrmann,     *King Arthur's Knights and the Myths of the Round Table: A New Approach to the French 'Lancelot in Prose'* (Paris, 1972). (Interpretation of Vulgate Cycle in Christian terms as demonstrating the need for repentance.)

Carman, J. N.,     *A Study of the Pseudo-Map Cycle of Arthurian Romance* (Lawrence, Kans., 1973). (Relationship to contemporary history.)

Fox, M. B.,     *'La Mort le Roi Artu': Etude sur les manuscrits, les sources et la composition de l'œuvre* (Paris, 1933).

Frappier, J.,     *Etude sur la 'Mort le Roi Artu', roman du XIIIe siècle*, 3rd edn (Paris, 1972). (General study stressing narrative method and psychology of characters.)

Hartman, R.,     *La quête et la croisade: Villehardouin, Clari et le 'Lancelot en prose'* (New York, 1977). (Comparison of *Queste* and *Mort Artu* with two chronicles of the Fourth Crusade demonstrating interrelations of forms.)

Locke, F. W.,     *The Quest for the Holy Grail: A Literary Study of a Thirteenth-Century French Romance* (Stanford, Cal., 1960). (Sees basic pattern of work as pilgrimage, the search for the roots of existence.)

Lot, F.,     *Etude sur le 'Lancelot' en prose*, reprint (Paris, 1954). (On narrative interlacing in relation to unity of structure and subject.)

Matarasso, P.,     *The Redemption of Chivalry: A Study of the 'Queste del Saint Graal'* (Geneva, 1979). (Interprets as allegory of salvation based on Bible and writings of Cistercian monks.)

Pauphilet, A.,     *Etudes sur la 'Queste del Saint Graal' attribuée à Gautier Map*, reprint (Paris, 1981). (Deals particularly with symbolism.)

Robreau, Y.,     *L'Honneur et la honte: Leur expression dans les romans en prose du 'Lancelot-Graal' (XIIe–XIIIe siècles)* (Geneva, 1981). (On changing concepts of honour in an age of economic change.)

# English romance

## Literary histories

Baldwin, C. S.,     *Three Medieval Centuries of Literature in England: 1100–1400*, reprint (New York, 1968). (First published, 1932; still useful outline survey of evolution of narrative from epic to romance.)

Baugh, A. C.,     *The Middle English Period (1100–1500)*, in *A Literary History of England*, I, Part 2, ed. A. C. Baugh, 2nd edn (New York, 1967). (Highly condensed but well-balanced and readable survey.)

Bennett, H. S., *Chaucer and the Fifteenth Century*, The Oxford History of English Literature, II, Part 1 (Oxford, 1947). (Useful coverage of Caxton, Lydgate, and the later Romances.)

Bolton, W. F. (ed.), *The Middle Ages*, The Sphere History of Literature in the English Language, I (London, 1970). (Sound introductory survey treating romance in the literary context of the period.)

Brewer, D., *English Gothic Literature*, Macmillan History of Literature, (London, 1983). (Deals with individual romances in the general literary context and includes a chapter on Malory and Caxton.)

Chambers, E. K., *English Literature at the Close of the Middle Ages*, The Oxford History of English Literature, II, Part 2 (Oxford, 1945). (Ch. 3: popular narrative poetry and the ballad; Ch. 4: Malory.)

Everett, D., *Essays on Middle English Literature*, ed. P. Kean (Oxford, 1955). (Valuable essays on the nature of Middle English romance, Layamon's *Brut*, the alliterative *Morte Arthure*, and the *Gawain*-poet.)

Kane, G., *Middle English Literature*, rev. edn (London, 1971). (Section on the romances evaluates them critically on literary grounds.)

Ker, W. P., *Medieval English Literature*, reprint (Oxford, 1969). (Ch. 4: the Romances: classic outline survey, now somewhat dated.)

Oakden, J. P., *Alliterative Poetry in Middle English*, I: *The Dialectal and Metrical Survey*; II: *A Survey of the Traditions* (Manchester, 1930, 1935). (Relates alliterative romances to each other and their cultural context.)

Pearsall, D., *Old English and Middle English Poetry*, The Routledge History of Poetry, I (London, 1977). (Individual romances briefly treated in period context with stress on metrical forms and manuscript make-up.)

Schlauch, M., *English Medieval Literature and its Social Foundations* (Warsaw, 1956). (Limited outline placing romances in social context.)

Schofield, W. H., *English Literature from the Norman Conquest to Chaucer*, reprint (Westport, Conn., 1970). (First published, 1906; still useful survey of the romances in context of Anglo-Latin and Anglo-Norman literature.)

Spearing, A. C., *Criticism and Medieval Poetry*, 2nd edn (London, 1972). (Textual analysis exemplified on parts of *Sir Gawain and the Green Knight*.)

Speirs, J.,          *Medieval English Poetry: The Non-Chaucerian Tradition*, 2nd edn (London, 1962). (Emphasizes folklore elements in romance and other genres.)

Turvill-Petre, T.,   *The Alliterative Revival* (Cambridge, 1977). (Treats alliterative romances in relation to the tradition, largely metrically.)

Wilson, R. M.,       *Early Middle English Literature*, reprint (London, 1968). (Ch. 9: Romance–general survey of thirteenth-century texts in relation to linguistic and cultural context.)
                     *The Lost Literature of Medieval England* (London, 1952). (Cites evidence of romances on the various 'Matters' no longer extant.)

## Studies of romance

Barrow, S. F.,       *The Medieval Society Romances* (New York, 1924). (Analysis of social context and literary techniques of a group of romances, French and English.)

Donovan, M. J.,      *The Breton Lay: A Guide to Varieties* (Notre Dame, Ind., 1969). (Analyses of French and English examples for purposes of defining genre and determining Breton affiliations.)

Dürmüller, U.,       *Narrative Possibilities of the Tail-Rime Romance* (Berne, 1975). (Study of stanza structure in relation to narrative structure.)

Hibbard, J.,         *Medieval Romance in England: A Study of the Sources and Analogues of the Non-cyclic Metrical Romances*, rev. edn (New York, 1963). (Groups miscellaneous English romances on thematic grounds as 'Romances of Trial and Faith', 'of Love and Adventure', etc.)

Mehl, D.,            *The Middle English Romances of the Thirteenth and Fourteenth Centuries* (London, 1968). (Comprehensive survey and literary analysis of major texts grouped by length.)

Ramsey, L. C.,       *Chivalric Romances: Popular Literature in Medieval England* (Bloomington, Ind., 1983). (Views romances as escapist literature reflecting anxieties and desires of a popular audience.)

Richmond, V. B.,  *The Popularity of Middle English Romance* (Bowling Green, Ohio, 1975). (Fifteen texts studied in terms of their reflection of positive Christian values underlying and inspiring their escapism.)

Stevens, J.,  *Medieval romance: Themes and Approaches* (London, 1973). (Introduction to themes, motifs, and critical approaches dealing with selected texts from Chrétien to Malory.)

Taylor, A. B.,  *An Introduction to Medieval Romance* (London, 1930). (Introductory survey of themes and characteristics of English in relation to French Romance.)

Thompson, S.,  *Motif-index of Folk-literature*, rev. edn, 6 vols (Bloomington, Ind., 1955–58). (Alphabetic listing of narrative elements in folk-tales, ballads, romances.)

Wittig, S.,  *Stylistic and Narrative Structures in the Middle English Romances* (Austin, Tex., 1978). (Study of formulaic patterns underlying seemingly random narratives of non-cyclic romances.)

# Anthologies of romance texts

Broughton, B. B. (ed. and tr.),  *'Richard the Lion-Hearted' and Other Medieval English Romances* (New York, 1966). (Also includes: *Floris and Blancheflor* and *Amis and Amiloun*.)

French, W. H., and C. B. Hale (eds),  *Middle English Metrical Romances* (New York, 1930). (Includes: *King Horn, Havelok, Athelston, Gamelyn, Sultan of Babylon* (selections), *Sir Degaré, Sir Orfeo, Sir Launfal, The Earl of Toulouse, Emaré,* Layamon's *Brut* (sel.), *Ywain and Gawain* (sel.), *Sir Perceval of Galles, The Avowing of Arthur, Ipomadon* (sel.), *Eger and Grime, The Squire of Low Degree, The Seven Sages of Rome* (sel.), *King Alexander* (sel), *The Destruction of Troy* (sel.), *Floris and Blancheflour, Chevelere Assigne, Sir Cleges, The Tale of Beryn* (sel.), *Robert of Sicily, King Edward and the Shepherd, The Tournament of Tottenham.*)

Gibbs, A. C. (ed.),  *Middle English Romances* (London, 1966). (Includes extracts from: *King Horn, Havelok, Floriz and Blauncheflur, Sir Orfeo, Amis and Amiloun, The Gest Hystoriale of the Destruction of Troy, Sir Thopas, Emaré, Sir Degrevant.*)

Mills, M. (ed.),     *Six Middle English Romances* (London, 1973). (Includes: *The Sege of Melayne, Emaré, Octavian, Sir Isumbras, Sir Gowther, Sir Amadace*.)

Rumble, T. C. (ed.),     *The Breton Lays in Middle English* (Detroit, Mich., 1965). (Includes: *Sir Launfal, Sir Degaré, Lay le Freine, Emaré, The Erle of Toulous, Sir Gowther, Kyng Orfew*, Chaucer's 'Franklin's Tale'.)

Sands, D. B. (ed.),     *Middle English Verse Romances* (New York, 1966). (Includes: *Horn, Havelok, Athelston, Gamelyn, Sir Orfeo, Sir Launfal, Lai le Fresne, The Squire of Low Degre, Floris and Blauncheflour, The Tournament of Tottenham, The Weddynge of Sir Gawen and Dame Ragnell, Sir Gawain and the Carl of Carlyle*.)

Schmidt, A. V. C., and     *Medieval English Romances*, 2 vols (London, 1980). N. Jacobs, (eds),     (Includes: Vol. I: *Havelok, Athelston, Sir Orfeo*; Vol. II: *Sir Degarre, Ywain and Gawain* (sel.), Stanzaic *Morte Arthur* (sel.), Alliterative *Morte Arthure* (sel.), *Ipomadon* (sel.).)

Weston, J. L. (tr.),     *The Chief Middle English Poets* (Boston, 1914; reprint, New York, 1970). (Includes: *King Horn, Havelok, Arthur and Merlin* (sel.), *Richard Cœur de Lion* (sel.), *Sir Orfeo, Sir Tristem, Amis and Amiloun, Sir Launfal, Sir Amadace, Ywain and Gawain* (sel.), *Syr Percyvelle of Galles*, Stanzaic *Morte Arthur* (sel.).)

# Individual texts

(Alphabetically arranged; excluding the works of Chaucer, Lydgate, and Caxton)

*Alliterative Alexander Fragments*, ed. F. P. Mougan, *Gests of King Alexander of Macedon* (Cambridge, Mass., 1929).

*Amis and Amiloun*, ed. M. Leach, EETS, 203 (London, 1937).

Kratins, O., 'The Middle English *Amis and Amiloun*: Chivalric Romance or Secular Hagiography?', *PMLA*, 81 (1966), 347–54. (On subordination of purely chivalric values to concept of Christian fidelity.)

Kramer, D., 'Structural Artistry in *Amis and Amiloun*', *Annuale Medievale*, 9 (1968), 103–22. (On use of structural devices in conveying theme of perfect friendship tested.)

Baldwin, D. R., '*Amis and Amiloun*: The Testing of Treuþe', *Papers on Language and Literature*, 16 (1980), 353–63. (Demonstrates its relation to test literature in the variety of forms of fidelity involved.)

*Amoryus and Cleopes* (John Metham), ed. H. Craig, EETS, 132 (London, 1906; reprinted, 1973).

*Apollonius of Tyre*, ed. J. Raith, *Die alt- und mittelenglischen Apollonius-Bruchstücke*, Studien und Texte zur englischen Philologie, 3 (Munich, 1956).

*Arthour and Merlin*, ed. O. D. Macrae-Gibson, EETS, 268, 279 (London, 1973, 1979).

Sklar, E. S., '*Arthour and Merlin:* The Englishing of Arthur', *Michigan Academician*, 8 (1976), 49–57. (In adapting source English redactor made search for national unity the central theme.)

*Arthur*, ed. F. J. Furnivall, EETS, 2 (London, 1864; reprinted, 1965).

*Arthur of Little Britain* (Lord Berners), ed. E. V. Utterson (London, 1814).

*Athelston*, ed. A. McI. Trounce, EETS, 224 (London, 1951; reprinted, 1957).

Kiernan, K. S., '*Athelston* and the Rhyme of the English Romances', *Modern Language Quarterly*, 36 (1975), 339–53. (Significance of stanza structure in relation to complex narrative structure.)

Dickerson, A. I., 'The Subplot of the Messenger in *Athelston*', *Papers on Language and Literature*, 12 (1976), 115–24. (On role of the messenger, as common man, in rectification of royal injustice.)

*Avowynge of King Arthur, Sir Gawan, Sir Kaye, and Sir Bawdewyn of Bretan*, ed. C. Brookhouse, *Anglistica*, 15 (Copenhagen 1968); ed. R. Dahood, Garland Medieval Texts (New York, 1984).

*Awntyrs off Arthure at the Terne Wathelyne*, ed. R. J. Gates (Philadelphia, Pa., 1969); ed. R. Hanna, III (Manchester, 1974).

Hanna, R., III, '*The Awntyrs off Arthure*: An Interpretation', *Modern Language Quarterly*, 31 (1970), 275–97. (Interprets dual structure as two separate poems expressing opposed chivalric attitudes.)

Klausner, D. N., 'Exempla and *The Awntyrs off Arthure*', *Medieval Studies*, 34 (1972), 307–25. (First part of poem emphasizes lechery, second avarice.)

Spearing, A. C., '*The Awntures off Arthure*', in *The Alliterative Tradition in the Fourteenth Century*, ed. B. S. Levy and P. E. Szarmach (Kent, Ohio, 1981), pp. 183–202. (The dual structure offers deliberate parallelism with variation.)

*Ballad of Hind Horn*, ed. B. H. Bronson, *The Traditional Tunes of the Child Ballads*, 3 vols (Princeton, N.J., 1959–66), Vol. I.

*Bevis of Hampton*, ed. E. Kölbing, EETS, ES, 46, 48, 65 (London, 1885–94; reprinted as 1 vol., 1973).

Baugh, A. C., 'The Making of *Beves of Hampton*', in *Bibliographical Studies in Honour of Rudolf Hirsh*, ed. W. Miller and T. Waldman (Philadelphia, Pa., 1974), pp. 15–37.

Weiss, J., 'The Major Interpolation in *Sir Beues of Hamtoun*', *Medium Aevum*, 48 (1979), 71–76. (Interpolation, by increasing hero's stature, adds patriotic appeal to popular adventure.)

*Bone Florence of Rome*, ed. C. F. Heffernan (Manchester, 1976).

Lee, A. T., '*Le Bone Florence of Rome*: A Middle English Adaptation of a French Romance', in *The Learned and the Lewed*, ed. L. D. Benson (Cambridge, Mass., 1974), pp. 343–54. (On radical alterations which achieve economic structure and dramatic realism.)

*Book of Duke Huon of Burdeux* (Lord Berners), ed. S. L. Lee, EETS, ES, 40, 41, 43, 50 (London, 1882–87; reprinted in 2 vols, 1973).

*Buik of King Alexander* (Gilbert Hay) – no edition yet published.

*Cambridge Alexander-Cassamus Fragment*, ed. K. Rosskopf (Munich, 1911).

*Carle off Carlile*, ed. A. Kurvinen, *Sir Gawain and the Carl of Carlisle in Two Versions* (Helsinki, 1951).

*Chevalere Assigne*, ed. H. H. Gibbs, EETS, ES, 6 (London, 1868; reprinted, 1973).

Barron, W. R. J., '*Chevalere Assigne* and the *Naissance du Chevalier au Cygne*', *Medium Aevum*, 36 (1968), 25–37. (Identification of source version.)

Barron, W. R. J., 'Alliterative Romance and the French Tradition', in *Middle English Alliterative Poetry and Its Literary Background*, ed. D. Lawton (Cambridge, 1982), pp. 70–87, 140–42). (Nature of redaction.)

*Clariodus*, ed. D. Irving, Maitland Club, 9 (Edinburgh, 1830).

*Dublin Alexander Epitome*, ed. W. W. Skeat, EETS, ES, 47 (London, 1886; reprinted, 1973).

*Duke Roland and Sir Otuel of Spain*, ed. S. J. Herrtage, EETS, ES, 35 (London, 1880; reprinted, 1973).

*Earl of Toulous*, ed. G. Lüdtke, Sammlung englischer Denkmäler, 3 (Berlin, 1881).

    Reilly, R., '*The Earl of Toulouse*: A Structure of Honour', *Medieval Studies*, 37 (1975), 515–23. (On structure as a means of contrasting characters and the values they represent.)

*Eger and Grime*, ed. J. R. Caldwell, Harvard Studies in Comparative Literature, 9 (Cambridge, Mass., 1933).

*Emaré*, ed. E. Rickert, EETS, ES, 99 (London, 1908; reprinted, 1958).

    Donovan, M. J., 'Middle English *Emaré* and the Cloth Worthily Wrought', in *The Learned and the Lewed*, ed. L. D. Benson (Cambridge, Mass., 1974), pp. 337–42. (Use of concrete object as focus of narrative as in Marie's *lais*.)

*Firumbras* (Ashmole), ed. S. J. Herrtage, EETS, ES, 34 (London, 1879; reprinted 1966).

*Firumbras* (Fillingham), ed. M. I. O'Sullivan, EETS, 198 (London, 1935; reprinted 1971).

*Floris and Blauncheflur*, ed. A. B. Taylor (Oxford, 1927).

    Wentersdorf, K. P., 'Iconographic Elements in *Floris and Blauncheflur*', *Annuale Medievale*, 20 (1980), 76–96. (On erotic significance of such elements as the chess game, the flower imagery, etc.)

    Barnes, G., 'Cunning and Ingenuity in the Middle English *Floris and Blauncheflur*', *Medium Aevum*, 53 (1984), 10–25. (Redaction study demonstrates substitution of ingenuity for force of arms in French version.)

*Generides*, ed. W. A. Wright, EETS, 55, 70 (London, 1873; reprinted as 1 vol., 1973).

*Gest Historiale of the Destruction of Troy*, ed. G. A. Panton and D. Donaldson, EETS, 39, 56 (London, 1869, 1874; reprinted as 1 vol., 1968).

    Benson, C. D., *The History of Troy in Middle English Literature* (Cambridge, 1980).

*Golagrus and Gawain*, ed. G. S. Stevenson, STS, 65 (Edinburgh, 1918).

    Ketrick, P. J., *The Relation of 'Golagros and Gawane' to The Old French 'Perceval'* (Washington, D.C., 1931). (Source version identified.)

    Barron, W. R. J., '*Golagrus and Gawain*: A Creative Redaction', *Bibliographical Bulletin of the International Arthurian Society*, 26 (Nottingham, 1974), 173–85. (On fundamental reshaping of French original.)

*Grene Knight*, ed. F. J. Furnivall and J. W. Hales, *Bishop Percy's Folio Manuscript: Ballads and Romances*, 4 vols (London, 1867–68; reprinted, Detroit, Ill., 1968) Vol. II.

*Guy and Colbrond*, ed. F. J. Furnivall and J. W. Hales, *Percy Folio*, Vol. II.

*Guy of Warwick*,

    ed. W. B. Todd (Austin, Tex., 1968);

    ed., J. Zupitza (Caius MS), EETS, ES, 42, 49, 59 (London, 1883, 1887, 1891; reprinted as 1 vol., 1966);

    (fifteenth-century version), EETS, ES, 25, 26 (London, 1875, 1876; reprinted as 1 vol., 1966);

    G. L. Morrill, *Speculum Guidonis de Warwyk*, EETS, ES, 75 (London, 1898; reprinted, 1973).

    Klausner, D. N., 'Didacticism and Drama in *Guy of Warwick*', *Medievalia et Humanistica*, 6 (1975), 103–19. (Dramatic break between hero's career as knight and as pilgrim reinforces penitential theme.)

    Richmond, V. B., 'The Most Popular Hero: Guy of Warwick', in *The Popularity of Middle English Romance* (Bowling Green, Ohio, 1975), Ch. 6.

*Havelok the Dane*, ed. W. W. Skeat, 2nd edn (Oxford, 1915); rev. K. Sisam (Oxford, 1956).

    Reiss, E., '*Havelok the Dane* and Norse Mythology', *Modern Language Quarterly*, 27 (1966), 115–24. (Elements of Norse hero-myth in poem.)

Mills, M., 'Havelok and the Brutal Fisherman', *Medium Aevum*, 36 (1967), 219–30. (Inconsistencies in role of Grim derive from its folklore stereotype.)

Weiss, J., 'Structure and Characterisation in *Havelok the Dane*', *Speculum*, 44 (1969), 247–57.

Halverson, J., '*Havelok the Dane* and Society', *Chaucer Review*, 6 (1971), 142–51. (Sees basic story as 'a peasant fantasy of class ambition and resentment' ineptly adapted to chivalric mode in French *lai*.)

Delany, S., and V. Ishkanian, 'Theocratic and Contractual Kingship in *Havelok the Dane*', *Zeitschrift für Anglistik und Amerikanistik*, 22 (1974), 290–302. (Basic theme is nature of kingship.)

Staines, D., '*Havelok the Dane*: A Thirteenth-century Handbook for Princes', *Speculum*, 51 (1976), 602–23. (Havelok a portrait of the ideal king.)

Jack, G. B., 'The Date of *Havelok*', *Anglia*, 95 (1977), 20–33. (Concludes date cannot be more precisely fixed than within period late twelfth century to *c*. 1272.)

*Helyas, the Knight of the Swan* (Copland). (No modern edition; the edition by Wynkyn de Worde was reprinted by the Grolier Club (New York, 1901) ).

*History of the Holy Grail* (Lovelich), ed. F. J. Furnivall, Parts i–iv, EETS, ES, 20, 24, 28, 30 (London, 1874–78); D. Kempe, Part v, EETS, ES, 95 (London, 1905); the whole reprinted in 2 vols, 1973.

*Horn Child*, ed. J. Hall, *King Horn* (Oxford, 1901).

*Ipomadon*, ed. E. Kölbing, (couplet, stanzaic and prose versions) (Breslau, 1889); ed., T. Ikegami, (Couplet version) (Tokyo, 1983).

*Jeaste of Syr Gawayne*, ed. F. Madden, *Syr Gawayne* (London, 1839).

*Joseph of Arimathie*, ed. D. A. Lawton, Garland Medieval Texts (New York, 1983).

Barron, W. R. J., '*Joseph of Arimathie* and the *Estoire del Saint Graal*', *Medium Aevum*, 33 (1964), 184–94. (Identification of source version.)

Lagorio, V. M., 'The *Joseph of Arimathie*: English Hagiography in Transition', *Medievalia et Humanistica*, 6 (1975), 91–101. (Arthurian associations modified in favour of Joseph's apostolic role.)

*King Arthur and King Cornwall*, ed. F. J. Furnivall and J. W. Hales, *Percy Folio*, Vol. i.

*King Arthur's Death*, ed. F. J. Furnivall and J. W. Hales, *Percy Folio*, Vol. i.

*King Horn*, ed., J. Hall (Oxford, 1901); ed., R. S. Allen, Garland Medieval Texts (New York, 1984).

French, W. H., *Essays on King Horn* (Ithaca, N.Y., 1940).

Gellinek, C., 'The Romance of *Horn*: A Structural Survey', *Neuphilologische Mitteilungen*, 66 (1965), 330–33. (Central section of tripartite structure unites dual themes of love and loyalty with special emphasis.)

Ziegler, G., 'Structural Repetition in *King Horn*', *Neuphilologische Mitteilungen*, 81 (1980), 403–08.

*King of Tars*, ed. J. Perryman, Middle English Texts, 12 (Heidelberg, 1980).

*King Pontus*, ed. F. J. Mather (Baltimore, Md., 1897).

*Knight of Curtesy and the Fair Lady of Faguell*, ed. W. C. Hazlitt, *Remains of the Early Popular Poetry of England*, 4 vols (London, 1864–66), Vol. ii.

*Kyng Alisaunder*, ed. G. V. Smithers, EETS, 227, 237 (London, 1952, 1957; reprinted 1961, 1969).

Richmond, V. B., 'Kyng Alisaunder' in *The Popularity of Middle English Romance* (Bowling Green, Ohio, 1975), pp. 35–42.

*Lai le Freine*, ed. M. Wattie, Smith College Studies in Modern Languages, 10.3 (Northampton, Mass., 1929).

*Lancelot of the Laik*, ed. M. M. Gray, STS, n.s. 2 (Edinburgh, 1912).

*Laud Troy Book*, ed. J. E. Wülfing, EETS, 121, 122 (London, 1902, 1903; reprinted as 1 vol., 1973).

*Layamon's Brut*, ed. G. L. Brook and R. F. Leslie, EETS, 250, 277 (London, 1963, 1978);

ed. and tr. W. R. J. Barron and S. C. Weinberg. *Layamon's Arthur* (Cambridge, forthcoming). (Parallel text and prose translation of the Arthurian section of the text.)

Kirby, I. J., 'Angles and Saxons in Layamon's *Brut*', *Studia Neophilologica*, 36 (1964), 51–62. (Suggests Laymon's anti-English sentiments were confined to the Saxons alone.)

Lewis, C. S. *Studies in Medieval and Renaissance Literature*, ed. W. Hooper (Cambridge, 1969), pp. 18–33. (Literary appreciation.)

Stanley, E. G., 'Layamon's Antiquarian Sentiments', *Medium Aevum*, 38 (1969), 23–37. (Relation of archaisms to patriotic theme.)

Frankis, P. J., 'Layamon's English Sources' in *J. J. R. Tolkien, Scholar and Storyteller: Essays in Memoriam*, ed. M. Salu (Ithaca, N.Y., 1979), pp. 64–75.

*Legend of King Arthur*, ed. F. J. Furnivall and J. W. Hales, *Percy Folio*, Vol. I.

*Libeaus Desconus*, ed. M. Mills, EETS, 261 (London, 1969).

Mills, M., 'A Medieval Reviser at Work', *Medium Aevum*, 32 (1963), 11–23. (MSS revisions show attempt to rationalize incongruous elements by use of romance commonplaces.)

*Marriage of Sir Gawaine*, ed. F. J. Furnivall and J. W. Hales, *Percy Folio*, Vol. I.

*Melusine*. ed. A. K. Donald, EETS, ES, 68 (London, 1895; reprinted, 1973).

*Merlin* (Lovelich), ed. E. A. Kock, EETS, ES, 93, 112, EETS, 185 (London, 1904, 1932; reprinted 1961, 1971, 1973).

*Morte Arthure* (Alliterative),

ed. L. D. Benson, *King Arthur's Death: The Middle English Stanzaic Morte Arthur and Alliterative Morte Arthure* (Indianapolis, Ind., 1974). (Marginally glossed texts of both poems.);

ed. V. Krishna (New York, 1976);

ed. M. Hamel, Garland Medieval Texts (New York, 1984);

tr. V. Krishna, *The Alliterative Morte Arthure: A New Verse Translation* (New York, 1983).

'The Alliterative *Morte Arthure*: An Annotated Bibliography, 1950–1975', ed., M. Foley, *Chaucer Review*, 14 (1979), 165–87.

Matthews, W., *The Tragedy of Arthur: A Study of the Alliterative Morte Arthure* (Berkeley, Cal., 1961). (Sees poem as a tragedy of fortune much influenced by Alexander romances.)

Finlayson, J., 'The Concept of the Hero in *Morte Arthure*', in *Chaucer und seine Zeit: Symposium für Walter F. Schirmer* (Tübingen, 1967), pp. 249–74. (Traces Arthur's degeneration from Christian champion to fallen sinner.)

Keiser, G. R., 'The Theme of Justice in the Alliterative *Morte Arthure*', *Annuale Mediaevale*, 16 (1975), 94–109. (Sees Arthur, having failed as agent of divine justice, eventually submitting to divine will.)

Göller, K. H., ed. *The Alliterative Morte Arthure: A Reassessment of the Poem* (Cambridge, 1981). (Twelve original studies by various authors.)

*Morte Arthur* (Stanzaic),

ed. L. D. Benson, *King Arthur's Death* (see under Alliterative *Morte* above);

ed. P. F. Hissiger (The Hague, 1975).

Wertime, R. A., 'The Theme and Structure of the Stanzaic *Morte Arthur*', *PMLA*, 87 (1972), 1075–82. (Poem a tragedy of consequence moderated by narrator's compassion.)

Beston, J., and R. M. Beston, 'The Parting of Lancelot and Guinevere in the Stanzaic *Le Morte Arthure*', *AUMLA*, 40 (1973), 249–59. (Sees the lovers' parting as originating with the English poet.)

Knopp, S. E., 'Artistic Design in the Stanzaic *Morte Arthur*', *ELH*, 45 (1978), 563–82. (Coherence rooted in non-realistic, iconographic art.)

*Morte Darthur* (Malory),

ed. E. Vinaver, 3 vols (Oxford, 1947; revised, 1973);

ed., E. Vinaver, Oxford Standard Authors (London, 1954; revised, 1977);
ed., P. J. C. Field, Tales Seven and Eight (London, 1978).
*Sir Thomas Malory and the 'Morte Darthur': A Survey of Scholarship and Annotated Bibliography*, ed. P. W. Life (Carlottesville, Va., 1980).
Knight, S., *The Structure of Sir Thomas Malory's Authuriad* (Sydney, 1969). (Sees tragic ending not structurally unified with preceding adventures.)
Lambert, M., *Malory: Style and Vision in 'Le Morte Darthur'* (New Haven, Conn., 1975). (Central interest of work seen as chivalry not human conflict.)
Benson, L. D., *Malory's 'Morte Darthur'* (Cambridge, Mass., 1976). (Analysis in terms of romance tradition and concept of chivalry.)
Takamiya, T. and D. Brewer, eds, *Aspects of Malory* (Cambridge, 1981). (Eleven previously unpublished essays by various authors.)
Whitaker, M., *Arthur's Kingdom of Adventure: The World of Malory's 'Morte Darthur'* (Cambridge, 1984). (On changing settings for adventure as reflection of changing reality as romance becomes tragedy.)
Kennedy, B., *Knighthood in the 'Morte Darthur'* (Cambridge, 1985). (On shaping of Malory's work by contemporary concepts of knighthood.)
*Octavian*, ed. F. McSparran, Middle English Texts, 11 (Heidelberg, 1979).
*Otuel a Knight*, ed. S. J. Herrtage, EETS, ES, 39 (London, 1882; reprinted, 1969).
*Otuel and Roland*, ed. M. I. O'Sullivan, EETS, 198 (London, 1935; reprinted, 1971).
*Partonope of Blois*, ed. A. T. Bödtker, EETS, ES, 109 (London, 1912; reprinted, 1973).
*Prose Alexander*, ed. J. S. Westlake, EETS, 143 (London, 1913; reprinted, 1971).
*Prose Merlin*, ed. H. B. Wheatley, EETS, 10, 21, 36, 112 (London, 1865–99; reprinted in 2 vols, 1973).
*Prose Siege of Thebes*, ed. F. Brie, *Archiv für das Studium der neueren Sprachen und Literaturen*, 130.40, 269 (Braunschweig, 1913).
*Prose Siege of Troy*, ed. F. Brie (see under *Prose Siege of Thebes* above).
*Richard Coer de Lyon*, ed. K. Brunner (Leipzig, 1913).
Broughton, B. B., *The Legends of King Richard I, Cœur de Lion: A Study of Sources and Variations to the Year 1600* (The Hague, 1966).
*Robert of Cisyle*, ed. R. Nuck (Berlin, 1887).
Hornstein, L. H., '*King Robert of Sicily*: Analogues and Origins', *PMLA*, 79 (1964), 13–21. (Demonstrates superiority over Continental versions in synthesizing folklore themes with history and biblical commentary.)
*Roland and Vernagu*, ed. S. J. Herrtage, EETS, ES, 39 (London, 1882; reprinted, 1969).
*Romauns of Partenay*, ed. W. W. Skeat, EETS, 22, rev. edn (London, 1899; reprinted, 1973).
*Roswall and Lillian*, ed. W. C. Hazlitt, *Early Popular Poetry of Scotland*, 2 vols (London, 1895), Vol. II.
*Scottish Alexander Book*, ed. R. L. G. Ritchie, STS, n.s.12, 17, 21, 25 (Edinburgh, 1921–29).
*Scottish Troy Fragments*, ed. C. Horstmann, *Barbour's Legendensammlung nebst den Fragmenten seines Trojanerkrieges*, 2 vols (Heilbronn, 1881), Vol. II.
*Seege of Troye*, ed. M. E. Barnicle, EETS, 172 (London, 1927; reprinted, 1971).
*Sege of Melayne*, ed. S. J. Herrtage, EETS, ES, 35 (London, 1880; reprinted, 1973).
*Siege of Jerusalem* (Titus and Vespasian), ed. E. Kölbing and M. Day, EETS, 188 (London, 1932; reprinted, 1971).
Moe, P., 'The French Source of the Alliterative *Siege of Jerusalem*, *Medium Aevum*, 39 (1970), 147–54.
*Sir Amadace*, ed. C. Brookhouse, Anglistica, 15 (Copenhagen, 1968).
*Sir Cleges*, ed. J. H. McKnight, *Middle English Humorous Tales in Verse* (Boston, 1913).
*Sir Degaré*, ed., G. Schleich (Heidelberg, 1929).
Faust, C. P., *Sire Degaré: A Study of the Text and Narrative Structure* (Princeton, N.J., 1935).

Stokoe, W. C., Jr, 'The Double Problem of *Sir Degaré, PMLA*, 70 (1955), 518–34. (Distinguishes two distinct versions in surviving texts accounting for varying critical evaluation.)

Kozicki, H., 'Critical Methods in the Literary Evaluation of *Sir Degaré*', *Modern Language Quarterly*, 29 (1968), 3–14. (Sees work as well-knit domestic epic of growth to maturity, augmented by vegetation-myth symbolism.)

Rosenberg, B. A., 'The Three Tales of Sir Degaré', *Neuphilologische Mitteilungen*, 76 (1975), 39–51. (Suggests origin in conflation of three folk-tales.)

*Sir Degrevant*, ed. L. F. Casson, EETS, 221 (1949; reprinted, 1970).

*Sir Eglamour of Artois*, ed. F. E. Richardson, EETS, 256 (1965).

*Sir Gawain and the Green Knight*,
    ed. M. Andrew and R. Waldron in *The Poems of the Pearl Manuscript* (London, 1978);
    ed. and tr. W. R. J. Barron (Manchester, 1974). (Conservative edition with parallel prose translation);
    tr. M. Borroff (New York, 1967). (Alliterative verse translation.);
    tr. B. Stone, Penguin books, rev. edn (Harmondsworth, 1974). (Verse translation.);
    ed. J. R. R. Tolkien and E. V. Gordon, 2nd edn, rev. N. Davis (Oxford, 1967);
    tr. J. R. R. Tolkien (London, 1975). (Alliterative verse translation.)

*The Gawain-Poet: An Annotated Bibliography: 1839–1977*, ed. M. Andrew (New York, 1979). (Comprehensive coverage of all four poems.)

'*Sir Gawain and the Green Knight': a Reference Guide*, ed. R. J. Blanch (Troy, N.Y., 1983). (More selective than Andrew above, concentrating on critical and interpretative studies to end of 1978.)

Benson, L. D., *Art and Tradition in 'Sir Gawain and the Green Knight'* (New Brunswick, N.J., 1965). (Discusses issues of source, style, meaning, and literary method in relation to romance tradition.)

Burrow, J., *A Reading of 'Sir Gawain and the Green Knight'* (London, 1965). (Seminal study focused on use of comedy and realism in establishment of an idealism rooted in complex concept of *trawthe*.)

Blanch, R. J., ed., *Sir Gawain and the Green Knight and Pearl: Critical Essays* (Bloomington, Ind., 1966). (Six previously published essays.)

Fox, D., ed., *Twentieth Century Interpretations of 'Sir Gawain and the Green Knight': A Collection of Critical Essays* (Englewood Cliffs, N.J., 1968). (Fourteen essays and extracts from books previously published.)

Howard, D. R. and C. Zacher, eds., *Critical Studies of 'Sir Gawain and the Green Knight'* (London, 1968). (Twenty-three reprinted essays.)

Spearing, A. C., *The 'Gawain'-Poet: A Critical Study* (Cambridge, 1970). (*Gawain* section concentrates on interrelation of plots as key to meaning.)

Borroff, M., '*Sir Gawain and the Green Knight': A Stylistic and Metrical Study*, reprint (Hamden, Conn., 1973). (Detailed analysis of vocabulary, metre, and alliteration in relation to poetic technique and meaning.)

Davenport, W. A., *The Art of the 'Gawain'-Poet* (London, 1978). (Emphasizes use of antithesis and ambiguity in mixed mode of romance.)

Barron, W. R. J., '*Trawthe' and Treason: The Sin of Gawain Reconsidered* (Manchester, 1980). (Analyses relationship between hunting and bedroom scenes and discusses Gawain's fault in terms of law and theology.)

*Sir Gowther*, ed. K. Breul (Oppeln, 1886).

Marchalonis, S., '*Sir Gowther*: The Process of a Romance', *Chaucer Review*, 6 (1971), 14–29. (Sees folk-tale elements as artistically integrated to form an exemplum embodying the chivalric ethic.)

*Sir Isumbras*, ed. J. Zupitza and G. Schleich, Palaestra, 15 (1901).

Braswell, L., '*Sir Isumbras* and the Legend of Saint Eustace', *Medieval Studies*, 27 (1965), 128–51. (On adaptation of framework of the legend to romance genre.)

*Sir Lambewell; Sir Lamwell* ed. F. J. Furnivall and J. W. Hales, *Percy Folio*, Vol. I.

*Sir Lancelot du Lake*, ed. F. J. Furnivall and J. W. Hales, *Percy Folio*, Vol. I.

*Sir Landeval, Sir Launfal* (Thomas Chestre), ed. A. J. Bliss, *Sir Launfal* (London, 1960).

    Martin, B. K., '*Sir Launfal* and the Folktale', *Medium Aevum*, 35 (1966), 199–210. (On folk-tale conventions surviving in the poem.)

    Williams, E., '*Lanval* and *Sir Landevale*: A Medieval Translator and His Methods', *Leeds Studies in English*, n.s. 3 (1969), 85–99. (On adaptation of courtly lay for popular audience.)

    Lane, D., 'Conflict in *Sir Launfal*', *Neuphilologische Mitteilungen*, 74 (1973), 283–87. (On conflict of good and evil, harmony and discord.)

    Anderson, E. R., 'The Structure of *Sir Launfal*', *Papers on Language and Literature*, 13 (1977), 115–24. (On pattern of moral opposites forming symmetrical structure focussed on hero's manhood.)

*Sir Orfeo*, ed. A. J. Bliss, 2nd edn (Oxford, 1966).

    Knapp, J. K., 'The Meaning of *Sir Orfeo*', *Modern Language Quarterly*, 29 (1968), 263–73. (Poem not a fantasy but an affirmation of power of love, self sacrifice and loyalty.)

    Bristol, M. D., 'The Structure of the Middle English *Sir Orfeo*', *Papers in Language and Literature*, 6 (1970), 337–47. (Sees mythic pattern not as tragic but as a process of liberation and redemption.)

    Friedman, J. B., *Orpheus in the Middle Ages* (Cambridge, Mass., 1970). (Illustrated survey of the influence of the myth in art and literature.)

    Hanson, T. B., '*Sir Orfeo*: Romance as Exemplum', *Annuale Medievale*, 13 (1972), 135–54. (Contrasts function and treatment of two versions.)

    Lucas, P. J., 'An Interpretation of *Sir Orfeo*', *Leeds Studies in English*, 6 (1972), 1–9.

    Riddy, F., 'The Uses of the Past in *Sir Orfeo*', *Yearbook of English Studies*, 6 (1976), 5–15. (On emotional patterns of loss and restoration.)

*Sir Perceval of Galles*, ed. J. Campion and F. Holthausen (Heidelberg, 1917).

    Griffith, R. H., *Sir Perceval of Galles: A Study of the Sources of the Legend* (Chicago, Ill., 1911). (Sees little if any influence of Chrétien's version in multistage development of poem.)

    Baron, F. X., 'Mother and Son in *Sir Perceval of Galles*', *Papers on Language and Literature*, 8 (1972), 3–14. (On filial duty as a replacement for chivalric adventure and pursuit of the Grail.)

    Eckhardt, C. D., 'Arthurian Comedy: The Simpleton Hero in *Sir Perceval of Galles*', *Chaucer Review*, 8 (1974), 205–20. (Sees simpleton role of hero, sustained throughout, as positive contribution to theme.)

    Fowler, D. C., '*Le Conte du Graal* and *Sir Perceval of Galles*', *Comparative Literature Studies*, 12 (1975), 5–20. (A creative response to Chrétien's poem consciously parodying romance conventions.)

*Sir Torrent of Portyngale*, ed. E. Adam, EETS, ES 51 (London, 1887; reprinted 1973).

*Sir Triamour*, ed. A. J. Erdman-Schmidt (Utrecht, 1937).

*Sir Tristrem*, ed. G. P. McNeill, STS, 8 (Edinburgh, 1886; reprint, New York, 1966).

    Rumble, T. C., 'The Middle English *Sir Tristrem*: Toward a Reappraisal', *Comparative Literature*, 11 (1959), 221–28. (On rationalization of French original to suit tastes of English audience.)

    Pickford, C. E., '*Sir Tristrem*, Sir Walter Scott and Thomas', in *Studies in Medieval Literature and Languages in Memory of Frederick Whitehead*, ed. W. Rothwell *et al.* (Manchester, 1973), pp. 219–28. (Interest of narrative and nature of audience for translations of French romance.)

*Song of Roland*, ed. S. J. Herrtage, EETS, ES, 35 (London, 1880; reprinted, 1973).

*Sowdon of Babylon*, ed. E. Hausknecht, EETS, ES, 38 (London, 1881; reprinted, 1969).

*Squyr of Lowe Degre*, ed. W. E. Mead (Boston, 1904).

    Rivers, B., 'The Focus of Satire in *The Squire of Low Degree*', *English Studies in Canada*, 7 (1981), 379–87.

*Syre Gawene and the Carle of Carelyle*, ed. R. W. Ackerman (Ann Arbor, Mich., 1947).

*Tale of Gamelyn*, ed. W. W. Skeat, (Oxford, 1884).

    Shannon, E. F., 'Medieval Law in the *Tale of Gamelyn*', *Speculum*, 26 (1951), 458–64. (Illustrates exactness of legal references in poem.)

    Menkin, E. Z., 'Comic Irony and the Sense of Two Audiences in the *Tale of Gamelyn*', *Thoth*, 10 (1969), 41–53. (On presentation of hero to appeal both to upper- and middle-class audience.)

*Taill of Rauf Coilyear*, ed. F. J. Amours, *Scottish Alliterative Poems*, STS, 27, 38 (Edinburgh, 1892, 1897).

    Smyser, H. M., '*The Tail of Rauf Coilyear* and Its Sources', *Harvard Studies and Notes in Philology and Literature*, 14 (1932), 135–150. (Defines degree of parody in use of epic motifs in popular romance.)

    Walsh, E., '*The Tale of Rauf Coilyear*: Oral Motif in Literary Guise', *Scottish Literary Journal*, 6 (1979), 5–19. (On use of formulaic diction in literary romance on folklore theme.)

*Three Kings' Sons*, ed. F. J. Furnivall, EETS, ES, 67 (London, 1895; reprinted, 1973).

*Turke and Gowin*, ed. F. J. Furnivall and J. W. Hales, *Percy Folio*, Vol, I.

*Valentine and Orson*, ed., A. Dickson, EETS, 204 (London, 1937; reprinted, 1971).

*Wars of Alexander*, ed. W. W. Skeat, EETS, ES, 47 (London, 1886; reprinted, 1973.)

    Cary, G., *The Medieval Alexander*, ed. D. J. A. Ross (Cambridge, 1956).

    Duggan, H. N., 'The Source of the Middle English *The Wars of Alexander*', *Speculum*, 51 (1976), 624–36. (Sole source was $I^3$ recension of the *Historia de preliis Alexandri Magni*.)

    Hill, B., 'Alexanderromance: The Egyptian Connection', *Leeds Studies in English*, n.s. 12 (1981), 185–94. (On surrogate paternity of hero as an addition to English versions of legend.)

*Weddynge of Sir Gawen and Dame Ragnell*, ed. L. Summer, Smith College Studies in Modern Languages, 5.4 (Northampton, Mass., 1924);

    reprinted by B. J. Whiting in *Sources and Analogues of Chaucer's Canterbury Tales*, ed. W. Bryan and G. Dempster (Chicago, Ill., 1941; reprint, London, 1958);

    tr. G. B. Saul, *The Wedding of Sir Gawain and Dame Ragnell* (New York, 1934).

*William of Palerne*, ed. G. H. V. Bunt, Mediaevalia Groningana, 6 (Groningen, 1984); ed., N. Simms (Philadelphia, Pa., 1969).

    Dunn, C. W., *The Foundling and the Werwolf: A Literary-Historical Study of 'Guillaume de Palerne'* (Toronto, 1960). (Literary background.)

    Turville-Petre, T., 'Humphrey de Bohun and *William of Palerne*', *Neuphilologische Mitteilungen*, 75 (1974), 250–52. (Patron and audience.)

    Barron, W. R. J., 'Alliterative Romance and the French Tradition', in *Middle English Allitertive Poetry and Its Literary Background*, ed. D. Lawton (Cambridge, 1982), pp. 70–87, 140–42. (Relationship to French source and nature of redaction.)

*Ywain and Gawain*, ed. A. B. Friedman and N. T. Harrington, EETS, 254 (London, 1964; reprinted, 1981).

    Finlayson, J., '*Ywain and Gawain* and the Meaning of Adventure', *Anglia*, 87 (1969), 312–37. (Narrative method contrasted with Chrétien's.)

    Harrington, N. T., 'The Problem of the Lacunae in *Ywain and Gawain*', *JEGP*, 69 (1970), 59–65. (Supposed lacunae due to redactor's radical method of freeing the action from Chrétien's elaborations.)

    Hamilton, G. K., 'The Breaking of the Troth in *Ywain and Gawain*', *Mediaevalia*, 2 (1976), 111–35. (On change of thematic emphasis from love to the keeping of a pledge and the search for justice in society.)

# Index

285